JUDSON BOYCE ALLEN is a member of the Department of English at Marquette University.

This study of the definition of literature in the late medieval period is based on manuals of writing and on literary commentary and glosses. It defines a method of reading which may now profitably explain medieval texts, and identifies new primary medieval evidence which may ground and guide that reading.

Allen chooses texts whose commentary tradition provides the greatest opportunity for completeness. The most important of these is Ovid's *Metamorphoses*. Medieval reading of Ovid brings into focus a number of major literary questions – the problems of fable and fiction, of unity imposed by miscellany poetry, of allegorical commentary, and of Christian use of pagan culture – all in connection with a text which furnished medieval authors with more stories than any other single source except possibly the Bible.

Allen also studies commentaries on the *Consolation of Philosophy* of Boethius, the *Thebaid* of Statius, the *De nuptiis* of Martianus Capella, the medieval Christian hymn-book, and the *Poetria nova* of Geoffrey of Vinsauf.

Together these texts represent the range of medieval literature – a literature which, Allen concludes, was taken as direct ethical discourse, logically conducted and artfully organized, within a system of language that also assimilated the natural world and sought to absorb its audience.

JUDSON BOYCE ALLEN

The Ethical Poetic
of the Later Middle Ages:
A decorum of
convenient distinction

UNIVERSITY OF TORONTO PRESS
Toronto Buffalo London

© University of Toronto Press 1982
Toronto   Buffalo   London
Printed in Canada

ISBN 0-8020-2370-3

Canadian Cataloguing in Publication Data

Allen, Judson Boyce, 1932–
  The ethical poetic of the later Middle Ages
  Includes index.
  ISBN 0-8020-2370-3
  1. Criticism – Europe – History. 2. Poetry, Medieval –
  History and criticism. 3. Poetics – History. I. Title.
  PN688.A44   801.9510902   C81-094850-8

Publication of this book is made possible by a grant from the subsidized publica-
tions fund of the University of Toronto Press.

In piam memoriam
HATTIE BELL McCRACKEN ALLEN
1896–1981

Contents

Introduction

I first began to be a medievalist in the Bodleian Library, seated before a manuscript I could not read, written in a language I could but laboriously translate. In that experience, despair was mitigated by the pleasure that I was in physical contact with something medieval, and the hope that if I were patient I would learn what the manuscript could teach. The nature of my project forced me to begin with manuscripts, and being in Bodley encouraged me to continue in that habit. As a result, I made in ignorance a large number of discoveries which had already been made, and probably wasted a good deal of time.

But there is one inestimable benefit to be gained from getting first impressions directly from the primary evidence – one is considerably less likely to be betrayed by false expectations. When Beryl Smalley first began to work on the exegetes she calls the 'classicizing friars,' she did not expect secular storytellers. Her classic study of them was, as she says, 'born in a trap.' Its excellence is the result of the great historian's willingness to give up expectations in the face of what was, in this instance, a new kind of fact.

In my own case, I had no settled expectations, except those rooted in my own modern sensibility, which I soon learned I had axiomatically to distrust. Eventually, of course, I found out from modern scholarship what I was supposed to expect, but by that time the manuscripts themselves had had their way, and I was able clearly to realize that medieval ideas were more various and more different from our own, than we had thought.

This book is a report on fifteen years' reading of what medieval commentators wrote about their classic literature, and about the making of their own. This material includes a few texts which have long been familiar, such as the *Poetria nova* of Geoffrey of Vinsauf and Dante's letter to Cangrande. Most of it, however, comes from manuscript, and occurs as the introductions and glosses which preserve with poetry the medieval version of its reading. It is this kind of reading – this theory of literature, which I will define here. It is a theory which will seem strange to modern critics in the habit of presuming, as the basis of their work, an autonomous category of literature, toward which one relates with some kind of aesthetic attitude. But it is the theory which the medieval evidence insists on, with a clarity that derives in part from the strong impression made by contact with manuscripts in large numbers.

My work has been based on one obvious assumption: that the literary criticism of an age will, after an interval of time, cease simply to explain the texts to which it was addressed, and become evidence for the particular literary attitudes and presumptions which were, when it was made, satisfied with it. Thus, in architecture, the nineteenth-century designers of Balliol College looked upon their work as medieval, and we see it as Victorian. Thus, in literary biography, Johnson's *Lives of the Poets* now tell us more about Johnson than about Shakespeare and Milton. Only Aristotle's *Poetics* and perhaps the *Biographia* of Coleridge have escaped this voracious progress of context; if so, it is because they have been canonized as true, and are adapted by commentary after the manner of all sacred texts to speak to the needs of the commentator.

We do not now, however, write poetry under the guidance of the *Poetria nova* of Geoffrey of Vinsauf, nor indeed of any other rhetoric, though the *Rhetoric of Fiction* may tell us what we have implicitly done when we have finished our work. Geoffrey's book, and the others which were in the Middle Ages followed to the same end, address themselves to medieval problems and medieval needs; through it, and others like it, I propose, we may discover and define those problems and needs, and with them in mind, understand the late medieval theory of literature.

My work is new in two ways. First, I have taken medieval commentaries, which survive in large numbers, as my central evidence for the character of the medieval understanding of the texts which were then read. I have tried to read as many commentaries as possible – on literary texts representing a variety of genres, and having some claim to be widely admired by medieval readers. One of these texts, naturally, is the *Poetria nova*, which context of commentary makes me understand in a medieval way. In modern terms, the analogous procedure would be to read, as a way of making certain that I understood Derrida, Krieger, Wellek, and Wimsatt, et al., the critical apparatus of a large number of sophomore survey textbooks, and a large sample of book review pages from the more provincial newspapers, as well as the *Times* and the *New York Review*. In the second place, I have presumed that what medieval critics wrote about poetry was for them not only a true accounting but also a sufficient accounting. I have not, of course, read every surviving commentary. But I have read enough to have some confidence that I will not be surprised by any new one I might read. Since the evidence I have read is remarkably consistent in its concern, I have reported it as such. Matters which medieval critics discussed with concern, I presume concerned them – matters which they ignored, dismissed, or seemed unable to see, I presume did not concern them, and did not need to concern them. I have felt obliged to construct my definition of medieval literary theory, therefore, out of what the critics said, and I have felt obligated to refrain from supposing what they should have said, had they 'really' understood poetry.

My results were startling, and at first unwelcome. I went to the medieval commentaries on literary texts, and to the manuals for writers, expecting to find a theory of poetry. I expected, for instance, to find discussions of imaginative metaphor, and for this expectation at least I had some encouragement from the twelfth-century allegorists and from such modern expositors of twelfth-century doctrine as Brian Stock and Winthrop Wetherbee. But I did not find what I expected.

In the largest sense, I expected three things, which, of course, seem to me so obviously intrinsic to any discussion of poetry that one might claim to find no poetic where they were not discussed. I expected first to find a category for poetry – that is, an entity corresponding to what we call literature or belles-lettres, in which we could securely find such texts as the *Divina commedia* and the *Canterbury Tales*, and in which we could confidently fail to find any *Summa theologica* or treatise *de regimine principum*, or merely mnemonic verse, or any other such 'non-literary' text. In the second place, I expected to find a sense of literary form which was intra-textual. I expected medieval critics to see that any given poetic text has its own integrity, and that its form and coherence should be generated and defined by constraints, intentions, and forces internal to that text. Third, I expected the discourse of poetry, in so far as it was rhetorical, to achieve or enact with audience an instance of contact with an Other. In short, I was essentially a New Critic, though I was in this position compromised by having some awareness of the literary problems caused by the existence, in our own day, of the possibility of solipsism. My project, to trace the notion of poetry past the twelfth century, was a classic exercise in the history of ideas.

But the evidence refused to behave. I knew intuitively that *Piers Plowman* and the *Romance of the Rose*, different as they are, are more like each other than either is like the *Anticlaudianus*. I should not have been surprised to find substantial discontinuity in literary attitudes after the end of the period dominated by the sensibility we define as Chartrean. But I was indeed surprised, and for a long time baffled, by the fact that the late medieval commentators refused to satisfy any of my three basic expectations: for discourse from an Other, for a literary form defined by its text alone, even for a single category which might properly be called 'literature.'

What the evidence finally forced me to see was that, if I would give up 'literature,' I could have everything back, and in an even more powerful and admirable mode. This mode, as the title of my book announces, is the mode of the ethical. I shall not attempt to define it here; the medieval commentators must do that, in their own words, as they are given their turn. But by way of introduction to what they say, I must try to explain two things: how it can be that one can give up the category 'literature' and still keep for poems their full richness, power, and value; and, in a factual and historical way, what presence and manner of address gave to these medieval commentators that I quote the right to be, for medieval writers and readers, a sufficient accounting for poetry.

First, then, how can one begin a book on literary theory by giving up literature? For some readers, I know, this attitude is and will remain an a priori impossibility. No one who went first hand through the wars that rescued poetry from Irving Babbit and the McGuffey readers can easily face the possibility that what one rescued does not exist. These readers will feel, on a priori grounds, that the medieval commentators are talking beside the point, and that even when their talk actually illuminates, or permits me to illuminate, some medieval poem, this happy result has occurred because a poet has been able to exploit for the sake of poetry something alien to it. With this attitude there can, obviously, be no communication, since what is involved is a basic difference of ideology.

I can at least illustrate this difference, and perhaps defuse it, by resorting to a deliberately frivolous analogy. A motorcycle may be deemed, with equal propriety, a mode of transportation or a sex symbol. In either case, the object itself remains the same. It is a two-wheeled thing, with handlebars, a saddle which usually accommodates no more than two in-line embracing passengers, and an internal combustion engine, usually noisy, capable of lively acceleration and quite dangerous speeds. In riding it, one is exposed to considerable kinetic stimulation, and in owning it, to the insistent presence of obviously well-made and finely tuned machinery. Both in owning and in riding, one is stimulated to an awareness of that virtue which Plato defined in terms of virtuous skill – if one does not deal with one's motorcycle expertly, one will be killed.

Beyond this is context and ideology. In a poor country, the motorcycle is a mode of transportation whose real alternative is a bicycle; in a rich one, it is a frivolous and dangerous alternative to the automobile. When one trades up from bicycle to motorcycle, one attains a mode of getting around which is no more exposed in wet weather, and otherwise vastly superior. But one gains this improvement at a price – there is greater speed, greater danger, and therefore a greater requirement of virtuosity. All these achievements, however, are subsumed under transportation, and give to the act of simply getting from place to place a certain mythic quality which comes with the virtuosity required in operating the beast.

In a rich country full of automobiles, a motorcycle is an inferior mode of transportation, which one chooses, if at all, as a deliberate exercise of the virtuosity it requires, for the sake of that virtuosity alone. That is, one extracts from the existence of the motorcyclist those features which can be enjoyed aesthetically, and prizes them only. Being on the road is more important than the destination, and because of the danger, power, and posture involved, this being is very often interpreted in terms of metaphors of sexuality.

It is important to see that, because the motorcycle is what it is, every feature of the aesthetic use of it persists when one uses it as transportation. One does not make the trip any less dangerous and exciting and kinetic, simply because one intends to get somewhere – rather, one transforms the practical act of travelling into something with a mythic dimension. In giving up the use of the motorcycle for its own sake, one gives up nothing – rather, one is forced to transform the practical by experiencing it, as such, by including a dimension whose content might, if taken separately, be called aesthetic. To do so does not abolish or omit the aesthetic. Rather, it de-trivializes it by integrating it into the very essence of the real.

What the medieval critics asked me to do was give up literature, in order that I might get back poetry de-trivialized, delivered from that dismissal into which the category 'literature' had put it. Poems, of course, in so far as they are objects, or instances of human behaviour, remained the same – all their decorum, virtuosity, textual richness, emotional power, remain. But under the definitions of the medieval critics, they enjoy a different status, they benefit from a different ideology. They are not literature, but ethics; thus their presence to and in affairs we are pleased to call practical transforms the practical itself into something pleasing as well as useful.

These critics were present to medieval poets and to the audience of medieval poetry in two ways. First, these critics were schoolteachers, and so determined what readings of school poetry would be made. Second, their glosses are pervasively present in book margins; it would be possible to conceive of a medieval reader who had never read commentary on some single poem, but not possible to believe one could remain innocent of commentary if he read many poems. Thus Dante, Langland, Chaucer, Jean de Meun, or whoever – no medieval poet could have learned his Latin without having submitted his reading to a school accessus, nor could he have read at all widely without having encountered more or less marginal commentary. One may as little imagine that a medieval poet could be unaffected by these experiences as imagine that a modern one could have passed through sixteen years of normal, liberal education without ever having acquired an aesthetic attitude.

These facts become obvious to anyone who will take the trouble to order up, from any great manuscript collection of Europe, ten random medieval copies of Ovid's *Metamorphoses*.[1] The extensive quotations from the medieval critics, which I have arrayed in this book, are intended to reproduce, in organized and accessible form, the sense of the being of poetry one gets from reading it in a glossed manuscript, with the mind of one trained by the methods of the medieval accessus. My claim that medieval poets both did and necessarily must have read in this way is first and most fundamentally the result of my having read behind them, out of the same physical books which in general they read, and made to read. My modern sense, at least at first, that this way of reading was both unnatural and unpoetic, is utterly beside the point; the fact that the manner of reading whose clear nature and procedure medieval books preserve seems to be eccentric is a problem which I must overcome, and not a cause for rejecting medieval evidence.

In these manuscripts, many glosses betray explicitly that they are school lectures, or lecture notes.[2] On the other hand, it is clear that some material is more advanced than others. The classic and well-known example is that given by Alanus in his introduction to the *Anticlaudianus*, in which he distinguishes several different levels of ability and appreciation in his expected audience.[3] Even when a reader finds some one poem in a copy with clean margins, he will know from elsewhere the usual way of reading. Robert Holkot, who apparently read his *Metamorphoses* without commentary, or at least without repeating material from any commentary now known, invented for his advanced classes in theology the same kinds of interpretation which the commentaries would have taught him.[4] Dante, writing to his patron, clearly thinks that school procedures of commentary explanation are suitable for the presentation of his *Paradiso* to Cangrande;[5] he also formed his *Vita nuova* after the model of text and gloss. Whether created by schoolmasters or made up by adult readers following their example; whether transcribed in a formal school situation or encountered when 'inventing' from some auctor the matter of one's poem – the glosses of the commentators, and their implicit theoretical attitudes, would have been unavoidable.

Of this pervasive presence of a lore which exists between school and life and partakes of both, the existence of Vatican manuscript Vat. lat. 1479 is an excellent illustration. This book, an elegant large folio, on vellum, made in fourteenth-century France, is obviously some wealthy adult's personal library. The volume contains the *ars major* of Donatus, with other grammatical material and an anonymous treatise on prosody, plus the *Distichs* of Cato, the *Eclogues* of Theodulus, the *Remedia amoris* and the *Metamorphoses* of Ovid, the versified *Tobias* of Matthew of Vendôme, and the *Alexandreis* of Walter of Chatillon. All but the first two texts are elaborately surrounded by commentary. Such a book, partly reflecting the elementary curriculum of the schools and partly the cultivated reading of the schooled adult, set in a dense frame of gloss and commentary written large for old eyes, is ideal testimony to the character of medieval literary culture.

In collecting glosses, I have tried to cast as wide a net as possible. At the same time, I have tried to find some valid focus in this wilderness of glosses, by choosing certain texts whose commentary tradition might be covered with something like completeness. The most important of these texts was Ovid's *Metamorphoses*. Medieval reading of Ovid, particularly in the later period of his greatest popularity, brings into convenient focus a number of major literary questions – the problem of fable and fiction, the problem of unity posed by miscellany poetry, the problem of allegorical commentary, the problem of the Christian use of pagan culture – all in connection with a text which furnished late medieval authors with more stories than any other single source with the possible exception of the Bible. Other than the *Metamorphoses*, the texts on which I have studied a substantial and representative number of commentaries are the *Consolation of Philosophy* of Boethius, the *Thebaid* of Statius, the *De nuptiis* of Martianus Capella, the medieval Christian hymn-book, and the *Poetria nova* of Geoffrey of Vinsauf. Other texts and other commentaries will be referred to from time to time, but they are of the same sorts as these. Altogether they represent fairly the kinds of literature which cover the medieval range: a story book, an epic history, a personal meditation, an allegorical encyclopedia, a piece of criticism, and a collection of Christian lyric. In addition, I have used the Averroistic version of Aristotle's *Poetics*, which medieval critics knew in the translation of Hermann the German, and on which there survives one Paris commentary.

As a parallel, and control, I have used also at least some of the major collections of commentary on the Bible: the *Glosa ordinaria*, the compilations of Hugh of St Cher, and the works of Nicholas of Lyra, Pierre Bersuire, and Denis the Carthusian. In using Bible commentary I do not intend to prejudge any questions of interpretation, though I am convinced that distinctions which clearly obtained in the twelfth century to separate exegesis from the interpretation of literary integumenta tended later to weaken if not disappear entirely in practice. Rather, I look for procedural parallels – common accessus schemata, common ways of making divisions and naming parts, common areas of reference or concern in interpretation – that is, for things which are either narrowly technical or merely human, which might be expected to surround the specifically theological essence of exegesis. Where these procedural parallels do occur, the exegetical evidence can quite properly add corroborative detail to what is found in poetic contexts.

In presenting this material, I have tried to let the medieval critics speak for themselves, both by quoting extensively, and by conducting my discussion of their doctrines, as far as possible, by using their technical vocabulary in Latin. In my translations, I have tried to avoid misleading with cognates, and thus have had to try for a quite free but just interpretation where a literal translation would not mean much. Thus 'inventio' does not mean invention in the sense of imaginative creation so much as it means something like 'research'; 'dicendum est qualiter agat' literally means 'it must be discussed how it proceeds,' but since the commentators conventionally use this phrase to introduce discussion of the kind or mode in which a text occurs, I have in some cases interpreted: 'Genre must be discussed.' But even in these cases, my translations are intended to be no more than utilitarian, and my hope is that these commentators, strange though their notions be, will by sufficient speaking become intelligible in their own terms.

In presenting the writings of these commentators, I have tried to serve two purposes at once. I have tried first to explain the literary theory which seems to lie behind what they wrote – that is, behind the kind of reading which they made of the poems they read. Second, I have tried at every stage and step of definition to test my conclusions in the light of great medieval poetry – I have tried to read medieval poems in a medieval way, to confirm that the theory I was defining was true in the only way that matters to us – that is, could help us better understand Dante, Chaucer, Piers Plowman, the Gawain poet, and others.

My exposition has been organized so as to proceed from general to particular. I have dealt first with the large category in which medieval critics put their poems, that is, the category of ethics. Under this topic I try to explain what difference it makes both to poetry and to ethics that they occupy the same category. Next, I notice that under medieval definitions a poem has two forms, not one. The first form is external, modal, procedural, thematic. The second form is the poem's literal outline. I give a chapter to each kind of form. Since under most modern assumptions a poem has only one form, I am primarily concerned in these two chapters to distinguish clearly between these two quite different medieval forms which separately determine any given text. In addition, of course, I give some consideration to the critical significance of the fact that there are two forms rather than one. Fourth, I deal with the material of poetry – what the forms contain or form. By material, of course, I do not mean the content to which the words refer. Rather, I mean the words themselves, or rather the acts of language themselves, taken medievally, and so centrally defined by the word 'assimilatio' or likening. Finally, I deal with audience, which paradoxically, under medieval standards, does not stand outside or over against a poem, but ideally is contained within it. Thus I proceed from the category which contains poems, through their external and internal features, to that which poems contain. This centripetal procedure fits both the material with which I deal and the ideal requirements of logic. It has the further advantage of leaving the audience, at the end, inside the material. This happy conclusion will, I hope, not prove too uncomfortable. What the medieval critics demand of their modern audience is an axiomatic conversion. They are not repeating modern literary theory in a funny way. They are saying something quite different and incommensurable. One cannot understand what they are saying without first admitting that it is indeed different, so that one may then follow their words so as to be, eventually, taken in by them. Only by being so taken in can one avoid mistaking what the medieval critics have to say.

In the making of this book, I have incurred many happy debts – to librarians, colleagues, friends, benefactors, and books. To the American Philosophical Society I owe a summer's travel, and to the National Endowment for the Humanities one year in Rome and another in France, during which this book first became visible and finally was written. By virtue of their generosity, I am able to be grateful to the medieval critics themselves, with whom I am in fellowship both by virtue of our common enterprise of scholarship and because they have communicated to me an esteem for literature in which their rich human commitments and values are a living presence. One of the central pleasures of being a medievalist is that the books and documents of the period survive physically in sufficient numbers to permit genuine acquaintance with the people of that time, and thus to enrich one's own mind and position by living contact with a very different one. To the staffs of the great libraries – the Bodleian, the Vatican, the Bibliothèque nationale, the British Library, and the state libraries of Munich and Vienna –

I owe the customary thanks of the American, given the freedom of national treasures not his own. To colleagues and friends who encouraged me to trust what I was reading when none of us understood it, and who supported me in the work and pleasure of making sense of it, I owe large debts. To my some-time student R.A. Shoaf I am grateful both for the rigour of his conversation over the years, and for his reading of my earliest and latest drafts in a way which permitted me to distinguish between the possibly profound and the merely unintelligible. For help of the same kind, in the course of revision, I am also happy to thank John Alford, Patrick Gallacher, John Leyerle, and Glending Olson. For their improvements of my latinity, I thank Jeanne Krochalis and an anonymous reader for University of Toronto Press. Janet Black, my typist, coped admirably with a manuscript tedious both in bulk and in detail. My research assistants, Zarine Bana, Carol Briggs, and Patricia Hefner, helped with verification; Judith Jablonski worked with me through the copy editing, and prepared the indexes. At the University of Toronto Press, Prudence Tracy and Judith Williams supported me and the manuscript through our several ordeals of consideration and editing with kindness, efficiency, good humour, and unusual dispatch.

All these specific debts permit me to express, through them, a final grati-tude: for the pleasure of knowing myself in a field whose practitioners are friends rather than rivals. As medievalists, we each have so many happy things to work at that we are free to be glad that our friends are also busy, and free also to share. From this capital I have been given much, and so am pleased to repay, from time to time, what I can.

NOTES

1 The whole experience of dealing with medieval literature and its Latin context by directly confronting manuscripts is radically important, in ways which can-not be adequately explained to persons whose readings are normalized on modern printed editions. Auctoritas in its medieval form comes only weakly and much relativized into print. The best explanations I know of the effect of manuscript format on texts are Richard A. Dwyer 'The Appreciation of Hand-made Literature' *Chaucer Review* 8 (1974) 221–41; and Rossell Hope Robbins 'Mirth in Manuscripts' *Essays and Studies* NS, 21 (1968) 1–28.

2 A fifteenth-century Italian gloss on the *Thebiad*, for instance, says: 'Iste est quartus liber in quo proponuntur quedam carmina qui secundum quosdam duobus capitulis consumatur, sed secundum magistrum meum preceptorem quinque capitulis consumatur. / This is the fourth book, in which are pre-sented certain songs which according to some take two chapters, but according to my teacher take five.' Yale University, Beinecke Library, ms 166, f E6v.

3 *Anticlaudianus: texte critique avec une introduction et des tables* ed R. Bossuat (Paris 1955) pp 55–6

4 And used some of the same source books. For a study of Holkot's use of mythographic materials, see Judson B. Allen 'The Library of a Classicizer: The Sources of Robert Holkot's Mythographic Learning' *Les Arts libéraux et philosophie au moyen âge: Actes du quatrième congrès international de philosophie médiévale, 27 août–2 septembre, 1967* (Montréal 1969) pp 721–9.

5 'Itaque, formula consummata epistolae, ad introductionem oblati operis aliquid sub lectoris officio compendiose aggrediar. / Thus, now that I have finished the letter formula, I turn briefly to introduce this book I am sending by behaving like a schoolteacher.' Epistola X, in *Le Opere di Dante Alighieri* ed E. Moore (Oxford 1963) p 415. (All future references to Dante's works, other than the *Commedia*, are to this edition.)

THE ETHICAL POETIC OF THE LATER MIDDLE AGES
A DECORUM OF CONVENIENT DISTINCTION

1

Ethical poetry, poetic ethics, and the sentence of poetry

The enterprise of this chapter is to locate a particular occurrence of poetry. I wish to look at the universe of late medieval Europe in order to see where and under what guise we might find in it the thing which we are now accustomed to call a poem. To announce this purpose is both to presume the possibility of historical criticism, and in this presumption to imply that finding poetry in late medieval Europe can be done clearly and obviously. It can, but only after a considerable modern critical adjustment. To impose at the outset a proper sense of the difficulty of this enterprise, as well as the character of its goal, I would like to indulge an analogy.

When Claude Lévi-Strauss escaped from Vichy France in 1941, he found himself on the same steamer with Victor Serge, a former companion of Lenin in the Russian Revolution. His reaction to Serge defines structures which are precisely the same as the ones which this chapter will attempt to construct, and through which it will be possible to locate poetry in the late medieval universe. Of Victor Serge, Lévi-Strauss says:

I was intimidated by his status as a former companion of Lenin, at the same time as I had the greatest difficulty in identifying him with his physical presence, which was rather like that of a prim and elderly spinster. The clean-shaven, delicate-featured face, the clear voice accompanied by a stilted and wary manner, had an almost asexual quality, which I was later to find among Buddhist monks along the Burmese frontier, and which is very far removed from the virile and superabundant vitality commonly associated in France with what are called subversive activities. The explanation is that cultural types which occur in very similar forms in every society, because they are constructed around very simple polarities, are used to fulfil different social functions in different communities. Serge's type had been able to realize itself in a revolutionary career in Russia, but elsewhere it might have played some other part. No doubt relationships between any two societies would be made easier if, through the use of some kind of grid, it were possible to establish a pattern of equivalences between the ways in which each society uses analogous human types to perform different social functions. Instead of simply arranging meetings on a professional basis, doctors with doctors, teachers with teachers and industrialists with industrialists, we might perhaps be led to see that there are more subtle correspondences between individuals and the parts they play.[1]

In this casual reference to a 'grid' and a 'pattern of equivalences,' we have the essence of Lévi-Strauss' structuralism. His genius has been, not only to see individuals (whether people or actions) as elements in a system, but even more to achieve the comparison of systems themselves.

In these terms, late medieval Europe was a system – a universe with no parts left over, corresponding as a whole, but only as a whole and not part by part, with all other systems. In this late medieval system, texts were made whose textuality we still possess, and which we are pleased to call poems. Between our system and the late medieval one, this textuality persists – an ordered series of words in a particular language. Beyond this, of course, there is nothing – no certain correspondence. Our enterprise must begin by admitting this nothing, lest we impose our categories on the past. Just as a Russian revolutionary from one system corresponds to a Buddhist monk from another, so what we in our system call poems will indeed correspond to something in the medieval system – but nothing in our system except the textuality of those poems must be allowed to predict what that something will be.

Fortunately, the search is made easier by the structure of the medieval system itself. One of the favourite intellectual procedures of medieval scholars was classification. For us, this activity ranks relatively low, and we delegate it to file clerks and electronic morons, in order to think about processes and systems, and make flow charts. But medieval culture is full of lists of headings. There are seven sins, seven virtues, four elements, four humours, twelve zodiacal signs and their corresponding cosmic and human temperaments. It may be that some sense of the power and fitness of this use of lists is being now recovered – one is beginning to hear people classifying themselves and others as Pisces or Leo or Virgo with no sense of violated human integrity and with some considerable sense that a significant interpretation has been made, and this not many years after most intellectuals felt that to be called, or to call someone, a communist was inadmissible, not only because of possible factual inaccuracy, but even more because such classificatory labelling was felt to violate the existential uniqueness of the human individual.

Medieval classifications were made, apparently, in the faith that any given entity – act, person, or fact – was enhanced by being so classed. One's label, one's context, was properly a part of one's essence and definition, and one could not do without it. It seems simple enough to say that there are, for instance, seven liberal arts – or more specifically, that the trivium consists of grammar, rhetoric, and logic. In practice, however, when one confronts medieval thinkers grappling with application – deciding just which linguistic activities were grammar, which rhetoric, and which logic, and dealing with the fact that these three headings must be taken as exhaustive as well as descriptive – it becomes clear that the decision to classify, and to classify under these three headings, is a decision of enormous structural importance.[2] When, therefore, we know where in their system of classification medieval critics put poems, we obviously know already a great deal about their definitions of poetry.

Medieval critics conventionally began their commentaries on the poem they read by making an 'accessus,' or introduction, in which a number of obligatory topics were discussed.[3] Among these topics was the assignment of the work under consideration to its proper part of philosophy. Conrad of Hirsau, in his *Dialogue super auctores*, explains the possibilities:

Restat nunc in calce nostri dialogi que sint partes philosophie perpaucis ostendere, quod constat nos in fronte suscepte collationis posuisse.

(D) Partium enim distinctio tocius unde partes constant elucidatio est; dic ergo.

(M) In tres partes philosophia distinguitur, in logicam que rationalis dicitur, in phisicam que naturalis dicitur, in ethicam que moralis dicitur. de physica quadruuium habes, arithmeticam geometriam musicam astronomiam, de logica triuium, rhetoricam dialecticam grammaticam; de ethica: iusticiam prudentiam fortitudinem temperantiam: hec enim de moribus tractat; porro de rethorica: natura usus doctrina; de grammatica: lectio enarratio emendatio iudicium; de dialectica: propositio assumptio probatio conclusio.

Now it remains at the end of our dialogue to show briefly what are the parts of philosophy, which we did at the beginning of the undertaken comparison.

(D) It is an explanation of a whole to distinguish the parts which compose it. Tell on.

(M) Philosophy is divided into three parts: logic, or rational philosophy, physics or natural philosophy, and ethics or moral philosophy. From physics you derive the quadrivium – arithmetic, geometry, music, and astronomy. From logic, the trivium – rhetoric, dialectic, and grammar. From ethics – justice, prudence, fortitude, and temperance, for this [ethics] deals with behaviour. Next, rhetoric, which includes character, custom and prescription; grammar includes reading, interpretation, correction, and criticism; dialectic includes proposition, hypothesis, proof, and conclusion.[4]

Thus there are many available parts of philosophy to which a work may be assigned. Conventionally, medieval critics assigned poems to ethics, as we shall see. But there were occasional exceptions, either because the subject matter of a particular poem seemed so clearly something other than ethics as to demand a special classification, or because the poem dealt with poetry itself, and so demanded to be classified as a verbal art. These exceptions, however, really prove the rule, because in practice the habit of assigning poetry to ethics was so strong as to have some influence even where it clearly or conventionally did not belong.

A perfect example occurs in an accessus to a commentary on the *Ars poetica* of Horace; it shows the author actually changing his mind after having followed the convention:

Ethice sub ponitur [sic] quia ostendit qui mores conveniant poete. Vel potius logice, quia ad noticiam recte et ornate locutionis et ad exercitationem regularium scriptorum nos inducit.

It is classified as ethics because it shows which behaviour is appropriate to the poet. Or rather as logic, because it teaches us correctness and elegance of expression, and the use of the rules of writers.[5]

The crucial phrase here, which we shall see substantially repeated in accessus after accessus, is 'ethice subponitur quia ostendit qui mores conveniant ...' Any text which has anything to do with human behaviour 'subponitur ethice.' But in this case the commentator is wrong; he has ignored the distinction between an art and that which may exist as a result of the exercise of an art. So he changes his mind, and puts the *Ars poetica* under logic. It could have gone well enough under grammar, or even rhetoric, but as a verbal art, it would normally have had to be put under one of the three.[6] This is true because, as a verbal art, it has no content of its own, but contains the rules for correct and attractive writing about any content whatever. At the same time, one can sympathize with the commentator's mistake. Rhetoric came out of Roman law and politics, and grammar in practice included both much rhetorical doctrine and many actual poetic examples.

What is at stake is well explained by Alanus de Insulis. He deals with this distinction between ethics, on the one hand, and the proper understanding of a verbal art, on the other, in his commentary on the *Rhetorica ad Herennium*, which I quote from a St Victor manuscript, probably of the late fourteenth century. Alanus, dealing with his text with full appreciation of its practical usefulness to the lawyers and civic leaders for whom it was originally written, first relates rhetoric to 'civil science.'

Est igitur civilis sciencia in dictis propter rethoricam que est pars litigandi sive causas agendi, quod idem est. Doceret enim dicere, idest causas agere. Est ita in factis propter sapienciam que est in legibus quibus cives disceptant idest quid iustum quid utile quid honestum, quid ita faciendum sit et quid non, indubitanter agnoscunt. Et hec quidem partes civilis sciencie non ad agendum spectant sed pocius ad sciendum qualiter dicendum et qualiter agendum. Unde et civilis ratio que ex his est civilis appellatur sciencia. Et si quis ad verum inspiciat inveniet opportere quemvis esse peritum in civili sciencia ut ad civilem digne promoveatur administracionem. Manifestum est autem ex prius dictis artem rethoricam integralem partem esse civilis sciencie.

It is a civil science in its words, because of rhetoric, which is a part of litigation or the pleading of cases, which is the same thing. For it teaches speech, that is, the pleading of cases. It exists in deeds because of the wisdom embodied in the laws by which citizens make judgments, that is by which they know without any doubt what is just, useful, and honest, and what should or should not be done in such and such a way. And these parts of civil science have less to do with action than with the knowledge of how speech and action should be. Therefore the theory of government based on these things is called civil science. And whoever has regard to the truth will find it fitting for someone to be expert in civil science, so that he might worthily be promoted to public office. Thus it is manifest from the above that the art of rhetoric is an integral part of civil science.[7]

Then, after discussing a number of conventional accessus topics, to which he refers in concluding, 'et hec sunt que circa opus quod exposituri sumus consideranda proposuimus, / and these are the things which we propose should be considered about the work we shall expound,' he turns to the obligatory assignment to a part of philosophy. The pressure of the convention must be resisted:

Amplius utrum rethorica ad philosophiam pertineat superfluum est inquirere, quoniam non est de philosophia nec ad aliquam partem eius aliquo modo spectat.

Philosophia nimirum studium est et amor sapiencie per quam veritas inquiritur et reperitur circa generales questiones. Sed in rethorica nulla est omnino veritatis inquisitio, nec et in grammatica, quia orator non intendit veritatem inquirere, sed persuadere. Est enim rethorica animorum commotiva sicut grammatica est recte locutionis inquisitiva. Unde manifestum est quod rethorica non est de philosophia nec ad aliquam partem eius spectat. Philosophie namque tres partes sunt: ethica, speculativa, rationalis idest logica. Sed rethorica ad nullam harum partium spectat philosophie. Quare non est de philosophia est est [sic] notandum quod in hoc libro ut nobis videtur, non est inquirenda materia, sicut nec in ceteris libris. Materie quippe non sunt librorum sed artium tantum.

It is superfluous to inquire further whether rhetoric has to do with philosophy, because it does not, neither does it in any way pertain to any part of philosophy. Philosophy, obviously, is the study and love of wisdom, by which the truth involving general questions is investigated and discovered. But in rhetoric there is no investigation of the truth at all, neither in grammar, because the orator does not intend to investigate the truth, but to persuade. Rhetoric has to do with stirring souls, as grammar has to do with determining correct language. Therefore it is obvious that rhetoric does not belong to philosophy nor pertain to any part of it. For there are three parts of philosophy: ethics, speculative philosophy, and rational philosophy or logic. Rhetoric pertains to none of these parts of philosophy. Therefore it is not philosophy; and it should be noted that in this book, as it seems to us, one should not inquire about the material, just as one does not in other books. The material involved is not that of the book, but of the art only. (ff 5v–6r)[8]

This same oscillation we find reflected in commentaries on Geoffrey of Vinsauf's *Poetria nova*. The commonest choice is to treat the work as an art. Thus:

Parti quidem phylosophie supponitur rationali sive per grammaticam sive per loycam sive etiam per rethoricam, quibus poetica diversimode supponitur ut ut [sic] patet ex prius dictis. In quam vero ad musicam pertinet, supponitur mathematice philosophie. Musica enim est una de mathematicis scientiis.

It is classified as rational philosophy either because it is grammar, or logic, or rhetoric: poetry may be variably classified as one of these, as is clear above. In so far as it pertains to music, it is classified as mathematics, for music is one of the mathematical sciences.[9]

Another accessus in the same manuscript says simply, 'Supponitur autem phylosophie rationali' (f 74v). Another commentator carelessly leaves his sentence unfinished, but his meaning is clear: 'Et si queratur cui parti philosophie supponatur cum qualibet scientia sit in sermonem ut in subiecto ... / And if one asks to what part of philosophy it belongs, since every science may have a linguistic aspect, so with regard to this subject ...'[10] On the other hand, still another commentator says: 'Cui parti phylosophie supponatur? supponitur arti poetice que supponitur phylosophie morali? / Under which part of philosophy is it classified? / under the art of poetry which is a part of moral philosophy.'[11] In so saying, he not only reflects the convention which associates poems with ethics; he goes further and makes it explicit that he thinks so because the thing he is classifying is a poem, and therefore specifically is 'poetice' before generically 'phylosophie morali.'

In most late medieval accessus and commentaries, this convention is pervasively obvious. In the materials edited by R.B.C. Huygens, one normally finds simply, 'Ethicae subponitur quia de moribus tractat. / It is classified as ethics because it deals with behaviour.'[12] In commentary on the *Metamorphoses* of Ovid, the commentators not only classify the poem as ethics, but generalize, saying that this is normal for poets:

Intentio Ovidii est omniumque fabulas scribentium utpote Terentii maxime delectare et delectando tamen mores instruere, quia omnes auctores fere ad ethicam tendunt.

Ovid's intention, and that of all writers of fables, such as Terence, is to delight as much as possible, and by delighting, to instruct in behaviour, because virtually all authors have to do with ethics.[13]

The *Metamorphoses*, of course, is the test case; in the age of Ovid, it is more than any other work the exemplary poem. It would be tedious to pile up citation after citation; they all say virtually the same thing.[14] The only exceptions I have found occur in three probably related manuscripts, whose commentary recognizes that the *Metamorphoses* includes cosmological material at its beginning. But they also reflect the ethical classification. The earliest commentary says:

Videndum est qualiter agat. Agit enim heroyco metro colligens mutationes diversas a prima creacione mundi usque ad suum tempus, quod signat sua invocatio ubi dicit *primaque ab origine mundi etc*. Physicus est auctor iste assignando generationem elementorum. Ethicus est in assignatione mutationum que faciunt ad mores.

We must see what is the genre of the book. Generically, it is in the heroic metre; it is a collection of diverse changes from the first creation of the world up to his own time. This its invocation indicates where it says, 'and from the first origin of the world, etc.'

This author is a physicist when he points out the generation of the elements; he is ethical in pointing out the changes which have to do with behaviour.[15]

What is true of the *Metamorphoses* seems to be true generally. The conventional assignment is to ethics; when an exception occurs, it seems clearly an exception – and in no case have I found either assignment to any category which one might consider literary or aesthetic in the modern sense, or any willingness to consider a category consisting of literature, or poetry, as having any existence as such.[16] Narrative poetry, obviously, one must take as ethics; I have found in commentary on the *Thebaid* of Statius no exception to this rule.[17] Ovid's *Heroides* are ethics;[18] so is the *Facta et dicta* of Valerius Maximus,[19] so is Boethius' *Consolation of Philosophy*,[20] so, by clear implication, are at least some of the various genres of Languedoc lyric,[21] so, by virtue of Dante's own accessus, is the *Divina commedia*,[22] so, to descend into medieval trivia, are the pseudo-Virgilian *Copa*[23] and John Garland's *Cornutus*.[24] Only the medieval hymn-book, whose liturgical associations make it naturally theological,[25] and the *Anticlaudianus* of Alanus,[26] whose commentary tradition was substantially defined very early, are not related to ethics explicitly, but they are not exceptions which permit one to make anything essential of poetry as such.

In my documentation of this relation between poetry and ethics, I have been at great pains to emphasize exceptions, not because there are so many, but because there are so few. My work began as an attempt to find, in the work of the late medieval critics, a theory of 'poetry,' properly so called. The evidence was recalcitrant; no such theory could be found. Medieval critics insisted, both in their conventional classification of their texts as ethics, and in their tendency to moralize and make moral allegories, that their texts constituted no special, aesthetic, poetic category. Their awareness of the difference between a verbal art and the text which results from its practice, and their very occasional awareness of the fact that a particular text's content was theological, scientific, or speculative, have, indeed, a great deal of medieval doctrinal importance, but cannot be taken as proving the existence of anything like a modern definition of poetry. I must admit that for some years I tried to make the evidence do so – I tried to read forward from the speculative and mythic poems of the twelfth century, and backward from the extraordinary humanist honour paid to 'litterae humaniores' in the Renaissance, in order to use these few exceptional glosses as claims for poetry as such. I was, therefore, searching with special diligence for these exceptional glosses, as I thought glittering in a wilderness of trite morality, and I here record every one of the few I have found, in order to admit, and demonstrate, that they are worse than useless as proof of what I wanted them for, but that they make quite good sense as a part of a morality really more garden than wilderness.

What needs to be emphasized first and above all is that all poetry – in fact, anything made of words – belongs to some branch of philosophy or other (or to the contentless trivium, which some would classify as philosophy also). For the most part, texts we would call poems were, in general conventionally, classified as ethics. This fact means two complementary things. First, it means that in the later Middle Ages, there existed no intellectual category precisely corresponding to the one we mean when we say 'poetry,' or 'literature.' There were, indeed, a number of medieval categories one might try to mistake for 'poetry,' such as the 'auctores,' or even 'poetria.' But these are not the same. Our Russian revolutionary has become a Buddhist monk, and we must take him with his yellow robe or not at all. On the other hand, all the features of a poem's textuality which we admire by the word 'poetry,' continue to exist – ostentation of formal strategies, material involving heightened decorum or attention or both, that assumption of self-importance which we label with such words as 'mythic' or 'archetypal.' These features continue to exist, but now not as qualities of poetry but as qualities of ethics.

This fact, that late medieval poems were classified as ethics, and therefore that no medieval category existed precisely corresponding to our 'literature,' involves me in a practical problem. The ostensible subject of this book has disappeared. In absolute terms, there is no such thing as medieval literary theory, because there is no literature to be theoretical about. There are, however, poems, and my real difficulty consists in continuing to use the word 'poem' and the word 'poetry,' because no other words exist to describe the collection of verbal objects whose textuality we possess in common with the medieval critics. My practical need for the word conflicts precisely with the heuristic necessity of avoiding it. I might be tempted to substitute such a phrase as 'the class of verbal objects distinguished by ostentatious and apparently deliberate virtuosity and decorum,' but there is already enough jargon in the world, and one must guard against it as much as possible. I also must admit that in the course of having gotten myself to the intellectual point of wishing to write this book, my own notion of what a poem is, in absolute terms, has been much influenced by these medieval categories. My use of the term 'poetry,' therefore, involves a certain amount of duplicity even apart from the enterprise of describing medieval definitions and theories, in that I mean by it something rather more anthropological than I would suppose is generally held. I know no way out of this dilemma except to plead guilty and go on. I shall therefore use the words 'poem,' and 'poetry,' and 'literature,' freely to mean simply, and no more than, the class of objects (it may be that not all of them, medievally speaking, will turn out to be verbal) defined by the existence of such examples as the *Consolation of Philosophy* of Boethius, the *Metamorphoses* of Ovid, the *Commedia* of Dante, the 'Can vei la lauzeta mover' of Bernard of Ventadour, the *Quadrireggio* of Federigo Frezzi,[27] and the *Morte Darthur* of Malory.

One might be tempted to protest that, since Dante's poem continues to exist, it makes no difference what one calls it. The *Commedia* is so much more important than either Benvenuto da Imola or Benedetto Croce that one should merely be satisfied *that* it is, and in this satisfaction discover all that one needs to know of *what* it is. Such a protest cannot be refuted; having presumed already an existential world, it leaves no ground for arguing one's self out of it. I can, however, protest in return that for minds having any sympathy at all for Platonism, or even for the Aristotelian version of it that dominated late medieval thought, the enterprise of definition contributes powerfully to and indeed is a necessary part of the existence of any single thing. Just as it makes a great deal of difference to one's appreciation of a human being to know that he is a Russian revolutionary or that he is a Buddhist monk, so it should make an enormous difference, both to our appreciation of Dante's *Commedia* and to our use of it, that we should know what it is. A definition is both a complement to a thing, and a compliment to it. A definition gives a thing its use – furnishes to it an orderly cosmos of which it is both a constituted and a constitutive part.[28] Thus to wish to dispense with definition, or to claim that the world in its existence has deprived us of definition, is to admit the desirability or the possibility of getting along without a universe, or of making one's own existence the sole basis for all interpretations. Medieval thinkers, of course, would admit no such chaos; their example is instructive.

If, then, poems are classifiable under ethics, to define ethics is to define the genus of which poetry is the species. Given the medieval evidence which I am about to present, it is fair to make the equation even more direct, and say that to define ethics in medieval terms is to define poetry, and to define poetry is to define ethics, because medieval ethics was so much under the influence of a literary paideia as to be enacted poetry, and poetry was so practically received as to be quite directly the extended examples for real behaviour.[29] What we are dealing with is a category which does not precisely correspond to any modern one, partly because it includes a much larger rhetorical component than modern ethics, partly because it is differently normative, and partly because it does not confront the question of sincerity. What we have, in a word, is a category which can only be designated 'ethics-hyphen-poetry'; which contains most elements of both, and which is distinctive by virtue of its existence as a single, self-consistent category, rather than as the paradox which my hyphenated piece of jargon implies today. It is particularly difficult to define, because it was clearly so obvious to medieval thinkers that they did not really discuss it as such, so much as make distinctions within and about it, presume it, and analyse its elements; what we are after is a piece of the medieval axiom system, and so we must get at it by hints and indirections.

The category is enacted in a complex of Dantean puns, of which R.A. Shoaf has kindly informed me. At the very beginning of the *Commedia*, Dante found himself ('mi ritrovai,' *Inferno* I.2); etymologically, the word connects his act to that of the trouvères, and names a poetic invention, of which Dante's use of the word 'per' makes the dark wood an agent or means as well as a location. Dante then promises to treat ('trattare') of the good he found there. What results from such a treating, verbally, is a tractate or commentary – in this case, Dante's poem, which treats his invention, himself. Nearly two cantiche later, at what is certainly at the moral level the climax of the poem, Virgil says to Dante,

'Tratto t'ho qui con ingegno e con arte;
  lo tuo piacere omai prendi per duce;
  ...
 per ch'io te sovra te corono e mitrio.'

'I have led you here with genius and with art; / from here on take your pleasure as your guide ... because I crown and mitre you over yourself.' (*Purgatorio* XXVII.130–42)

These two places frame the area of the poem in which sin is possible, and in which, therefore, ethical considerations are obtrusive. The word that begins by 'tractating' ends by literally leading, and both are the same, as the word is the same. The verbal act which makes a poem and the moral act which leads a life are the same, and both operate on a trouvère's invention, and both are accomplished by means of the exercise of genius and art.

What Dante's language enacts other medieval books presume. I shall discuss two, which frame the area of the ethical from opposite sides. One, the *De regimine principum* of Aegidius Romanus, defines the purposes and strategy of an ethical treatise by using terminology normally used to describe something literary. In another place, he distinguishes rhetoric from ethics and politics in a way which relates ethics to logic. From the other side, there occur in the version of Aristotle's *Poetics* accepted by the Middle Ages analyses of remarkably ethical terminology. The ethical treatise talks in literary terms; the treatise on poetics talks in ethical terms. In combination, they bracket our needed definition. Further, all this material is clearly defined as relating, in one direction, to logic, and in the opposite, to the praise and blame of human behaviour, or 'mores.' In trusting these materials to provide a definition of the medieval ethical poetic, I am of course trusting a certain logic of analogy – that literary and ethical terminologies carry with them consistent meaning when used in foreign contexts. That they must have done so is obvious from the accessus of the medieval critics, whose classification of poetry as ethics presumes the combination. The *De regimine* and the *Poetics* put together make that presumption both explicit and intelligible.

The discussion in the *De regimine*, which deals with the modus agendi of an ethical book through the use of essentially literary terms, is both short and straightforward; the terms are ones familiar both to twelfth-century poetic and to modern discussions of it. It is thus enough to make the point that I specify the terms, and show that they were indeed used. The discussion in the *Poetics*, by contrast, is enormously complex. It displaces, in the medieval theory of literature, the six parts of tragedy familiar from the authentic Aristotle. This displacement, and the ethical significance of the terms involved, have not been hitherto properly appreciated, and I shall therefore have to deal with them far more carefully and at much greater length than with the *De regimine*.

The first chapter of the *De regimine* is entitled 'Quis modus procedendi in regimine Principum.' The modus procedendi, or, as other accessus schemata would have it, the forma tractandi which is half of formal cause, refers to the intellectual posture or kind of activity by means of which a particular subject is dealt with. This notion of modus procedendi, or forma tractandi, is of enormous importance for medieval poetic theory; it will be the primary concern of the chapter to follow. However, it is important here to realize that ethical thinking, which Aegidius here sets out to define, is clearly a kind of thinking – a mental posture first, and the result of that mental posture second. Aegidius will make the point that the object of this thinking is action rather than knowledge; nevertheless, the radical connection in this as in other features of medieval culture between fact and thought, between what is and some category of mental capability, is entirely clear.

Sciendum ergo, quod in toto morali negotio modus procedendi secundum Philosophum est figuralis et grossus: oportet enim in talibus typo et figuraliter pertransire, quia gesta moralia complete sub narratione non cadunt.

15 Ethical poetry, poetic ethics, and the sentence of poetry

It should be known, that the [intellectual] procedure in moral matters according to the Philosopher is figurative and approximate; in such matters it is appropriate to deal by means of models and figuratively, because moral actions are not treated fully by simply telling what happened.

Aegidius goes on to explain that this is true in three ways: one because of the material involved, one because of the end or purpose, and one because of the audience. Then we have a slightly more expanded version of what he means by 'figuralis et grossus.'

Cum enim doctrina de regimine Principum fit de actibus humanis, et comprehendatur sub morali negocio, quia materia moralis (ut dictum est) non patitur perscrutationem subtilem, sed est de negociis singularibus: quae (ut declarari habet 2. Ethicorum) propter sui variabilitatem, magnam incertitudinem habent. Quia ergo sic est, ipsa acta singularia, quae sunt materia huius operis, ostendant incedendum esse figuraliter et typo.

Since the doctrine of the training of princes deals with human actions, and is comprehended under morality, it is not subject to strict analysis, but concerns individual transactions, because (as was said) its material is moral. Individual transactions, as is declared in the second book of the Ethics, are most uncertain because they vary. Because this is true, the singular acts, which are the material of this book, prove by their nature that they can only be treated figuratively and with a model.

He distinguishes this treatment of ethics, which involves persuasion, from geometry and other deductive sciences, which involve demonstration, and then turns to the treatment of purpose or end.

Opus morale suscipimus non contemplationis gratia, neque ut sciamus, sed ut boni fiamus. Finis ergo intentus in hac scientia, non est sui negocii cognitio, sed opus: nec est veritas, sed bonum. Cum ergo rationes subtiles magis illuminent intellectem [sic], superficiales vero et grossae magis moveant et inflamment [sic] affectum: in scientiis speculativis, ubi principaliter quaeritur illuminatio intellectus, procedendum est demonstrative et subtiliter, in negocio morali, ubi quaeritur rectitudo voluntatis, et ut boni fiamus, procedendum est persuasive et figuraliter.

We do not undertake a moral work for the sake of contemplation, nor that we might know, but that we might be made good. The purpose of this science therefore is not knowledge of its material, but action; not truth, but the good. Therefore since precise reasoning more illuminates the intellect, subject matter drawn from what appears to be, and what is approximate more moves and inflames the affections: in speculative fields, whose principal object is the illumination of the intellect, one proceeds strictly and by demonstration; in moral matters, whose object is right will, and that we might be made good, one proceeds by persuasion and figurally.

He then explains that, though the primary audience of this book is the Prince, who is by it to be taught to rule, others will learn in it how to be ruled. They, of course, since 'pauci sunt vigentes acumine intellectus, propter quod ... quanto maior est populus, remotior est intellectus, / few people are very intelligent, because of which ... the larger the population the scarcer the intelligence,' will have to be taught 'in morali negocio figuraliter et grosse.' To do so requires the use of 'rationes superficiales et sensibiles' and therefore 'oportet modum procedendi in hoc opere esse grossum et figuralem.'[30]

It is not necessary, I think, to react excessively to what might seem the pejorative implications of this introduction. Aegidius is making a distinction, not a value judgment. It is not scholastic barbarism, but an obvious truth, that the general and the rational and the speculative are more specifically intellectual exercises than is attention to the particular, the concrete, and the contingent. Some defenders of poetry have made extremely exalted claims for the knowledge derived from poetry, and therefore for the concrete particulars which it contains; the distinction which Aegidius makes would not be congenial to them. But poetic theorists have also been prone to intellectualism – Coleridge's explanation of the 'Sum,' and his definitions of fancy and the imagination, pay the same honour that Aegidius does to modes of thought considered properly higher or more certain than others. What we must learn from Aegidius' distinction is not that moral thinking, by using intellectual procedures we think of as poetic, fails to be rationalist; rather we must try to pay close attention to what it is and how it works. Moral thinking is 'gross' or approximate and 'figurative'; it cannot be dealt with fairly or completely by simple 'narration.' It involves the use of 'types.' It moves the affections and the will, and persuades to action. It is suited to the non-philosophical mind – it is capable of being popular.

In his use of the words 'typo' and 'figuraliter,' Aegidius has placed his definition squarely in the centre of modern discussions of medieval literary theory. It is fruitless to ask just how much of the full meaning developed by biblical exegesis for these terms Aegidius meant to imply; rather, one must suppose that the distinction between exegesis and other forms of interpretation worried him less than it worried us. He is here dealing, of course, with facts – with the possible kinds of human moral action which one might need to understand, evaluate, and imitate – and his concern is to define the shape of the thought process required to deal with these matters. What he seems to say is that one cannot deal with moral questions simply by describing what happened (narratio); one must also make comparisons (figuraliter), and bring to bear examples which imply or seem to embody a definition (typo). John Balbus defines 'figura' as a locution in which 'unum dicimus et aliud intelligimus, / we say one thing and mean another,' and refers us for an illustration to his definition of 'leo,' under which he indulges a good deal of Christ-figure typologizing.[31] We must suppose that when Aegidius used the word 'figuraliter,' he meant by it that what related the one thing said and the other thing meant was a relation in some sense given in the nature of things; otherwise the figure would not signify. We must also suppose, since what is being treated here is moral action, that the things related 'figuraliter' will be concrete appearances, taking 'rationes superficiales et sensibiles' to mean 'subject matter drawn from what appears to be, and what one can deal with empirically.'[32] The word 'typus' could not be taken, of course, in its full exegetical sense of that which prefigures Christ, but certainly must be taken in the analogous sense of something whose shape and character resemble the central truth of which it is a sufficient example – that is, something communicating a sense of the normative or definitional. This is the sense appropriate to a science which deals, not with 'quod credas,' but with 'quod agas'; not 'contemplationis gratia, neque ut sciamus, sed ut boni fiamus.' In order to be made good; and as good in order to deal with action rather than just cognition, one must achieve in existence precisely the mode which the word 'typus' denotes: that is, a mode of action which is at once concrete, particular, and acted, on the one hand; and true, decorous, intelligible, and related to the form of the good, on the other. All this is involved in the modus procedendi of a form of words (in this case, the *De regimine principum*) which is classifiable under ethics. It is a modus procedendi, obviously, which makes sense as a definition of ethics – equally obviously, it is a discussion which makes a good deal of sense of poetry.

In his discussion *De differentia Rhetoricae, Ethicae et Politicae*,[33] Aegidius Romanus places rhetoric in a middle position between the moral and rational sciences:

Nam ethica et politica sunt scientie speciales et sunt determinati generis. Circumcernunt, enim, actus humanos, tanquam specialem materiam circa quam versantur. Rethorica autem non sic; sed ut dicitur primo Rethoricorum: 'rethorica est assecutiva dyalectice.' Ambe, enim, sunt de talibus que communiter quodammodo est cognoscere, et nullius scientie determinate. Sed, si sic dicimus, quod credimus bene dicendum, consurgit quedam dubitatio, nam rethorica videtur quasi media inter scientias morales et rationales; videtur enim composita ex utroque negotio, videlicet, dyalectico et politico.

For ethics and politics are particular sciences, and are of definite kind. They are concerned with human actions, and have them as their particular content. Rhetoric is not like this, but as it is said in the first book of the *Rhetoric*, 'Rhetoric is what follows dialectic.' For both deal with what in some manner it is to know of such things, and are of no definite science [that is, field having content]. But if we say thus, which we believe properly should be said, there arises a certain question, because rhetoric seems to be a mean between the moral and the rational sciences, for it is composed of both matters, that is, dialectic and politics. (pp 5–6)

In so doing, he reflects the same position which we have already seen in operation in Alanus' treatment of the *Rhetorica ad Herennium*, and in accessus assignment of Geoffrey of Vinsauf's *Poetria nova* now as a verbal art, and now to ethics. It is a position which sees in the art of morally persuasive language – that is, the art of writing things classifiable as ethics – an ability to combine fact and truth. On the one side, this art treats of mores; on the other, it is a logical art, and therefore an art of the true. Formally, the position of the art is exactly the same as the mode of the action it seeks to recommend: action which is at once real, and therefore contingent rather than a matter for pure cognition, and at the same time good, and therefore connected to truth.

It is for this reason that Hermann the German classifies the *Poetics* of Aristotle, along with the *Rhetoric*, in the logical *Organon*, and at the same time finds in it a great deal of treatment of moral and ethical matters – that is, matters involving content, and not, strictly speaking, assignable to the verbal arts. In so far, that is, as an art involved the relation of words to actions, it necessarily had to occupy a position on both sides.

In the light, then, of the classification of poems normally under ethics, and in the light of the relation between the verbal arts and the parts of philosophy which this classification implies, poetry as such disappears, as a medieval category, to be replaced by something far more largely normative on the one hand, and far more unambiguously true of history and morality on the other, than we would now consider it. It remains to see what has happened to ethics, on the other hand, as a result of the same merger.

If poetry is ethics, then the subject matter, the sentence, of poetry must be ethical, and we can therefore find out what ethics is, in the sense defined by its inclusion of poetry, by considering medieval definitions of the content of poetry. The clearest such example is in the Averroistic version of Aristotle's *Poetics*, translated by Hermann the German from Arabic to Latin in 1256. It has the added advantage, for my purposes, of being explicitly a distortion of the ancient text on poetic now most widely canonized as definitive; no modern reader can confront Averroes' theories without being constantly reminded, because of his knowledge of the authentic text, of the fact that Averroes is different.

The story of the career of this text in the Latin West has been several times repeated.[34] The translation was made in Toledo in 1256 by Hermann the German, who had already translated the *Rhetoric*. Twenty-four manuscripts survive. Its suitability for its medieval audience is best proved by the fact that it held its readership in spite of the existence, after 1278, of a quite faithful Latin translation of the *Poetics* from the Greek by William of Moerbecke, who was both an important man and the author of other books popular in the Middle Ages. A recension of the text was made, sometime before 1307, by which it was shortened slightly, divided, and glossed with attributions of its material to Aristotle and Averroes. This recension was the subject of an extra-curricular lecture at the University of Paris, made by Bartholomew of Bruges in 1307, and was in addition excerpted in several florilegia. The Averroistic *Poetics*, and not the authentic one made by William, was the one normally cited, even into the Renaissance, by such diverse persons as Roger Bacon, Thomas Aquinas, Benvenuto da Imola, Coluccio Salutati, Alessandro Piccolomini, and Torquato Tasso.

In Averroes' theory, tragedy is the art of praising, and comedy is the art of blaming. He must have known, of course, that the word 'tragedy' customarily also had something to do with the fall of the great, and that comedy might be expected to have a happy ending. A commentary on the *Rhetorica ad Herennium* from St Victor defines tragedy as

compositio fictitia et apparens factum facta de viris potentibus per multas fluctuationes et excellentias habitas inter eos tandem ad exitum tristem decus declinantibus [cod declina'].

a fictional composition which seems true made about powerful men who go through many vicissitudes and have among them many excellent qualities, declining finally to a sad decorous end.[35]

Dante defines comedy as that which 'vero inchoat asperitatem alicuius rei, sed eius materia prospere terminatur / truly begins badly for someone's business, but ends with his affairs prospering.'[36] John Balbus, in his *Catholicon*, discussed both; his definitions are comprehensive, and typical of medieval treatment of the subject:

Tragedia ... est cantus vel laus componitur cum tragos quod est hircus. Et dicitur hec tragedia idest hircina laus vel hircinus cantus idest fetidus. Est enim de crudelissimis rebus sicut qui patrem vel matrem interficit vel comedit filium vel econverso vel huiusmodi. unde et tragedo dabatur hircus scilicet animal fetidum. Non quod non haberet aliud dignum premium, sed ad fetorem materiae designandum ... et differunt tragedia et comedia, quia comedia privatorum hominum continet facta. Tragedia regum et magnatum. Item comedia humili stilo describitur tragedia alto. Item comedia a tristibus incipit, sed cum letis desinit. Tragedia econtrario, unde in salutatione solemus mittere et aptare tragicum principium et comicum finem.

Tragedy ... is song or praise. It comes from 'tragos' which means 'goat.' And tragedy is named this, that is goatish praise or goatish song, that is, stinking. Tragedy deals with horrible matters, such as the killing of a father or mother or the eating of a child or a parent or such like. Whence to the tragedian is attached the goat, that is a stinking animal; not that it has no other worthy reward, but to designate the stench of the material ... Tragedy differs from comedy because comedy contains the deeds of private men; tragedy of kings and magnates. Also, the comic is described in the low style, tragedy in the high style. Also, comedy begins with sad things, and ends with happy ones. Tragedy is the opposite, so that in greetings we are accustomed to send or wish a tragic beginning and a comic end.[37]

Medieval critics, of course, did not bring to their sense of these terms either a modern or a classical awareness of theatre; their definition would give primary importance to words read as opposed to words mimetically performed. Naturally enough, therefore, the style of language and the character of the material or content would be more important, and all overtones which we might want to supply deriving from our assumption of a dramatic spectacle would need to be suppressed. In these terms, there is nothing paradoxical about Averroes' claiming simply and without argument or amplification the ethical definition: 'tragedia, idest ars laudandi' (p 19), and by implication, since 'omnis oratio poetica aut est vituperatio aut est laudatio' (p 3), that the comedy which Aristotle never gets around to treating is ars vituperandi. In neither case is his sense of the morally exemplary essence of the material he wishes to describe compromised by any idea of the 'well made' play, or of plot in the University of Chicago sense as something intrinsically attractive, or of mimesis as anything more profound than skilful discursive description. He is not interested in the individual, but in the type,[38] in the exemplary, not the merely concrete or realistic, and his understanding of the kind of words in which awareness of these things can be properly communicated is thoroughly discursive and rhetorical. This is not to say, of course, that he was unaware of 'individua cadentia in sensum,' or of the fact that any given human affair 'incipit' and then eventually 'desinit.' It is to claim, however, that they exist differently as a part of ethics from the way we see them as poetic particulars enacting our 'sense of an ending.'

It is perhaps paradoxical to suggest that the art of praising should deal with 'crudelissimis rebus sicut qui patrem vel matrem interficit vel comedit filium vel econverso vel huiusmodi.' It is admittedly inconvenient that the definitive tragedies which medieval readers had among their auctores were the sensational Senecan ones, but even there, one must recall, the people involved were kings, heroes, and gods. What governed, I think, was the sense of hierarchy – the medieval desire to have connection between social superiority and moral superiority, as well as between those and high language. Tragedy deals with the 'facta regum et magnatum,' comedy only with the 'facta privatorum hominum.' Archetypally as well, the fall of the great is occasion for eulogy, while the successes of ordinary people are liable to be pretentious in a way demanding laughter, if not ridicule. If the fallen great had, in their lives, been involved in 'crudelissimis rebus,' then the pathos of their ends becomes the basis of praise of what might have been; laughter, on the other hand, is always distancing, and for an age which would have avoided the category of the absurd, would have also been normative. The Chaucerian ironies, in particular, make exact definition of this normative quality a slippery and subtle enterprise, but even, or especially, in the *Canterbury Tales*, our laughter as well as Chaucer's must properly be taken as based on moral as well as emotional security.

The first, and most obvious, characteristic of medieval ethics – of poetic ethics, in the sense in which I have been trying to develop the term – is that it involves, or expects, praise and blame, within a set of assumptions that include both a sense of social hierarchy and an answering sense of a hierarchy of styles. In anthropological terms, this kind of ethics belongs as much in the 'shame culture' category as in the 'guilt culture' category which its Augustinian theological inheritance might suggest. In these terms, no unambiguous classification is possible, but at least we must recognize and allow for the sense of 'shame culture,' which alone can account for the highly rhetoricized quality of this ethics. It defines a morality always conscious of its audience; a way of being good as a human being which exists, unfolds itself, as an act of communication as well as an act which accomplishes whatever it intrinsically does. The most literal representation of this shame culture, in its medieval form, is the romance, and its antecedent epic and chanson de geste. The characters in these stories are constantly concerned for appearing well, for avoiding occasions of shame, for what Malory calls their 'worship.' Real life, of course, has equivalent concerns. A king must behave as a king should, a villain may be suspected of acting villainously, and the quite obvious financial success of the ars dictaminis and its practitioners proves that the ability to produce an answerable style was sufficiently valuable that magnates were willing to pay to be well expressed.

The essential character of this ethics, then, is rhetorical. Within this specification, a number of elements can be distinguished. These elements, I suggest, are usefully and clearly specified in Averroes' treatment of the six parts of tragedy. This treatment corresponds to a famous section of Aristotle's authentic text, and so has been much liable to misunderstanding by being interpreted in a sense as close to Aristotle's as the words can possibly sustain, rather than being allowed to speak for itself. In its own right, it really has almost nothing in common with proper Aristotelian doctrine, but what it does say is, once its complexities are explained and the barriers generated by our false expectations of something Aristotelian are penetrated, most useful and important. The amount of text involved is substantial, but its doctrine is central to my argument, and the terminology on which this doctrine is based is subtle and difficult of definition. I therefore quote fully, and present a translation which attempts two opposite purposes at once: to present the literal sense of the passage in English, and to attempt an interpretation of the crucial terms. The translation, therefore, oscillates between very free paraphrase and slavish literalism. The crucial terms of the passage are difficult primarily because they have misleading English cognates; I shall therefore argue my interpretation in terms of the original more than in terms of my translation.

Et oportet ut tragedie, idest artis laudandi, sex partes sunt: scilicet sermones fabulares representativi; et consuetudines, et metrum seu pondus; et credulitates, et consideratio; et thonus. Et signum huius est quoniam omnis sermo poeticus dividitur in assimilationem et in id per quod fit assimilatio et ea per que fit assimilatio – tria sunt: representatio et metrum et thonus. Et ea que assimilantur in laudando etiam tria sunt: consuetudines et credulitates et consideratio, idest probatio recte credulitatis. Sunt itaque necessario partes tragedie sex, et partes maiores carminis laudativi sunt consuetudines et credulitates. Tragedia etenim non est ars representativa ipsorummet hominum prout sunt individua cadentia in sensum, sed est representativa consuetudinum eorum honestarum et actionum laudabilium et credulitatum beatificantium. Et consuetudines comprehendunt actiones et mores; ideoque ponitur consuetudo una sex partium et per eius positionem excusatur positio actionum et morum in illa divisione. Consideratio autem est declaratio recte credulitatis per quam homo laudabilis existit. Istud vero totum non reperitur in poematibus arabum, sed reperitur quidem in sermonibus legalibus. Et representant hoc tria, scilicet consuetudines et credulitates et significationes, per tres maneries rerum per quas fit representatio, scilicet per sermonem imaginativum et metrum et tonum. Dixit: Et partes sermonis fabularis secundum quod est representativus due sunt. Omnis enim representatio aut imperat sibi locum per representationem sui contrarii et post permutatur ad suam intentionem, et est modus qui dicitur apud eos circulatio; aut rem ipsam non faciens mentionem aliquam sui contrarii, et hoc est quod ipsi nominabant significationem. Et hoc quod se habet ex hiis partibus tanquam principium et fundamentum est sermo fabularis representativus. Et pars secunda sunt consuetudines. Et est illud in quo primitus usitata est representatio, scilicet est illud quod representatur. Et est quidem representatio seu imitatio sustentamentum et fundamentum in hac arte propterea quod non fit delectatio ex rememoratione rei cuius intenditur rememoratio absque sui representatione, sed fit delectatio quidem et receptio ipsius quando representata fuerit. Ideoque multociens non delectatur homo ex aspectu forme ipsius rei existentis in natura et delectatur in eius representatione et formatione per picturas et colores, et propterea utuntur homines arte pingendi et describendi. Et pars tertia tragedie est credulitas, et hec est potentia representandi·rem sic esse aut non sic esse. Et hoc est simile ei quod conatur rethorica in declaratione quod res existat aut non existat, nisi quod rethorica conatur ad hoc per sermonem persuasivum et poetria per sermonem representativum. Et hec representatio reperitur etiam in sermonibus legalibus. Dixit: et iam alkedemonii legum positores contenti fuerunt ad firmandum credulitates in mentibus hominum sermonibus poeticis quousque posteriores ceperunt adinvenire vias rethoricales. Et differentia inter sermonem poeticum preceptivum et instigativum ad credulitates et preceptivum et instigativum ad consuetudines est quoniam ille qui instigat ad consuetudines instigat ad operandum et agendum aliquid aut recedendum et fugiendum ab eo. Sermo vero qui instigat ad credulitatem non instigat nisi ad credendum aliquid esse aut non esse, sed non ad inquirendum ipsum aut respuendum. Quarta autem pars est metrum seu pondus. Et de perfectione ipsius est ut proportionatum sit proposito seu intentioni. Fortassis enim pondus quoddam pertinet uni proposito et non pertinet alteri. Et pars quinta que consistit in ordine est thonus, et est maior partium ad imprimendum anime et operandum in ipsam. Et pars sexta est consideratio, scilicet argumentatio seu probatio rectitudinis credulitatis aut operationis non per sermonem persuasivum. Hoc enim non pertinet huic arti neque est conveniens ei, sed per sermonem representativum. Ars nempe poetrie non est consistens in argumentationibus neque in speculatione considerativa et proprie tragedia. Ideoque non utitur carmen laudativum arte gesticulationis neque vultuum acceptione sicut utitur hiis rethorica.

And it is proper that there be six parts to tragedy, or the art of praising: these are fictional descriptions, customs, conscious formalism of language in some mode or other, beliefs, the persuasiveness that is based on descriptions, and charisma or expressive power. This is true because all poetic language is divided into two: likening, and that by which likening is made. And likening is made by means of three things: description and formalism of language and expressive power. And the things which are likened in praising are also three: customs and beliefs and persuasiveness, that is, the fit encouragement of belief. Therefore necessarily there are six parts of tragedy. The most important parts are customs and beliefs. For tragedy is not an art which describes men as perceivable individuals, but which describes their honest customs and praiseworthy actions and sanctifying beliefs. Customs, of course, include both actions and manners, and therefore custom is put as one of the six parts, making it unnecessary to list action and manners as separate headings in the classification. Credibility is the fit declaration of the belief by which the praiseworthy man exists. Not all of this is found in Arabic poetry, but it is certainly found in law-court speeches. And three things represent all this; they are customs and beliefs and meanings, by means of three sorts of things by which representation is made – these are description and verbal formalism and expressive power. He said: and the aspects of fictional language according to which it is representative are two: for all representation either refers [literally, orders a place for itself] through the representation of its contrary and afterward it is changed to its proper intention (and this is the mode which is called among them 'indirection'), or it is representation of the thing itself without making any mention of its contrary, and this is what they call signification. The principle and foundation of these six parts is fictional description. The second part consists of customs. These were at first the primary object of representation; that is, what were represented. And certainly it is representation or imitation which is the basis and foundation of this art because there is no delight in recalling anything one recalls without its representation, but the delight clearly occurs, along with insight, when the thing has been represented. Thus often one takes no delight in seeing the form of something existing in nature, but does delight in its representation and forming in drawing and colour, and therefore people use the art of painting and describing. And the third part of tragedy is belief, and this is the power of representing a thing as thus-and-so or not thus-and-so. And this is like what rhetoric attempts by declaring that an affair exists or does not exist, except that rhetoric achieves its effect by persuasive speech and poetry by representative speech. And this representation is found also in legal language. He said: And the framers of the laws of the Spartans were content to establish belief in the minds of men with poetic language, until later people began to invent rhetorical ways. And the difference between poetic language which leads to belief and that which leads to behaviour is that what leads to behaviour makes one work or enact something, or reject and withdraw from it, while language which leads to belief achieves nothing except the belief that something is or is not, without making one investigate it or reject it. The fourth part is conscious formalism of language in some mode or another; it is well done when it is appropriate to what is proposed or intended, since perhaps one kind of expression may fit one proposition and not another. And the fifth part in order is expressive power, and this is the most important of the parts for impressing and manipulating the emotions. And the sixth part is credibility, that is argument or proof of the rightfulness of a belief or a deed, not by persuasive speech, since this does not pertain to the art of poetry nor does it fit it, but rather by description. Obviously the art of poetry, and especially tragedy, is not something which consists of arguments nor of reflective speculation, and so poems of praise do not use the tricks of gesture or facial expression as rhetoric does. (pp 19–23)

The first thing which must be emphasized in this extraordinary piece of literary criticism is that the six parts of tragedy are specified not just once, but four different times and in four slightly different ways. First we have the list right at the beginning, which runs from 'sermones fabulares representativi' through 'thonus.' Then we have the list of the three 'per que fit assimilatio' and the three 'que assimilantur.' Then we have the three things which 'representant,' and the three means by which 'fit representatio.' Finally, we have a numbered list of six 'partes tragedie,' in which each is more extensively explained.

Both Hardison[39] and Weinberg[40] attempt to make sense of this discussion by taking the first list, and lining it up as closely to Aristotle's original specification as possible. Thus plot corresponds to 'sermones fabulares representativi,' character to 'consuetudines,' thought to 'credulitates,' diction to 'metrum,' spectacle to 'consideratio,' and song to 'thonus.' This interpretation, obviously, allows us to keep plot and character in their traditional place of theoretical honour. Then, with 'consuetudines' translated as character, we can slide past Averroes' crucial sentence, 'partes maiores carminis laudativi sunt consuetudines et credulitates,' without seeing just how alien and important it is. In the end, we are left with the sense that Averroes is more confused than different, and that all this theory is more significantly bad Aristotle than it is good Averroes. Such is the power of canonical authority – as much in our own day as in the Middle Ages. Aristotle's basic definitions have for so long seemed such a part of the eternal fitness of things, so obviously and simply true, that it requires a deliberate and stubborn effort of the imagination even to suppose, much less describe, a set of definitions incommensurable with his. It is this effort of the imagination which I attempt to achieve, obviously at the risk of some error in the opposite direction, but with the conviction that what seems to be the plain sense of Averroes' doctrine, as Hardison recognized, 'made the work intelligible to the medieval audience.'[41]

Averroes says that 'consuetudines' and 'credulitates' are the most important parts. We can best understand what he means by seeing, at the outset, that these are the terms that displace the genuinely Aristotelian plot and character. The Averroistic art of praising is not concerned with 'perceivable individuals' but rather with their 'honest customs' and their 'laudable actions' and their 'beatifying beliefs.' Therefore, since 'consuetudines comprehendunt actiones et mores,' consuetudo displaces action, or plot, and makes it unnecessary to specify as separate parts either 'actiones' or 'mores.' Credulitas, correspondingly, is the universal or general category of which the mental postures of human beings in the face of the truth, by which they are made blessed, are instances and examples. As consuetudo comprehends actions in material reality, so credulitas comprehends acts of mind of which the Truth is the measure and judge. Both of these terms, in practice, mean two things, in that they refer both to the content of praise, and to the effect of it. Speech which encourages consuetudo exhorts to the performance or avoidance of some action; speech which encourages credulitas exhorts to the belief that something either is or isn't. This distinction is developed at somewhat more length in Averroes' treatment of credulitas. In the first place, along with consuetudo, it is one of those things which 'assimilatur,' which something 'representat'; at the same time, it is 'potentia representandi rem sic esse aut non sic esse ... per sermonem representativum.' Thus it is at once something which is described in praise, and something which generates itself in the mind of an audience. This generation, this effect, however, is not to be achieved by rhetorical means, that is, by persuasive speech, but rather by 'sermonem representativum.' Whatever belief is involved is intrinsic to the praise as words, rather than based on some feature of its performance. The effect, then, is in some sense a part of the content – a part of what is 'assimilated' by means of the techniques of 'representatio et metrum et thonus.' As content, it is not, any more than consuetudo, a means to the end of mimetic presentation of individuals; rather, it is specified as 'beatificans.' It is that quality of which the mental attitudes of given persons are exemplary.

There are three ways to get at what Averroes means by all this. First, we can consider just what difference it makes to substitute consuetudo and credulitas for plot and character as the essence of poetry – and, by medieval equations, of ethics as well. Second, we can consider just what kind of primary ontology is implied by such words as consuetudo and credulitas. Third, we can deal with the implicit relation between words and the world defined by the existence of a poetic content which claims also to be a poetic effect, and so seeks to abolish the distinction between the poem's inside and its outside.

I have several times noticed in passing that Averroes does not consider poetry the representation of sensible individuals, but rather of their customs and beliefs. The Aristotelian terms 'plot' and 'character' emphasize the particular; whatever universal quality or impression one may in the end reach, its essence is the existence and significance of a particular action, at a particular time, by particular persons. Averroes is just the reverse; whatever is particular in poetry is exemplary rather than essential. The real essence of poetry is something universal. The particulars of which, empirically, representation must be made are instrumental, not absolute; their presence has normative overtones which they define but do not dominate. Thus the primary ontology of this poetry, qua words, tends toward or desires the philosophically realist, not nominalist. At the same time its modus procedendi is gross, typical, figural; what it literally contains, as material, can only be particular. Thus it is wrong to deny, for instance, that the Wife of Bath 'assimilates' a verisimilar human being. But it is equally wrong to affirm that she is only that, because her words and her career resonate so strongly and obviously a sense of the normative, of definition. I have tried to explain, in another place,[42] that this sense of the normative is generated, not only by Chaucer's treatment of the wife herself, but even more by the fact that her biography and her tale appear in a series, an array of tales and prologues, whose presence to one another can only be defined in discursive and normative terms. Such dependence on array, on the grouping of particulars which, as it were, triangulate a norm, is only to be expected in an age whose philosophical convictions tended to be more and more nominalist, but whose sense of God made it impossible for the normative, and even the philosophically realist, to be given up altogether. No medieval philosophical position is as nominalist, in absolute terms, as is the modern existentialism which centers our ethics and even our metaphysics, such as it is. It is therefore impossible to suppose that medieval particulars would have been seen, as ours are, as indefinite, various, possibly absurd, simply existent. Medievally, what one knows, at the beginning, is particulars; but what one comes to know through them, by the aid of reason and faith, is truth. What the ars laudandi achieves, therefore, is the representation of the true, of the universal, as both enactable (consuetudo) and credible (credulitas).

These features of consuetudo and credulitas are well illustrated by medieval practical criticism. My example is an anonymous commentary on the *Heroides* of Ovid, probably from late in the fourteenth century, and now preserved in ms 302 of the Biblioteca Communale in Assisi. A part of its accessus is as follows:

Hiis visis dicendum de hiis que solent inquiri in primo cuiuslibet libri scilicet que materia, que intentio, que utilitas, cui parti phylosophie supponiatur [sic], quis libri titulus et que causa suscepti operis. Materia libri sunt mores et vicia dominarum. Intentio versatur circha mateream [sic]. Intendit enim tractare de moribus et viciis dominarum et casto amore cum mendace et de incesto vituperare. Utilitas est duplex, scilicet communis et propria. Propria utilitas huius libri est quia cognito hoc libro cognoscemus dominas vel amicas nostras et cognantas [sic] caste amare. Utilitas communis est duplex, scilicet pulcritudo conditionum que sunt in hoc libro et pulcritudo vocabulorum. Cui parti phylosophie supponatur; supponitur ethice idest mortali [sic]: tractat videlicet de moribus dominarum. Libri titulus dictus est Publii Ovidii hic liber incipit. Causa suscepti operis supradicta est, ut benivolentiam dominarum Romanarum caperet et has ystorias de greco in latinum transtulit.

Having seen these things, the subjects which it is usual to treat at the beginning of any book must be discussed – that is, what material, what intention, what usefulness, to what part of philosophy it should be attached, what is the title of the book, and what is the cause of the work's being undertaken. The material of the book consists of the behaviour and vices of ladies. The intention depends on the material. For it intends to treat the behaviour and the vices of ladies, and chaste love with false, and to condemn unchastity. Its usefulness is double, that is common and personal. The personal usefulness of this book is that when we have understood it we can understand ladies or our mistresses, and in understanding chastely love them. The common usefulness is double, that is the beauty of the human situations in the book and the beauty of the words. To what part of philosophy is it attached? it is attached to ethics that is morality; for it deals with the behaviour of ladies. The title of the book is 'Publii Ovidii hic liber incipit.' The cause of the work's being undertaken was explained above – that Ovid might gain the favor of the Roman ladies and he translated these stories from Greek into Latin.[43]

The material consists of 'mores et vicia dominarum.' It represents the general and the normative. It has fundamentally practical and ethical use – that we might understand our ladies and girl friends and love them chastely. Otherwise, the distinction between the two modes of general usefulness reflects precisely the distinction which Averroes makes among his six parts of tragedy – on the one hand, there are the techniques by which likening is done (here simply 'pulcritudo vocabulorum') and on the other that which is likened. Conditio is a reasonable equivalent of the sum of consuetudo and credulitas. It is also the fundamental and initial concern of Chaucer's art, in his picture gallery of pilgrims:

> Me thynketh it acordaunt to resoun
> To telle yow al the condicioun
> Of ech of hem, so as it semed me.[44]

That it is conditiones, and not pilgrims as existential individuals merely, which Chaucer assembles in this prologue, Jill Mann has argued with great learning and convincing detail.[45] Moreover, she accounts for Chaucer's apparent realism in moral terms which precisely reflect Averroes' concern for the artes laudandi vituperandique:

[Chaucer's] general aim of complicating the reader's emotional responses ... is more comprehensible as a development from *descriptio* when described in medieval terms 'for praise or blame' than when it is anachronistically analysed in terms of the 'artificial' and the 'real.' (p 184)

This same concern for the general or universal instead of the particular also appears in Dante's theory of language, as Dragonetti explains it in connection with a discussion of the myth of Babel.[46] Averroes' emphasis on consuetudo and credulitas, thus, finds reflection in the implicit and explicit concerns of both commentators and poets.

Averroes' third term, first specified as 'consideratio' and then, by a clear process of elimination, as 'significationes,' is rather more subtle. It is clear from the outset that consuetudo, credulitas, and consideratio constitute, as it were, the content of poetry; Averroes, submitting like all medieval theorists to the productive character of art, distinguishes fundamentally between that which art makes and that by which the art is exercised. It is also clear that consideratio is not spectacle, though it does, probably, displace spectacle in the genuinely Aristotelian list. Consideratio is not, narrowly, rhetorical; it is not persuasive; it does not depend on 'arte gesticulationis neque vultuum acceptione sicut utitur hiis rethorica' (p 23). It is, rather, 'argumentatio seu probatio rectitudinis credulitatis aut operationis non per sermonem persuasivum ... sed per sermonem representativum' (p 23). This is, fundamentally, a definition in negative terms: consideratio is not like rhetoric, because its means is description rather than persuasive actions – at the same time, it is like rhetoric in its effect. Averroes' use of 'significatio' as a synonym for 'consideratio' is most helpful, because it points us toward what it is that makes words persuasive when they are not literally and formally argumentative – that is, rhetorical in the narrow sense. The quality of language to which 'significatio' and therefore 'consideratio' refer is both subtle and simple – in practice, it is what we mean when we call language 'meaningful.' One distinguishes, of course, between nonsense and the meaningful constantly; at all levels of experience, one decides that some things, acts, descriptions, and events are significant, and others are insignificant or make no sense. What we have in Averroes' term 'consideratio' is a specification of that quality of descriptions of customs and beliefs which renders those customs and beliefs important, normative, definitional, connected with the eternal fitness of things. In the face of consideratio, our belief is like that belief generated by rhetorical performance, but it happens without our being exposed to any performance at all. Consideratio exists in and is a feature of the descriptive language itself. Therefore consideratio in a sense displaces or replaces rhetorical performance, and must therefore be categorically distinguished from rhetorical performance. This distinction, for Hermann, reflects the distinction between the book of rhetoric and this book of poetic, both of which are branches of the large art of logic in Hermann's implicit logical *Organon*.

On the other hand, consideratio is not a quality of the words, qua words; we have three more terms to describe the means 'per que fit assimilatio.' Consideratio is rather a quality of words as made by means of representatio, metrum, and thonus. It is one of the things to which the words refer, which they constitute by having been brought into existence in a particular order and arrangement. When we ask why it is, we can talk about verisimilitude, but that is a characteristic of description. We can talk of the power of heightened language, but that has to do with metrum, thonus, and assimilatio. Once again, as in consideration of consuetudo and credulitas, we cannot deal properly with this word without that double philosophic reference, to particulars, and to that philosophic realism in reference to which particulars become significant.

In practice, the quality is easy enough to illustrate. The best example I know of it as experienced, and not as simply there, occurs of course in modern literature, which always provides itself with a phenomenological filter. C.S. Lewis, in *Perelandra*, reports that Ransom perceived the eldils as slanting, within the norms defined by his own senses, but at the same time as vertical, in absolute terms which were felt to correct and displace his own. This sense of being corrected or of confronting the absolute is, I think, a fit example of the sense of consideratio. Modern criticism might be disposed to call it the archetypal element. Medieval examples abound, if we but have the sense to see them – if, that is, the probatio which consideratio achieves produces 'recta credulitas' in us as well as in what its words themselves constitute. The best example, to me, is Dante's angel in the *Inferno*, who comes to open the gates of Hell before which even Virgil is for a moment stopped, puzzled, perhaps afraid. When he comes,

> Ahi quanto mi parea pien di disdegno!
>   Venne a la porta e con una verghetta
>   l'aperse, che non v'ebbe alcun ritegno.

> How full of disdain he seemed to me!
>   He came to the gate and with a wand
>   he opened it, and there was no resistance. (*Inferno* IX.88–90)

Such bored excess of power, obvious in the description of the act itself, and needing no argument or underlining! This is an event which argues itself. Another, perhaps more impressive to the modern mind because more provided with atmosphere, is the encounter between Chaucer's rioters, in the *Pardoner's Tale*, and the old man at the stile. In both these events we have, or should have, a perception of that sense of background, of the requirement to interpret, which Auerbach so well explains as the quality of the paratactic Abraham story.[47] The difference between the two, in that Dante's incident expects one to know very clearly something about the nature of angels, and the relative power of heavenly and hellish agents, while Chaucer exploits the power of folk tale atmosphere, is of more importance to the modern than to the medieval reader, whose response to the angel would have been more total than ours, and whose response to the certainly Pauline 'old man' would have been more doctrinal. Again, the hilarious reversals of the *Miller's Tale* – the series of kisses which lead inexorably to the cry of 'Water' for which the old fool in the attic waits – possess by the very fact that they are funny, that at certain predictable points the audience laughs, this same quality of consideratio. The only difference, of course, is that comedy is the ars vituperandi – but the act of assent to the normative which is expressed by laughter is, with regard to the norm itself, exactly the same as the quieter but no less definitive assent generated by well-deserved praise – that is, by the effective description of the admirable.

It must, of course, be admitted that writing has been convincing in other ages than the medieval, and that both beliefs and customs are frequently treated, both implicitly and explicitly. To the extent that, as in the Renaissance, literature merely continued to exist as the ars laudandi vituperandique, there is no problem. In the case of such genres as the comedy of manners, however, the theoretical conclusion one must draw is exactly the opposite from the medieval one, since here one is being asked to praise the ingenue (usually) at the expense of the manners, rather than understand the normative manners which all good ingenues achieve when they grow up, or are recognized as grown up. Such is the difference between Sir Gareth, or any other Bel Inconnu, and the country wife. Comedy of manners also involves the inherent contradiction of the spectacle – of the art of the piece – in that the claim that 'all the world's a stage, and all the men and women merely players' defines the world in terms of a heightened decorum of manners, that is, of rhetorical existence, which the laughter of the comedy of manners explicitly reproves. The logical ends of this contradiction are, on the one hand, an aestheticism which takes the theatre as either a diversion or an art form purely, and on the other, an absurd life which finds itself trapped by the modern incommensurability of life and art, as in Anouilh's *The Rehearsal*. Again, the Bildungsroman, in all its protean forms, deals with customs and beliefs, but chronicles not so much the hero's achievement of them as the hero's achievement of some unique identity in spite of them. The moral centre of most modern art is the value of the particular as such, taken either in the personalist sense exemplified by Wordsworth's *Prelude*, or in the verbal and lapidary sense most perfectly illustrated by 'Twas brillig, and the slithy toves ...' The two come together in *Finnegans Wake*, as the world of literature achieves perfect verbal solipsism. All these works, of course, make truth claims of various sorts, but they all have in common the axiomatic divisions of post-Renaissance times: life from art, mind from matter, science from religion, fact from value, word from thing. Whether these are accepted or opposed makes no difference; they are there. The medieval claim that poetry contains, assimilates, consuetudo, credulitas, and consideratio presumes as axiomatic that these divisions do not exist – before Descartes, obviously, there was a profound sense in which they had not yet been thought of. Late medieval theory, then, took the particulars of story, and of mental posture as defined by lyric, as immediately exemplary. Affirming that poetry was ethics, and therefore necessarily that the norms of ethics participated in the virtuoso decorousness which is in fact characteristic of poetry, medieval theory achieved a reality for that decorum, and a genuinely normative essence for daily life. If one wished to be a good man, he must behave as if in a story.[48] Then he will both be and exemplify, not 'individua cadentia in sensum,' but that consuetudo and credulitas which has the power of consideratio. In response, a story, in its decorous telling, and even if fiction, was true.

It is for these reasons that we can take with perfect seriousness the advice of the medieval critic quoted above, who tells us that reading the *Heroides* will help us love our girl friends. He meant exactly that. The distance between his world and ours can be no better illustrated than by this, that for us such courting 'by the book' can exist neither in literature nor in life except as ridiculous comedy. We must not, of course, presume that the medieval reader of the *Heroides* was ridiculous and did not know it; rather, we must presume that his quality of life, his set of moral axioms, was such as to make it both plausible and effective that he relate his amorous behaviour to Ovid. In the same way, it takes a real effort of the imagination even to begin to reconstruct the situation in which Thomas' *Tristan* could be, as it may in fact have been,[49] a compliment to Eleanor of Aquitaine for having substituted Henry for Louis. The intimacy of the love story in the romance must be taken to have celebrated in public the private passion of the Queen and her Henry. It is not, of course, 'kiss and tell,' but it is kiss and let somebody else tell, and the telling, once attached to history, violates both the literary decorum of love's secrecy and any possible sense that public figures might have private lives. The daily ceremonial bedding and rising of the Louis the Sun King must have been treated with considerable public seriousness at the time, because Louis had the power to demand it, but it becomes comic to modern minds as soon as one thinks of all the physical particulars it had to include, and may well have become so to the occasional cynic of that time. Yet we must, if we are to take seriously the medieval critics who classify literature as ethics, who insist that it is about consuetudo and credulitas validated by consideratio, believe that in some manner a medieval person's sense of his own existence as a moral person was such as could successfully and decorously make love by the book, or feel complimented by having her intimacies celebrated under the name of Iseult. In this respect as in the more verbal ones we have already considered, there is a unity achieved between particular and definition. Here, it expresses itself as a unity between a private person's personal action and the various public and literary definitions it imitates and exemplifies.

And there is one further reconciliation involved – that betwen the audience of poetry, and the content of poetry. If, in some sense, the same consuetudo or credulitas, or both, are what the poem at once represents and achieves; if the poem's effect is a part of its content, then there is an absolute continuity between the people who read it and the people about whom they read. It becomes, or properly should become, impossible to tell or improper to ask where the world of the poem ends, and the world of the reader begins, or which is which. This situation is in fact the one which Shakespeare asserts in metaphor by speaking of the theatre as a microcosm; it is a fact which becomes more plausible because, as we shall see, medieval critics were much

less interested than we in positivist questions of verifiable historicity. Singleton put this fact in terms of literary criticism when he wrote that 'the fiction
of the *Divine Comedy* is that it is not fiction.'[50] In medieval terms, what the
Divina commedia asks of us is that we become its tropology, or even more
radically, that we see ourselves as ourselves characters in its allegory. Lydgate did in fact insert himself, telling the story of Thebes, in the *Canterbury
Tales*; donors of saint's life paintings had their own portraits inserted in the
paintings they gave; the kings of France enter Holy History in the windows
of St Denis. All exemplary existences inhabit, ultimately, the same world; to
the extent that one's submission to the ethical consideratio of a poem permitted one to achieve a normative resonance, a relation to credulitas and
consuetudo, one would exist as a part of that constitution of definition.[51]

The second three parts of tragedy, as Averroes defines them, are the formal or constructive parts. They are the parts, or techniques, 'per que fit
assimilatio' or 'representatio.' They, also, are more complex than they seem.
Averroes' discussion suggests commentary along two lines – first, in explanation of the fact that he has presented this array of six in two groups, and
second, in explanation of the terms themselves.

It would be wrong to interpret Averroes' division of the six parts of
tragedy into two groups by making any easy equation with modern categories. Form and content are tempting ones, but misleading, since custom,
belief, and consideration are in their way formal qualities, and the other
three are not so much forms as techniques by which forms are achieved.
Further, the late medieval understanding of literary form is defined, not in
terms of these six parts of tragedy or any analogue of them, but rather in
terms of the Aristotelian formal cause, divided into two aspects: 'forma tractandi' or form of treatment, and 'forma tractatus' or literal outline. These
terms and their full significance will be treated in subsequent chapters. Here
I must face the more inclusive issue, the ethical classification of literature,
and under that presumption try to explain why it is that discourse which is so
classified has defining features intelligible in two groups of three.

The critic of the *Heroides* whose introduction I have just quoted makes
two distinctions duplex which inform this one of Averroes. According to this
critic, the *Heroides* is a poem useful in two ways, one personal, and one
common. These, roughly, involve the difference between practical or moral
use, and what one might be tempted to call aesthetic but should call epideictic use. On the one hand, the poem is useful 'quia cognito hoc libro
cognoscemus dominas vel amicas nostras.' On the other hand, there are the
'pulcritudo conditionum' and the 'pulcritudo vocabulorum.' These second
two, as general values, must exist apart from the moral instruction of any

single person; they are rather that general quality of the good because of which its good may be recognized and valued. The commentator calls it 'pulcritudo.' Averroes, in talking about representation, refers to the pleasure one gets from some descriptions, qua descriptions, which happen to represent things literally repulsive in themselves. He defines 'thonus' as the 'maior partium ad imprimendum anime et operandum in ipsam.' It is in these terms that we must define this pulcritudo, this utilitas communis, as epideictic in the largest and profoundest sense, whose ultimate example, within the terms of medieval culture, is the recognition of the Creator in Genesis that his works are 'valde bona' (1:31). For literature, of course, this goodness is itself divided into two, the pulcritudo conditionum and the pulcritudo vocabulorum. These two do in fact correspond to our modern categories of form and content, with the difference that for the medieval mind form and content, or formal and material cause, are more ontologically separable than they are for us, to whom poems are hypothetical verbal objects having no ontology except linguistic, and with the further obvious difference that the beauty obviously must reside equally in both, and not be generated by either for the other. In these terms, then, Averroes' distinction must correspond to our commentator's larger one – that is, between the utilitas propria and the utilitas communis. Consideration, custom, and belief, narrowly and properly considered, are attended to for the sake of assimilating the reader or hearer to them, for the sake of the practical project of making him their allegory, or themselves his. They exist for his ethical profit. That they do so is good; this goodness, this power, this pleasure or impressiveness, is the basis for the existence of sermo imaginativus, metrum, and thonus. In the largest possible sense, it is these three factors which account for the fact that words can relate to things at all. It is they which achieve both the pulcritudo conditionum and the pulcritudo vocabulorum – that aspect of both form and content by which they may be recognized as 'valde bona.'

Here, as in his first three terms, Averroes is not verbally consistent. The problem is with his first item. First, it is 'sermones fabulares representativi,' then it is 'representatio,' then it is 'representatio, scilicet sermo imaginativus,' and finally it is 'representatio' of two kinds. Our problem is further complicated by the fact that this representatio not only 'represents,' but also is one of those things 'per que fit assimilatio.' 'Assimilatio,' a term which displaces but does not at all correspond to the Aristotelian 'mimesis,' seems to involve, in an undifferentiated array, that which relates words to referents, and descriptions to things described, as well as the separate terms of various kinds of analogies, contrasts, comparisons, and metaphors. I shall return to this term at much more length in connection with my discussion of metaphor and allegory. Here it is vitally important to notice that both assimilatio, and by implication representatio as well, suppress any distinction between those relationships which exist within the real world, or within the world of words, and those relationships which exist between words and things. In other words, they presume a kind of ontological continuity between language, thought, and fact – a continuity which is characteristic of medieval thought.

Positively, Averroes' first term involves fiction, because of his use of the word 'fabularis.' It involves the exploitation of mental images – it is sermo imaginativus. One might translate it simply as description, except that it may work, as Averroes explicitly emphasizes, by the use of contraries as well as by direct representation. Finally, it exists in a relation to what it assimilates or represents which does not either become, or tend toward, simple unity – there are always at least two terms, related, of course, but distinct. Sermo imaginativus is thus, in the most general sense, a form of words which both exists in and refers to a structure of relationships, within which one may become aware of, and impressed with the truth of, one or several instances of credulitas and consuetudo. As such, this sermo assimilates in one direction with all those non-verbal instances of representation possible in medieval experience – persons in office, coats of arms and liveries, ritual or sacramental actions, institutional buildings and their iconographic decorations, encounters with animals or other creatures having allegorical overtones – that is, with all instances of that great web of resemblance which structured medieval life. In the other direction, it assimilates to language as such – that which divides, names, and structures the world, the basis of meaning, whose definitive word was the Incarnate Word of God. This is not to say, of course, that the content of representatio is required to contain any particular allegory, by virtue of its status as a representation, nor that it is required to be pious, because of its status as language – rather, I mean only to suggest that the structures which it evokes and involves be as large and as powerful as these relationships involve.

Averroes' last two terms, 'metrum' and 'thonus,' are easy enough to translate as metre and melody. But they are really more complex than this. In the thirteenth century, there would have been practical awareness of both classical metres and of the newer possibility of accentual verse. Averroes uses 'pondus' as a synonym for 'metrum,' and defines its perfection in terms of its proportionateness to what is being said. In the most general terms, metrum is conscious formalism of language in some suitable mode or another; given the possibilities for poetry current in the time, plus what was being developed in the ars dictaminis and the increasing use of prose in romance, I do not think it is possible to go further than this. The important feature of metre, regardless of the quantities, accents, feet, or sounds in terms of which it is defined, is its ostentation of form. It is an ostentation of form which has countless parallels in other medieval decorums of behaviour, architecture, art, decoration, and thought; this is its essence, and this, I think, is what needs to be emphasized, lest we mistake metre for something in terms of which poetry can be made an autonomous category, rather than a species of ethics.

'Thonus' literally means something musical, and the amount of music that survives attached to medieval poetry, especially lyric poetry, demands that we take it seriously as at least that. But it is more. Guided by Dragonetti's discussion of Dante's similar definition of poetry as 'fictio rethorica musicaque composita' (*De vulgari eloquentia* II.iv.1) I take 'thonus' in the largest possible sense, as the presence of that harmony or sense of rightness which convinces one that one is in the presence of truth. It is that quality of poetry which especially enables it to assimilate, represent, consideratio; as Averroes makes clear by defining it as 'maior partium ad imprimendum anime et operandum in ipsam' (p 23). I would therefore propose the phrase 'charisma or expressive power,' not as a translation of 'thonus,' but as a formula for what can be taken as the twentieth-century equivalent of the medieval sense of being in the presence of musica mundana.[52]

All translations are distortions; after all this argument, I should hope that Averroes' terms will work well enough in Latin. Since, however, I shall have occasion to use them repeatedly, I prefer for reasons of style to have English equivalents, which I hope do not distort too much. 'Consuetudo' and 'credulitas' are easy enough; they equal custom and belief. For 'representatio,' 'sermo imaginativus,' and 'sermo fabularis representativus' I propose 'resemblance making'; for 'metrum,' 'heightened language,' for 'thonus,' 'expressive power.' For 'consideratio' there is nothing; one must resort to the cognate: 'poetic consideration.'

In his ethical, rhetorical poetic, Averroes treats many other topics of great importance, in addition to this one having to do with the six parts of the art of praising. I shall return to other parts of his text in subsequent chapters, especially to his complex use of the term 'assimilatio.' It is not, I think, any distortion of his doctrine to deal with it thus topically. My method is to proceed from most general to most particular; the most general of all is the universal under which medieval literary criticism must operate. This, as is clear from accessus language, from Aegidius Romanus' discussions both in literary and non-literary contexts, and from this Averroistic treatment of the six parts, is ethics. Poetry is that body of texts which concerns itself with the

value-laden description of human behaviour; it leads to and permits normative judgments of mores – of what real people really do, and above all of the
patterns which their doing implies and establishes. All the more particular
features of poems – the kinds of thinking that make them, the nature of their
outlines and internal coherences, their potential effect on an audience – can
only make medieval sense in terms of a clear understanding of this ethical
universal within which poems are classified, and within which they operate.

In practical terms, this medieval assertion that poetry is to be classified as
ethics, and by necessary implication that ethics therefore is a body of truth
within which the strategies and decorums empirically characteristic of poetry
have some intrinsic place, makes possible a number of very important and
perhaps even new twentieth-century activities, and prohibits others. These
activities may be broadly grouped under three generalizations. In the first
place, this medieval doctrine flatly contradicts purely aesthetic approaches to
literature, unless they are undertaken merely as the first step in an analysis of
rhetorical effectiveness – that is, as the first step in an analysis of poetic consideration, expressive power, or heightened language, as these relate to and
demonstrate ethical values. In the second place, this medieval doctrine permits one to use literature with considerable rigour and force as evidence in
ethical discussions in the broadest sense. Thematic studies of literature
become more than mere speculation and paraphrase, because the doctrines
of the medieval critics predict the logic whereby these themes shall be
expressed, related, and linked to historical fact. Both the occasionality of
most medieval poetry, and in some cases its specific occasions, may be more
safely specified and defined. In the third place, this medieval doctrine provides a basis for the analysis of particular medieval poems as integrated,
well-made, intelligible things – a basis more congenial than the theories on
the basis of which we have searched for the most part in vain for such features as the 'unity' of most long medieval poems, and some shorter pieces as
well.

The first of these generalizations, obviously, seeks to displace not only such
unfashionable positions as those defined by Croce for Dante and by the New
Critics for any poetry susceptible of being read as ironic or ambiguous, but
also would seem to attack the linguistic version of aestheticism being argued
with great subtlety and popularity by Paul Zumthor and others. To the extent
that their position is a mere aestheticism, an argument which admires something solipsistic on the basis of its formal values, I do indeed intend such an
attack. To the extent that it is more than that, there may be a good deal of
common ground. But I am not primarily interested in arguing relationships
with schools of modern critics, so much as in presenting these medieval
ideas as, in the first place, true – in that intelligent medieval people can be

proved to have believed them – and, in the second place, as of considerable use to the modern critic who wishes to appreciate the full value of Dante's *Commedia* or Malory's *Morte*, or Chaucer's *Canterbury Tales*, or any other medieval poem.

The use of literature in ethical discussion is not properly the concern of this book. I rather am involved in defining the opposite proposition – the use of ethics in literary discussion. However, for the sake of completeness of outline,[53] it is appropriate to suggest some of the possibilities. I have published elsewhere a discussion of the medieval literary paideia, and its usefulness, both as the basis for the training of medieval administrators, and as an analogical model on the basis of which one might project an education for modern public figures.[54] C.W. Westfall's *In This Most Perfect Paradise*[55] is an analysis of Nicholas V's plans for the reconstruction of Rome which makes it clear that Nicholas had in mind, as the basis of city planning, precisely the kind of ethical resemblance-making which is for Averroes the major resource of poetry. Similarly, one can use the concepts of custom, belief, and poetic consideration to define models for institutions which can give people life-enhancing roles rather than merely bureaucratic ones – that is, medieval notions of the relation between particular and definition, which poetry enacts and which life enacted, have the power both richly to inform and to reform the dehumanizing structures of modern and urban life.[56] Thus, as Liebeschütz observes, John of Salisbury was apparently unable to conceive of a governmental abstraction without a person in it. 'In John's mind the State consists simply of the actions of the officials who command in the ruler's name, and the actions of the subjects who react to these commands ... [He] avoids any idea of a corporation as the executant of political action.'[57] At the same time, of course, the sovereign had, as person, a sacramental as well as a merely biological existence. The possibility of this kind of existence, which at once connects individual human beings to their meanings, and avoids that reification of abstractions which is the most significant and most totalitarian achievement of modern political science of the extreme left and right, is one which ethical literary theory both recommends and defines. To the extent that this possibility recommends itself as a solution to pressing modern problems, then the medieval critical method is one which can permit the rigorous use of literary models in sociological and political contexts. Such a use seems to me at least both important and timely, and, in practical terms, an obvious better use of the time of specialists in literature than at least some of the Laputan speculations we are wont to indulge.

On the other hand, and with regard to literary criticism, it will, I hope, become increasingly obvious that the ethical poetic of the medieval critics is a powerful instrument for the analysis and rationalization of medieval poems. My purpose here is not so much to apply this poetic as to explain it; my illustrations and examples in application are intended to be only suggestive and tentative, and as such will necessarily run the risk of being briefly and imperfectly argued, or too allusively documented. It is a risk which must be assumed, however, since there must be illustration, but there is not space for much elaboration of it. Here, at the level of the defining ethical universal under which medieval poetry operates, examples must be large and general. They appear in asking and answering the question: 'What difference does it make to our approach to a poem that we have, by our awareness of the medieval ethical poetic, already decided what it is about?'

I have tried to show, in another place, that Chaucer's *Canterbury Tales* are about society, and therefore about what in modern terms would be called social bonding. In Chaucer's terms, real human marriages are, as real, to be taken also as paradigmatic, so that on the basis of an array of stories of marriage, and of relationships analogous to marriage, Chaucer discusses the promises and structures of act and promise by which society constitutes itself. The definition of society and the social bond which results from this analysis is in no sense a reductionist one. It does not merely express the predictable medieval clichés, nor any modern ones either. Rather, it proves that Chaucer was, within the large terms and materials with which a fourteenth-century man could work, a remarkably thoughtful and distinctive social thinker.[58] William Langland, on the other hand, makes it frequently clear that his poem of *Piers Plowman* should be classified as theology; its persistent question has to do with the salvation of the soul. Nevertheless there is a great deal of society in it, and the ethical place of poetry resonates strongly in what Langland has to say. I have already said, in what I hope is not too dark an epigram, that *Piers Plowman* constantly raises its question in the singular only to have it answered in the plural. To date, the best analyses of the poem, in my opinion, have been those which address themselves to the explanation of riddling details.[59] Langland is a man whose education seems to have been quite profound but not wholly conventional; in a way unusual for the Middle Ages but formally somewhat like Browning or Emily Dickinson, he is a private poet, and his poem has something of the quality of a commentary somehow loose from its text. In fact, as John Alford has shown in a seminal article, the quotations in the poem can function more as its independently existing structure than as illustration.[60] In larger terms the poem has been especially well studied as an apocalypse,[61] and in terms of its doctrine of salvation.[62] What the medieval critics make possible, I think, is not so much a new interpretation as a clearer focus. The poem's central character is Will – that is, I think, Voluntas. In the later Middle Ages, the will was of course the principle of action, but it was also related to cognition, and was of increased importance in theological speculation. The will therefore must obviously be central to that search for salvation which involves action as well as knowlege, which is social as well as thoughtful. For this search the Averroistic doctrines of consuetudo and credulitas, and Aegidius' claim that the modus procedendi of arts of action proceeds 'grosse et figuraliter,'[63] must be important glosses.

The test case, however, is Dante. I shall depend heavily on the *Commedia* for illustration as I develop this definition of late medieval theory, not with any pretence of being a Dantista, nor with the hope of shedding more than modest light on his work. Rather, I take him as the expert witness. Dante's greatness is not based on any absolute and self-existent genius, universalized out of time and space. More even than Shakespeare, he is a poet of a particular time and place, of whose cultural and theological achievements he is the supremely typical exemplar. In practice, therefore, his testimony should be expected to confirm and exemplify the theories of the time, in so far as I have gotten them described correctly. Fortunately, there can be no mistaking Dante's subject. He defines it himself:

Est ergo subiectum totius operis, literaliter tantum accepti, status animarum post mortem simpliciter sumptus. Nam de illo et circa illum totius operis versatur processus. Si vero accipiatur opus allegorice, subiectum est homo, prout merendo et demerendo per arbitrii libertatem iustitiae praemiandi et puniendi obnoxius est.

The subject of the whole work, taken literally as such, is simply the state of souls after death. For the process of the whole book treats this state and its context. If we take the book allegorically, its subject is man, in so far as he is liable to the justice of reward and of punishment by the exercise of free will in having or not having merit. (p 416)

Dante's subject is man, as something deserving of reward and punishment, or, by obvious implication, of praise and blame. In addition, he clearly defines the serried levels and ranks into which he places his characters in terms of consuetudo and credulitas – here or there one finds people who practise this or believe that. It is therefore surprising that so little notice has been given to the fact that anagogy, for Dante, is the letter. That level, by the norms of exegesis, to which we should attain only at the mystical end, is for Dante the starting place. That this literal place, the 'status animarum post mortem,' has itself a clear hierarchical arrangement, does not alter the fact that it is all anagogy, and it is all literal. The *Commedia* is – shocking truth –

only literally about hell, purgatory, and heaven. It is only literally a journey, only literally ordered in terms of an ascent, and that into a heaven which literally presents itself, not as it is, but in a metaphoric or similitudinous manner suited to the capability of its observer. The allegory of the poem, on the other hand – that is, the meaning we are supposed to reach, as goal, through and by the means of the letter – is 'homo, prout ... praemiandi et puniendi obnoxius est.' The allegorical subject of the poem is man in this life, man deserving of reward and punishment as a political animal, in a world whose ultimate value is justice – but, of course, whose ultimate instrument of justice is the love which both made and made possible the Incarnation. Thus, though the literal anagogy of the poem must never be discarded or denigrated, it must be taken as instrumental. Any single statement must always be an oversimplification; nevertheless, it is true to say that the subject of the *Commedia* – what is it about – is much more to be seen as Florentine (or imperial) politics than God, or heaven, or Beatrice, or any other being or belief that presents itself in transcendent or anagogical terms. That level has already been appropriated; it is literal. What the poem is about is ethics.

There is some excellent recent work which analyses Dante's *Commedia* implicitly in these terms, and without falling into the opposite error of discarding the texture of the work itself in order to collect and exhibit mere dicta implying political ideas. The meaning of the poem is not to be found merely in what Farinata, or Cacciaguida, or any other person, including Virgil or Dante, says. Rather it is to be found through what they all are, both as themselves and in a pattern of relation to one another. In these terms, I especially admire two studies of Dante: the essay by David Thompson, *Dante's Epic Journeys* (Baltimore 1974), which compares the Dantean journey to the journey of civilization accomplished by Aeneas, and the magisterial recent study by Giuseppe Mazzotta, *Dante, Poet of the Desert: History and Allegory in the 'Divine Comedy'* (Princeton 1979). Both are properly figural in their approach, and both make happily clear important aspects of Dante's clarifying interest in this world, and in the human affairs which constitute its history. Erich Auerbach's *Dante, Poet of the Secular World* (tr Ralph Manheim, Chicago 1961), on the other hand, is disturbingly and puzzlingly unsatisfactory, though of course brilliant in detail – I think because Auerbach reaches his notion of the secular Dante by avoiding, rather than affirming and enjoying the necessity of, the theology which for Dante must always be basis of every truth whatever.

At this stage, in my enterprise of definition, since I have established only the relationship between poetry and ethics, and still not defined the strategies, arrangements, and effects internal to this ethical poetry, there is not much in the *Commedia* which can be used as illustration, except for its announced subject. The most obvious and most important feature of Dante's poem, beyond the fact that it is full of exemplary historical characters, is that it is an ordering. More than for any other work I know, this is a poem whose geography is its outline. Literally of course, this outline is the geography of a journey. But beyond the journey is a discursive intent, to which Dante explicitly refers when he speaks of the forma tractandi and the forma tractatus. His practice, more clearly and explicitly than that of any other medieval poet, illustrates the powers and intentions of a poetry whose form is defined in these scholastic terms, and I shall return to it at some length after having presented the related discussions of the medieval critics. Here, however, there is at least one specific topic which may adequately illustrate the terms of the definitions already presented – that is, the relation between poetry and ethics, the fact that the background happens to be the twelfth century, and the obligation of the critic to begin his work by deciding what the poem under discussion is about. This topic is Dante's treatment of poetry in the *Commedia*.

This treatment falls into two parts. First, there is the dramatic material in which poets are met and poetry (much of it Dante's own) is quoted and admired. Second, there are Dante's comments and actions, both as pilgrim and as remembering author, which have to do with his words – their adequacy or inadequacy, the difficulty of finding them, and finally, the inexpressibility topos and the failure of that fantasia after which all possible words must be inadequate. This is a very large topic, which I shall be using as illustration rather than as critical occasion, and which I shall in no sense exhaust. In discussing it I am very conscious of the fact that reading poems as about poetry is a critical posture now fashionable in Dante studies,[64] and that this posture involves a certain pessimism – 'language is an inherently unstable and murky instrument.'[65] In part, this pessimism is but a part of the larger fashionable affection for an 'illisibilité' imported from France; in part, it is a suggestion that a dependence upon the mediation of signs is a result of the fallen condition of man. But this fallen condition is, for Dante, redeemable – it is both true and good that the 'Christian universe is, ultimately, a verbal universe of which the Logos made flesh is the divine center.'[66]

I therefore claim that Dante's work does not add up to any ultimate rejection either of poetry or of the power of words. The *Commedia* is not finally about itself; making words is an act which is not in itself either a sin or an impossibility – and even those passages in which the *Commedia*, a thing made out of signs, informs us truly of the duplicity of signs, must be taken themselves as examples of the success of signs, and not of the paradox of the 'lying' Cretan. To dwell too much on Dante as a man fascinated with language, or worse, fascinated with the fact that (especially in the *Convivio*) he finds language fascinating, is to mistake him for the same Narcissus in terms of whom Zumthor defines the grand chant courtois. At the centre of every solipsism, even every mere self-preoccupation, there is an absurd despair, but this despair is neither Dante's condition nor his point. Rather, his point is that poetry, or more generally, words, may be misappropriated but need not be – may be the occasion of sin or despair, but should not be. Instead, words, and especially the words of poetry, and even more especially the words of this poetry which imitates the figural language of the Bible,[67] exist to achieve the enactment of the Word whose Incarnation makes healthy language possible.

My primary point here is that Dante's treatment of poetry in the *Commedia* rejects one kind of poetry only in order to recommend another. This treatment, however, exists within the larger question of language – of signs, to which I should refer briefly by discussing that locus where the subject is dealt with most densely – canto XXVI of the *Paradiso*.[68] Here, in the context of his meeting with Adam, Dante defines what language was and is. The crucial passage is Adam's definition of the fall:

> Or, figliuol mio, non il gustar del legno
> fu per sé la cagion di tanto essilio,
> ma solamente il trapassar del segno.

> Now, my son, the taste of the tree
> was not in itself the cause of so great an exile,
> but only the trespass of the sign. (*Paradiso* XXVI.115–17)

Singleton translates the crucial passage 'the overpassing of the bound' – a dignified version of 'running the Stop sign.' This, theologically, is what it must mean; but this translation ignores the pun. Absolutely, the fall is the trespass of signs – that is, the enacted desire for immediate rather than mediate knowledge. Language existed in Paradise – Adam made it and used it (line 114, cf Genesis 2:20). If sin is the trespass of the sign, then innocence is the acceptance of the sign, in anticipation, of course, of the Logos who would have become the Incarnate sign even had there been no fall. If the sign was wounded in the fall, it was only by becoming mutable –

> ché l'uso d'i mortali è come fronda
> in ramo, che sen va e altra vene.

> For the usage of mortals is like a leaf
> on a branch, which goes away and another comes. (*Paradiso* XXVI.137–8)

Yet this image is corrected and redeemed by being a repetition of Dante's good image of love, earlier in the very same canto – his right love is the love of 'le fronde onde s'infronda / the leaves which enleave' (line 64), that garden which presumably is all of enduring creation, and this love corresponds to God's goodness because of the successful mediation of those leaves – 'am'io cotanto / quanto da lui a lor di bene è porto. / I love them as much as good is carried from him to them' (lines 65–6). The tree image, whose sign was trespassed, bears and sheds and bears again those linguistic leaves whose changing reflects mortality but still does not fail to communicate good.

Adam himself, who has explained this to Dante, is a sign of a sign – he appears covered with 'la'nvoglia' of light, but in spite of (or perhaps because of) this involucrum he, his meaning, and his intention are perfectly clear, as is Dante's wish, whose mirror-nature is described in a formula properly descriptive of God (lines 97–108). Moreover, this is the canto in which Dante is examined in love, whose teeth (line 51) evoke Augustine's metaphor of the teeth of the church in the *De doctrina christiana*.[69] His examiner is the apostle John, who by promising him in Beatrice the power of Ananias equates him with the blinded and converted Saul, and by so equating him corrects the Pauline pessimism for signs with his own confidence in the flesh which can became the Word. Unlike Honorius in the *Elucidarium*,[70] Dante does not make linguistic mediation the defining feature of man's fallen condition, so much as one of the goods salvaged from his innocence – the good, in fact, whose rejection was the fall.

It is the context of this optimism about language that we must view Dante's comments about poetry. It is true that these comments, both in dramatic situation and in propriis personis, add up literally to no compliment. In the whole of the *Commedia*, poetry's only unqualified success is the conversion of Statius:

> Per te poeta fui, per te cristiano:

> By you I was a poet, by you a Christian: (*Purgatorio* XXII.73)

Beside this, Dante's own devotion to Virgil is something that is finally compromising:

> ... Virgilio dolcissimo patre,
> Virgilio a cui per mia salute die'mi;
>
> né quantunque perdeo l'antica matre,
> valse a le guance nette di rugiada
> che, lagrimando, non tornasser atre.

Virgil sweetest father, Virgil to whom I have given myself for my salvation, nor could all the ancient mother lost keep my cleansed cheeks from turning dark with crying. (*Purgatorio* XXX.51–4)

Beatrice's stinging reproof for Dante's tears[71] evokes, by her words, a contrast with the Siren of Dante's slothful dream, whose song represents to Dante the terrible accidia of the wrong kind of poetry.[72] He must repent of this, as well as for that other preoccupation, with philosophy, and whatever else were those 'imagini di ben ... false / Images of false good' (*Purgatorio* XXX.131), before he will be fully admissible to Lethe, and from thence to Paradise. This repentance is presumed in Dante's dramatic references to poetry within the frame of the journey. He is proud when he reports that the great poets of Limbo made him the sixth, and therefore last of their company.[73] Brunetto's expectation that writing a quite conventional encyclopedia in French will make him immortal is indeed a sodomy, in which Dante by a certain writer's sympathy participates.[74] Casella's song is Dante's to which both Dante and Virgil listen in rapt sloth.[75] Sordello, poet and admirer of Virgil, corresponds to Farinata, the heretic.[76] Bonagiunta quotes Dante's *Donne ch'avete intelletto d'amore* in the context of the purgation of gluttony,[77] and Arnaut Daniel, who is the 'miglior fabbro del parlar materno, / better workman with the mother tongue' (XXVI.117), is, save Dante, the last sinner we hear in the *Commedia*.[78] All these references add up to an act of contrition for poetry gone wrong – for poetry that is merely the 'dolce stil nuovo,' for poetry that is merely aesthetic or merely self-expressive. In these terms, the reference in the Paradise of Venus to Dante's canzone, *Voi che'ntendendo il terzo ciel movete*,[79] spoken, of course, after Dante's experience of Lethe, informs him that here are those true 'principi celesti' to whom, in eternal truth and beyond all merely earthly power of knowing, the poem here quoted had addressed itself. Dante has already told us what he thinks of his own intention for the poem, by putting the next one, the one which in the *Convivio* it introduces, back at the beginning of *Purgatorio*, in the song of Casella, the occasion of that slothful disregard of the ascent.[80]

In this complex web of references, what Dante is finally doing is rejecting, not only the 'donna gentile,' but also the allegory of the poets in terms of which she is discovered, described, and praised. This allegory, of course, is the one elaborately defined in the *Convivio* in connection with Dante's commentary on the *Voi che'ntendendo il terzo ciel movete*. Heaven, of course, knows what this poem really means, but Dante did not, and therefore such poetry must be rejected, not only in so far as it is an occasion for pride or slothful self-preoccupation on the part of poet or audience, but also in so far as it claims or presumes a theory of the relation between letter and sentence which is less than figural. It is in these terms that Dante's increasing use of the inexpressibility topos, and his final admission of the failure of fantasia, must be understood. What fails, at the end of the poem, is not quite cognition, because there is a flash of overpowering insight, too great for fantasy to receive, memory to record, or words to define. Nevertheless, the achievement of the end is not cognitive, but active; Dante's desire and will achieve their submission to the love that moves the sun and other stars.

In terms of the ethical poetic of the later Middle Ages, this end is not a failure of language, but an overwhelming success. What Dante reports achieving, or rather reports realizing that he had already achieved, is a perfect state of consideratio. He is, as it were, plugged in, involved, a part of the cosmos. He is true. His desire and his will are turned, like a perfectly turning wheel, so that his definition and his act (his intellect and his will) are perfectly the same. John Freccero has well explained this image, and in terms which permit Dante to be united with God without losing himself or the cosmos.[81] The fantasia which he had is beyond direct reporting – but it was had, and because of it Dante is true, and he knows that he is true, and this conviction of himself as true is based upon the fact that his 'mente fu percossa.' In modern terms, he had an insight – that most powerful and existence-altering experience of which mind is capable.

What the poem asks of its audience, from beginning to end, is exactly this same experience – to exist before it in a constant state of insight, of realization of consideratio, a realization, that is, that these exempla are true – that fact and definition fit. Given the fact that the poem's letter is anagogy, and its allegory is the tropology of human behaviour deserving reward or punishment, what it must represent or assimilate for its audience is consuetudo, credulitas, and a conviction of consideratio. It must proceed grosse et figuraliter. Implicit always, explicit often, the central strategy on which the ethical definition of late medieval poetic depends is that exemplification or representation by which particulars are seen as true – by which individua cadentia in sensum are seen, because the 'mente fu percossa,' as universal.

What strikes Dante's mind, and makes him realize that his will and his desire are already acting as perfect parts of the system of divine love, is the divine fact which makes all human truth possible – the doctrine of the Trinity, and the doctrine of the Incarnation. It is precisely in reflection of Dante's announced purpose – to use anagogy as a way of talking about human behaviour – that these two doctrines, generalized, permit one to explain, or at least behave, in human society so that one city is achieved by the unity of many different people, and so that particular, human, material actions may become so perfectly in accord with definition as to be true. Dante underlines this significance, I think, by his geometrical imagery, which evokes memory of the implicated circles of the *Timaeus* by which Plato represented the primal material of creation.[82] The whole poem is worldly, but the perfection of its worldliness is not realized until the end, when one is given, in the fact of the divine definitions which one is not required either to understand or describe, but merely realize, the reason why worldliness works and is true.

One insight remains – this one given to the audience. Dante never mentions it – indeed he cannot, for it is the image of the poem, and not some image in it. This is the image which is pictorially made by all of the heaven above the sun – that is, above knowledge – taken as a single, visual, whole icon. At the bottom is the cross in the circle of Mars – the cross on whose sacrifice all else stands. Above that is the band of the motto: *Diligite iusti-tiam* ... We must imagine this motto on its band as forming a circle. The M's become eagles – iconographically, of course, we will have both. Standing in this encircling band of inscription is the vertical of Saturn's ladder, at the top of which is the great globe of the heavens with its band of Zodiac, and in particular the twins: Gemini. Above them is the great cup of the rose, in the company of angels, and above that, poised in space, is the divine emblem of the interlocked circles, containing the image of man. The result, drawn in the literal words of a journey, is a chalice, with an elevated host above.[83]

That this stack of icons will make a chalice is conceptually obvious; to construct its literal image in the mind is more difficult. Fortunately, there is a convenient medieval version of it. In Siena, in the middle of the thirteenth century, Pacino di Valentino, a goldsmith, invented a new kind of chalice.[84] Traditionally, chalices had been rather squat, with large hemispherical cups, sometimes with handles. They could be decorated with incised or low relief ornament, some of it representational. The new Sienese chalice was taller, with a narrower and more parabolic cup and without handles, much more elaborately decorated with strapwork and stampings, and featuring large numbers of enamels in medallions. It is clear from surviving examples that the enamels were made separately, so that it would be possible to make substitutions, and to order a chalice with some particular iconographic program.

The fashion for this type of chalice spread quickly throughout Italy, and became the dominant form until long after Dante's time. The spread and acceptance of the fashion occurred, obviously, during Dante's impressionable years; the earliest surviving example, commissioned by Nicholas IV for the basilica of St Francis about 1290 and inscribed, 'Niccolaus papa quartus. Guccius Manniae de Senis fecit,' Dante may well have known. This chalice has an elaborate iconographic program, executed in enamels, most of them still in place. Around the foot, the knop, the stem, and the cup, there are nine series of enamels, all but the lowest of which include eight medallions. The bottom series, around the foot of the chalice, contains eight large and eight small enamels. The large ones represent the Crucifixion, the Virgin, St Francis with the stigmata, St Anthony or St Bonaventure, the Virgin with child, Pope Nicholas IV, St Claire, and St John of the Crucifixion. The smaller medallions alternating contains various beasts and an angel. The next series represents birds of prey, in flight in attack posture. The third is a series of faces and angels, and includes what appears to be a winged bull. The fourth and fifth are again birds of prey. The sixth, a series of large circular medallions on the equator of the knop, are apostles and saints; one represents Christ blessing. The seventh and eighth are once again birds of prey, and the ninth, which consists of the petals supporting the chalice cup, represents angels in various postures of praise.[85] It is an enormously impressive object, even to a modern scholar who has necessarily been exposed to the even larger and more elaborated church plate of baroque and later styles. It must have been even more impressive to a late thirteenth-century Italian whose possibilities for comparison lacked the baroque.

Its iconographic program is not, of course, the same as Dante's. But it is similar in some respects, and it formally permits a complexity equal to that of this part of the *Commedia*. Other surviving examples confirm this impression. All the ones which I have seen or seen described have a medallion of Christ on the cross on their bases, at the place which must correspond to Dante's cross in Mars. The two which I have seen personally – at Assisi and at Princeton – have many medallions representing birds of prey, which may well be eagles, in various active postures. On one of them, now at Princeton, 'the cup proper is set into a collar of six petals on which are incised seraphs with red enamelled wings.'[86] I have not seen any example with a zodiacal knop, but one exists which has a stem decorated with columns in a ladder-like fashion.[87] The inscription on the Assisi chalice mentions the donor and maker; this may be customary,[88] but is of course not necessary.

I would not, of course, argue that Dante copied the *Paradiso* detail for detail from some then existing Sienese chalice. Rather, I would suggest that the iconography of the Eucharist is powerfully suggested by a visualization of the canti from Mars up, and that the chalice style new in Dante's day is impressive chiefly for its iconographic complexity – a complexity suggesting, at least, that of Dante's own poem. The two together are a happy convergence, which lend external plausibility to an insight. Ultimately, of course, the poem must argue itself.

There is, however, a discursive version of the same experience, with all the terms filled in. This is the experience of the dreamer-poet in the Middle English *Pearl*, who also confronts a blessed and loving lady in the environs of paradise. Like Dante, the dreamer of the *Pearl* comes to the end of the poem in desire. But the dreamer, seeking to satisfy it, goes further than Dante takes his pilgrim, so that the narrative of the poem includes the departure from the dream and the return to this life. In this return, the dreamer is given the experience of Christ in the Mass, which the priest 'shows us, each a day.' The same experience, of course, was Dante's once he left his poem. Both for Dante and for the dreamer, this is as it should be, because it is in the mode and under the appearance of the Eucharist that the Incarnation presents itself, as the continuing and continuously re-enacted spectacle at the centre of life, meaning, and society. One is not required to understand it, but merely attend to it, realize it, and submit to it. Then, not it, but everything else, is clarified. This is not the enterprise of the cognitive achievement of the ideal, which so preoccupied the twelfth century. Rather, this is the enterprise of the proper use of this world, whose empirical base and whose theological coherence, and their unity, were the preoccupation of the less platonist age which followed. The poetry which is of use to Dante is not the poetry of a refined, idealist fin amour consciousness, conscious primarily of itself; ultimately, it is not even the poetry of cognition, after the manner of the *Anticlaudianus* where the journeying is superficially similar. The poetry which is of use to Dante is the poetry of things, viewed sub specie aeternitatis in order that their ethical value in this life might be perceived, defined, ordered, and, most important of all, enacted.

NOTES

1 Claude Lévi-Strauss *Tristes tropiques* tr John and Doreen Weightman (New York 1974) p 25
2 The literature on the seven arts in general, and the trivium in particular, is properly enormous, and I cite only a few works which seem especially to illustrate my particular point. The collection of the SIEPM, *Les Arts libéraux et philosophie: Actes du quatrième congrès international de philosophie médiévale* (Montréal 1969), contains a number of articles sufficiently specialized to

bring us into contact with specifics, and therefore with the act of classification itself. J.J. Murphy's long-continued study which seeks to determine just what is and what is not rhetoric is an exemplary account of the difficulties and achievements generated by bringing theory and practice together.

3 The early history of this convention of commentary is by E.A. Quain 'The Medieval Accessus ad Auctores,' *Traditio* 3 (1945) 215–64. The difference between an accessus to a book and an accessus to an art is discussed by R.W. Hunt 'The introductions to the "Artes" in the twelfth century,' in *Studia Mediaevalia in honorem R.J. Martin O.P.* (Bruges 1948) pp 85–112. A representative, if somewhat old-fashioned, collection, is R.B.C. Huygens ed *Accessus ad auctores, Latomus* 12 (1953), and collection Latomus xv (Brussels 1954). An excellent recent treatment, which focuses on late rather than early medieval materials, is Bruno Sandkühler's *Die frühen Dantekommentare und ihr Verhältnis zur mittelalterlichen Kommentartradition* (Munich 1967) pp 13–46; another, with a difference of focus which makes it independently useful, is Bruno Nardi 'Osservazioni sul medievale "Accessus and Auctores" in rapporto al' Epistola a Cangrande' in *Saggi e Note di Critica Dantesca* (Milan 1966) pp 268-305. My discussion here is a development of my 'Commentary as Criticism: Formal Cause, Discursive Form, and the Late Medieval Accessus' in *Acta Conventus Neo-Latini Lovaniensis* ed J. IJsewijn and E. Kessler (Munich 1973) pp 29–48.

4 Conrad of Hirsau *Dialogus super auctores* ed R.B.C. Huygens (Leiden 1970) p 65. Alanus de Insulis, in his commentary on the *Rhetorica ad Herennium*, makes a somewhat different division: 'Philosophie namque tres partes sunt: ethica, speculativa, rationalis idest logica. / Philosophy has three parts: ethics, speculative philosophy, and rational philosophy or logic.' Paris, Bibliothèque nationale, ms lat 7757, 5v. William of Conches, in his commentary on Boethius, divides 'scientia' into 'sapientia' and 'eloquentia.' Under eloquentia are grammar, rhetoric, and logic. Sapientia is divided further into 'theorica' or 'contemplatio,' under which are theology, mathematics (comprising the quadrivium), and physics; and 'practica,' under which are economics, politics, and ethics: Vatican Library, ms Ottob 1293, ff 2v–3r. The differences among these three explanations are in part more terminological than real, but in part quite important. I give Conrad emphasis only because his work is more simplemindedly to be classified as literary criticism than that of the others.

5 Munich, ms Clm 19475, f 15r. Cf Huygens ed *Accessus ad Auctores* p 50. Another commentary on Horace, this one from a twelfth-century manuscript, reflects the total convention without making the mistake: 'Cum alii plures tractatus ethice supponantur, iste loyce supponi videtur. / Though many other works are classified as ethics, this one seems to belong under logic.' Paris, Bibliothèque nationale, ms lat 7641, f 106v.

6 Medieval classifications of the verbal arts, more often than not, omit explicit reference to poetry; for a discussion of the most important exception to this habit, Domenicus Gundisallinus, see O.B. Hardison Jr *The Enduring Monument: A Study of the Idea of Praise in Renaissance Literary Theory and Practice* (Chapel Hill 1962); and Hardison's 'The Place of Averroes' Commentary on the *Poetics* in the History of Medieval Criticism,' in *Medieval and Renaissance Studies: Proceedings of the Southeastern Institute of Medieval and Renaissance Studies, Summer 1968* ed John L. Lievsay (Durham, NC 1970).

7 Paris, Bibliothèque nationale, ms lat 7757, 2r

8 Hermann the German believes that rhetoric is a part of logic, but he does allow for 'Cicero's' rhetoric as a part of civil science, in an observation which nicely covers all the possibilities: 'Quod autem hi duo libri (Aristotle's *Rhetoric* and *Poetics*) logicales sint, nemo dubitat qui libros perspexerit arabum famosorum, Alfaribi videlicet et Avicenne et Avenrosdi et quorundam aliorum. Imo ex ipso textu manifestius hoc patebit. Neque excusabiles sunt, ut fortassis alicui videbitur propter Marci Tullii rhetoricam et Oratii poetriam. Tullius namque rhetoricam partem civilis scientiae posuit et secundum hanc intentionem eam potissime tractavit. Oratius vero poetriam prout pertinet ad grammaticam expedivit. / That these two books are logic, no one doubts who has looked at the books of the famous Arabs, that is, of Alfaribi and Avicenna and Avenrosdi and certain others. This is even more clear from the text itself. Nor is it excusable to think, as some may, that the book is rhetoric because of Cicero or poetry because of Horace. For Cicero made rhetoric a part of civil science and treated it chiefly according to that application; Horace developed poetic in terms of its pertinence to grammar.' Quoted in O.B. Hardison, Jr 'The Place of Averroes' p 78.

9 Assisi, Biblioteca communale, ms 309, f 2r

10 Vatican Library, ms Chigi L.IV. 74, f 1r

11 Venice, Biblioteca Marciana, ms lat XII 244 (10531), f 32v

12 Huygens ed *Accessus ad auctores* p 25. The author so classified is Maximianus. Among the others so classified are Prudentius (p 20), Cato (p 21), Avianus (p 22), Homer (p 26), Arator (p 27), Ovid's *Ars Amatoria* (p 33), etc.

13 Munich, ms Clm 4610, quoted in Fausto Ghisalberti 'Medieval Biographies of Ovid' *Journal of the Warburg and Courtauld Institutes* 9 (1946) 17. Another is similar: 'Quoniam uniuscuiusque poete finis mentes sit hominum informare in omnibus, unde in principio istius libri sicut alibi dictum est quod ethice, idest philosophie morali supponitur iste liber. / Since the end of every poet is to inform the minds of men in everything, therefore at the beginning of this book, as was said elsewhere, it is classified as ethics or moral philosophy.' Milan, Biblioteca Ambrosiana, ms D 76 inf (2), f 33r.

14 Arnulf of Orleans: 'Ethice supponitur quia docet nos ista temporalia, que
transitoria et mutabilia, contempnere, quod pertinet ad moralitatem. / It is
classified as ethics because it teaches us to disvalue temporal things, which are
transitory and changeable; this pertains to morality.' In Fausto Ghisalberti
'Arnolfo d'Orleans, un cultore di Ovidio nel secolo XII' *Memorie del reale
istituto Lombardo di scienze e lettere*, 24 (1932) 181.

Giovanni del Virgilio: 'Sed cui parti phylosophie supponatur dico quod sup-
ponitur ethyce idest morali phylosophie, nam omnes poete tendunt in mores. /
But as for the part of philosophy to which it belongs, I say that it belongs to
ethics, that is, moral philosophy, for all poets deal with behavior.' In Fausto
Ghisalberti 'Giovanni del Virgilio, espositore delle "Metamorfosi"' *Il Giornale
Dantesco* 34 (1933) 19.

Honofridus Angelus de San Gemignano (1398): 'Quoniam uniuscuiusque
poete sit mentes hominum moribus informare, ideo in primordio huius libri
praecipue scire debemus quod hic liber Ethice, idest morali scientie suponitur,
ideoque omnis transmutatio in hoc libro transcripta merito ad mores est peni-
tus reducenda. / Since it is a characteristic of any poet to inform the minds of
men with regard to their behaviour, therefore at the beginning of this book
we should know above all that it is classified as ethics, that is, moral science,
and thus every metamorphosis transcribed in this book must be totally referred
to behaviour.' Florence, Biblioteca Laurenziana, ms Plut 36.16, f 1v. Cf also
London, British Library, ms Harl 1014, f 12r.

An anonymous commentary dated 1406: 'Iste liber supponitur parti philo-
sophice scilicet ethice morali philosophie. / This book is classified under that
part of philosophy which is ethics, or moral philosophy.' Florence, Biblioteca
Laurenziana, ms Plut 36.3, f 11r.

15 Leiden, Bibliotheek der Rijksuniversiteit, ms BPL 95, 1v. The manuscript is of
the thirteenth century, from France. A fourteenth-century manuscript (Paris,
Bibliothèque nationale, ms lat 8253, f 1v) is slightly more developed: 'Phisice
supponitur quia de naturalibus loquitur, scilicet quomodo elemente nature prin-
cipalis separata fuerunt a prima materia scilicet yle. Omne illud est yle quod est
quid et de quo est quid. Unde diffinicio: yle est vultus nature antiquissimus gen-
erationis uterus indefessus formarum prima susceptio materia corporum sub-
stancie fundamentum. Ethice supponitur quia tractat de moribus. / It is classified
as physics because it deals with natural things, that is, how the principal elements of nature were separated from the prime material which is hyle. Hyle is all
that which is something, and from which something is. Whence the definition:
Hyle is the antique face of nature, tireless womb of generation, the first assumption
of forms, the material of bodies, and the foundation of substance. It is classi-

fied as ethics because it deals with behaviour.' Cf also the accessus preserved in London, British Library, ms Harl 2769, f 2v.

16 That is, before the Renaissance, and the development of such concepts as the poet as 'vates.' But these Renaissance concepts are not fully like our aesthetic ones, and even these are rare in commentary, which tends to be conservative. The earliest example I know, and one of the very few, is an Italian commentary on Geoffrey's *Poetria nova* dated 1394. The accessus begins in conventional piety and conventional terminology: 'In nomine domini nostri yesu christi. Hic incipit divisiones huius [libri?] premissis primo causis operi cuilibet convenientibus. / In the name of our Lord Jesus Christ. This begins the divisions of this book, after discussion of the causes which relate to all works.' It ends with the thoroughly Renaissance opinion, cast in the medieval framework: 'Tertio querebatur cui parti philosophie supponeretur; dicimus quod supponitur ipsi poesi que est philosophia velata. Amen. Dictis ergo hiis et omnibus causis veniendum est ad huius libri divisionem. / Third it was asked in what part of philosophy it should be classified; we say that it is classified as poetry itself, which is philosophy veiled. Amen. Having discussed these and all causes we must consider the divisions of this book.' Florence, Biblioteca Laurenziana, ms Strozzi 137, f 1r.

17 A commentary from the late twelfth or early thirteenth century makes it clear that the assignment is obvious: 'Ad quam partem philosophie liber iste spectatur? satis patet quod ad ethicam. / To which part of philosophy does this book belong? Clearly enough to ethics.' London, British Library. ms Royal 15.A.29, f 4v. An Italian commentary, which quotes Dante and defines poetry as 'integumentorum scientia, incredibili superficie paliens veritatem, / the science of figurative language, shrouding the truth with an incredible surface,' classifies, 'Supponitur morali philosophie quia de moribus hominum dicitur. / It is classified as moral philosophy because it treats the behaviour of men.' Florence, Biblioteca Nazionale, ms II.II.55, f 123r. Another Italian commentary, probably fifteenth-century, has: 'Hetice [sic] supponitur per polliticam, quia nobis morum informat doctrinam. Hetice autem due sunt partes: echonomica, qua propria disponimus familie (echonomus enim dispensator interpretatur), politica vero est scientia que ad regimen civitatum est necessaria. Pollis enim civitas dicitur. / It is classified as ethics because it is about politics, because it informs for us the rule of our behaviour. There are two parts of ethics: economics, by which we manage the goods of a family ("Echonomus" means "dispenser"), politics is the science which is necessary for the government of a city. "Polis" means "city."' Florence, Biblioteca Riccardiana, ms 842, f 1r. Cf also Vatican Library, ms Vat lat 3280, f 103v; ms Reginensis lat 1375, f 140v; Leiden, Bibliotheek der Rijksuniversiteit, ms BPL 191A, f 214r.

18 From a thirteenth-century miscellany of commentary: the *Heroides* 'hetice subponitur que morum instructoria bonorum est et extirpatrix malorum. / It is classified as ethics because it is instructive in good behaviour and roots out evil behaviour.' Paris, Bibliothèque nationale, ms lat 5137, f 97r. Cf also Assisi, Biblioteca communale, ms 302, f 138v.

19 A fifteenth-century Italian commentary has 'Causa finalis est ad virtutes inducere et a viciis removere. Nam hic intendit in toto opere homines a viciis retrahere et virtutibus informare. Ex hiis sequitur quod liber iste supponit [sic] ethyce cuius est virtutes cognoscere et de ipsis docere et scientiam tradere. / Its final cause is to lead to virtue and remove from vice. For in the whole work this is the purpose – to take men away from vice and inform them in virtue. For these reasons it follows that this book is classified as ethics, whose concern is to recognize the virtues and teach and transmit the knowledge of them.' Yale University, Beinecke Library, ms Marston 37, f 5r.

20 'Ethice supponitur quia de moribus loquitur. / It is classified as ethics because it speaks of behaviour.' William of Conches' commentary, Vatican Library, ms Vat lat 5202, f 1r.

21 The Provençal treatise *De doctrina de compondre dictats*, written about 1290, edited by J.H. Marshall in *The 'Razos de Trobar' of Raimon Vidal and Associated Texts* (London 1972) pp 95–8, distinguished the various genres of lyric almost entirely in terms of their content, and clearly specifies that the rhetorical object of much of the poetry shall be praise or blame. For instance, to make a 'vers,' 'deus parlar de veritatz, de exemples e de proverbis o de lauzor, non pas en semblant d'amor. / you should speak of truth, of exempla or proverbs or praise, without representing love.' In making a 'sirventes,' among other things, 'per proverbis e per exemples poretz hi portar les naturaleses que fan, o ço que fan a rependre o a lausar. / with proverbs or exempla you can bring in the characteristics of his character, or criticize or praise what he does.' The word 'naturaleses' will become clearer when we have considered its best Latin equivalent in this material, that is, 'consuetudo' as used by Hermann the German. In making a 'cançо' one should write 'ses mal dir e ses lauzor de re sine d'amor. / without praising or blaming anything but love.' The relation of all this vocabulary to human mores, and therefore to ethics, is obvious. We lack for this poetry the conventional accessus which were made for Latin works, and for such works as the *Commedia*. Nevertheless, this language, added to the tendency of thirteenth-century and later compilers to explain twelfth-century fin amour lyric in terms of the biographies of the poets, relates this material more to ethics than to anything else.

22 'Genus vero philosophiae, sub quo hic in toto et parte proceditur, est morale negotium, sive ethica; quia non ad speculandum, sed ad opus inventum est

totum et pars. Nam si in aliquo loco vel passu pertractatur ad modum speculativi negotii, hoc non est gratia speculativi negotii, sed gratia operis / The kind of philosophy, under which this [that is, the work of helping people out of misery, and into a state of felicity, to which Dante has just referred] proceeds as a whole and in part, is the matter of morality, or ethics, because the whole and every part is chosen not for the sake of speculation, but for the sake of this work. For even if some place or passage is written in the manner of speculative matter, this is not for the sake of the speculation, but for the sake of the work.' Epistola X (to Cangrande) in Dante *Opere* ed Moore p 417. Among the commentators there is a bit of waffling, but the strength of the convention is clear. Boccaccio classifies the *Commedia* as ethics following Dante's opinion: 'La terza cosa principale, la quale dissi essere da investigere, è a qual parte di filosofia sia sottoposto il presente libro; il quale, secondo il mio giudicio, è sottoposto alla parte morale, o vero etica: per ciò che, quantunque in alcun passo si tratti per modo speculativo, non e perciò per cagione di speculazione ciò posto, ma per cagione dell'opera. / The third principal thing which it is conventional to investigate, is to what part of philosophy this present work should be assigned; according to my judgment, it should be assigned to the moral part, or to ethics, because, even though certain passages are speculative in their manner, this is not for the sake of speculation as such, but for the sake of the work.' *Exposizioni sopra la Comedia di Dante* ed Giorgio Padoan (Milan 1965) p 10. Benvenuto da Imola, following a different accessus outline, says: 'Hic namque poeta peritissimus, omnium coelestium, terrestrium, et infernorum profunda speculabiliter contemplatus, singula quaeque descripsit historice, allegorice, tropologice, anagogice, ut merito de ejus opere totius sapientiae et eloquentiae plenissime dicere possim ... Hic autem christianissimus poeta Dantes poetriam ad theologiam studuit revocare, quae tamen de se magnam convenientiam habet cum illa; potest namque theologia dici quedam poetria de Deo. / This supremely expert poet, having contemplated speculatively the profundities of heaven, earth, and hell, described every detail historically, allegorically, tropologically, and anagogically, so that I could say truthfully that his work was full of all eloquence and wisdom ... This most Christian poet Dante strove to bring poetry back to theology, though the two already fit each other quite closely, for indeed certain poetry about God can be called theology.' *Benvenuti de Rambaldis de Imola, Commentum super Dantis Aldigherii Comoediam* ed J.P. Lacaita (Florence 1887) vol I, pp 7–9. Dante's son, on the other hand, says simply: 'Nunc videndum cui parti philosophiae supponatur. Unde dico quod supponitur ethicae, idest morali philosophiae. / Now it must be seen to what part of philosophy [the book] belongs. I say it belongs to ethics, that is, moral philosophy.' *Petri Allegherii super Dantis*

ipsius genitoris Comoediam Commentarium ed V. Nannucci (Florence 1845) p
11. Jacopo della Lana distinguishes: 'Puossi dire che questa opera sia sottoposta a morale filosofia in quanto ella ha per suo subietto atti umani, et
puotesi dire che a nulla specialmente de filosofia sia sottoposta in quanto in
essa si tratta della divina essenzia che appartiene alla supereccelentissima
theologia. / It can be said that this work should be classified as moral philosophy in so far as it has for subject human actions, and it should be said that it
should not be classified as any special kind of philosophy in so far as it deals
with the divine essence, which has to do with the most high theology.' *Commedia de Dante ... col commento di Jacopo della Lana* ed Luciano Scarabelli
(Bologna 1866) vol I, p 97.

23 The accessus also contains a very rare emphasis on the delight to be found in
poetry: 'Materia sua est hec: Scopa Calibidam ad amorem suum invitans.
Intentio sua est tractare de hac materia, ad ostendendam mulierum impacienciam, que si non rogentur tum rogant. Unde Ovidius in Arte: Conveniat
maribus ne quam nos ante rogemus. Utilitas solum est delectatio. Quia aut
prodesse volunt aut delectare poete. Ethice supponitur liber iste quia agit de
moribus mulierum, que impacientes viros ad amorem sollicitant. / Its material
is this: Scopa inviting Calibida to her love. Its intention is to treat of this material, to show the impatience of women, who propose if they aren't proposed
to. Whence Ovid in the *Art of Love*: "Did it suit us males not to ask any
woman first, the woman, already won, would play the asker" [adding the next
line: "Femina iam partes victa rogantis agat." I.277–8]. Its usefulness is
delight alone, for poets wish either to profit or delight. This book is classified
as ethics because it deals with the behaviour of women, who are impatient
and invite men to love.' Paris, Bibliothèque nationale, ms lat 8207, f 9v.

24 The commentator is aware of the distinctly minor character of his text; he
manages to be both utterly conventional and a bit personal at the same time.
Since his treatment is economical, I quote slightly more at length, to give an
example of the kind of context in which an assignment to ethics occurs: 'Sicut
enim in aliis actoribus quedam inquirere solemus, ita in isto libro non minus
celebri quedam digna inquisitione censemus. Unde primo videndum est que
materia, que intentio, quis titulus, quis actor, que causa suscepti operis, quis
modus agendi, cui parti philosophie supponatur. Materia huius libri potest
esse duplex, scilicet vocabulorum diversitas et eorundem moralitas. Intencio
versatur circa materiam. Intendit enim nos docere dictionum diversitates, et
per eas nobis mores exponere speciales. Titulus talis est: Incipit distigium
magistri cornuti. Et dicitur titulus a titane, quod est illuminatio, quia sicut sol
illuminat mundum, ita titulus opus sequens. Actor tangitur in titulo, scilicet
cornutus, qui multos libros prosaice dicitur compilasse, sed tandem metrice

hunc incepit, quem preventus morte non terminavit. Sed quadraginta duos versus solum composuit. Causa suscepti operis motus pietatis. Modus agendi mediocris. Ethice supponitur, quia agit de moribus. Et hiis visis ad litteram accedamus. / As in other authors there are conventional topics for criticism, so for this book, which is not less famous, I think a certain serious investigation is appropriate. First we must see what the material is, and the intention, the title, the author, the reason for making the book, the genre, and to what part of philosophy it should be assigned. The material of this book can be double – the diversity of words and their morality. The intention depends on the material. For he intends to instruct us in the diversities of terms, and by means of them explain to us particular kinds of behaviour. The title is thus: Here begin the distichs of Master Cornutus. And the etymology of "title" comes from "titan," which means illumination, because as the sun illuminates the earth, so the title the work that follows. The title refers to the author, Cornutus, who is said to have written many books in prose, but finally began this one in verse, which he died before he could finish, composing only forty-two lines. He was moved by piety to undertake the work. Its genre is the low style. It is classified as ethics, because it deals with behaviour. Having seen these things, let us turn to the text.' Paris, Bibliothèque nationale, ms lat 8207, f 10v.

25 A fourteenth-century commentary on the hymns: 'Et nota quod iste liber est liber ymnorum idest liber laudis divine quia ymnus grece laus est latine. Liber iste supponitur theoloyce philosophie idest divine contemplationi. / And note that this book is the book of hymns, that is, of divine praise, because "ymnus" in Greek means praise in Latin. This book is classified as theological philosophy, that is, divine contemplation.' London, British Library, ms Arundel 512 (II), f 21r.

26 One commentator on the *Anticlaudianus*, for instance, says: 'Liber vero nulli parti vel speciei philosophie tenetur obnoxius, nunc ethicam tangens, nunc phisicam delibans, nunc in mathematice subtilitatem ascendens, nunc theologie profundum agrediens. / The book is related to no part or kind of philosophy: now touching ethics, now tasting natural science, now ascending into the subtlety of mathematics, now approaching the profundity of theology.' Paris, Bibliothèque nationale, ms lat 8299, f 13v.

27 I deliberately include one 'bad' poem; one important feature of the medieval definition is that the question 'what kind?' is more important than the question 'how skilful?' Ethical behaviour, however, also admits of hierarchical classification and in terms partly involving virtuosity. But there are important distinctives.

28 Modern Italian, in the word 'divisa,' preserves precisely the value-laden concept I wish to communicate. The word means a uniform, or a motto, or a coat

of arms, and in this combination defines that identity-enhancing power which the English word 'uniform' denies.

29 This relation between ethics and literary studies is described as a way of grounding the study of medieval ehtics, in Ph. Delhaye '"Grammatica" et "Ethica" au XIIe siècle' *Recherches de théologie ancienne et médiévale* 25 (1958) 59–110.

30 *Aegidii Columnae Romani ... De regimine principum Libri III* (Rome 1607, repr 1967) pp 2, 3–4

31 *Catholicon* (Mainz 1460, rpr 1971), np, sv 'Figura'

32 This sense of the word 'ratio' had by the end of the thirteenth century penetrated the Romance vernacular; see the 'De doctrina de compondre dictats' Marshall *The 'Razos de Trobar'* 95ff.

33 G. Bruni ed in *The New Scholasticism* 6 (1932) 1–18

34 The edition which I use is by W.F. Boggess, 'Averrois Cordubensis Commentarium medium in Aristotelis poetriam' (PHD Dissertation, University of North Carolina, Chapel Hill, 1965). All future references to this text will be to this edition. See also his 'Aristotle's *Poetics* in the Fourteenth Century,' *Studies in Philology* 67 (1970) 278–294; and O.B. Hardison Jr 'The Place of Averroes.' The text has been translated by O.B. Hardison in *Classical and Medieval Literary Criticism, Translations and Interpretations* ed Alex Preminger, O.B. Hardison Jr, and Kevin Kerrane (New York 1974) pp 349–82. (Introduction, pp 341–8). Further bibliography may be found in all these studies. I am happy here to thank Professor Hardison for having first brought this text to my attention, and for his continuing helpful interest in my work with it. It is universally admitted that Averroes' theories are congenial to the medieval mind; but once this is said, discussion of the text to date has concentrated on its mistakes – its lack of agreement with the true doctrines of Aristotle. The result of this concentration has been, on the one hand, to minimize some differences, and, on the other, to neglect the possibility that Averroes' theories are, in themselves, a coherent and sufficient definition of poetry. It is this possibility to which I addressed myself in 'Hermann the German's Averroistic Aristotle and Medieval Poetic Theory' *Mosaic* 9 (1976) 67–81; my treatment here is an amplification of that study. For a contrary view, see H.A. Kelly 'Aristotle-Averroes-Alemannus on Tragedy: the Influence of the "Poetics" on the Latin Middle Ages' *Viator* 10 (1979) 161–209. Kelly concludes that the Averroistic poetics had little influence because medieval readers found in it no doctrine of tragedy; this is like saying that baseball has had no influence on the Japanese because it has not led them to play cricket.

35 ['Exitum decus' is not good grammar, but the meaning is much the same however one construes or emends 'decus.'] Paris, Bibliothèque nationale, ms lat 14716, f 261r. The manuscript is from the late fourteenth or early fifteenth century.

36 *Opere* p 416
37 sv 'Tragedia'
38 'Tragedia etenim non est ars representativa ipsorummet hominum prout sunt individua cadentia in sensum, sed est representativa consuetudinum eorum honestarum et actionum laudabilium et credulitatum beatificantium. / Tragedy is not an art which represents men in so far as they are individuals perceived by the senses, but it represents their honest customs and praiseworthy actions, and beatifying beliefs.' Boggess p 20.
39 'The Place of Averroes' p 70. In his translation, Hardison puts 'meter or accent' for 'metrum,' and 'deliberation' for 'consideratio.' But he underlines the Aristotelian equivalence by bracketing 'plot' after 'representational speeches in the form of fables,' by bracketing 'thought' after 'belief,' and by translating 'consuetudines' without comment consistently as 'character' (p 355).
40 Bernard Weinberg *History of Literary Criticism in the Italian Renaissance* (Chicago 1961) p 360. Weinberg's discussion of Averroes' text, and of other similarly medieval matters, gives them only the rights of precursors. With regard to Averroes, Weinberg reveals his attitude in such phrases as 'philosophical naiveté' (p 56), 'complete failure to understand either text' (p 56), 'careless or unintelligent handling of terms' (p 63), 'weakness of logical method' (p 64), concluding with: 'By constantly asking what virtues or vices of method are present in a given document, we shall without doubt be able to discover some simplicity in complexity and some clarity in confusion' (p 70). For a critic whose obvious interest is in univocal Aristotelian clarity, such strictures are of course appropriate, but they are not a happy basis for the enterprise of positive understanding of medieval theory.
41 'The Place of Averroes' pp 64–5
42 In so far as these theories apply to Chaucer's *Canterbury Tales*, my discussion appears in a book written with Theresa Moritz, *A Distinction of Stories: The Medieval Unity of Chaucer's Fair Chain of Narratives for Canterbury* (Columbus 1981).
43 Assisi, Biblioteca communale, ms 302, f 138v
44 F.N. Robinson ed *The Works of Geoffrey Chaucer* (2nd ed, Boston 1961) I.37–9 (p 17). All future references will be to this edition.
45 Jill Mann *Chaucer and Medieval Estates Satire* (Cambridge 1973)
46 R. Dragonetti 'Aux frontières du langage poétique' in *Romanica gandensia* 9 (Ghent 1961) 23 ff
47 Erich Auerbach *Mimesis: The Representation of Reality in Western Literature* tr Willard R. Trask (Princeton 1953) chapter 1
48 Actual medieval behaviour enacting this principle can be endlessly cited; the best kind of example is probably the behaviour of knights who imitate romances. For a discussion, see Larry D. Benson *Malory's Morte Darthur* (Cambridge 1976).

In religious terms, the supreme example is Christ himself, who deliberately behaved so as to fulfil prophecy. A particularly striking medieval case is Richard Rolle, whose distinctive behaviour was deliberately imitated from biblical precedent – the connection was elegantly presented in a paper by John Alford, to a section on medieval mysticism of the Midwest Modern Language Association in 1976.

49 For a discussion of these possibilities, see the essay by A.T. Hatto in his translation of Gottfried von Strassburg's *Tristan* (Harmondsworth 1976) pp 355–66, and Rita Lejeune 'Rôle littéraire d'Alliénor d'Aquitaine et de sa famille' *Cultura Neolatina* 14 (1954) 31–6. Both these studies presume that only the eventual lack of good relations between Eleanor and Henry would have made the Tristan story an unacceptable compliment; they do not raise the question of privacy. As distinguished from secrecy, which of course in all ages has both personal and diplomatic uses, and to which Chaucer is referring in using the word 'privetee' in the *Miller's Tale*, privacy may well not be a medieval value.

50 Charles Singleton 'The Irreducible Dove' *Comparative Literature* 9 (1957) 129

51 Milton's masque, *Comus*, is the analogous case from the perhaps more accessible world of fantasy. The Earl of Bridgewater's presumably virgin daughter, who acts the personification of chastity by sitting charmed in a chair, is in fact presiding over her own homecoming party; the double roles which she simultaneously acts relate to one another as universal to particular. The ethical poetic of the Middle Ages would tend to assert, as the ideal paradigm of normal ethical existence, a remarkably similar structure. The Baroque elaboration of the Renaissance spectacle may well result from a loss of faith in the reality of the relationships being poetically represented, and the masque, as a form, survives today only as the object of scholarly interest. But one can, and does, still find both moral pleasure and profit in placing one's own contemporaries in their fit places in Dante's *Commedia*.

52 Dragonetti 'Aux frontières' 52 ff

53 Cf Augustine's *De doctrina christiana* II.1, tr D.W. Robertson Jr (New York 1958) p 34.

54 Judson B. Allen 'The Education of the Public Man: A Medieval View' *Renascence* 26 (Summer 1974) 171–88

55 Westfall *In This Most Perfect Paradise: Alberti, Nicholas v, and the Invention of Conscious Urban Planning in Rome, 1447–55* (University Park 1974).

56 Some of the implications of this thesis I have explored in oral presentations, working toward an eventual book: eg 'Life as Story: The Constitutive Rhetoric of the Middle Ages and the Human Definition of the City' to the Amherst College Public Seminar on the City, March 1972; and 'Cities in Expectation of Leopards: The Rhetorical Design Process' to the Interdisciplinary Seminar on

Design, College of Architecture and Art, University of Illinois Chicago Circle, February 1974.

57 Hans Liebeschütz *Medieval Humanism in the Life and Writing of John of Salisbury* (London 1950) p 82; cf p 6

58 Allen and Moritz *A Distinction of Stories*

59 Among these studies, the one which is exemplary and definitive in bulk and method is R.E. Kaske '*Ex vi transicionis* and its passage in *Piers Plowman*' JEGP 62 (1963) 32–60. Its basis is a grammatical gloss, evidence of the importance of grammatical lore; for this see also the important article by Anne Middleton 'Two Infinities: Grammatical Metaphor in *Piers Plowman*' ELH 39 (1972) 169–88. The poem abounds in cruxes – a few articles, representing kinds of problems, some of them by Kaske's students, are as follows: Mary C. Schroeder '*Piers Plowman*: The Tearing of the Pardon' *Philological Quarterly* 49 (1970) 8–18; Kaske 'Piers Plowman and Local Iconography' *Journal of the Warburg and Courtauld Institute* 31 (1968) 159–69; Stephen A. Barney 'The Plowshare of the Tongue: The Progress of a Symbol from the Bible to *Piers Plowman*' *Mediaeval Studies* 35 (1973) 261–93; Katharine B. Trower 'The Figure of Hunger in *Piers Plowman*' *American Benedictine Review* 24 (1973) 238–60; Joseph S. Wittig '*Piers Plowman* B. Passus IX–XII: Elements in the Design of the Inward Journey' *Traditio* 28 (1972) 211–80; Edward C. Schweitzer '"Half a Laumpe Lyne in Latyne" and Patience's Riddle in *Piers Plowman*' JEGP 73 (1974) 313–27.

60 John A. Alford 'The Role of Quotations in *Piers Plowman*' *Speculum*, 52 (January 1977) 80–99. On the other hand, R.E. Kaske's 'Holy Church's Speech and the Structure of *Piers Plowman*' in *Chaucer and Middle English Studies in Honour of Rossell Hope Robbins* ed Beryl Rowland (London 1974) 320–7, argues that the ostentatiously partitioned speech of Holy Church with which the poem begins implies an outline for the whole – this rhetorical, discursive strategy of beginnings, of course, the medieval critics confirm as proper in their discussions of forma tractandi and forma tractatus.

61 Morton W. Bloomfield *Piers Plowman as a Fourteenth Century Apocalypse* (New Brunswick NJ [1961])

62 Robert Worth Frank Jr *Piers Plowman and the Scheme of Salvation* (New Haven 1957)

63 Study of the poem as allegory is of course important. D.W. Robertson's and Bernard Huppé's *Piers Plowman and Scriptural Tradition* (Princeton 1951) is the most important, ambitious, and procrustean of the studies in this genre. Here, more than anywhere else perhaps, the theories of the late medieval critics can provide clear correction and guidance, because they define an allegory which is not reductionist, whose material is particular and individual, and

whose procedure is more accumulative, associative, and analogical than figurative. In this respect *Piers Plowman* is more like the *Prelude* than like the *Anticlaudianus*; its object is to attain a state of being more than a state of knowing – though of course the being which interests Langland is far more comprehensive than is the poetic mentality which interests Wordworth. Langland ends his poem in action; Wordsworth's end, on Mount Snowdon, is the achievement of a merely epistemological symbol. But the thick literal stuff of both poems is irreducible, and the obligation of allegory (or interpretation) is not so much to go through it as to add it up.

64 The best recent example, to my mind, is Giuseppe Mazzotta's 'Dante's Literary Typology' *MLN* 87 (January 1972) 1–19. The fashion, of course, extends beyond Dante studies. For Paul Zumthor, *Essai de poétique médiévale* (Paris 1972), the grand chant courtois is about itself; for Larry Benson, *Art and Tradition in Sir Gawain and the Green Knight* (New Brunswick NJ 1965), the *Gawain* is a romance about romance. R.A. Shoaf ' "Mutatio Amoris:" Revision and Penitence in Chaucer's *Book of the Duchess*' (unpublished PHD dissertation, Cornell University, 1977), makes the analogous point about Chaucer's poem; and his 'Dante's *Colombi* and the Figuralism of Hope in the *Divine Comedy*' *Dante Studies* 93 (1975) 27–59, contains, among other things, considerable discussion of the *Commedia*'s treatment of poetry. The subject, of course, is a legitimate object of study, and medieval poems are in interesting ways 'self-conscious' texts; some modern interest in it, however, may have something to do with the fact that our age contains Wallace Stevens and Roland Barthes.

65 Giuseppe Mazzotta 'Poetics of History: *Inferno* XXVI' *Diacritics* 5 (1975) 37

66 Mazzotta 'Dante's Literary Typology' 19

67 The latest and best treatment of this much vexed subject, which retraces some of the author's own excellent previous work, and which contains exhaustive bibliography, is Robert Hollander 'Dante *Theologus-Poeta*' *Dante Studies* 94 (1976) 91–136.

68 My discussion of this Canto grows out of a number of most fruitful conversations with R.A. Shoaf, who first made me face its importance, and whose disagreement with me about its ultimate effect has made it possible for me to find out what I think of it.

69 Augustine's image both honours interpretation and, by reference to 'errors,' means interpretation, and thus doubly praises language. *De doctrina christiana* II.6, p 37–8.

70 Honorius distinguishes knowledge 'per scientiam' and knowledge 'per experientiam' – the first less direct than the second, and therefore presumably mediated through signs. Before the fall, men knew good 'per experientiam'

and evil 'per scientiam' – after the fall, his condition was reversed. See the *Elucidarium* I.14, in J.-P. Migne *Patrologiae cursus completus, series latina* (Paris 1895), vol CLXXII, col 1119.

71 *Purgatorio* XXX.73–4

72 Beatrice announces herself 'Ben son, ben son Beatrice'; the Siren: 'Io son,' cantava, 'io son dolce serena' (*Purg.* XIX.19). It is this monster to which Beatrice refers in *Purgatorio* XXXI.45. For an excellent analysis of these parallels, on which I largely depend, see Charles Williams *The Figure of Beatrice: A Study in Dante* (New York 1961) pp 165–7.

73 Presuming the usual medieval meaning of six – ie that it is a perfect number, the sum of whose factors equals their product. The number acquired the expectable variety of allegorizations 'in bono' and 'in malo.' See for example Macrobius *Commentary on the Dream of Scipio* tr W.H. Stahl (New York 1952) pp 102–3; Pierre Bersuire *Dictionarium seu repertorium morale* (Venice 1589) vol III, p 323, sv 'Sex.' Dante here implies that six poets is a canonically complete group; as poet of anagogy, he must be seen as having pre-empted the possibility of a sabbatical seventh. *Inferno* IV.102. When six and seven are related, six is seen as earthly, seven as cosmic or heavenly, perfection.

74 *Inferno* XV. A Pézard's argument, in *Dante sous la pluie de feu* (Paris 1950), that Brunetto is not literally a sodomite, but that his use of French is morally equivalent, seems to me largely convincing. Dante's habit of letting the place in which something occurs in the *Commedia* be an unglossed but powerful part of his meaning is especially effective in the case of Brunetto, whose sin, in the largest sense, is the sin against language, not just against Italian. He expects words to be constitutive of reality in general, and his own immortality in particular. The opposite sin is John Locke's, for whom language is the mere result of reality. The medieval critics would define the truth in terms of an assimilatio between language and its reality, based ultimately on creation and incarnation. For a most sophisticated discussion of this view of language, by an author who probably has not been helped by living this side of Kant, see Bernard Lonergan *Verbum: Word and Idea in Aquinas* ed David B. Burrell (Notre Dame 1967).

75 *Purgatorio* II.106ff. There are three great dove images in the *Commedia*, which occur here, in *Inferno* in connection with Paolo and Francesca, and in *Paradiso* in connection with Dante's examination in faith, hope, and love by the apostles. For an explanation of these images, which much informs the sense in which here poetry is both a great wrong, and, as wrong, a version of the truth, see R.A. Shoaf 'Dante's *Colombi*.'

76 *Purgatorio* VI–VII

77 *Purgatorio* XXIV.51

78 *Purgatorio* XXVI.139ff. The most dangerous sins are the most idealistic ones. It is impossible to say for sure why Dante chose Arnaut Daniel, out of all the troubadours, for the last word; but it is obvious that this series of references to the grand chant courtois which climaxes here is a most perceptive and important piece of literary criticism, by a poet who was himself a master both of the chant itself and of the writing of its razos, and whose final judgment is that it is an abuse, both of love and of language. That Dante puts his own poem on the cornice of gluttony and the repentant poetry of another on the cornice of love probably means that this self-preoccupied act of lyric is more dangerous for its authors than for its audience, though dangerous enough for both. In either case, it is a preoccupation with consciousness, rather than with either act or with that which may be known. Only later did philosophy discover its name – the solipsism. Dante's final judgment of the grand chant courtois, not coincidentally, is thus based on the same definition of that poetry which Zumthor makes. Three distinctions must be made, however, lest that correspondence be misappropriated. First, Dante's value judgment is precisely the opposite of Zumthor's; what Dante condemns as the failure or the apostasy of poetry Zumthor admires as its achievement. In the second place, however, one must admit that Dante's condemnation makes no proper allowance for twelfth-century sensibility. Dante was not an historical critic, obviously; he was dealing with the grand chant courtois not as something valid at a particular time and place, but as a possible, and dangerous, posture for his own action of poetry. Zumthor, oppositely, both denies the possibility of historical criticism and achieves in practice an excellent example of it, in his chapter 'La nuit des temps' (*Essai* pp 19ff). The result is again the reverse of Dante's; the grand chant courtois becomes something at once impossibly distanced in time and at the same time immediately accessible as poetry. Neither Dante nor Zumthor, I think, make proper allowance for the fact that the grand chant courtois, in its own twelfth-century context, is one of the proper modes of philosophical idealism. The third and most important distinction is that Zumthor, along with all critics whose ontology is no more than aesthetic or linguistic, is absolutely interested in poetry for its own sake, while for Dante that self-preoccupation which the phrase 'for its own sake' implies is precisely the sin he comes to realize he must avoid.

79 *Paradiso* VIII.37

80 Cf note 75

81 'The Final Image: Paradiso XXXIII,144' *MLN* 79 (1964) 14–27

82 *Timaeus* 36; see *Timaeus a Calcidio translatus commentarioque instructus*, ed J.H. Waszink (London and Leiden 1962) pp 29ff. For Chalicidius' comment, see pp 144ff. John Freccero treats this image from the *Timaeus* in a number

of places: 'Dante's Pilgrim in a Gyre' PMLA 76 (1961) 172–4; 'Paradiso X: The Dance of the Stars' Dante Studies 86 (1968) 102; and 'Dante e la tradzione del Timeo' Atti e Memorie, Accademia di scienze, lettere ed arti di Modena 4 (1962) 107–23. He does not, however, relate the Platonic crossed circles to Dante's final image of the Incarnation and the Trinity – in which Dante, by a complex image of circles, the squared circle, and the image of man in the godhead, appropriates both the Platonic anima mundi and the notion of microcosm-macrocosm to the higher, but analogous, Christian notions of unity in Trinity and man's parallel to God in created image.

83 I am ashamed to admit, and happy to acknowledge, that I did not see this for myself. An undergraduate, Jeanne Von Hoff, first suggested it to me.

84 Ippolito Machetti 'Orafi Senesi' La Diana: Rassegna d'Arte e Vita Senese diretta da Aldo Lusini e Piero Misciattelli 4, fasc 1 (1929) 5–110. This is the standard article on the subject; Pacino is dealt with on p 9. See also Charles Oman 'Some Sienese Chalices' Apollo 81 (1965) 279–81 and Marvin J. Eisenberg 'A Late Fourteenth Century Italian Chalice' Record of the Art Museum, Princeton University 10 (1951) 3–11.

85 I am happy here to thank the authorities of the Basilica of St Francis in Assisi, and especially Father Gerhard Ruf OFM for making it possible for me to examine this chalice during a time when it was not on museum display.

86 Eisenberg 'A Late Fourteenth Century Italian Chalice' p 7

87 Alinari N. 52246; Perugia Gall. Naz. (early fourteenth-century)

88 Another chalice with the inscription 'Picinus de Senis me fecit' is in the Museum at Lyons: Eisenberg, p 10, n 12.

2

Poetic thinking and the forma tractandi

At the end of the twelfth century, medieval people who occupied themselves with what we now call information retrieval began to make much increased use of the fact that the alphabet has an order as well as a content, and therefore that the arbitrary relationship between names and their spellings could be of practical use. The result was the biblical concordance. Richard and Mary Rouse have described this factual development in happy and useful detail;[1] they pay less attention, however, to what might be called the theology of it; that is, to the larger significance of a cultural decision to begin lists with 'Aaron' (or more modernly, 'aardvark') instead of with God. At the time, of course, it must have been a merely practical and pragmatic event – the result of a decision to adopt a technique of arrangement for reference of obvious immediate value to people who had large quantities of data, and who needed to be able to turn up any given bit of that body of data when needed. Implicitly, however, it was in this momentous cultural act that data, as such, were invented. At this point, one might say, sociology and the computer became possible, and myth began to die.

Alphabetization, then, is a structure within which thought can take place, and within which, because of that structure, it must take place in a certain range of ways. As a structure, it is intrinsically powerful, because it determines a priori what contents and relations of content can be thinkable. There is, in fact, something almost Kantian about it – once one makes the connection – and it is heuristically useful to keep Kant's categorical achievement in mind, because it is axiomatically familiar to the modern sensibility. I shall eventually try to replace it with something medieval, by dealing in more Aristotelian terms with the causality of forms.

The medieval equivalent of this word 'structure' is difficult to determine. Medieval thinkers were of course as wont to indulge a priori thinking as those of any era, but their tendency was to focus upon entities rather than upon the nature of the organizing spaces between entities. For this reason the possible medieval equivalents of structure which might first come to mind, such as 'forma' in the Platonic sense, or 'esse' in the sense of intrinsic or defining being, will not really do. In so far as structure is a conceptual invention of the later Middle Ages one may get quite far by supposing, as the best candidate, the word 'modus.'

In scholastic terms, a modus is a manner or procedure of thought – a way of thinking. More broadly, 'modus' may refer to the manner, context, or kind of activity within which or in terms of which an entity may exist. In so far as the word applies to the making of poems, the scholastic usage seems to have made the term more powerful, more 'structuralist' than it had been before. Literary accessus in the twelfth century and before, for example, refer frequently to the modus agendi of a work; what is often specified is simply whether or not the work in question is in prose or verse. During the scholastic period, however, the equivalent subject was discussed in terms of modes of a forma tractandi, or form of treating, under which a number of quite rigorous modes could be specified, and in terms of which the resultant poems were of a much more determined character than would have been the case under a specification of merely prose or verse.

In medieval terms, then, we may say that alphabetization, which we would call a structure of thought or of data processing, is a modus. Because it is a structure, or a modus, it has a powerful limiting effect. By studying the structures, or modi, of a culture, we study the limits within which whatever happens must happen, and therefore can know the character of a culture at the level of axiomatic definition. It is at this level that I wish, in this chapter, to deal with poetry.

The medieval term under which the modi of poetry were specified is as I have said, forma tractandi. It occurs regularly in late medieval accessus, as one of a pair under the more general subject of formal cause – its complement is the forma tractatus, which specifies the literal arrangement of the parts of a text, and which obviously must follow, logically, the forma tractandi. The critics specify the forma tractandi of a particular text by naming for it one or several (very often, as we shall see, a conventional five) modi. They do not, so far as I have seen, specify alphabetization as a modus – obviously, because poems are not dictionaries. But the ones they do specify must be seen as analogously powerful, analogously structural, analogously literal, and analogously a priori, and tending toward the same character of influence. What the presence of these scholastic modi in the poetic process makes distinctive about late medieval poetry is its character as discourse.

Because of these modi, operating at the level of formal assumption and definition, both the language of late medieval poetry and the matters which that language could treat were distinctively shaped. In being so shaped, the language of poetry endured the same kind of influence which happened to data because of alphabetization – it became more literal, more discursive, more empirical.

The enterprise of this chapter is to explain this distinctive quality of poetry, which results from its being a medieval discourse enacted by modi. This distinctive quality, I think, can be best explained by considering it in its own terms, rather than by comparisons, and this is what I have chiefly done. I should point out, however, that the poetry enacted by late medieval modal thinking is, as a distinctive thing, obviously different both from the twelfth-century poetry which preceded it, and from the modern poetry whose nature we mistakenly find in the verse of all periods. I shall from time to time consider these differences, but I shall be primarily concerned with two direct approaches to definition: first, to explain just what the forma tractandi is, and, second, to explain just what difference it makes that poems have a forma tractandi as well as a forma tractatus, that is, that poems have two distinct and simultaneously operating forms, involving two distinct intellectual levels, which must not be confused or even reconciled into one. In order to explain these things, I shall begin by pointing out certain differences which distinguish twelfth-century poetry from this later poetry, which are of particular relevance to definition at this level of formal cause. Next I will try to give enough particular examples of medieval usage, both of the term 'forma tractandi' and of various specifications of the modes, to make clear both what the details of terminology are, and what they mean. Finally, I will show that this way of forming poetry makes it possible to understand the concept of genre in a medieval way, and makes clear how exemplification, one of the most important modes of forma tractandi, can be both particular and normative. In all this discussion, what is important is the structural fact – the a priori fact – that is, that late medieval poetry is what it is because one reached the making of it through certain forms of thought.

The difference between this late medieval sensibility, with its modal forms of thought, and the earlier sensibility which it transformed involves a difference in relation between instance and definition, or between particular and universal, which can be very roughly and tentatively expressed as the difference between an exemplum and the letter of an allegory. Of the earlier sensibility, which of course in some form persisted throughout the Middle Ages and still survives at the folklore level of popular thought, Jean LeClercq provides a telling example in his book on the monastic mind, *L'amour des lettres et le désire de Dieu: Initiation aux auteurs monastiques du Moyen Âge* (Paris 1957). There, quoting G. Geenen, he records that monastic defences of the doctrine of immaculate conception are not based on the few explicit biblical texts which may be read as literally supporting that doctrine. Rather, these monastic defences are based on other scriptural passages, literally irrelevant, but rich already in allegorical elaborations, and capable of being elaborated further into a devotional affirmation of the doctrine in question (pp 209–10). This intellectual procedure depends, for its plausibility, upon two presumptions – first, that in the givenness of all that is, God guarantees a priori a unity founded upon the truth of the Christian faith; and second, that the human mind which partakes of that faith is capable, by allegorical meditation, of discovering some aspect of the relatedness that that unity generates. Twelfth-century thinkers, for the most part, had no difficulty in believing *that* the universe was one of God's books of self-disclosure, nor in believing *that* the God so disclosed was the one in whom, on dogmatic and revealed grounds, they already believed. Their problem, or rather their poetic privilege, was to work out the detailed explication of the disclosure. In this working out, of course, it made no difference where one started – if the whole of the universe were about God, then any part of it was also about God, and one's information about the universe, the data so to speak, might be arranged in hierarchical order descending from God, because from the intellectual point of view it was never necessary to find any particular bit of data to prove anything. The connections were meditative, symbolic, allegorized. The interpretations, and even the poems, which resulted from this meditation were therefore unoriginal by definition. They stated what was, because true, already true – as distinguished from an originality which could only be heretical, or simply false.

Such a definition, in a period as lively as the twelfth century, necessarily leads to instability. Elaboration cannot continue indefinitely. The interest that alphabetization betrays is an interest in literal proof. The conviction that truth existed and could somehow be found persisted, of course, but there were more rigorous ways to search for it than intuitive allegorization beginning at random, no matter how devout. One needs data. The need for specific data under literal names expresses an interest in facts – in what exists or has happened. The modi in general tend toward the same focus; their result is a sensibility far more empirical than the one seeking for the cognitive achievement typical of twelfth-century thought and poetry. At the same time, of course, medieval empiricism is very different from modern positivism; medieval empiricism is still very much the servant of an enterprise at heart theological, or at least rationalist, in that late medieval attention to the mere data of nature and experience generally included some desire for judgments of value, whether narrowly theological, more broadly devotional, or simply moral. If St Bernard's meditation on the nuptial raptures of the Church and her Christ, and Bernard de Ventadour's reconstruction of the rapt mind of love, are typical of the twelfth century; then Dante's use of an anagogical journey to God as the framework for an ordered definition and evaluation of the political and moral universe of this life, and St Francis' fascination with physical poverty and the innocence of Nature's creatures are typical of the empiricism which succeeded it. It is therefore not surprising that this is the era of the exemplum, of the fabliau, of the Merton school of research in light and optics, of Jean de Meun, of the developed and certain practice of portraiture in art, and of the great Flemish climax of medieval manuscript illumination. All of these cultural events include a focused and very material attention to physical reality; all of them likewise include a certain achievement of truth. The particular mode of relationship by which this combination is achieved can be understood, for poetry at least, by considering the kinds of poetic thinking defined by the forma tractandi of the medieval critics.

The tradition which precedes and defines this discussion of forma tractandi has been briefly defined by Curtius, in his analysis of the modi which Dante specifies in his letter to Cangrande.[2] Bruno Sandkühler, in his study of commentaries on Dante, discusses and illustrates these matters at considerably more length.[3] My treatment owes much to them, though I do bring to bear a quantity of manuscript evidence which they do not consider, much of which comes from a late medieval tradition of commentary on the hymns of the Church. At the outset, however, I should suggest two nuances of difference between their discussion and the position I try to define. First, Curtius implies more originality for Dante's letter to Cangrande, in speaking of Dante's 'carefully considered choice' of modi, than is probably just – a slightly different, and I think rather more interesting, point can be made by beginning with the fact that Dante is here very conventional. Second, Sandkühler implies that the medieval use of these modi imply a tendency to distinguish between that which is 'Wissenschaftlich' and that which is 'Dichtung.'[4] This distinction is close to the proper one, I think, but it is not completely fair to the evidence in that it presumes for some modi, which I shall classify with the Averroistic 'things that assimilate,' a significance not properly distinguished from modern notions of poetry.[5]

Before the terminology derived from Aristotle became popular in the accessus, this notion of form tended to be treated either under the rubric of 'qualitas carminis,' deriving from Servius, or under the rubric of 'modus agendi.' These meant much the same thing, as far as texts which we would call poems were concerned, and the definition usually given for the 'modus' or the 'qualitas' was something having to do with metre or genre. The modus agendi is 'metricus,' or 'prosaicus,' or 'heroicus.' When the schema of the four Aristotelian causes became popular, one was of course the formal cause. Commentators habitually distinguished two as I said above: the forma tractatus and the forma tractandi. The first of these was universally defined in terms of the ordered books, chapters, divisions, paragraphs, or other parts which the work under discussion contained, and betrays a critical concern for that unity of a work which is achieved by the ordering of its parts. This concern is the chief subject of the chapter to follow. Here, at a more general level than that which defines the disposition of parts, or the form, of any single work, we are concerned with the medieval sense of those mental and verbal procedures by which a text is made. These are discussed and defined by the medieval critics under the rubric of forma tractandi.

In this discussion three features are most important. First, it is clear that the forma tractandi has a normal, conventional, fixed definition, which the medieval critics often adopt, reflect, or refer to as they define the form of the treatment of the particular texts they discuss. Second, the older formulae of the modus agendi persist, in part as an alternative approach, in part in mixture with the newer formulae of the forma tractandi, and from this persistence and mixture one may define concepts which may replace, though they are not equivalent to, modern notions of literary genre. Third, the concern of these critics with what is in scholastic terms a modus, or way of thinking, defines for medieval poetry a truth value of a discursive rather than a poetic character, and, more important, bases it in mental activity so as to make it a kind of philosophy, rather than something to be distinguished from philosophy. The distinction between *Wissenschaft* and *Dichtung* simply does not apply; critics who insist on reading these texts 'as poetry' ignore what they really are, and impoverish their interpretations a priori. Definitions of the forma tractandi, thus, agree with and reinforce the normal critical assignment of poems to ethics, and refine and confirm our notions of what ethics is.

In the medieval documents, the best-known citation of the forma tractandi is undoubtedly Dante's in his letter to Cangrande:

Forma sive modus tractandi est poeticus, fictivus, descriptivus, digressivus, transumptivus; et cum hoc definitivus, divisivus, probativus, improbativus, et exemplorum positivus.

The form or mode of treatment is poetic, fictional, descriptive, digressive, and meta-phoric, and with this it defines, divides, proves, refutes, and gives examples. (p 416)

The second five of these modi are a conventional group, to which Thomas Waleys, for instance, refers as items which may be specified 'secundum com-muniter loquentes.'[6] The same presumption appears in a commentary on Ovid's *Metamorphoses*:

Causa formalis est duplex, forma tractatus et forma tractandi. Est autem modus quintuplex scilicet divisivus, diffinitivus, exemplorum positivus, probativus, et reprobativus et collectivus. In hoc libro tripliciter, scilicet divisivus, diffinitivus, et exemplativus.

The formal cause is double, the form of the treatise and the form of the treatment. This is a fivefold mode, that is dividing, defining, putting examples, proving, refuting, and inferring. In this book triply, that is dividing, defining, and putting examples.[7]

Sandkühler gives other examples to the same effect, and says that they occur customarily in philosophical, grammatical, and scientific commen-taries of the thirteenth and fourteenth centuries (p 32). The conventional list, obviously, specifies the ways in which knowledge occurs, and by being connected to poetry, these ways clearly imply that the content of poetry is a legitimate object of knowledge. In addition, by being the modes in which or because of which knowledge occurs, they define and delimit knowledge itself. Clearly, this knowledge is something closely related to logic and reason, since it involves proof and refutation. It affirms the normative, because it involves definition. Its relation to division reflects the medieval sense of composite wholes, understood in terms of homologous parts and parts of parts, and intellectually reflected in the late medieval strategy of distinctio, to which I shall return at length. Finally, its use of exempla raises in the most helpful possible way the large question of the relation between the particular and the concrete, on the one hand, and the intellectual or definitional on the other, and relates to the ethical kind of knowing which proceeds 'grosse et figuraliter' and which has already been discussed in chapter one. The fact that these modi are conventional – so much so that even when they are specified in terms which in fact vary, there still exists in the background a sense of their presence – means that whenever forma trac-tandi occurs, as a term, there is some implication that knowledge is being treated – and that a kind of knowledge which exists because the mind has exercised a modus of thought.

Against this norm of a fivefold forma tractandi, customary for the discussion of texts containing knowledge or information of some sort or other, the commentaries related to texts we would consider poetic vary a good deal. The most important variation involves the persistence of material from the older specifications of 'modus agendi,' or 'qualitas carminis.' Otherwise, there is a good deal of obvious care being exercised, to make one's discussion actually fit the text being considered, so as to relate it properly, rather than merely automatically, to the modi of knowledge which the convention supplies. The material upon which I base my conclusions consists of commentaries on a substantial array of poetic texts, and texts relating to poetry, including the *Metamorphoses*, the *Thebaid*, Dante's *Commedia*, Alanus' *Anticlaudianus*, Aesop's *Fables*, the *Rhetorica ad Herennium*, the *Doctrinale* of Alexander of Villa Dei, the *Aeneid*, the *Ars poetica* of Horace, the *Consolation of Philosophy* of Boethius, the tragedies of Seneca, the *Facta et dicta* of Valerius Maximus, the *Poetria nova* of Geoffrey of Vinsauf, and, finally, the medieval tradition of hymns and sequences.

The hymns at least, and by extension also probably the sequences, should be taken as poetry.[8] The commentaries on these hymns and sequences, which were elaborated most fully in the fourteenth and fifteenth centuries,[9] preserve the most intricate discussion of the forma tractandi which the medieval critics made, and at the same time are clearly in agreement with the kinds of things which other commentators were saying. I have therefore freely included the hymn commentaries with all the others, and dealt with all this evidence as having more or less equal status.

The older convention based on the qualitas carminis, or the modus agendi, persists in a variety of contexts. A fifteenth-century commentary on Aesop's *Fables* equates the forma tractandi with the modus agendi, and defines it as 'metricus.'[10] The *Thebaid*, according to a commentary probably from the late fourteenth century, has as its 'qualitas carminis' 'metrum heroicum' – though the commentator hedges a bit, as we shall see, by defining this metrum heroicum in terms of content, and by specifying also a 'modus materiei.'[11] A hymn commentary, doubtless confused by comment on the sequences, says that the 'forma tractandi est modus agendi et ille est prosaicus.'[12] Dante's own specification of 'poeticus,' at least, is undoubtedly also a reflection of this convention. What all these definitions imply is a distinction between poetry and prose that is purely formal and metrical,[13] a matter of heightened language. This is a common sense distinction, which causes no trouble unless we take it for more than it is – that is, unless we fail to grant that it makes one category out of everything metred, from the grandest epic to the most utilitarian mnemonic doggerel.

Other specifications are more complex. Sometimes, the simple opposition between poetry and prose brings with it an awareness of formal tradition. A commentary on Boethius' *Consolation*, for instance, says:

Sed forma tractandi est modus agendi quem servat autor sive tenet quia scribit metrice et prosaice, et secutus est marcianum capellam idest illum poetam qui scripsit unum librum de nuptiis deorum per carmina et prosas, et ante illum poetam nullus latinus scripserat per prosas et carmina. Et boecius est secundus qui fuit secutus ipsum, et bernardus sylvester fuit tertius, et alanus de complantu [sic] nature etc.

But the form of the treatment is the mode of doing [genre] which the author observes or holds to because he writes in verse and prose, and follows Martianus Capella, that is, that poet who wrote a book of the marriage of the gods in metres and proses, and before him no Latin poet wrote in proses and metres. And Boethius is the second who followed him, and Bernardus Sylvestris was the third, and Alanus in the Complaint of Nature etc.[14]

A late fourteenth-century German commentary on the hymns avoids the issue, while allowing for variety and for the basic concept of the modus:

forma tractandi diversitatur in libris secundum quod et operarii aliter et aliter operantur.

The form of the treatment differs in books according to the practice of different authors.[15]

Giovanni del Virgilio, a friend of Dante's, includes both the traditional information and the new Aristotelian definitions in his *Metamorphoses* commentary.

Sed forma tractandi est modus agendi qui est duplex, scilicet generalis et specialis, generalis est stili qualitas et genus poematis, sed specialis est multiplex quia diffinitivus, discursivus, collectivus et sic de aliis sicut apparebit in processu.

But the form of the treatment is the mode of doing, which is double, that is, general and special. The general is the quality of style or the genre of the poem; the special is multiple, because it defines, it is discursive, inferential, and on other topics as will appear further in the commentary.[16]

Another commentary on the *Metamorphoses*, which I have already noticed as testimony to the conventionality of the fivefold definition of the forma tractandi, specifies that for the *Metamorphoses* there are only three modi: 'scilicet divisivus, diffinitivus, et exemplativus.' But the commentary continues, defining terms: 'divisivus quia dividit in quindecim libros, collectivus quia colligit multa et omnes fabulas.' Apparently there are four modi.[17] The notion of collection turns up again in a Leiden commentary: 'Videndum est qualiter agat, agit enim heroyco metro colligens mutationes diversas a prima creacione mundi usque ad suum tempus. / It must be seen what the genre is; it is in heroic metre collecting diverse transformations from the first creation up to his own time.'[18] A late fourteenth-century commentary on the *Doctrinale* of Alexander de Villa Dei adds reference to the author, plus examples – the passage is misleading, because it follows the usual form of a divisio, and is not one. The lemmata are simple examples:

Forma tractandi est modus agendi penes quem modum agit [auctor] in suo toto libro et iste modus agendi est triplex [sic]: diffinitivus ut ibi *quod nomen proprium*, divisivus ibi *ingeminans species*, epilogutivus ut ibi *deo deo deque geo*, probativus ut ibi *iungit diversa quo significata*, improbativus ut ibi *sed non est nobis natura congrua talis*, exemplorum positiva ut ibi *o sicut cento*.

The form of the treatment is the mode of doing according to which the author operates in his whole book, and this mode of doing is triple: definition, as at 'what is a proper name [line 114]'; division, at 'doubling the species [line 1370; Alexander's text is properly 'in geminas species']'; after the manner of an epilogue [that is, having to do with endings of words], as at 'of -deo and of -geo [line 767; reading 'de deo deque geo']'; proof, as at 'by which it joins diverse meanings [cf Alexander's line 1532, 'iungit diversa coniunctio significata']'; disproof, as at 'but such nature is not congruent to us [cf Alexander's line 1492, 'sed non est nobis constructio congrua talis']'; exemplary, as at '-o as an *cento* [line 552].'[19]

For Bartholomew of Bruges, in his commentary on the Averroistic *Poetics* of Aristotle, the forma tractandi is 'multiplex'; from the usual list, he omits 'reprobativa.'[20]

Other specifications of the forma tractandi go beyond the simple mentioning of prose or verse, but do not really repeat or correspond to the scholastic modi. Commentaries on the *Thebaid* of Statius tend to be this sort. A Leiden manuscript, for instance, says: 'Modus tractandi tripartitus est, nunc historiam tangit, nunc figmenta subiungit, nunc allegorice scribit. / The mode of treatment is tripartite – now it deals with history, now it adds something imaginary, now it writes allegorically.'[21] Another is more elaborate, but says what amounts to the same thing:

Qualitas carminis est metrum heroicum et est metrum heroicum continens tam divinas quam etiam humanas personas, vera falsis admiscens ... modus materiei est tripartitus, quia nunc istoriam tangit, nunc figmento subseruit poetico, nunc scripto utitur allegorico. Nota tria esse scribendi genera, humile, mediocre, grandilocum, quibus omnibus utitur virgillius, quod alii kracteres [sic] alii stilos vocant.

The quality of the poetry [genre] is heroic metre; heroic metre is a genre which contains both divine and human characters, mixing the true with the false. The mode with regard to its material is tripartite, because now it deals with history, now it serves a poetic fiction, now it uses something written allegorically. Note that there are three kinds of writing: low, middle, and high, all of which Virgil used, which some call 'kracteres' and others call styles.[22]

With these comments we are close to a definition of the forma tractandi in terms of content, but under generic labels which preserve contact with mental procedure. The early commentary of Raoul de Longchamp on the *Anticlaudianus* goes all the way in this direction: 'Modus et ordo agendi talis est. Finitis praepositione et invocatione introducitur Natura cum sororibus conquaerens et omnium suorum operum imperfectioni condolens et allegans unicum esse consilium et unicum remanere solatium, ut unum scilicet fabricetur opus, in quo tot munera fundat quaelibet. / The mode and order of the doing is thus: after the proposition and the invocation Nature is introduced lamenting with her sisters and suffering over the imperfection of all her works and proposing that only one plan and one consolation remains – that a work should be made endued with every possible gift.'[23] There follows a kind of summary of the action of the book. At the other extreme, there are two *Thebaid* commentaries which multiply modes much more extensively, almost into a list of kinds of thought or speech. The first of these makes its specifications in an accessus:

Modus quem in tractando servavit est multiplex: secundum quod infra librum poterimus ostendere, quia quandoque laudat, quandoque vituperat, et invehit reprehendo, vel exclamat et alios varios modos quos poete docent, qui potest dici generaliter modus tradendi per exempla et typicus [sic] sermones ut mos est rethoricis et poetis.

The mode followed in the treatment is multiple, according to what our commentary will show, because sometimes it praises, sometimes it blames, and attacks by reproving, or it exclaims, and [uses] the other various modes which poets teach, which can generally be called the mode of treating by examples and by speech containing conventions, as the custom is for rhetoricians and poets.[24]

The second is simply full of modus terms, in the form of verbs. Gloss by gloss, the commentator says, Statius 'comparat, describit, declarat, ponit, tangit, apostrophat, concludit, manifestat, dat, specificat, ostendit. / compares, describes, declares, puts, touches, apostrophizes, concludes, manifests, gives, specifies, shows.'[25] Some of this, obviously, is nothing more than elegant variation, but some of it must reflect an awareness of an array of modes. More careful, but still unconventional specifications can be found in the hymn commentaries, and in the commentary of Robert of Sorbona on the *Anticlaudianus*. Robert relates the modi to the basic divisions of knowledge:

Modus agendi triplex est, aliquando procedit rationaliter scilicet quantum ad naturalem proprie dictam et trivium, quandoque disciplinaliter quantum ad quadrivium, quandoque intelligibiliter quantum ad metaphysicam.

The mode of the doing is triple: sometimes it proceeds rationally in terms of the natural as such and the trivium, sometimes by disciplines in terms of the quadrivium, sometimes intelligibly in terms of metaphysics.[26]

One hymn commentary defines the modes briefly as 'laudativus et supplicativus, ut dictum est. / Praise and supplication, as is said.'[27] Another, with examples, specifies a modus 'monologi,' another, 'invocationis,' and a third, 'commonitorii.'[28] A third commentary is much more elaborate:

Sed si queritur de causa formalis [sic] deducendum est quod causa formalis scientie theologie est eius modus procedendi, qui duplex est, petitorius et instructius. Modos [sic] procedendi petitorius idest supplicionibus tenetur in libro ympnorum et sequentiarum. In hiis enim deo supplicitur et gratiarum actiones referuntur ut patebit in processu. Modos [sic] autem procedendi instructius in theologia estque quadruplex [cod duplex]. Est enim hystoriacus, allegoricus, tropoloycus, anagoycus; hiis enim quattuor instructionibus utitur theologia ... Ideo de causis huius libri quem pre manibus habebis videamus ... Forma tractandi est modus agendi procedendi que in hoc libro triplex est: [supplicativus ...] narrativus. Narrat enim quandoque vitam sanctorum, petens quia deo supplicat ut sepe gratiarum actiones deo referuntur, ut patebit.

But if there is question of the formal cause, it must be explained that the formal cause of the science of theology is its mode of proceeding, which is petitionary and instructive. The petitionary mode of proceeding, that is, with supplications, is found in the book of hymns and sequences. For in these supplication is made to God and acts of thanksgiving are related, as will appear in the course of the commentary. The instructive mode of proceeding in theology is fourfold: it is historical, allegorical, tropological, and anagogical, for theology uses these four instructions ... therefore let us consider the causes of this book which you will have to hand ... the form of the treatment is the mode of doing and proceeding, which in this book is triple: supplicative ... narrative. For sometimes it tells the life of the saints; [it is] petitionary because it makes supplication to God as also he is given thanks, as will be clear.[29]

The manuscript is careless and incomplete, but its sense is clear enough. The hymns contain knowledge, and relate to theology. Their modi have to do both with generic matters – that is, with content and with the way words work in relation to their significations – and with the mental postures and procedures of authors and readers (or singers, in this case). The first of these concerns relates to Bernardus Silvestris' twelfth-century definition of the modus agendi in terms of description 'in integumento';[30] the second is an attitude on which Alanus de Insulis, also twelfth-century, generalizes when he says, in a commentary on the *Rhetorica ad Herennium*, that 'artifex est efficiens causa, ars ipsa est formalis secundum quam artifex agit in materiam. / the artist is the efficient cause; the art itself which the artist uses on his material is the formal.'[31] The form of the text is the art which the maker exercises when he makes it. And art, of course, is for the Middle Ages not something aesthetic, but rather the codified array of rules and procedures by which anything which can be done by rule is to be so done. But, especially in the later Middle Ages, this art which poets exercise, this form or mode which they follow or exercise as they make texts which we today consider poetic, was not something either autonomous, arbitrary, or merely, in our terms, 'formal.' Rather, it had some connection with the truth. A fifteenth-century Italian commentary on the *Facta et dicta* of Valerius Maximus puts it best: 'Forma tractandi est ipsam veritatem breviter et lucide tradere. / the form of the treatment is the brief and lucid passing on of truth itself.'[32]

At the same time, we must be very careful to distinguish this truth from the merely empirical or verifiable. Alanus' comment is here very much to the point – in very concrete terms, what he is saying is that the formal cause of, for example, a chair, is not 'chairness,' but cabinet-making or joinery. Thus formal causes are not merely intellectual, not ideal pictures, but something active, dynamic, procedural, capable of being in actual exercise an art. 'Chairness' would, to pursue the analogy, correspond merely to the forma tractatus – the outline, picture, or organization of the work; forma tractandi is the art – that procedure, validated by the nature of things, by which individual things, be they poems or chairs or human lives, achieve their nature, that is, achieve their 'ipsa veritas.'

In all this material, what we primarily have is terminology. There is, from time to time, some discussion, some definition, some illustration; but on the whole, there is not much. Fundamentally, we are confronted with terms, being used within a culture which understood them at the level of presumption. In understanding them, we have some help, of course, from their literal meaning. A great deal can be learned, as I have said repeatedly, by simply taking the medieval critic at his word, and assuming that what he said about his texts, however conventional it seems, was for him a fully adequate explanation. We also have the help which comes from knowing these words in other contexts, as Curtius has so well, if briefly, shown.[33] There is, moreover, much to be learned from the cumulative effect of this language, in seeing it repeated with small variations in attachment to a wide variety of texts.

In one area, however, we have more. In a few of the hymn commentaries, these terms, and the relationship between poetry and the forma tractandi defined in terms of the scholastic five modes, are quite elaborately discussed. The problem under discussion, in these commentaries, is the problem of knowledge, or 'scientia.' On the one hand, it is argued that the hymn-book has no forma tractandi because the forma tractandi is a schema which relates to a demonstrative science, and the hymn-book is not a science in that its points are made by narration rather than demonstration. On the other hand, it is argued that the hymn-book has no forma tractandi because it does indeed contain knowledge (scientia), which, by 'modern' definition, has only efficient and final causes. In both these discussions, the problems raised exist only because the commentator is, in a sense, splitting hairs – because he is being very careful, in the light of fine points of definition fashionable in the philosophy which is his background, to get his terminology applied precisely and validly to the hymn-book. Paradoxically, the two discussions come to literally opposite conclusions, because they relate to slightly different parts of the larger philosophical context. But they both make the same point – that poetry (in this case, the poetry of the hymn-book) is something of which one fundamentally asks questions which have to do with its truth value, that is, with its relation to knowledge.

The first of these discussions, which is preserved in only one manuscript, is as follows:

Causa formalis distinguitur communiter quod sit duplex, scilicet forma tractatus et forma tractandi. Forma tractatus consistit in ordinatione partium ... Sed forma tractandi secundum quosdam dicitur esse triplex in hoc libro, scilicet forma probandi, quia probat scientiam irregularem idest aliorum formacionem, reprobandi quia inprobat reprehensiones sanctorum, forma exemplaris quia diverse dant[ur] exempla. Sed licet illud dictum sit sapientum attamen non videtur esse verum. Ratio huius est illa quia tractatus de illis meretur dici scientiam quia per Aristotelem scientia est habibilis consequens per demonstrationem acquisitus, in illo autem libro nulla questio demonstratur sed narratione proceditur. Similiter in illo libro nulla questio inprobatur ut exempla aliqua ponuntur secundum quod ipsi dicunt, hic inprobantur persecutores. Hoc, salva reverencia harum [sic], non dicitur inprobare sed plus reprobare. Sciendum est igitur in hoc quod illius libri non sit aliqua forma tractandi quia illa per omnes solum potest esse quintuplex, scilicet forma divisa ... diffinitiva ... probativa, 4a inprobativa, 5a exemplaris positiva. Sed quia nulla illarum in presenti libro reperitur derelinquitur quod ille non habet formam tractandi sed solum forma tractatus.

The formal cause commonly involves a distinction because it is double, that is there is a form of the treatise and a form of the treatment. The form of the treatise consists in the ordering of the parts ... But the form of the treatment according to some is said to be triple in this book, that is, the form of proving, because it proves an unusual science (that is, the result of education by a different set of teachers); of reproving, because it refutes the condemnations of the saints; the form of exemplification because exempla are given variously. But granted that this saying be of wise people, nevertheless it does not seem to be true. The reason for this is that a treatise on a subject deserves to be called a science because, according to Aristotle, a science involves a derivable consequent acquired by demonstration, but in this book no question is demonstrated, but it proceeds by narration. Similarly in this book no question is refuted as some kinds of exempla are proposed, according to what they say, 'Here the persecutors are refuted.' With all due respect, this does not mean refute, but reprove. Therefore it should be known by this that there is not properly any form of treatment of this book, because the form of treatment according to all authorities can only be fivefold, that is the form which divides ... defines ... proves, fourth refutes, fifth gives examples. But because none of these is found in the present book, it follows that it does not have a form of treatment, but only a form of the treatise.[34]

The meaning is clear enough. The hymn-book is not a science, because the truth it contains is not presented in a scientific way – not by demonstration, but by narration. The same point is made by Alexander of Hales, as Curtius has shown,[35] and is a part of that whole tradition whereby the kind of truth contained by poetry on the one hand, and the Bible on the other, which also uses modes which are narrative, historical, and metaphoric, is to be distinguished from the kind of truth established by logic. Implicitly, however, we have here the admission that, if one could have a forma tractandi composed solely of the modes narrativa and exemplorum positiva, then indeed the hymn-book would have such a form.

There are here, also, several interesting betrayals. Most obviously, this commentator agrees with many others that I have cited that the forma tractandi quintuplex is indeed a conventional schema, that its home ground is scholastic, and that it defines the manner by which one deals scientifically with truth. In addition, it is especially clear here that this tradition of literary criticism, of discussion of the hymn-books, is indeed a tradition. In this case, one can even speculate that it is a tradition which involves living people in discussion, as well as involving people with books – one is not generally careful so politely to save the reverence of books. Third, and most interesting of all, there is here clear proof of something which otherwise would have had to have been left at the level of overtone and possibility – that is, that the mode 'reprobativa' or 'refutativa,' which of course properly means 'refutation' or 'disproof,' was confused with the ethical mode of 'vituperatio.' Thus the possible punning relation between proof and refutation on the one hand, and approval and reproof on the other, has at least here, because one critic denounces it as a mistake, some place in medieval opinion.

The second discussion is preserved in three substantially similar versions, in manuscripts now in Munich and Vienna. The treatment in the Munich manuscript is quite detailed; the following excerpts contain the gist of the argument:

Sed ad propositum, hec verba sic exponi possunt ita quod quivis studens scientie theoloycalis potest dicere, Ego sponsa, idest studens, sedi, idest moram feci, sub umbra, idest sub doctrina illius ... Et sic propositio prehabita diversimode exposita est pro commendacione dei et salute nostra et diligencia studii huius libelli [that is, the sequences]. Sunt ergo in verbis propositis tria notanda: primo tangitur sublimitas huius scientie cum dicitur illius quem desiderabam; secundo tangitur fructuositas illius scientie cum dicitur sub umbra; tertio tangitur delectabilitas illius scientie cum dicitur et fructus eius etc. ... Notandum primo dicit Aristoteles primo phisicorum unumquodque sciencie arbitramur cum causas eius cognoscimus, ideo de causis et de quibusdam aliis inponendis videamus que continentur in hiis versibus: Quolibet in opere debemus quinque notare, primo materiam, post hec intencio que sit, post hec utilitas, tytulum, subiungite causas. Circa primum est notandum quod antiqui posuerunt cuiuslibet sciencie quatuor causas scilicet causaum materialem formalem efficientem et finalem iuxta dictum Aristotelis secundo phisicorum: cause sunt quatuor etc. Causam materialem dixerunt esse istam de quo ista sciencia consideraret. Sed formalem dixerunt esse istam scilicet modum et ordinem procedendi in tali scientia. Sed causam efficienem dixerunt collectorem illius scientie. Sed causam finalem rationem cuius scientia talis acquiritur. Sed moderni hoc reprobant videlicet quod secundum eos nulla scientia potest habere causam materialem proprie loquendo. Et nulla scientia potest habere causam formalem ... Ergo moderni dicunt quod cuiuslibet sciencie tantum due sunt cause scilicet efficiens et finalis proprie loquendo. ... Sed diceret aliquis de hoc tamen Aristoteles assignat quatuor causas in philosophia naturali ut iam dictum est, ergo scientie habent quatuor causas. Ad hoc respondetur quod proprie loquendo tunc scientie non possunt habere nisi duas causas ut volunt moderni sed loquendo inproprie tunc quelibet scientia potest habere quatuor causas ... Simili modo capiunt causam formalem inproprie puta pro ordine quo scientia adipiscatur vel acquiritur, et sic est valde inproprie dictum quia proprie loquendo talis ordinatio partium in scientia non est aliqua res a sciencia secundum quod moderni concedunt. Et sic inproprie loquendo istius possunt sciencie assignare quatuor cause. Unde causa formalis huius sciencie est modus procedendi in ista sciencia. Sed efficiens inproprie dicta et mediata fuit beatus Gregorius quantum ad aliqua cantica et beatus Dyonisius et Ambrosius etiam ad aliqua ymo plures sunt novi doctores qui ad laudem dei quedam nova cantica composuerunt que in hoc libro sunt exponenda.

But with regard to the text, these words may be expounded thus, that anyone studying may say of the science of theology, *I the bride*, that is the studying one, *sat*, that is made a delay, *under the shade*, that is under its doctrine ... And thus the above text is expounded in many ways, for the sake of the commendation of God, and our salvation, and the diligence of our study of this little book. Therefore there are three points to be noted in this text: first it touches the sublimity of this science when it is said, *of him whom I desired*; second it touches the fruitfulness of this science when it is said, *under the shade*; third it touches the delectability of this science when it says, *and its fruit*, etc. ... It should be noted first, as Aristotle said in the first book of the Physics, we consider each part of science, when we know its causes, so let us consider the causes and certain other attributes which are contained in these lines of verse: We should note in any given work five things: first the material, after that what is the purpose, after that the usefulness, the title, join on the causes. Concerning the first it should be noted that the ancients put four causes for any science, that is, the material cause, the formal, the efficient and the final, according to the saying of Aristotle in the second book of the Physics, there are four causes, etc. The material cause they said is this: what the science treats. But the formal cause they said is this, that is, the mode and order of proceeding in the science. But the efficient cause they said is the developer [by analogy with 'collectivus,' inferential] of the science. But the final cause is the reason why such a science is learned. But the moderns disagree with this; according to them no science can have, properly speaking, a material cause. And no science can have a formal cause. Therefore the moderns say that there are only two causes for any science, that is the efficient and the final, properly speaking. But someone might say to this that Aristotle nevertheless assigned four causes in natural philosophy as is already said, therefore sciences have four causes. To this it is responded that properly speaking then sciences can have only two causes, as the moderns claim, but improperly speaking then any science can have four causes ... In like manner they attack the formal cause improperly, for example, for the order by which the science is approached or acquired, and it is very improperly said thus because properly speaking such an ordering of parts in a science is not anything scientific according to what the moderns grant. And thus improperly speaking one can assign four causes for this science. Whence the formal cause of this science is the mode of proceeding in this science. But the efficient cause, improperly said, and mediate, was the blessed Gregory for some songs and the blessed Dionysius and Ambrose, also for some, in fact, there are many new doctors who to the praise of God have composed certain new songs which are to be expounded in this book.[36]

I have here included a slightly larger sample of context than usual. The witty derivation of this essentially pedestrian material from a text, in this case Canticles 2:3, is normal for this period; accessus tend to be written in the form of sermons, even when the material they contain is blandly formulaic. As is customary, this commentator lists his obligatory topics, though with rather more justification from Aristotle than one usually finds. The formal cause, as usual, is equated with the modus procedendi. Then we must deal with the moderns, who, doubtless with nominalist motivation, insist that knowledge has neither form nor material. The willingness to equate the form of an art with its pedagogy, which this commentator reproves, is indeed to be found elsewhere – Aegidius Romanus assumes a form of it, which in effect equates the forma tractatus and the forma tractandi, in his commentary on Canticles. In the end, the commentator gets what he wants, by the device of 'inproprie loquendo' – the hymn-book is, even if to some improperly, a book of science, and it does have a modus procedendi or a form.

Up to this point in this chapter, I have tried to let the medieval critics speak in their own voice. I have presented their theory of modal discourse by quoting their terminology in action. What is most obvious in all this commentary is the willingness of the medieval critics to be conventional. This conventionality presents two difficulties to the modern reader. Obviously, the passage of time has turned terminology into jargon, which must be decoded. Even more, this conventionality is but one aspect of the medieval desire to celebrate the normative in thinking and writing. The fundamental appeal on the basis of which knowledge is to be achieved, for a medieval critic, is appeal to definition. Philosophically, this is an idealist thing to do; as such, it is characteristic of medieval thought, even at its most nominalist and empiricist, far more than it is characteristic of our own modern thought.

The philosophical difficulty is intrinsic to the enterprise of this book, and I can only deal with it by frequently evoking it. As for the terminology itself, I have already tried to quote a great deal of it, in order at least to establish usage. It remains to interpret it. I shall do so in two ways. First, very briefly, I shall show that the terminology of the forma tractandi permits a generic discussion of texts which is quite unlike anything we would now conduct, but is nevertheless of considerable critical power. Second, I shall confront the fact that the chief formal difference between the medieval theory and modern theories of poetic form is that the medieval theory of modal discourse posits two forms simultaneously, instead of one. In distinguishing the two, I shall deal with limiting cases, first by discussing features of these two forms which might be taken as the same, but must nevertheless be distinguished. Then I will deal with an analogous twelfth-century case, and then with the very peculiar case in which the two medieval forms are taken as the same, in a way which is of course not modern at all.

Questions of literary genre seek to know what kind of a thing any given text is. Tragedy and comedy, novel, epic, lyric and sonnet are kinds that we all recognize, and among modern discussions of them the best general definition has probably been made in terms of degrees of verisimilitude, by Northrop Frye in his *Anatomy of Criticism* (Princeton 1957). As written, his *Anatomy* is a Chinese box of system, beautiful both in its self-contained integrity and in its intricacy, which sometimes I think succeeds in describing literature only by taking that also into the box. But the fundamental point upon which the whole is based, that is, that there is an observer, an empiricist, before whom and in terms of whose world some things are high and impossible, others are low and impossible, and others are at various levels in between – this point is a telling and wholly appropriate one, even though in Frye's hands it becomes more Kantian than empirical-relativist. No matter how pure, this point is still a point of view, to which all system-making is relative, and in terms of which any system can be entered and used.

The notion of genre implied by the forma tractandi and its modes is quite different from this modern one. The modi, though they indeed name mental operations, are not to be subsumed under the operation of any particular mind. They are pre-Cartesian, and are vulnerable neither to the solipsism nor to private point of view. Rather, they are epistemological only in that exalted and confident sense achieved by philosophies which know their knowing absolutely, as it were from the outside, as Plato confidently can predict what is outside the cave of his particular existence. The modi, then, constitute an analysis of the act of knowing which is not, in the modern sense, epistemological, that is, which does not analyse knowledge or mental process in terms of actions intrinsic and limited to personal sensibility but rather in terms of actions or procedures intrinsic to knowledge itself, or to the world within which and about which knowledge exists, and of which the operations of any given mind are a resultant. Thus the mode 'demonstrativus' implies the possibility of truth, rather than mere credibility; the mode 'laudativus' that the person praised is intrinsically praiseworthy, and not just socially superior to the critic or poet. Further, both these modi, and all the rest, make normative presumptions about mental process – if one wishes to make a poem, he must think his thoughts into and along the decorous tracks already determined by the nature of his art.

At the same time, these modi, which are the form of poems, are mental processes – poetry cannot be ontologically self-existent in its genre. A poem is not a thing, rather it is both an example of and the result of behaviour. It is for this reason that we must be especially careful of medieval genre words which are linguistic cognates of some of our own – there is no easy equivalence between them. Their existence in this different medieval modal system, this different context, interrupts equation. Tragedy, medievally defined, is the art of praising, and not the imitation of an action of determinate size, tending to the evocation of pity and fear. Tragedy therefore disappears, in a sense, and we are left with praise as the activity on which to base our generic notion. Our situation with regard to genre is thus far more rhetorical and practical than aesthetic and phenomenal.

The first and most obvious feature of the modi is that they involve action – tractandi is a process word. Further, the gerundive has a strong sense of obligation. Both these grammatical features are precisely appropriate to describe something which is behaviour but not behaver – that which exists as act but is not actor. In the second place, obviously, the modi all have to do with the use of language. Otherwise, they seem to divide into three great groups. One group seems to be concerned with the kinds of things that words can make their referents do – that is, define, exemplify, narrate, distinguish, or whatever. Another group seems to be essentially about the character of the language as such, but defined in terms of its kind of relation to its referent – metaphoric, allegorical, even metrical, if we take the Averroistic definition of metrum as including the power to impress. Finally, there is a group which exists to name, or guarantee the presence of, a value judgment – this is the group which gives to the modi their rhetorical dimension.[37]

It would seem from these features of the modi that the notion of genre, that is, the idea of the kinds into which verbal activity can be classified, must be defined in a way which takes into account both word and world. Genre, in medieval terms, is not a concept which applies to texts as verbal constructs, but to verbal events which include both reference and rhetorical effect. Just as Frye's genres constitute a range, from myth to irony, which is at once a hierarchy and a closed circle (in that extreme irony becomes mythic); so the medieval verbal events which some notion of genre must classify constitute a range – from universal to particular. This range is, like Frye's, both a hier-archy and a closed circle, in that universal is higher than particular, but the highest universal, God, manifests himself in the perfect particular of the Incarnate Christ, upon whose existence all universals and particulars per-fectly depend, and whose double nature is the ontological ground of meta-phor. It is in terms of this range that medieval reality arranges itself, in such a way that nearly every item on that range may be taken as word, or thing, or both. Language and world are a single system, and not two, as we shall see in some detail in the discussion of assimilatio in chapter four and chapter five. At the same time, the relationships that may exist among parts of this single system – relationships which we would call linguistic reference – may be more or less indirect. There are various kinds and degrees of assimilatio. At one end, there is direct description; at the other, the typological mode of meaning achieved by the paralleling of two distinct entities or realities, which was developed by exegesis, and which by this period had achieved in Dante and others a secular existence as well, with ironic and affirmative modes. Thus, in order to identify any given genre, one must account for two ranges. On the one hand, there is the range from particular to universal, in which one attends to subject matter; on the other hand, there is the quality and character of the indirection with which language is used. These two corre-spond precisely to the two kinds into which Hermann the German distin-guished his parts of tragedy – that is, those things which are assimilated, and those things which assimilate. It is in terms of the range of possible combina-tions of these two kinds that medieval genres can properly be defined.

We have already seen that what is assimilated is custom, belief, and poetic consideration; the techniques which make assimilation are heightened lan-guage (metrum), expressive power (thonus), and resemblance-making or description (sermo fabularis representativus). All of the modi which the commentators use or imply, relate to, explain, or illustrate one of these six terms, or relate more generally to the praise or blame which is their global intention. Consideration, or that quality by which a thing seems true, obviously is the same as the mode probativus, and by implication, the mode refutativus. Customs and beliefs at one extreme equal the mode definitivus, and at the other the mode of exemplification. All the modes that have to do with the way words work – descriptivus, transumptivus, the specifications of stili qualitas, metrum heroicum, and the like, correspond either to heightened language, expressive power, resemblance-making, or description, or to some combination of these. All together, they praise or they blame.

It is more at this level of generality than at a more specific level of classification that the notion of genre has medieval value. In the great array of kinds of things that any given genre or kind can be, it is most important to emphasize the whole notion of modus, or kind of act of thought, and within that the particular modus which this great array of names defines. The genre to which poetry belongs, as ethics (and of course to which ethics belongs, as poetry) is the genre which has the particular duty of relating words and things. One can, of course, name the included genres: praise by definition, allegorical exemplification, proof by convincing description, definition by means of examples, and many more. All that is required is the combination of some form or technique word, and some content word, understanding, either implicitly or explicitly, the rhetorical dimension of intention for audience. In the work of the medieval critics, the best explicit illustration of this possibility of naming genres, which as such remained more implicit than explicit for them, is their definition of the hymn: 'laus Deo in canticum.' More comprehensively, this is what Dante is doing, when he defines the forma tractandi of his *Commedia* in terms of two groups of five modi.

Genre, then, or the kind of a thing that any given text is, is more than merely textual. Forma tractandi is the form of a text, it is true, but in terms of modes of thought, reference, and effects which implicate the text in a great deal that would now be thought external to it. When we think now of the form of a text, we think of something more sharply limited and literal – something much more equivalent to the forma tractatus. In order to complete my definition of forma tractandi, it is appropriate to proceed by contrast, and show just how it is not forma tractatus. In order to do so, I must have them both explicitly present at the same time.

Dante's accessus permits me to begin. One of his modes is digressivus; another is divisivus. Both have to do with the identification of parts, and with the understanding of their order and relationship one to the other. Both are specified under forma tractandi. But it would seem that they also implicate forma tractatus, which is the form defined by the divisions into which a text outlines itself – division into books, chapters, sections, paragraphs, assertions. If the essence of forma tractatus is partition – division – then why is divisivus a mode of forma tractandi? In a sense, of course, division operates at both levels. But it is vitally important to distinguish that act of division which recognizes the point at which a certain chapter one ends and a certain chapter two begins, from that consciousness of ideal structures, normative wholes and their normative parts, on the basis of which it possible to say that chapter one is rightfully ended, and chapter two is meaningfully begun. An artist and a surveyor divide a terrain differently, even though both may recognize, in their different ways, the presence of the same fences and hedgerows; even though the fence is a part of the literal tract, the artist's mode of appropriating it is an exercise of forma tractandi.

The clearest medieval illustration of this situation is, as might be expected, not an example of the direct use of the terms. Terminology is a shorthand, which often conceals as much as it reveals. The best example comes from a critic who needs the terminology before it has been invented, and so has to improvise and explain himself. His situation is not precisely the same, because he is not accounting for a text and its mode, but rather for a text and its allegory, but his need to account for parts and their order produces a definitively clear analogous case. The critic is Bernardus Silvestris; his work, the commentary on the *Aeneid* of Virgil.

At the beginning of his commentary, Bernardus argues that the book literally begins in medias res; its order is therefore artificial. But at the same time he notes that its allegorical interpretation generates a natural order in the same material: the six ages of man, in order from infancy on, correspond seriatim to the first six books of the *Aeneid*. Thus, says Bernardus, the poet 'utrumque ordinem narrationis observat, artificialem poeta, naturalem philosophus. / observes both orders of narration: the artificial as a poet, the natural as a philosopher.'[38] The book has two orders at the same time, and thus two different actions of division superimposed on one another. First, there is the division of the literal material of the *Aeneid* into six books, beginning at sea just before the arrival at Carthage and ending with the descent into hell, artificially ordered. Second, there is the chronological treatment of the life of man, divided into the same six parts. The first ordering, which violates chronology and is artificial, satisfies one of the meanings of 'digressivus' – that is, going from one part of one's material to another which is not naturally next. Thus the first ordering, which is literally visible as a forma tractatus in six books, obeys as a literal ordering the mode digressivus of the forma tractandi. The second ordering enacts the poem's simultaneous obedience to the modus tractandi of divisivus; it is an ordering of which we become aware when we see what this division into six literally digressive

books means. Medieval commentators habitually divide their texts. This is
the initial act of critical analysis. In making this division, the commentators
of course recognize and delineate the parts which define the forma tractatus
of the literal text. But their goal is the mode divisivus of the forma tractandi;
their goal is to identify some normative array of parts or some normative
sequence, in terms of which the author's literal material has its full significance. The significance which Bernardus explains is, to modern minds,
imposed allegory, but this would not have mattered to him. Medieval commentary language regularly presumes that meanings allegorically imposed
were indeed fully intended by the original authors of the texts under consideration.[39]

Thus there are two kinds of division enacted by the *Aeneid*. The first, that
presumed by the mode divisivus of the forma tractandi, permits understanding of something discursive in terms of its natural parts, naturally ordered,
under strongly paradigmatic presumptions. The second is the result of this
first paradigmatic analysis by division, achieved by the exercise of another
mode of forma tractandi, digressivus, on literal material – as it happens, the
narrative of the adventures of Aeneas. The result of the simultaneous activity of both these modes is a literal text with a literal form – the forma
tractatus – which enacts its literal division in six parts. This second division is
the result of the first, as well as its literal parallel; it involves a complex act of
ordering, with a great deal of artificiality and manipulation of digression,
whereby the textual parts of something which can be written are so arranged
as to correspond exactly to all the already divided elements of material and
meaning intended for that text. Divisivus and digressivus are both, of
course, modes of the forma tractandi, in that they describe mental operations
which produce texts, rather than literal features of texts; at the same time the
text 'contains' both, and it is the duty of analysis to discover the one in the
other. What authors intend – or rather, what medieval definitions of modus
define as the mental procedure through which authorial intentions discover
themselves – is discovered in the act of commentary or criticism by following
the process backwards. One begins with the parts of the text, and finds
implied in their order and in their ordonnance the prior acts of analysis by
digression and division in terms of which understanding of significance
begins to be possible. Bernardus, as it happens, discovers by this process his
text's 'allegory' – a meaning which to modern sensibilities seems more
imposed than intended. In so doing he is fortunately explicit about the
process itself – the fact that the text has two orders, and that he must analyse
the one to elucidate the other. But the process does not require allegorization
as its critical result – rather, it requires merely that the commentator be

extremely sensitive to the fact that medieval texts have parts, and that these parts occur as they do and in the order they do for reasons which literal narrative requirements will never completely explain. Meaning may not be allegorical, but meaning and letter are always double, because form is double. Behind all the artificialities of texts, there is an intention of parts that is naturally ordered and paradigmatic, in terms of which both the meaning and the unity of a given text may be explained.

The most complex possible illustration of this process is the *Commedia*. I have already suggested that Jupiter and the eagle and Saturn and his ladder follow Mars for iconographic as well as astronomical reasons – that Dante is here drawing two pictures at once. Generalizing, I would propose that the most profitable question to be asked of the *Commedia* is the question of order: why does what come next, or how does the material in a given book of *Inferno* correspond to and gloss the material in the corresponding books of the other two cantiche? I shall return to the *Commedia* after discussing, in the next two chapters, the processes of poetic disposition or forma tractatus, and of assimilatio, or likening (the general name for all kinds of relationships which obtain among textual parts, and between those parts and their referents). These two terms, properly understood, will confront us with a correctly defined textuality which we can see operating in dialectic with this level of modus which I have just defined. There is, however, one special case, which should be introduced at this point. This is the case of the text whose forma tractatus is the same as its forma tractandi, for which the normal medieval doubleness of form is collapsed into unity. I present two illustrations, one certain because affirmed by a medieval authority, and one speculative. The first, and certain case, is the biblical Canticles, as defined by Aegidius Romanus:

Consuevit enim distingui duplex forma, scilicet forma tractandi, que est modus agendi: et forma tractatus, quae est ordinatio capitulorum adinvicem. Modus autem agendi in aliis scientiis est approbativus et improbativus.[40] In doctrina vero sacra potissime in canone esse videtur inspirativus, idest revelativus, quia magis talis textus innititur revelationi quam probationi. Modus autem in isto libro specialiter videtur esse affectivus, desiderativus, et contemplativus. Unde et glossa tenet quod modus huius libri est ostensivus quali desiderio membra capiti adhaereant, et ei placere contendant, et quali affectione sponsus ecclesiam diligat. Unde modus agendi huius libri convenienter notatur per huiusmodi dulcedinem, cum dicit, (Vox tua dulcis.) quia complacentia, affectio, et desiderium, quandam dulcedinem amoris important. Ex hoc etiam potest haberi forma tractatus, quae talis debet esse, quale requirit modus agendi, immo quia ipse ordo capitulorum adinvicem bene intellectus

animam demulcet et delectat, non inconvenienter forma tractatus per dulcedinem
(cod dulcedine) intelligitur.

It is customary to distinguish a double form, namely the form of the treatment, which
is the mode of doing, and the form of the treatise, which is the ordering of the
chapters one after the other. The mode of doing in other sciences is approving and
disproving. In sacred teaching, and above all in the Bible, the mode of doing seems to
be inspirational, or revelationary, because such a text depends for its effect more on
revelation than on proof. In this book the mode seems to be especially emotional,
contemplative, and full of desire. Thus the glosa says that the mode of this book is to
show with what desire the members adhere to the head, and contend to please him,
and with what affection the husband loves the Church. Therefore the mode of doing
of this book can be conveniently defined in terms of this sweetness, when he says,
'Your voice is sweet,' because pleasure, affection, and desire imply a certain sweetness of love. And from this is also found the form of the treatise, which must be what
the mode of doing requires, because the very order of the chapters one after the
other, when well understood, soothes and delights the soul. So it is fitting that the
form of the treatise be understood as the effect of sweetness.[41]

This is an enormously complex bit of criticism. In the first place, in equating
the modus agendi and the forma tractatus, it subtly alters both. Second, it is
clear that the agent of the modus here is not merely a human author; since
God is involved, the implicated human being is at least in part the rhetorical
audience, rather than maker, of the text. Third, the specific names of many
of these modi are affective rather than purely intellectual. This last point
raises problems which I shall avoid;[42] the second one, in so far as it raises the
problem of audience as something other than author read backwards, I shall
deal with in chapter six. Here, it is important simply to notice what happens
when the literal ordering of a text's material corresponds exactly to the order
of that mental process whereby that material was invented and made significant. The result of this equation of the modus agendi and the forma tractatus
is that the modus agendi becomes itself the subject, rather than or in addition
to, the agent, of the book. The book is about its own making. But this making, therefore, must be at once something which is a modus – which is the
existence of the active intellect in some one of its aspects – and at the same
time something worth asking the audience of the book to repeat, not for the
sake of making the book (since that has been done) but for the sake of
whatever else it is that the modus can do. In the case of Canticles, it is the
affective process itself which must be understood since that is what both is
and makes possible the contemplation which is the book's (and the reader's)
achievement. This process is not something that the book can be about – can

refer to, can assimilate by making descriptions or examples of it. Rather, this process is something which the book itself must be, as it exists in the serial ordering of its parts, which the reader experiences thus serially, thus reproducing for himself the act of modus which is the book's subject. In practical terms, this kind of book, in which modus agendi is what is being treated, and in which therefore modus agendi and forma tractatus are the same, is a profoundly medieval way of handling, and instructing in, the act of knowing. This act, as I said before, is not epistemologically treated; rather, it is an act which achieves, for any reader who submits to it, his assimilation into what is intrinsic to knowledge itself.

It is these terms that I wish to propose my second, and most speculative, example of a text in which the modus agendi and the forma tractatus are the same: *Piers Plowman*. In a way, Mary Carruthers makes precisely this point, when she recommends that we look for the 'meaning in the poem' rather than the 'meaning of the poem.'[43] I think, in the end, her analysis is too epistemological, too concentrated on the mental, moral, and linguistic faculties of human nature which are the instruments of knowledge, rather than on some modus whose enactment would *be* knowledge, or, in this case, salvation. But her sense of the poem's process, of the fact that its meaning must arise out of the dialectic motion through its parts that is the experience of its characters, is I think profoundly right. We shall not get much closer than this to the truth of the poem as a whole, I think, unless and until we have some help from the outside, in the form of discussions by medieval thinkers of modi and their parts, or in the form of some other authoritative definition of order for the parts of the experience of salvation and the Christian life. An important step in this direction, I think, was taken in a paper presented by Robert Adams to the 1976 MLA.[44] In that paper, the position of Need in Langland's poem, just before the appearance of Antichrist, is justified by reference to Job 41:13, 'Et faciem eius praecedit egestas. / And need goes before his [Leviathan's] face.' Surrounding commentary from Gregory's *Moralia* explains what Need means in this apocalyptic context, and the argument concludes with an apt quotation from Bloomfield: that reading Langland's poem is like 'reading a commentary on an unknown text.'[45] But what for Bloomfield was a telling insight into the poem's atmosphere and character becomes, in Adams' treatment, a very specific piece of external outline – Langland organizes his material, at this point, under the authority of an order recommended by Job 41:13. Before Antichrist, an author must put in Need.

That this ordering combines the forma tractatus and the forma tractandi is made clear in Adams' paper, though of course he does not use these terms – the poem is about, and explicates, its own apocalyptic process. The experience of it is its meaning – and the reason its meaning is so often dark to us is that we lack the paradigmatic forms of experience the medieval 'unknown text' can give us, and which Adams has so illuminatingly put behind this final bit of the poem.

In larger terms, I think it is possible to propose that the poem is the experience of Will – that is, Voluntas. If one proceeds on the basis of this hypothesis, then one is automatically protected from the mistake of Mary Carruthers. Though of course the will does have a certain cognitive significance, it is not the epistemological principle of personality. It is, however, the faculty which is especially involved in the processes that lead to salvation. Further, since it is an aspect of personality, rather than a person, it demands a critical focus in keeping with the general psychomachic atmosphere of the poem.

In an effort to define the 'unknown text' of *Piers Plowman* in terms of this hypothesis, I have begun to look at distinctiones on Voluntas. At this stage in my research, of course, I can make only the most speculative of comments, based upon one quite suggestive text. This is ms lat. 12424 of the Bibliothèque nationale, a collection of distinctiones attributed to Nicholas Byart, but containing what seems to be distinctive material. Its treatment of Voluntas begins 'Voluntas dei est multiplex. / The will of God is multiple.' What makes this text so interesting is that it deals, not with the will of man, but with the will of God; and that its treatment of the parts or aspects of the will of God reflects precisely the same dialectic oscillation between success and disappointment, hope and failure, which characterizes the process of *Piers Plowman*. I find no precise correspondence between the parts or aspects of God's will and the seriatim parts of Langland's poem; a medieval commentator could probably argue one, but I shall not. It is both too procrustean and too optimistic to expect a single distinctio passage to structure the entire poem – at the same time, it is proper to expect that a sufficient reading of this material, and of the biblical passages which this material orders, will indeed inform and define that process, that structure, whose commentary is the poem we have.[46]

Reading *Piers Plowman* as a process of will is, however, only meant in illustration; that is, as a way of making clear what is meant by the medieval critic who finds Canticles a text whose forma tractandi and forma tractatus are the same – whose process is its form. By modern definition, of course, Canticles and *Piers Plowman* differ considerably; by medieval definitions, they are alike in that they have the same form. To see them thus, of course, is to force upon us a readjustment of our notion of form. I hope that at the same time, once we have made the adjustment, we can also see from this new perspective just what kind of process *Piers Plowman* seems to be.

Except for this one special case, however, in which the modus agendi or forma tractandi and the forma tractatus are the same, all this exercise of modi, all this 'poetic' thinking, exists prior to the text of any given poem. The modi are not poems, or poetry; rather, they are the pre-condition, the context, and the definition of the possibility of any given text. One of the modi, however, more than any of the others, approaches textuality, in that it prescribes not only a mode of thought, but also its object. This is the mode of exemplification.

Logically, it is unfair to single out exemplification for special notice, because in terms of the reason even of late medieval texts, it is no more important than definition, division, proof, praise, blame, or any of the rest. Empirically, however, it is obviously necessary to make a special case for exemplification, because most of the text with which we have literally to do is a tissue of exempla. When, therefore, the medieval critics define, as one of the modes of thought which makes poetry, exemplorum positiva, they name a procedure which in fact is the one on which the rest depend, and which itself accounts for most of what poets actually said. As written, poetry does praise and blame, it does define, prove, refute, and imply partitions and divisions; it does contain heightened language and semantically complicated strategies of reference, but the material out of which all these things are made tends to be the description of concrete particulars – that is, in the most general sense of the term, exempla. I can, therefore, most directly account for the thinking that makes poetry by accounting for the late medieval logic of exempla, and for the implicit and explicit means whereby an exemplum, or a collection of exempla, may be significantly 'posited.'

Studies of exempla to date have been primarily occupied with problems of cataloguing, bibliography, and literary history.[47] I have myself touched upon this tradition of the exemplum in my *The Friar as Critic*. Here, there is no need to do more than repeat a few generalizations, which by now must have the status of common knowledge. First, the great period of exempla was the later Middle Ages – the thirteenth, and even more the fourteenth and the fifteenth centuries. Second, as exempla became more popular during this period, the traditional homiletic requirement that they be true weakened, and more and more exempla tended to contain the marvellous, the pagan, the fanciful – at the same time, as their literal truth value weakened, they tended to acquire that circumstantial detail, that empirical realism, which gave to them the truth of good fiction.

This last point, in particular, has been made already in so many medieval and modern ways that it scarcely needs even to be illustrated. It is this character of exempla which led Alan Gunn to claim for the *Romance of the Rose* the very carnal meaning which he found in it;[48] it is this empirical realism which made John Manly, many years ago, claim that Chaucer's characters had living models,[49] and which makes many critics willing to accuse those who allegorize late medieval literature of reductionism.

The same attention to circumstantial detail occurs also in the commentaries. Ghisalberti, for instance, notes that Giovanni del Virgilio summarizes Ovid's *Metamorphoses* in a way which turns Ovid's elegant narrative into realistic novella.[50] A fifteenth-century commentary on the *Rhetorica ad Herennium*, which might serve formally as a defining case for the use of exempla, since it is elaborately concerned with making analyses by division, and then with illustrating the resultant parts with examples, includes among the modes of captatio benevolentiae 'calamitatem, idest pauperiem cum debilitate corporis. / calamity, that is, poverty with bodily infirmity.' The commentator illustrates this by recommending the little speech which one might use in court: 'Cum iam vice necessaria mihi mense proxime lapso deficerent et miserabilem pati iam inciperem egestate dura subito usque nunc me corripuit egritudo, in qua ne media deficerem, compulsus sum librorum meorum quamplurimorum alienare. Vos ergo meo tanto dolori compatimini, meque vestro benigno patrocinio sublevate. / At the end of last month I ran out of money, and was so miserably poor that I fell ill, and had to sell most of my books to survive. You should sympathize with me in such a plight, and support me with your gracious patronage.'[51] Again, this commentator recommends that when one's client is clearly guilty, it is wise to put the best face on the matter one can. In this case, the commentator gives sample speeches for both sides, which are too long to quote fully, but of which the climax at least is vivid and amusing. The fact of the case in question is that one person has killed another by dropping a rock on him. For the defence:

Cernens se frustratum a labore suo furiens magis ac magis in dies, quadam nocte post primum sompnium fecit cum illis coniuratis impetum in domum meam. Cumque iam hoc quasi domus hostium [sic] cernerem prosterni metuens natis atque aliis domesticis meis potius quam mihi, cepi iacere de fenestra cuiusdam aule saxa deorsum existimans illum fugare, non perimere vel vulnerare, sed quo vehemencius vidit parari defensionem durius portam urgebat; et ideo si ut ait adversarius meus in eo loco faustus interiit, non fuit culpa mea qui hostes a domo mea expellebam sed magis fuit pertinacia[52] pereuntis, qui se cum poterat non retrahebat.

As he saw his project frustrated he became more and more enraged day by day; one night after everyone was asleep he attacked my house with his retainers. When I saw the man like an enemy of the house, I was afraid more for the ruin of my dependents and servants than for myself, and began to throw down rocks from the window of a certain hall, expecting to make him flee and not kill or wound him, but the more he saw the defence prepared the more strongly he attacked the door, and thus, if, as my adversary says, Faustus was killed there, it was not my fault who was merely defending my house, but rather it was his fault for being so stubborn in not leaving when he could.

For the prosecution:

[Faustus] accessit usque ad domum huius non ut eum perimeret sed solum ipsum ab illa proposita iniuria coherceret. Mox ut eo pervenit faustus, tunc publius cum posset alterum multiformiter aliter effugere ac repellere, lapidem ingentissimum ictu pertinaci iecit de quo virum illum celeberrimum tam crudeliter interfecit – nam summa pietas erat eum ita vulneratum et peremptum videre.

Faustus went to this man's house, not to kill him but only to prevent him from committing this premeditated crime. As soon as Faustus got there, Publius, who could have gotten him to go away and repelled him in a multitude of other ways, threw down an incredibly large rock with a crushing blow, which savagely killed that notable man – it was the greatest tragedy, to see him lying there so battered, dead. (f 261r–v)

Logically, exempla do not constitute the most rigorous or the most powerful kind of proof, but they do conform, especially, to the modus agendi of ethics. I have already dealt in some detail with the discussion of this fact made at the beginning of the *De regimine principum* of Aegidius Romanus. There, Aegidius made both clear and certain that ethics was a science which proceeded grosse et figuraliter, because it dealt with and was concerned to guide action, rather than generate pure knowledge. A kind of knowledge, nevertheless, is involved. Exactly what this knowledge is, and how it is achieved, Aegidius makes clear in another place – in his commentary on Romans. He is dealing with the fact that 'science deals with the universal and the necessary.' This is, of course, an Aristotelian commonplace;[53] its significance for poetic theory needs repeated emphasis, lest it be either ignored or abused. What Aegidius discusses is the logically extreme case. If any particulars could be the basis of scientia, then surely revealed biblical ones would be, but faithfulness to Aristotle requires that even here they be rationalized under universals:

Nam si diligenter aspicimus, maxima pars canonis Bibliae videtur esse de singularibus gestibus, et de particularibus actibus: sed cum particularium non sit scientia neque definitio, ut dicitur .vii. Metaphy. Videtur posse argui sacram Paginam, quae in canone Bibliae principaliter continetur, non esse scientiam. Si est scientia, est in intellectu, et intellectus principaliter, et per se, et recto aspectu non fertur in particulare, sed in universale; particularium gestorum impossibile est esse directe scientiam, sed sensus ipse est particularium discretivus. Itaque, ut sustineamus sacram Paginam esse scientiam, oportet particularia negotia in sacra pagina contenta, aliqua ratione Universalis induere. Inde est quod communiter dicitur, singulares personas in sacra pagina memoratas, per quandam signationem, Universalis rationem habere. Ut Iob, in quo eminenter commendatur patientia, significat universaliter quemlibet patientem: et Abraam, cuius fides abundantius commendatur, fidelem quemlibet repraesentat. Secundum hoc ergo, quanto plures conditiones alicuius singularis personae in canone Bibliae introductae competunt alicui, tanto ille per huiusmodi personam competentius significatur.

If we consider carefully, the greater part of the Bible's content seems to consist of singular deeds and particular acts, but there is no science or definition of particulars, as it is said in the seventh book of the Metaphysics. It would seem that Bible study, which deals principally with the content of the Bible, is not a science. If it is a science, it is in the intellect, and the intellect primarily and in itself, properly understood, asserts nothing in particular, but in universal; a direct science of particular deeds is impossible, but it is the senses which distinguish particulars. Therefore, if we are to uphold Bible study as a science, we must endue the treatment of particulars which Bible study involves with a certain universal content. Thus it is commonly said that the singular characters presented in Bible study have universal content because of a certain signing. Thus Job, in whom patience is supremely commended, signifies universally any patient person whatsoever; and Abraham, whose faith is abundantly commended, represents any faithful person. In this manner therefore, the more conditions pertaining to a Bible character fit someone, the more suitably are they illustrated by a person of this kind.[54]

Thus, particulars may be the basis of the true knowledge because they are exempla bearing a certain 'signationem'; they are examples of something definitive and universal. One might say that, implicitly at least, the customary philosophical relation of derivation between universal and particular has been here seen in reverse, and the 'signatio' exists in some fashion prior to the particular. Modistic grammar, for which the linguistic process 'depends on the interaction of three different modes or rationes: the mode of being, the mode of understanding, and the mode of signifying,'[55] can, I think, account in unusually elaborate fashion for meaning of this sort.

Absolutely, the relation of particulars in poems, and indeed in all art, to some sense of the universal, is the most habitual assertion of criticism.

Everyone who talks about art interests himself, in one way or another, in the fact that art is somehow 'true' – and the empirical fact that all art literally or pictorially or aurally contains particulars, whether of words, descriptions, shapes and representations and colours, or pitches, obviously requires that any assertion of truth value for art must necessarily involve some assertion of relation between particular and universal. Much of this talk about art, particularly that of the last century or so, has tended to make this assertion by claiming some universality for the particular itself, in itself. The logical extreme case of this tendency is existentialism, but it is pervasive in modern culture even when not carried to this extreme. There is thus a radical opposition between Aegidius, who will not trust a particular until he has, by the strategy of positing a 'signatio,' gotten safe hold on a universal; and the normal modern, be he critic, sociologist, or man of action, who tends to distrust abstractions until he can find some way safely to relate them to particulars, which he is pleased, if literate in the jargon, to call data or evidence. In both cases we have to do with an empiricist mentality – in both cases the particulars involved are real, hard, irreducible, rather than merely the appearances of a platonist sense of form. But the value judgments involved are different, and at the heart and basis of the medieval one is the willingness to make, and trust, normative or definitional statements as words which are and have a right to be comfortable and appropriate in the company of these irreducible and real particulars. An excellent illustration of the difference between these two sensibilities survives in modern times in the difference between the legal tradition of England, which is radically based on particular cases, and for which the constitution remains unwritten, and the legal tradition of France, which is philosophical, rationalist, and normative, and under which cases must be treated in a derivative manner. Analogously, one can see in the relatively recent adoption, in a number of different practical disciplines such a law, business, psychological counselling, etc, of the 'case study' method of training for practitioners, a rejection of the normative use of exempla and an affirmation of a trust of exempla as true only in themselves.

In modern reading of medieval literature, there has been a good deal of mere appreciation of particulars, as such. In the Robertsonian tradition, on the other hand, there has been what amounts to a platonist or twelfth-century reductionist approach to particulars, under which they do not merely relate to the normative, but disappear into it. It is vitally important to avoid both mistakes; we can do so, I suggest, by carefully considering two features of this late medieval use of exempla. One of them is explicit, named, and obvious in a long tradition of existing texts. The other is, I think, clearly implicit in actual late medieval use of exempla. The first of these is the tradition of the distinctio. The second is really nothing more than an interpretation of the first, for which I propose the term 'normative array.' The distinctio is the result of the exercise of a strategy of collecting data under general topics; the term 'normative array' is simply the assertion that this medieval data collecting was in fact, in its own terms, successful, and that exempla arrayed under a given topic did in fact relate to and define that topic.

The distinctio has been several times discussed in recent scholarship.[56] I doubt that its importance has yet been widely or strongly enough asserted to make it as much a commonplace as Curtius' notion of the topos, but it certainly deserves such status. Rouse defines it, in its earlier manifestations, as a strategy for collecting, and in collecting, distinguishing, the possible meanings of a biblical word or thing. Among the possibilities, of course, were the allegorical meanings, and the distinctio tended to emphasize these. Later, however, according to Rouse, the materials collected under the rubric of distinctio became so miscellaneous that the logical notion of distinction among meanings seems to have been lost, and what remained was merely anything collected, tending to be of use most obviously in the composition of sermons. This is of course true, and yet I think one can assert at least that, even though the material content of distinctio collections became more and more miscellaneous, fabulous, and incoherent, there still remained in the fact of the collecting under topics a basic impulse of definition, whose existence constitutes a clear definition of definition itself.

One of the most meaningful features of a culture whose books were handmade manuscripts, and in which authorship consisted so often of compilation and adaptation rather than absolute originality, is that any given book tends to be at once authoritative, complete, and sufficient, and yet at the same time different in small or large ways from all other books. This is not to deny, of course, that the Middle Ages had a sense of received texts, or of lacunae. Beryl Smalley's descriptions of the book-hunting activities of her classicizing friars is proof that such interests were in fact medieval.[57] At the same time, anyone who has had occasion to deal directly with late medieval manuscripts, particularly those which are utilitarian in cost and production, miscellaneous in content, and often anonymous, has confronted this very medieval claim.[58] At a much higher level of literary quality, the poem of *Piers Plowman* exists in many versions, all claiming in their individual manuscript existence authority as the poem, and classifiable even into three versions only by a modern editorial process which does not precisely respect the exact medieval sense of the way in which a text exists. Modern editors, in fact, sometimes admit that it is better to reprint a careful copy of a single manuscript's version of a text, rather than reconstruct some hypothetical 'authoritative' text which may never have had any medieval existence at all. And though *Piers Plowman* is a particularly vexed and complicated example of this problem, it is a pervasive one. I have argued elsewhere that the stories of the *Canterbury Tales* are not ordered in the same way in all manuscripts, and that each different ordering deserves therefore to be respected as a serious medieval attempt at edition.[59] What is true of *Piers Plowman* and of the *Canterbury Tales* is obviously even more true of impersonal medieval compilations. Any given collection of distinctiones, or any given collection of exempla and other material under a given distinctio topic, is a collection which some medieval compiler defined as both existent and sufficient by the act of making it, and from which a preacher took what was by definition both sufficient and authoritative material when he used it in the compilation of a sermon.

I said at the beginning of this chapter that the use of alphabetized arrangements of material was implicitly an assertion that a question involving the use of data can only be treated by relevant data, and not by just any data. Once this has been said, however, it is still necessary to define relevance, and to admit that by medieval standards, the relation between any given topic and the data which were admitted to explain and define it could be considerably more arbitrary, verbal, or even accidental than modern statistical or empirical procedures would admit. What the distinctio as a special genre, and the strategy of exemplification more generally, achieved for late medieval normative thinking was a sense of certainty, of adequacy of evidence, in spite of the fact that in broad terms the specific evidence involved was not uniform for any given case.

The term which I think best can describe the exemplary and particular data upon which any given late medieval sense of adequacy of evidence might be based is the term 'normative array.' This term accounts both for the late medieval willingness to take definition seriously, and the fact that exempla tend, in the later middle ages, to occur in batches. This willingness and this fact, taken separately, are obvious features of late medieval thought and culture; if I bring any insight at all to the matter, it is only in suggesting that they are related, and indeed depend on each other. One can illustrate this fact almost at random in late medieval literature; I choose five examples which make the point in a particularly telling manner. Supremely, there is the *Divina Commedia*. Over and over again, at level after level, Dante peoples his otherworlds with groups of characters. One or two may be singled out for special mention, description, or conversation, but Dante's continual strategy is to triangulate his definitions. As three points define a circle, and four a sphere, so two or three or a dozen characters, taken together, define great poetry, or carnal love, or heresy, or sodomy, or worldly preoccupation, or heavenly wisdom. Of all the great poets, Dante is quintessentially the master of the unstated implication; of the strategy by which an array of facts are presented, in a crucially important ordering which is both the expression and the basis of their logic, and are left to make their collective point purely by exemplification. This strategy, for instance, is the problem which Pézard poses for himself, in asking whether or not Brunetto Latini was actually a sodomite.[60] When he decides that Brunetto was almost certainly not literally such, he must conclude that Dante has put him where he has in order to assert a relation between an Italian who sought to immortalize himself in French, and the condition of homosexuality. Priscian keeps him company, at least in order to mention once more the subject of grammar.

A similar strategy governs the relationship between Farinata, Cavalcanti, and the topic of heresy which names the place of their tomb. Farinata is the extreme patriot; Cavalcanti, in his concern for his poet son, is an example of pride of family. Together, they constitute a normative array of two consuetudines and one credulitas – patriotism, family pride, and heresy – which mutually construct a definition of that complex human tendency to oversimplify into perverse rigidity some potential good, whose name is heresy and whose full dimensions we can now begin to understand.

Two much simpler examples of this same strategy of normative array, coming from very different fields of medieval interest, are John Bromyard's *Summa Predicantium* and John Gower's *Confessio Amantis*. The *Summa Predicantium* is, in fact, a distinctio collection, in its late and more miscellaneous guise. It is also a collection of exempla, arranged by topics and sub-topics, in which the weltering mass of exempla illustrate, and therefore collectively define, the topics to which they are related. The *Confessio Amantis* is even more obviously normative, since it is, as a whole, not a complication under an alphabetized list of topics, but an arraying of tales under the schema of the seven sins. Their normativity is complicated by the fact that this confession is that of a lover, who conceives of himself as a fit advisor of kings, but this complication is itself typically late medieval, in that it asserts of life a structure in analogous layers, mutually interpreting one another, and to which the array of tales Gower constructs is both a serious and an adequate definition.[61]

An analogous case may be found in commentary tradition. Both the *Ovide moralisé*[62] and Bersuire's commentary on the *Metamorphoses*[63] often supply more than one interpretation for a tale. At one level, this multiplicity of interpretation is simply the late medieval reaction to the richness of Ovid's meaning – or, more precisely, the medieval reaction to its own sense of the multiplicity or meaning in all things. At the same time, there is a good deal of repeating of levels and topics, which soon comes to have clearly normative implications. There are relatively few levels of meanings, apparently, which are possible. As an array, they are, as might be expected, similar to the four levels defined for exegesis; but they do not exactly correspond. What Bersuire's comments define for us is an array comprising natural or scientific meanings, theological meanings connected with the nature of Christ, theological meanings connected with the personal life of a Christian or sinner (that is, interpretations which have to do with salvation and damnation), moral meanings involving the behaviour of some individual moral type, and moral behaviour affecting social structures. By implication, these are all the kinds of events there are, and the elaboration of what might be called the tropological level into at least three different kinds is of course in keeping with the increasingly juridical and ethical approach to practical Christianity in the later Middle Ages.

Thus, for instance, the fable of Alpheus and Arethusa has a natural explanation, 'ad ostendendum [cod ostendeodum] fontis arethuse naturam qui subtus mare fluit in siciliam. / to show the nature of the fountain of Arethusa which flowed under the sea into Sicily.' But it also means the relationship between a soul and the God who loves that soul. 'Vel dic,' says Bersuire, with his customary formula, 'quod alpheus est prelatus Arethusa est subditus. / Or say, that Alpheus is a prelate, Arethusa is his subject' (f 48r). The fable of Latona, whom Juno forced to wander until she found the wandering island of Delos, where she bore Apollo and Diana, means first of all that evil vagabonds are hospitable to others of their own kind. In addition, it means that hospitable persons implicitly receive Christ and Mary; or, since Latona means charity or humility or grace, which are Christ-bearers, whoever receives these virtues gains Christ. Or, the story proves that people disliked by important people have a hard time getting help from anybody. Or, Latona is holy scripture, prophetically pregnant from the beginning with Mary and Christ, whom the synagogue would not receive, and who then went to the 'terra vaga idest gentilitas primum errans. / the wandering land, that is, the Gentile, which was at first in error' (f 51r–v). The fable of Ericthonius, the monster child associated with Athena, means 'historialiter' that no one can keep secrets, or that 'homo naturaliter nititur in vetitum. / historically, man naturally tries what is forbidden.' On the other hand, 'allegorice, / allegorically,' it means either the Incarnation, or the Eucharist (ff 27v–8r). Echo means either the flatterers of prelates and others, or those women and servants who always have to have the last word (f 35r–5v). These are quite random examples of Bersuire's procedure; what they illustrate is the fact that for the Middle Ages meanings tended to be multiple but not at all random or unpredictable; they existed in an array of possibilities which Bersuire's practice defines. In collecting these examples, and in naming their kinds, I have in fact myself made a distinctio, interesting for itself in that it shows how meanings tend to be events, or kinds of events, and therefore how exemplary particular and meaning tend to be presumed in relation in the act of interpretation as well as in exercise of forma tractandi to which interpretation is the proper response; and interesting also in that it shows how naturally and easily these late medieval data adapt themselves to distinctio patterning.

My final example of the normative array is Chaucer's *Canterbury Tales*. I have elsewhere made a full analysis of the *Tales* in these terms,[64] and obviously shall neither repeat nor summarize that analysis here. What must be repeated for the sake of illustration here is merely a description of the form or pattern which that analysis found by taking the *Tales* as an ordered collection of exemplary stories – that is, as a complex example of the exercise of a forma tractandi whose intellectual strategies emphasize definition and division, and whose material strategy consists largely of exemplorum positiva. As an ordered collection of stories, the *Tales* as a whole defines a four-part distinctio of moral orders or orderings. Each of these four parts itself constitutes a distinctio, with as many parts as there happen to be stories. The stories are in each part ordered so as to reflect in some way a progress from general to particular, or best to worst, or most true to least true. Thus ordered in an ostentatiously logical way, the stories themselves, including enclosed stories such as the exemplum of Midas in the Wife of Bath's Tale,[65] become defining arrays of exempla. Each array defines some important ethical truth. Taken all together, they converge into a definition of human nature in society as something morally based on both acts and words, that is, both relationships and vows. Thus defined, human nature exists precisely within that space between particularity and the universal which the Averroistic *Poetics* expects. Within fragments, the ordering of the tales upon which this analysis is based is completely Chaucer's, so far as we can know; the ordering of the fragments themselves is in a manner speculative, but it is nevertheless fully based on manuscript authorities. What the analysis achieves, I think, is a description of Chaucer's Tales as a unified collection with a subtle, important, ethical, medieval point. Objectively it is possible to claim that this description is the first one to argue for unity and at the same time find a logical place for all the tales and all the links. Whether this description in fact describes the *Canterbury Tales* as others read them must be left for others to answer. What is important here is to state that the notion of the normative array, and the medieval definitions of forma tractandi and distinctio which imply and define the notion of normative array, are the axioms which make that description at first thinkable and then achievable. Our approach to the *Canterbury Tales* was critically a priori. We presumed at the outset that Chaucer's intellectual and creative modus agendi would be that one which his contemporaries who wrote commentaries defined as normal for literary works. We presumed that definition, division, proof, refutation (with their probable overtones of praise and blame), and example-giving would be the strategy and form of the making of the tales. We further presumed that the material distinctio which would name what it was Chaucer sought to define would be found somewhere in medieval commentaries, and we found that a most promising one had in fact been applied to the story collection popular in Chaucer's culture which was nearest his in strategy – that is, the *Metamorphoses* of Ovid. Once we presumed these things, we found that the problems and difficulties usually encountered in trying to deal with the question of the unity of Chaucer's collection simply disappeared.

In the light of these examples, it is possible to conclude that the term 'normative array' really names only what a distinctio – or in broader terms, the mode divisivus of the forma tractandi – presumes: that is, since any medieval whole has parts, one can by inspecting the parts arrive at some conception of the whole. The fact that medieval exempla tend so often to occur, in medieval literature and in sub-literary and utilitarian collections, not singly or one at a time but in multiple, suggests for any such group of exempla the probability of a governing or outlining distinctio which implicitly arrays them, and whose name they, as an array, normatively define. This way of thinking is both natural and obvious for an age which wished to consider itself empiricist, and therefore confident of the meaningful existence of particulars, and at the same time metaphysical and theological, and therefore willing to think about particulars, and from particulars, in terms of normative universals. It is, in short, the way of thinking which is structurally necessary to any nominalist who wishes to discuss the truth. As a way of thinking, of course, it is structurally prior to what is being thought about. It is that pattern of thought which medieval critics betray in their terminology, in their approaches to material, in what and how they classify and divide, and in what implicit or explicit proofs, definitions, and refutations they have in mind to make.

I said at the beginning of this chapter that the pattern or procedure within which one decides to think has a powerful effect on what one then finds thinkable, and I admitted that this statement had about it a certain Kantian atmosphere. What relieves it from being in fact Kantian or phenomenological we can now see – it is that the pattern or procedure which the forma tractandi and the distinctio define is not, and is never thought to be, separate from or anything other than a feature of the real world which contains, of course, mind, and which mind does not contain. One must presume that the Aristotelian causes in fact were causes – did make things happen. Kant's classification of causality as a transcendental category was blessedly not yet thought of, and is beside the point. Both forms and purposes, as well as materials and tools, had reality, substance, and power. Medieval poems exist because modi tractandi have first made them possible, and then brought them into existence. These modi are of course exercised by poets, but the poets themselves were persons in submission to the world of possible words which the modi delimited and defined.

This very submission is what the critics' division into forma tractandi and forma tractatus especially emphasizes. Poems are not simply made in accordance with a pattern – they are not copies of an outline merely, a forma tractatus of which they are, each for its own, the actualization. More important, poems are the direct result of something far more central and important than their own private outlines – they are the result of modi tractandi. They are the result one might say, of active knowledge – of the same knowledge which makes possible and definite all the truth that is – acting in one or some of its modes.

My colleague Robert Boyle, who specializes in the works of James Joyce, told me once that the solipsism was the truest, safest, and most blessed refuge of poetry.[66] The little that I know of *Ulysses* and *Finnegans Wake*, and the slightly more that I know of modern philosophy, suggest to me that he is both critically correct and morally admirable to make this suggestion, which is the aesthetic equivalent of Thoreau's decision to accept jail as the only fit place for an honest man in an unjust country. Once the world gets itself beyond a certain point, only extreme remedies make sense. I would suggest, however, that it is precisely this predicament which the medieval forma tractandi permits one to avoid. In possessing what one might call a metaphysical Establishment that was capable of making poetry, the Middle Ages were automatically protected from having one from which poets might need to flee into a solipsism, or, since poetry is ethics, from which just men might need to take refuge in jail.

NOTES

1 R.H. Rouse and M.A. Rouse 'The Verbal Concordance to the Scriptures' *Archivum Fratrum Praedicatorum* 44 (1974) 5–30. See also their 'Biblical *distinctiones* in the thirteenth century' *Archives d'histoire doctrinale et littéraire du moyen*

âge 41 (1974) 27–37; and Lloyd W. Daly *Contributions to a History of Alphabetization in Antiquity and the Middle Ages* Collection Latomus 90 (Brussels 1967).

2 E.R. Curtius *European Literature and the Latin Middle Ages* tr Willard R. Trask (New York 1953) pp 221–5

3 Sandkühler *Die frühen Dantekommentare* esp pp 13–46

4 'Ob der Inhalt als Dichtung oder als Wissenschaft aufgefasst wird. / Whether the content is taken as poetry or as science' (p 41).

5 The same presumption about poetry is found in the very beginning of Sandkühler's book, where he says that 'Der Kommentar richtet sich daher in allererster Linie auf den Inhalt, nich auf die Form des Werkes; er is keine Literaturkritik, wie oft gemeint wird / The commentary is determined above all by the content, not the form of the work; it is not literary criticism, as is often supposed' (p 13).

6 In his commentary on the *Consolation of Philosophy* of Boethius: 'Causa autem formalis tractandi est modus agendi Boetii, et est dialogus ... vel potest dici secundum communiter loquentes quod causa formalis tractandi est quintuplex, diffinitiva, divisiva, probativa, improbativa, exemplorum positiva. / The formal cause of the treatment is the genre Boethius uses, and it is dialogue ... or it can be said as it is said conventionally that the formal cause of the treatment is fivefold: it defines, divides, proves, refutes, and gives examples.' *Boethius de consolatione ... cum Sancti Thomae philosophi profundissimi commentariis, necnon Ascensii Badii grammatici diligentissimi* (Venice 1524) f bb5v.

7 Florence, Biblioteca Laurenziana, ms Plut 36.3, f 11r. The manuscript is dated 2 August 1406; I have corrected the spelling of all these modes to '-ivus' from '-ius.' The only new term here is 'collectivus'; according to Sandkühler's evidence, it equals 'probativus' and 'improbativus' (p 38). For an independent confirmation of this conclusion, I am happy to thank Professor Richard McKeon for having told me that 'collectivus' means inferential. The same reflection of the causa quintuplex as something conventional and uniform may be found in Bodleian ms Hamilton 17, a commentary on the sequences of the Church: 'Sed forma tractandi in aliis libris est quintuplex scilicet diffinitivus, divisivus, probativus, inprobativus, exemplorum ponens. Sed tamen auctor in hoc libro solum habet duos modus tractandi, scilicet probativum et exemplorum positivum' (f 62v). Cf also Munich, ms Clm 13439, f 161r, 'forma tractandi ... per omnes solum potest esse quintuplex.'

8 A methodology presuming that hymns are poems is developed by Joseph Szövérffy 'L'hymnologie médiévale: recherches et méthode' in *Cahiers de civilisation médiévale* 4 (1961) 389–422.

9 I first called attention to the existence of the later and more elaborate of these commentaries in my article, 'Commentary as Criticism' pp 29–48. My dis-

cussion here is based on that article, though I now have more evidence. Perhaps the bibliographical data relative to the commentaries deserve repeating verbatim:

On Hymns:

1 Seneca dicit in quadam epistola: Scio neminem bene vivere. Österreichische Nationalbibliothek Vindob 4839, ff 5r–111r

2 Seneca in epistola sua undecima sic scribit: Nulla sapiencia naturalia cordis. Clm 13439, ff 160r–237r.

3 Accedite ad deum ... Hoc est verbum psalmiste sermonem suum ad nos dirigentis et incitantis nos ad deum. Clm 17543, ff 116r–158v. Clm 26874, ff 15–55. Clm 23856 (lacks accessus). Vindob 3818, ff 93r–175r.

4 Super salutem et omnem pulcritudinem dilexi sapientiam. Hec propositio scribitur in libro sapientie et quamvis sit in se satis lucida tamen in ea due commendationes scientie inveniuntur. Clm 11475, ff 3r–56r.

5 Sicut testatur philosophus in 41 ethicorum quod hominis ultima in hac vita felicitas consistit in optima operatione. Clm 12205, ff 25r–29r. Clm 14677, ff 89r–110v. (The beginning of the accessus is lost.) BL Arundel 512, vol II, ff 21r–8v (a fragment, including an accessus and only a few hymns).

6 Laudem dicite deo nostro omnes servi eius et qui timetis deum pupilli et magni. Hec sunt verba beati Johannis in apocalypsi xix ca. Et enim ut dicit beatus dionysius. Vat Reg lat 138, ff 282r–9v (the 'Liber scholasticus').

7 Etsi liricorum poetarum sit scribere communia choreas, locos virginum et huiusmodi, dicente Horatio libro primo carminum 6: Nos convivia, nos prelia virginum. Vat Palat lat 1709, ff 230v–40r.

8 Ad humanissimum principem, in tituli Sancti Eustachii cardinalem Senensem dominum suum, Cantalycii in sacros hymnos interpretatio ... In omni artium et scientiarum genere usque iam adeo sit scriptitatum. Vat Chigi C.IV. 141.

9 Implemini Spiritu Sancto ... In hac saluberrima divini apostoli exhortatione tanguntur. *D. Dionysii Carthusiani in omnes beati Pauli Epistolas Commentaria ... et Hymnos Ecclesiasticos, non minus piae quam eruditae Enarrationes* (Paris 1540).

10 In lumine tuo videbimus lumen. Hanc propositionem scribit propheta David et est theoloyca, et convenienter potest recitari circa istum librum qui etiam est theoloycus. (Includes sequences, without a separate accessus.) Vindob 14815, ff 2r–190r.

11 [P]hilosphus dicit primo ethicorum quod felicitas est bonum optimum pulcherrimum et delectabilissimum. In ista propositione tanguntur tria. Leiden University, ms BPL 191D, ff 25r–35v.

On Sequences:

1 Sicut dicit Aristoteles in libro de anima primo quod rerum notitiam certi-
tudinaliter estimamus quod honorabile et bonum. Clm 12205, ff 29v–36v.

2 Sub umbra illius quem desiderabam sedi et fructus dulcis eius gutturi meo
etc. Hec propositio scribitur canticis canticorum capitulo 20.
Et nota primo quod hec verba proposita primo exponuntur ratione amoris
ipsius Salomonis. Clm 6954, ff 141r–251r.

3 Sapiencia vincit maliciam. Hec propositio scribitur in libro sapiencie in qua
propositione duo tanguntur ad ipsius theoloye commendationem. Clm
11475, ff 58r–219r. Vindob 3818, ff 1r–91r. Clm 22405, ff 1r–120v.

4 Scribit Seneca in epistolis suis, Vir speculativus est quasi deus in humano
corpore hospitatus. Bodl Hamilton 17, ff 66r–112v.
Clm 23856, [Seneca in libro ethymoloyarum sic ait: Vir speculativis ...] f 1r
ff. Cf Bodl Hamilton 17, ff 62r–3v.

5 Grates nunc reddamus. Notandum est quod hic incipit liber sequentiarum
et aliquarum earum. Clm 22405, ff 169r–270v.

6 Gustate et videte quoniam suavis est. Verba proposita sunt propheta et
sunt dicta de pietate dei que comparabiliter et convenienter possent recitari de ipsa scientia. Vindob 4839, ff 113r–256r.

To this list I can now add the *Explanatio super hymnos quibus utitur ordo Cister-
ciensis*: 'Cum David ex mandato patris visitaturus fratres perrexisset ad castra ...' Troyes, Bib mun 658. An edition is now being prepared by Bro J.
Michael Beers OSFS.

10 'Forma tractandi est modus agendi qui est hic metricus.' Brussels, Bibliothèque royale, ms 2519, f 89r.

11 Florence, Biblioteca Riccardiana, ms 842, f 1r

12 'Causa formalis est duplex, forma tractandi et forma tractatus. Forma tractandi
est modus agendi et ille est prosaicus. Forma tractatus consistit in divisione, et
dividitur iste liber in tot partes que sunt ymni. / The formal cause is twofold,
the form of the treatment and the form of the treatise. The form of the treatment is the mode of doing [genre] and that is prose. The form of the treatise
consists of its division, and this book is divided into as many parts as there
are hymns.' London, British Library, ms Arundel 512 (II), f 21r–v.

13 As defined by Conrad of Hirsau, in his instructions for making an accessus:
'quomodo, idest utrum metrice vel prosaice, scripserit. / How, that is whether
he has written in verse or in prose.' *Accessus ad auctores* ed Huygens p 72.

14 To translate 'modus agendi' and 'qualiter agat' as 'genre' probably distorts the
medieval terminology by too much limiting it, but here, at least, what is being
described is a genre in the modern sense, that is, the 'prosimetrum.' Assisi,
Biblioteca communale, ms 555, f 3r.

15 Oxford, Bodleian Library, ms Hamilton 17, 125v

16 Edited by Fausto Ghisalberti in 'Giovanni del Virgilio,' 18

17 Florence, Biblioteca Laurenziana, ms Plut 36.3, f 11r. Clearly, this commentator does not mean 'inferential' by 'collectivus.'

18 Leiden, Bibliotheek der Rijksuniversiteit, ms BPL 95, f 1v

19 Vatican Library, ms Ottob 1293, f 33v. Cf Dietrich Reichling ed *Das Doctrinale des Alexander de Villa-Dei, kritisch-exegetische Ausgabe* Monumenta Germaniae Paedagogica, Bd XII (Berlin 1893).

20 Paris, Bibliothèque nationale, ms lat 16089, f 146r

21 Leiden, Bibliotheek der Rijksuniversiteit, ms Univ 191A, f 214r

22 Florence, Biblioteca Riccardiana, ms 842, f 1r. The same information can be found in London, British Library, ms Add 16380, f 144r. The distinction between history and figment, as far as *Thebaid* commentary is concerned, means a distinction between the material treating the history of Thebes, as such, which is history, and the material in which the interferences of the pagan gods are mentioned, which is poetic figment. Commentaries frequently point out which is which; the distinction corresponds to that betrayed by John Calderia's *Concordantia* of poetry, philosophy, and theology, (Vatican Library, ms Palat lat 985, printed edition Venice 1547), in which the poetry section is an elaborately allegorized mythography. The third category, however, that is, allegory, seems not of much importance; I have found only one gloss in *Thebaid* commentary which specifies a passage 'allegorice': At *Thebaid* I.303ff, 'In parte ista mercurius executir preceptum Iovis et acceptis alis et galero accipit virgam que dicitur caduceum cuius proprietas est quod homo vivus tactus ab ipsa moritur, et homo mortuus tactus ab eadem vivificatur. Per ipsam autem virgam allegorice scientia rethorice intelligitur. / In this part Mercury carried out Jupiter's orders and having put on wings and a helmet he took a rod which is called the caduceus whose property is that a live man touched by it dies, and a dead man touched by it comes alive. By this rod is allegorically understood the science of rhetoric.' London, British Library, ms Harley 4869, f 5v.

23 Raoul de Longchamp *In Anticlaudianum Alani Commentum* ed Jan Sulowski (Warsaw 1972) p 21

24 London, British Library, ms Harley 4869, f 1v

25 Vatican Library, ms Palat lat 1690, passim

26 Paris, Bibliothèque nationale, ms lat 8300, f 9v

27 Munich, ms Clm 11475, f 59v

28 Vatican Library, ms Reg lat 138, f 285v

29 Munich, ms Clm 17543, f 116r–v

30 *The Commentary on the First Six Books of the 'Aeneid' of Vergil commonly attributed to Bernardus Silvestris* ed Julian Ward Jones and Elizabeth Frances Jones (Lincoln 1977) p 3

31 Paris, Bibliothèque nationale, ms lat 7757, f 4v

32 Yale University, Beinecke Library, ms Marston 37, f 5r

33 Curtius *European Literature* pp 221–5

34 Munich, ms Clm 13439, ff 160v–1r

35 Curtius *European Literature* p 223

36 Munich, ms Clm 6954, ff 141v–2v. Cf Vienna, mss Vindob 4839, f 114r and Vindob 14815, f 2r–v.

37 The notion that the definition of a text includes its rhetorical object has already been treated, in a sense, in the discussion of consideratio in chapter one; the presence of consideratio as one of the six parts of tragedy in effect seeks to blur the distinction between the interior and the exterior of the text, as far as ethical belief is concerned, in order to include the audience. The usual definition of a hymn, as given in the *Expositio* of Hilarius, is thus: 'Hymnus dicitur laus dei cum cantico. / A hymn is called the praise of God with song.' The commentary in Vatican Library, ms Reg lat 138 clarifies explicitly, quoting Augustine on the Psalms: 'Hympnus ... est cantus, cum laude dei. Ubi [cod ibi] laudas deum et non cantas, hymnum non dicis; ubi [cod ibi] cantas et non laudas deum, non dicis hymnum; ubi [cod ibi] laudas aliud quod non pertinet ad laudem dei, et si cantando laudas non dicis hympnum. Hympnus ergo tria ista habet, et cantum et laudem et deum. Laus ergo dei in canticum hymnus dicitur. Sic Augustinus. / A hymn is a song, with the praise of God. Where you praise God and do not sing, you do not say a hymn; where you sing and do not praise God, you do not say a hymn, where you praise something that does not pertain to the praise of God, and if in singing you praise you do not say a hymn. Therefore a hymn has these three features, song and praise and God. Therefore the praise of God in song is called a hymn. Thus Augustine.' (f 286r)

38 Ed Jones pp 1–3

39 Judson B. Allen *The Friar as Critic: Literary Attitudes in the Later Middle Ages* (Nashville 1971) pp 59–60

40 In his use of the terms 'approbativus' and 'improbativus,' Aegidius doubtless commits the ambiguity reproved in the hymn commentary already cited (cf note 34) in failing to distinguish between categories implying proof and categories implying praise.

41 Aegidius Romanus *In librum Solomonis qui Cantica Canticorum inscribitur Commentaria* (Rome 1555) f 2v

42 Patrick Gallacher, in his 'Food, Laxatives, and Catharsis in Chaucer's Nun's Priest's Tale' *Speculum* 51 (1976) 49–68, deals with the problem of catharsis, and begins what will be a series of studies of this whole question of the affective, its relation to knowledge, and to the kinds of physical and mental health which proper ethical (and therefore literary) existence presumes. I am happy that it is possible, for full and fit treatment of this most complex matter, to trust the authority of another.

43 Carruthers *The Search for St. Truth: A Study of Meaning in 'Piers Plowman'* (Evanston 1973), p 3

44 The paper has since been published: Adams 'The Nature of Need in *Piers Plowman* xx' *Traditio* 34 (1978) 273–301. I am happy to thank Professor Adams for sharing with me a pre-publication copy.

45 *Piers Plowman* p 32

46 Though it has nothing to do with the point that *Piers Plowman* should be taken as a work whose forma tractatus and forma tractandi are the same, it is of significance for the poem as a general hermeneutic puzzle that this distinctio presumes that Voluntas is of God, rather than human. To suppose that the Will of the poem is, or at some level refers to, an aspect of God rather than a human faculty turns the whole notion of the quest for salvation upside down. It is, I think, a supposition worth pursuing, if only to bracket our eventual answer, since of course in ideal terms the achievement of the Kingdom involves the reaching of congruence between human and divine will.

The text of the distinctio is as follows:

Voluntas dei est multiplex. Primo vult omnium salvationem ut pater profectum filiorum. i thi. ii; Vult omnes salvos fieri. Sed hoc non impletur propter pigritiam sicut non illuminatur qui non aperit fenestram. Crisos. Deus vult omnes salvos fieri; rogo ut velis.

Item mandatorum eius implecionem ut rex in terra sua. Mt. vi: Fiat voluntas tua. Sed hoc non impletur propter vindicte dilacionem. Ecc. viii: Et enim quia non profertur cito contra malos sententia absque timore ullo filii hominum perpetrant mala.

Item fidei et morum unitatem, ut gallina pullos propter milvum. Mt. xxiii: Quociens volui congregare filios tuos quemadmodum gallina congregat pullos suos sub alas et noluisti. Sed hoc non impletur propter lasciviam et propter nimiam scienciam ut avis pennata fugit nidum. Os. xii: Effraym quasi avis avolavit.

Item anime sanitatem ut medicus egri. Eze. xviii: Nolo mortem peccatoris sed hoc non impletur propter diete inobservationem. Prover. 1: Despexistis omne consilium meum.

Item rubiginis peccati mundicionem sicut aurifaber metalli. Mt. viii: Volo mundare, sed hoc non impletur propter metalli pravitatem. Ie. vi: Malicie eorum non consumpte. Argentum reprobum vocate eos [cod eg']. Ideo Eze. xxii: Versa est mihi domus israel in scoriam; omnes isti: es per impacienciam, stannum per similacionem, ferrum per aliorum oppressionem, plumbum per exempli inquinacionem et instabilitatem in medio fornacis, idest tribulationis.

Item temporalium communicationem, ut largus domus largum senescallum. Mt. xii: Misericordiam volo et non iudicium. Sed hoc non impletur propter avariciam. Ion. ii: Qui custodiunt vanitates frustra idest temporalia, ut canis fenum; misericordiam suam deliquerunt.

Item cordis mundiciam. 1 thess. iiii: Hec est voluntas dei sanctificatio nostra ut magnus [sic] vasis mundiciam. Sed hoc non impletur propter luti et immundorum antectacionem [sic] Ecc. xiii: Qui tetigerit picem inquinabitur ab ea.

Item caritatem ut sponsus a sponsa vult amari. Luc. xiii: Ignem veni mittere in terram. Sed hoc non impletur propter filiorum et rerum dilectionem. Os. xii: Confusa est que accepit eos quia dixit, vadam post amatores meos.

Item bonorum participationem ut curialis non vult comedere solus nec iustus mercedem servi retinere. Io. xvii: Pater quos dedisti mihi volo ut ubi ego sum et ipsi sint mecum. Sed hec non impletur propter boni incepti dimissionem ut operarius non perficiens dietam. Mt. Qui perseveraverit usque in finem hic salvus erit. Et propter excusationem – exemplum de vocatis ad cenam qui se excusaverunt. Luc. xiiii. (f 301r–v)

The will of God is multiple. First he wills the salvation of all as a father the success of his sons. 1 Thi. 2. He wills that all should be saved. But this is not fulfilled on account of laziness – one gets no light if he won't open the window. Chrisostom: God wills that all be saved; I ask you to will [it].

Also the fulfilment of his commandments, as a king in his land. Mt. 6: Your will be done. But this is not fulfilled because of delayed punishment. Ecc. 8: And they do evil without any fear of the Son of men because he does not pass sentence quickly against the evil ones.

Also the unity of faith and behaviour, as a hen her chicks because of the hawk. Mt. 23: How often I desired to gather your children as a hen gathers her chicks under her wings, and you would not. But this is not fulfilled because of wantonness and because of too much knowledge – as a fledged bird flees the nest. Os. 12: Ephraim has flown away like a bird.

Also the health of the soul as the physician [the health of] the sick. Eze. 18: I do not desire the death of the sinner, but this is not fulfilled because of nonobservance of diet. Prover. 1: You have despised all my counsel.

Also the cleaning of the corrosion of sin, as the goldsmith [the cleaning] of metal. Mt. 8: I will clean, but this is not fulfilled because of the bad condition of the metal. Ie. 6: Their malices are not consumed. Call them waste silver. Also Eze. 22: The house of Israel is become dross to me; all these: bronze through impatience, tin through pretence, iron through the oppression of others, lead through the impurity and instability of example in the midst of the furnace, that is of tribulation.

Also the distribution of temporal things, as the generous house [has] a generous seneschal. Mt. 12: I desire mercy and not judgment. But this is not fulfilled because of avarice. Ion. 2: Those who take care for vanities in vain, that is temporal things, like the dog guarding straw, forsake his mercy.

Also cleanness of heart. 1 Thess. 4: This is the will of God – our sanctification, as the cleanness of a great vase. But this is not fulfilled because of contact with [?] filth and unclean things. Ecc. 13: He who touches pitch will be defiled by it.

Also charity, as the bridegroom desires to be loved by the bride. Luc. 13: I came to send fire into the earth. But this is not fulfilled because of affection for children and things. Os. 12: Confused is she who receives those because she said, I will go after my lovers.

Also the sharing of good things, as the courtly person who does not wish to eat alone, or the just man who does not keep back the wages of a servant. Io. 17: Father, those whom you have given me, I wish that they might be with me where I am. But this is not fulfilled because of leaving off after a good beginning, as a worker who does not finish the day's work. Mt.: He who perseveres to the end, he shall be saved. And because of making excuses – for example, the ones called to the feast who excused themselves. Luc. 14.

47 The best book on the subject is still J. Th. Welter *L'exemplum dans la littérature religieuse et didactique du moyen âge* (Paris 1927). J.A. Herbert's *A Catalogue of Romances in the Department of Manuscripts in the British Museum* vol III (London 1910) is an excellent indication of the character of late medieval exempla collections, of which the British Library contains a typical and extensive sample. G.R. Owst's *Literature and Pulpit in Medieval England* (Cambridge 1933), and *Preaching in Medieval England* (Cambridge 1933), and J.A. Mosher's *The Exemplum in the Early Religious and Didactic Literature of England* (New York 1911) are representative and still standard studies depending on exempla. Most collections of exempla, as well as most of the largely homiletic material containing exempla in use, remain in manuscript; the *Summa praedicantium* of John Bromyard is a large and representative printed collection, the *Gesta romanorum* a more specialized one. See also the collections of Jacques de Vitry, John Mirk, and Étienne de Bourbon.

48 Alan M.F. Gunn *The Mirror of Love: A Reinterpretation of 'The Romance of the Rose'* (Lubbock 1952)

49 John Manly *Some New Light on Chaucer* (New York 1952)

50 Ghisalberti 'Giovanni del Virgilio' pp 20–30

51 Paris, Bibliothèque nationale, ms lat 14716, f 257r

52 The text has 'culpa'; the commentator has cancelled it and inserted 'pertinacia' from the margin. Obviously, we have here an autograph, in process of composition.

53 Étienne Gilson *History of Christian Philosophy in the Middle Ages* (New York 1955) p 502

54 *In epistolam B. Pauli Apostoli ad Romanos commentarii* (Rome 1555) f 1r

55 R.C. Godfrey 'The Language theory of Thomas of Erfurt' *Studies in Philology* 57 (1960) 24. This brief article is the clearest presentation I know of this most complex subject. Otherwise, see Jan Pinborg *Die Entwicklung der Sprachtheorie im Mittelalter* Beiträge zur Geschichte der Philosophie und Theologie des Mittelalters (Münster 1967); G.L. Bursill-Hall tr and ed *Grammatica Speculativa of Thomas of Erfurt* (London 1972), and Bursill-Hall, *Speculative Grammars of the Middle Ages* (The Hague 1971). These contain extensive references.

56 Most recently by Richard and Mary Rouse, 'Biblical *distinctiones*' 27–37. Beryl Smalley, *The Study of the Bible in the Middle Ages* (Oxford 1952) pp 264ff explains the distinctio's beginnings, and gives bibliography. I used the distinctio as evidence for certain arguments about allegory in *The Friar as Critic* pp 32–3, 102–8, but did not really address there the larger questions which the distinctio permits one to ask and answer.

57 Beryl Smalley *English Friars and Antiquity in the Early Fourteenth Century* (Oxford 1960)

58 An excellent discussion of this quality of manuscripts is Richard A. Dwyer 'The Appreciation of Handmade Literature' *The Chaucer Review* 8 (1974) 221–40.

59 Allen and Moritz *A Distinction of Stories*. I must admit, however, that even in affirming this we went that one, perhaps modern, step further, and reconstructed from this manuscript evidence a proposal for a proto-ordering.

60 Pézard *Dante sous la pluie de feu*

61 Though Patrick Gallacher does not, of course, argue his point in terms of the notion of normative array, his study, *Love, the Word, and Mercury* (Albuquerque 1975), does prove both that Gower had a mind capable of this architectonic approach to definition, and that Gower in fact makes his points by touching and retouching them in tale after tale, thus implicitly making a normative array.

62 C. de Boer *Ovide moralisé, poème du commencement du 14ième siècle* 5 vols (Wiesbaden 1966–8)

63 Pierre Bersuire *Metamorphosis Ovidiana Moraliter ... explanata* (Paris 1509). Bersuire's prologue indicates that there were at least three recensions of this work, of which this Badius edition, wrongly attributed to Thomas Waleys, represents the second. For full presentation of what is at present known about Bersuire's work on Ovid, see Joseph Engels 'Berchoriana I: Notice Bibligraphique sur Pierre Bersuire, Supplement au Repertorium Biblicum Medii Aevi' *Vivarium* 2 (1964) 62–112, continued, ibid, 113–24; and also his 'L'Édition critique de l'Ovidius moralizatus de Bersuire' *Vivarium* 9 (1971) 19–24, containing a list of sixty-two manuscripts of Bersuire's work, and followed by an edition (pp 25–48) of his commentary on book I of Ovid's *Metamorphoses*, made by Maria S. van der Bijl. I have not seen all these manuscripts, but I have seen enough to believe both that Engel's description of Bersuire's revision in at least three stages is substantially accurate and that, from the point of view of the medieval reader, Bersuire's text deposited into circulation such a variety of glosses that only an editing of material, rather than some supposedly critical text, can fairly represent Bersuire's influence on the use of allegorized Ovid in literary allusions after about 1350.

64 Allen and Moritz *A Distinction of Stories*

65 Judson B. Allen and Patrick Gallacher 'Alisoun Through the Looking Glass, or Every Man his own Midas' *Chaucer Review* 4 (1970) 99–105

66 As a Jesuit who has made his vocation an impressive resource in the understanding of Joyce's ostentatiously modern works, Robert Boyle is both an unusual and an unusually helpful colleague, to whose insight and counsel my own quite different criticism owes a great deal.

3

Poetic disposition and the forma tractatus

Both in the Middle Ages and now, well-made sermons customarily have three points. One late medieval ars predicandi explains why: 'because of the Trinity, because a triple cord is hard to break, because Saint Bernard's sermons had three points, and because three points take up about the right amount of time.'[1] Here definition, precedent, and practical experience meet in a way that is characteristically medieval. Texts have parts, and these parts exist as such for every possible good reason. The non-organic character of medieval wholes has already been quite elaborately defined, analysed, and argued;[2] but I think in a way which claims more than it proves about the unity of either medieval cathedrals or medieval texts. In this chapter and in the next, I shall be particularly concerned with parts and partitions in medieval literary texts, and with what was thought to relate and array them. Medieval critics made a great deal of the fact that texts had parts, and customarily devoted great care and attention to dividing what they discussed. Both implicitly and explicitly, their concern for parts of wholes, for their precise delimitation, and often for their naming, not only justifies the term 'homologous parts and parts of parts,' which has been proposed to describe the medieval position, but also makes quite clear just what kind of whole it is that is being divided into its parts.

The medieval understanding of the parts of a whole text depends upon a number of related concepts, which it is the project of this chapter to define and distinguish. First, of course, is the notion of the forma tractatus itself, in terms of which texts were defined as the result of the presence of parts. The fact that many medieval texts contain, or consist of, narratives suggests consideration of the notion of plot as a factor in medieval analysis, but in fact medieval discussion of beginning, middle, and end is concerned not for Aristotelian plot, but for essentially discursive and rhetorical organization. It is in terms of this discursive organization that parts of any given text exist, and in terms of which the critic must make the answering act of division. But division itself is complicated by the fact that, for the medieval critics, there were at least three kinds: dispositio, divisio, and distinctio. Understanding of these kinds is further complicated by the fact that divisivus is one of the modes of the forma tractandi; this mode divisivus must be clearly distinguished from dispositio and divisio, or the two levels of form, the forma tractandi and the forma tractatus, collapse into one. Distinctio, as we shall see, operates at both levels.

In the previous chapter, I defined the forma tractandi. Here, I turn to the second element in the medieval sense of the form of a text, the forma tractatus. The forma tractatus was always defined in terms of a text's outline; it was that which named the work's division into books, chapters, parts of chapters, etc. 'Forma tractatus est divisio libri in suas partes. / The form of the treatise is the division of the book into parts.'[3] This language is thoroughly conventional;[4] most commentators simply repeat the formula and go on, presuming that it is understood. A few, however, say things which are a little more revealing. For instance, Bartholomew of Bruges, in his lecture on the Averroistic *Poetics*, says, 'Forma tractatus est ordinatio libri in omnibus enim que constant ex pluribus partibus ordinem ad invicem habentibus; ordo est sua forma. / The form of the treatise is the organization of the book in terms of all the factors which arise out of the relationships which obtain among many parts; the order is its form.'[5] Giovanni del Virgilio, in his commentary on the *Metamorphoses*, says:

Forma tractatus est compositio et ordinatio[6] 15 librorum in hoc volumine et capitulorum in dictos libros et partium in capitulis descendendo usque ad partes minutas que per se sententiam aliquam important. Que scilicet compositio apparebit per divisionem, eo quod unum oppositum per aliud declaratur, ut dicitur libro elenchorum, nam oppositio iuxta se posita maiora et minora esse videtur.

The form of the treatise is the composition and organization of the fifteen books in this volume, and of the chapters in those books, and of the parts in those chapters, descending even to the minute parts which as such have some meaning. This composition will appear when the text is divided, for the reason that one opposite is interpreted by another, as is said in the book of the Elenchorum, for an opposition put next to itself seems to be a major and minor premise.[7]

Walter Burley, in his commentary on Aristotle's *Ethics*, makes it very clear that this dividing is meaningful, rather than merely formal or symmetrical:

In exponendo totum textum dividam quemlibet librum in tractatus, et tractatus in capitula, et capitula in partes, et partes in particulas, faciendo istas divisiones secundum diversitatem sententie et non secundum quantitatem littere quemadmodum plurimi diviserunt.

In expounding a whole text I should divide every book into tractates, and the tractates into chapters, and the chapters into parts, and the parts into bits, by making these divisions in terms of the separate meanings involved, and not in terms of the quantity of text after the manner many divide.[8]

Several betrayals in this language need to be emphasized at the very outset. First of all, it is clear that the basis of division is sententia, or meaning. Parts are not necessarily of equal size, but a part is a part because it 'importat aliquam sententiam.' There is, in Walter Burley's comment, proof that some commentators tried harder for symmetrical divisions than meaning would permit – what we should make of this, I think, is that the medieval sense of a book's form included some sensitivity to length and material balance, but that these factors were not finally determinative. The form of a medieval book, properly understood and arranged, was dominated by meaning. One example which must have influenced their thinking was Augustine's *De doctrina christiana* (II.i.2), in which Augustine at one point dutifully and ostentatiously treats a subdivision of his subject, although that topic is not really to the point, because his outline logically requires it.

In the second place, it is clear from Giovanni's comment that this order, based as it is on meaning, is as an order related to logic. Bartholomew of Bruges, in his phrase 'partibus ordinem ad invicem habentibus,' is less specific, but I think makes the same point. In these comments, two problems are raised. First is the problem of the ordering as such – the fact that parts range themselves serially one after the other in an order which can be given a name. Second is the problem of the relationship between parts – what is it that binds part to part, or makes it inevitable that part three follow part two and precede part four? The ordering as such in medieval texts tends to derive from some structure such as the distinctio; this is most important, as a critical principle for medieval literature, because it means negatively that the modern principle of plot is usually not determinative, even though the material involved is literally narrative and does more or less vaguely have a plot. The relationship between parts is, in a manner, logical, at least in that the ordered parts develop an argument or a definition, but it is not always, as Giovanni says, formally syllogistic. At the most general level, this relationship is defined by Averroes' term 'assimilation'; to define this term will be the chief concern of the next chapters. Here, however, it is necessary at least to suggest that the assimilatio or likening, defined by Bartholomew as 'partibus ordinem ad invicem habentibus' and by Giovanni as 'unum oppositum per aliud declaratur,' poses in the profoundest possible way the medieval strategy whereby one detail is explained by the next – whereby the parts of medieval texts constitute to each other mutually interlocking and mutually explicating glosses. The power of this kind of organization, and its character, I can best explain by comparing the medieval question which it answers with the modern critical question which it ignores. In any modern analysis which presumes the genuine Aristotelian notion of plot, the crucial question is, for any given series of parts, 'Why does this part come next?' The answer bases itself on an analysis of causality, and reaches an aesthetically satisfactory conclusion when it announces some kind of tragic or comic inevitability. The crucial question which the medieval analysis asks is superficially similar, but in essence utterly different. It is, 'Why do this part and the next one go together?' The answer bases itself on an analysis of logical, analogical, and allegorical relationships. The analysis reaches a conclusion that is both sententially and morally satisfactory by showing that the two parts whose relationship is in question have, because of their relationship, more significance and definition than either would have had in isolation. In addition, of course, both parts taken together can be expected to form parts of a normative array.

In practice, most late medieval literature which is still admired is, or is substantially composed of, narrative. Lyric is far more important in Romance than in English, but the greatest Romance lyric is twelfth-century, and therefore strictly speaking not accountable to the theories I am trying to define. In the later Middle Ages, what one confronts above all are the masterpieces of Dante, Chaucer, and Arthurian romance; Dante's *Commedia* is full of exempla at least, even when the full narrative is left implicit, and both the romances and the *Canterbury Tales* are stories. Otherwise, in works as varied as the *Romance of the Rose*, *Piers Plowman*, the Middle English *Pearl*, or even such lyrics as 'Blou northerne wynd' and 'De clerico et puella,' what dominates in content is either story, or exemplary characters who are the result of story, or who implicate a story. The temptation, therefore, to take all this narrative as such, rather than as narratio or exemplum or both, is very great. But to do so imposes on all this narrative the kinds of expectations to which modern approaches to plot accustom us, and ensures that we miss its full medieval significance. I can begin to deal with this temptation, and at the same time begin to define the medieval doctrine of the forma tractatus, by presenting Averroes' medieval replacement for the well-known Aristotelian doctrine of plot, as defined in terms of beginning, middle, and end.

Averroes' treatment, in the translation of Hermann the German, is quite long and detailed. As before, when dealing with his discussion of the six parts of tragedy, I shall quote as much as makes his doctrine clear, and then discuss his meaning in some detail. Here, as before, the syntactical translation of the passage offers few difficulties; the problem consists not so much in knowing what he says, as in understanding what he means by what he says.

Dicamus de rebus per quas fit decor et bonitas eorum ex quibus processit poetria. Necessarium est enim dicere de hiis rebus in tragedia et in ceteris. Sunt namque eis tamquam principia et initia existendi. Res namque ex quibus procedunt artes duorum sunt modorum. Quedam enim sunt eis necessarie et quedam completive et meliorative. Dicemus igitur quoniam oportet ut sit tragedia conferens sufficienciam finibus operationis sue, scilicet ut pertingat in assimilatione et representatione ad finem ad quem potest pertingere secundum naturam suam. Et hoc erit per aliqua quorum unum est ut sit ei quod intenditur magnitudo quedam determinata per quam fit totum et completum. Totum autem et completum est quod habet principium et medium et ultimum. Principium autem ante rem est, nec oportet ut sit cum eis quibus est principium. Et ultimum est cum eis quibus est ultimum, neque est ante. Medium autem est ante et cum. Ipsum ergo melius est utrisque extremis, cum sit medium in loco qui est inter id quod est ante et inter id quod est post. Talem enim locum optinent in bello illi qui fortes sunt, scilicet locum medium inter locum timidorum et locum audacium seu protervorum. Et hic est locus medius, et hoc modo terminus bonus in compositione est medius, et est qui componitur ex extremis et ex quo non componuntur extrema. Neque oportet ut medium sit solummodo medium in compositione et ordine et loco sed in quantitate et bonitate. Et quando hoc sic fuerit, tunc oportet ut id quod intenditur habeat primum et medium et ultimum, et ut sit unaqueque istarum partium media in quantitate. Et similiter oportet in summa composita ex ipsis ut habeat quantitatem determinatam, non ut existat secundum quamcumque magnitudinem indifferenter. Bonitas quippe in composito ex parte duorum existit quorum unum est ordo et alterum quantitas. Et propter hoc non dicitur de animali parvi corporis in comparatione individuorum sue speciei quod sit bonum seu pulcrum. Et dispositio in locutione poetica in tali est, sicut dispositio in doctrina demonstrativa, scilicet quoniam si doctrinalis sermo brevior fuerit quam oporteat obscurat intellectum, et si longior fuerit difficilis erit retentionis et inducet discipulo oblivionem. Est igitur dispositio in hoc sicut est dispositio in aspectu alicuius sensibilis. Erit enim aspectus talis bene se habens quando distantia fuerit equalis inter aspicientem et aspiciendum, non nimis propinqua neque nimis longinqua. Et quod accidit in doctrina, idem accidit in sermonibus poeticis, scilicet si fuerit carmen laudativum brevius et compendiosius quam exigat laudandi materies non complebit debitum laudandi, et si prolixius fuerit non potuerunt partes eius retineri in memoria auditorum. Continget ergo eis ut cum audierint partes postremas in oblivionem cadant partes prime. Sermones autem rethorici quorum usus in controversia est in collatione seu obviatione non habent quantitatem determinatam secundum naturam ... Oportuit ut haberet ars poetica terminum naturalem sicut se habet in quantitatibus naturalibus rerum existentium secundum naturam. Quemadmodum enim omnia generabilia quando non impediuntur in generatione ab aliqua mala occasione perveniunt ad magnitudinem definitam a natura, sic oportet ut se habeat in sermonibus poeticis et proprie in duabus maneriebus representationum, quarum una fit permutando a representatione contrarii ad contrarium, altera autem representando ipsam rem non connotando contrarium.

We must discuss those matters by which arise the fitness and value of those things from which poetry proceeds. It is necessary to deal with these matters in tragedy and for other genres, because they are the first principles of the existence of poetry. The things from which arts come exist in two modes – certain ones are necessary conditions, and others are supplementary or beneficial. We should say, therefore, that there must be a factor in tragedy which makes it adequate to the end it works for, that is, able to attain by means of likening and representing to the end appropriate to its nature which it can reach. There are several such; one is that it be, in terms of its end, of a certain determinate size which makes it whole and complete. Anything whole and complete has a beginning, a middle, and an end. The beginning is what comes before something, without needing anything with it to make it a beginning. The end is with what makes it the end, but it is before nothing. The middle is both before and with. This middle is better than either extreme, since it is the middle in place which is between that which comes before and that which comes after. In battle, this is the place which the strong obtain, that is, the middle place between the place of the timid and the place of the audacious or rash. And this is the middle place, and in this manner the good term in composition is the middle one, which is composed of the extremes, and of which the extremes are not composed. Nor is it fitting that the middle should be middle only in composition and order and place, but also in quantity and merit. When the middle has been arranged in this way, then it is proper that the whole have a beginning, a middle, and an end, and that all these parts be of moderate size, and similarly it is proper that the whole composed of these parts be of determinate size, and not of some indifferent magnitude. Thus the merit of a composition comes from two factors, one the order and the other the quantity. It is for this reason that one does not say of an animal that is small by comparison with other members of its species that it is good or pretty. The arrangement in a poetic speech is just like the arrangement in a lecture, because if a lecture is too short for its material it is confusing, and if it is too long it is hard to remember and makes the student forget. Disposition in this field is like disposition as it relates to looking at something sensible. One can see a thing best when the distance between it and the observer is appropriate, neither too close nor too far. And the same thing happens in poetry that happens in lecturing – that is, if the song of praise is shorter and more condensed than the material of praise requires, the due praise will not be accomplished, and if it is too prolix the audience will not remember its parts; it could happen that as they hear the last parts, they forget the first ones. Rhetorical speeches used for controversy in conference or argument have no determinate natural length. But the art of poetry should have a natural end, like the natural sizes of things existing according to nature. Just as everything that lives, unless it is hindered by some accident, reaches a size defined by its nature, so also should poetry, and properly in its two manners of representing, of which one is made by dealing with a thing in terms of its contrary, and the other by representing the thing itself without evoking a contrary.[9]

This section in Averroes' treatment follows immediately upon his discussion of the six parts of tragedy. After defining tragedy and its parts, in this section he turns to the discussion of various characteristics of tragedy (or praise, or poetry) as such, taken as something definite and whole. These, according to the analysis of Bartholomew of Bruges, have to do with the determinate size of tragedy, with its thematic unity, with the fact that it does not deal in fictions, with its entire dependence on representation, and with its possible dependence upon contrast as well as upon direct description. The part that I have quoted is that which deals with the questions of determinate size.

Throughout this whole discussion, it is presumed that poetry has a nature, that this nature is related to its end or purpose, and that its defining characteristics are what gives it its 'decor et bonitas.' The greatest attractiveness that poetry can attain, it would seem, is to be what it is. What it is involves, among other things, being of the right size. To be the right size is to be whole and complete, and to have a beginning, a middle, and an end. In this phrase we have an echo of the genuine Aristotle, which misleads only if we let it. Properly understood, this doctrine of beginning, middle, and end has nothing to do with plot. Rather, everything depends, really, on the middle. The beginning is something that comes before the middle, but after nothing. The end is that which comes with what makes it the end. The middle both follows the beginning and precedes the end – it is both before and with. All this becomes intelligible when we understand that the middle is the discursive substance of something sentential and expository, rather than that part of an action preceding a climax. As discursive substance, the middle dominates both beginning and end. What comes before is merely introduction or prologue; what comes after is summary, peroration, or proverbial close. This is not a definition of narrative, but of effective discourse. The fact that the discourse may take, rhetorically, the form of narratio in no way compromises its essence and formal character as discourse. Thus Chaucer, speaking of the end of narrative in the *Troilus*, becomes intelligible when we realize that he means, not plot, but discursive conclusion, the fulfilment of the purpose of the piece:

> How so it be that som men hem delite
> With subtyl art hire tales for to endite,
> Yet for al that, in hire entencioun,
> Hire tale is al for som conclusioun.
>
> And sithen th'ende is every tales strengthe,
> And this matere is so bihovely,
> What sholde I peynte or drawen it on lengthe ... (II.256–62)

Averroes, in fact, like Chaucer, finds length itself a natural topic in this context – that is, the question of appropriate size. As Averroes develops his definition, the word 'medium' takes on punning significance, and the virtue of the Aristotelian mean virtually takes over the accidental fact that what we are actually discussing is something that is materially located in the middle. This medium of poetry, like the centre of the army's line, is the best part. It is that which has the best features of both extremes, but gives nothing of own virtue away to them, though they must also be of fit size (media in quantitate). Averroes concludes his discussion of fit and determinate size with two comparisons. First, poetry is like any species of animal; it cannot be beautiful if it is small for its kind. Here, I think, Averroes betrays, in spite of the golden mean, the practical medieval preference for dilatatio. But on the other hand, there is a fit and proper relationship between the size of a poem and the number and complexity of its parts – just as there is a fit distance for viewing any object, a distance at which one can see the whole, and at the same time discern the parts. In this comparison, and as Averroes discusses in very practical terms the needs of an audience which is likened to an audience of students, it is very clear that poems are intended to be received as wholes – that one is supposed to remember the beginning as he hears the end, and at the same time one must allow for as many parts as are needed so that the poem 'complebit debitum laudandi.' Finally we find that the parts themselves may all treat univocally the same subject, or that the parts may involve the use of opposites and contraries. In either case, the quality of the piece is partly a function of the order in which these parts are presented;

presumably, all these parts, or certainly most of them, will belong to the great middle.

In his discussion of this treatment of beginning, middle, and end, Bartholomew of Bruges devotes all of his literal attention to specifying its parts, and in this practice of analysis by division he is both behaving in an understandably medieval fashion and exercising that critical faculty whose definition is the enterprise of this chapter. In making divisions, of course, Bartholomew implies an opinion of what his text means, and betrays this opinion further when, at least from time to time, he names his divisions. The most important feature of his treatment is that he never once mentions beginning or ending; his discussion is entirely concentrated on the words 'medium' and 'magnitudo' and their synonyms. The possibly confusing echo from the correct text of Aristotle absolutely disappears.

According to Bartholomew, the two most important points of this passage are these: 'primo ostendit quod sermo poeticus debet habere magnitudinem determinatam per quem [sic] fit totum et perfectum; secundo ostendit quod per hoc differt a sermone rethorico. / first he shows that a poem ought to have a determinate size by which it is made whole and perfect; second he shows that for this reason it differs from rhetorical language.'[10] Both Averroes and Bartholomew, as well as Dickens, know that litigation goes on forever, unless one puts a stop to it; rhetoric therefore has no intrinsic limits. But poetry does. Bartholomew defines this magnitudo which is natural to poetry thus:

Ostendit que et qualis debet illa magnitudo et in hoc exponit quod dixerat secunda ibi: *totum autem et completum*. Et hoc dividitur in duas, quia primo ostendit quod talis magnitudo consistit in medietate [sic] inter superhabundancia et defectum; secundo quia medium dicitur multis modis ostendit in quo et quali medio ibi: *neque oportet ut medium*.

He shows what this size is, and what its character is, and in this he explains when he said second, at: *whole and complete*. And this passage is divided into two parts, because first he shows that this size consists of something between too much and too little; second, because the word 'medium' can be used in many ways, he shows in what and of what character he means 'medium,' at: *nor should the medium*. (f 149r)

Rhetoric, on the other hand, is indeterminate: 'Quantitas determinata non invenitur in quibusdam sermonibus rethoricis secundum naturam; et dicit secundum naturam quia possent [sic] ex institucione humana habere. / Rhetorical language, by nature, does not have determinate size; and he says "by nature" because it may have such a limit because of human convention' (f 149r).[11]

In all this emphasis on an intrinsic and natural magnitude appropriate to any given poem we have something of the atmosphere of New Criticism, with its doctrine of the unparaphrasability of the unique poetic text. The difference is that for the New Critics this notion of a poem's inevitable and unique size and shape is a function of the poem's textuality, while for Averroes it is clearly doctrinal and discursive. His comparisons, except for the one military one, are drawn from obviously discursive uses of language; his conclusion makes clear that what he is talking about is content – is what the language is about. His acceptance both of treatment by contrast and univocal treatment of a subject is clear assent to the medieval notion of poems as things assembled rather than organic. And finally, his clear assumption that a given poem must have exactly the right amount of material – the right number of parts – according to its nature, is definitive agreement with the claim I made in the last chapter, that arrays of exempla or other material implied, in being arrayed, some sense of sufficiency. The normative array is normative because it is complete; a poem is a whole because it is of its natural magnitude, and has a complete number of parts. What in practice determines just what parts will be admitted and how they will be ordered and arrayed, is another question entirely. We begin to confront the textuality of a poem by admitting that by medieval definition and presumption, it is complete,[12] and that its completeness exists as an assembly of definite and separable parts.

The crucial act of medieval criticism, then, is division. Division exposes the forma tractatus, constitutes the first step toward realization of the forma tractandi, and is the basis of any possible serious consideration of a text's wholeness, subject, or meaning. I shall deal with this notion of division first by citing and discussing a helpfully detailed definition of division, which is itself found in one of the commentaries on which all these literary definitions are based. Second, I shall deal with three interrelated but distinguishable species of this general notion of division, or of the medieval sense that a text consists of an assembly of parts. These are dispositio, divisio, and distinctio. The first of these has to do with the ordering of material, and tends to emphasize consideration of natural and artificial orders, and the fitness of various ways of beginning. The second is division itself, used as an instrument both of analysis and of ordonnance, of which there are a host of examples both in commentary and in such related areas as preaching. The third we have already considered, in connection with the discussion of forma tractandi and normative array in chapter two; here, it must be seen both as an instrument of analysis, as the implicit basis of the visible outline of a text, and as a means of relating forma tractatus and the prior and more literally sentential dimensions of a text's existence, dimensions which are materially pre-textual but which in terms of medieval notions of causality are just as much present in and to a given text as its words. Third and finally, I shall array a number of examples of practical criticism, by which I show how this method of analysis by the kind of dividing which the forma tractatus and its antecedents defines is in fact a useful instrument of literary analysis. One of these examples, based on Dante's explanations of ordering in the *Commedia*, is medieval; the others are speculative, but attempt that version of the same explanation which can accomplish Dante's purpose for modern readers.

My definition of division comes from the commentary of Raoul de Longchamp on the *Anticlaudianus* of Alanus de Insulis. The commentary itself was written about 1216, or early in the period I have under consideration; the manuscript itself was made in France about 1400, and proves by its existence that these doctrines were still prized. The definition is as follows:

Sicut dicit Boethius, omnis logica aut deffinit, aut dividit, aut componit sive colligit ...

Divisionis autem sunt sex species principales: generis in species; totius in partes; vocis in significationes; subiecti in accidentalia; accidentis in subiecta; accidentis in accidentia.

Est enim divisio alicuius communitatis specificatio. Est enim multiplex communitas: communitas naturae, communitas vocis, communitas integritatis, communitas accidentis. Ex data descriptione patet, quod ad hoc, ut fiat divisio duo exiguntur, scilicet unio et diversitas. Oportet enim ut aliqua uniantur in diviso quae divisa esse ostenduntur per dividentia. Sic ergo non potest fieri divisio aliquorum nisi in aliquo conveniant et in aliquo differant.

Divisio autem generis in species fit tripliciter: quandoque fit in species et per species, ut:
'animalium aliud homo, aliud est asinus';
quandoque per substantiales differentias, ut:
'animalium aliud est rationale, aliud irrationale';
quandoque per finitum et infinitum, ut:
'animalium aliud est homo, aliud non homo';
Et notandum, quod divisio generis in species est quotiens superius dividitur in inferiora. Unde hic est divisio generis in species:
'hominum alius Socrates, alius Plato, alius Cicero'; similiter hic:
'coloratorum aliquod album, aliquod nigrum, aliquod medium'.

Alio tamen respectu est ibi divisio accidentis in accidentia.
Divisio totius in partes integrales est ut hic: 'Domus quaedam pars est tectum, alia paries, alia fundamentum'.

Divisio vocis in significationes sic habet fieri:
'Hoc nomen canis in una significatione significat latrabile, in alia marinum, in alia coeleste sidus'.
Subiecti in accidentia, ut:
'Hominum alius albus, alius niger'.
Accidentis in subiecta, ut:
'Alborum aliud nix, aliud cristallus'.
Accidentis in accidentia, ut:
'Alborum aliud molle, aliud durum'.

As Boethius says, all logic either defines or divides or orders or infers ... There are, moreover, six principal kinds of division: of a genus in species, a whole in parts, a word into its meanings, a subject into accidents, an accident into subjects, an accident into accidents. The specification of some truth is also a division, for truth is multiple: the truth of nature, the truth of a word, the truth of integrity, the truth of an accident. From this description it is obvious that two things are required for a division, unity and diversity. For it is appropriate that things be united in a division which are shown to be divided by dividing. Thus therefore division cannot be made among things unless they are both similar and different. Division of genus into species is made three ways. Sometimes it is made into species, or in terms of species, as in the case of animals – one is a man and another is an ass; sometimes it is made in terms of substantial differences, as some animals are rational and some are irrational; sometimes in terms of a finite class and an indefinite one, as of animals which may be either human or non-human. It should be noted that sometimes a division of genus into species involves dividing an inclusive class into its included parts; thus this is a division of genus into species – men may include Socrates, Plato, and Cicero. Similarly, of colours – they may be white, black, and grey. In another respect, there may be division of accidents. In accidental division the whole is divided into integral parts, as a house has a roof, foundation, and walls. The division of a word into its meanings has to be made thus: as this word 'dog' according to one meaning signifies by barking, according to another the marine being, according to another the star in the sky. Of a subject in accidents, as a man may be white or black. Of accident into subjects, as whiteness may be snow or crystal. Of accident into accidents, as a white thing may be either soft or hard.[13]

The most obvious, and most interesting, feature of this definition is that it is itself primarily a division – a distinctio. One defines division by dividing it into its parts and parts of parts, and by giving examples of many of them. Otherwise, what is most important is that a fit division requires parts that are both like and different – 'in aliquo conveniant[14] et in aliquo differant.' In the category which most nearly fits literary texts – that is, 'totius in partes,' what Raoul especially emphasizes is that the parts must be real and whole in themselves, they must be 'partes integrales,' they must make sense. More generally, however, each or all of these categories may fit a literary text, depending on the logical character of its subject and the logical arrangement of its material.

Two features of this definition are, for the purpose of literary analysis, most significant. First, it is clear by the very form of this definition that division was in the Middle Ages considered an instrument of definition. This fact is proved in practice by commentator after commentator; Dante's letting his analysis of the poems of the *Vita nuova* consist materially of little more than elaborate divisions is perhaps the most widely known example. Bartholomew of Bruges, in his commentary on the Averroistic poetics, even goes so far as to say 'dividit de' when what he probably means is 'defines' or 'states concerning.'[15] Second, it is clear from the array of examples which Raoul gives that the parts which a valid division specifies are logical parts, whose nature derives from and is consonant with the nature of the whole of which they are the parts. In these terms, and given the definitions established in previous chapters, we must expect the parts of a poem to be parts of the kind of whole which it must be – that is, of a whole which is verbal, discursive, and ethical. For instance, to take an example which I have argued at great length elsewhere, the parts of Chaucer's *Canterbury Tales*, as distinguished by the joints and rubrications surviving in the manuscripts, are prologues and tales, plus one envoi whose rubrication attributes it to Chaucer himself, all introduced by a somewhat longer general prologue. In some cases, especially when read thematically, prologues may introduce more than the one tale immediately following; in some cases, a tale lacks a prologue. A persistent tendency of modern criticism has been to ignore the obviously discursive significance of this medieval labelling of the parts of Chaucer's work, in order to divide by pilgrims – that is, in order to divide in a way which gives special importance to the teller-tale relationship. In modern hands, Chaucer's medieval unity disappears into dramatic relativism. But when seen as an array of exempla glossed by discursive prologue material, the *Tales* make clear doctrinal sense as a unified treatise. And it is no accident that the doctrine of this treatise is radically ethical and political, since, after all, this is the part of philosophy to which poetry is customarily assigned.[16]

In order, therefore, to understand any given medieval text, it is necessary to know where its divisions come, and what its parts are. The first question, grossly at least, is frequently decided for us by manuscript rubrication, though parts of books and parts of parts may still be left undivided, and initial letters may at least occasionally be inserted irresponsibly. The second question is more subtle, and must be answered by seeing what parts the medieval critics in fact recommended theoretically, and named in analysis. In the light of everything that has been argued thus far, one might presume a priori that parts will be discursive and sentential – that is, that they will be the kind of parts which can correspond to and fulfil the outline of an essay or a treatise, rather than the outline of a lyric, a drama, or a narrative. These are the parts which a text assignable to a part of philosophy must have; these are parts which can define, prove, refute, praise, blame, and all the rest. As an a priori, this is the presumption which explains John of Garland's willingness to treat poetry and dictamen in the same manual, since they all obey the same rules.[17] The clearest overt statement of it I know occurs in a commentary on the *Poetria nova* of Geoffrey:

Minus malum est ornare sententiam et non verba quam econtrario et hic ideo quia tota virtus materie principaliter consistit in sententia et non in verbis. Hoc etiam apparet per similitudinem: minus enim displicet pictura pulcra mulier in turpibus vestibus quam turpis in pulcris et nobilibus vestimentis.

It is less wrong to combine a decorated meaning with plain words than the reverse; this is true because what matters in material is principally the meaning and not the words. This is proved by a similitude: a picture of a pretty girl in ugly clothes displeases less than that of an ugly girl in pretty and elegant clothes.[18]

One must, therefore, find in poems parts whose sentence and whose ordering are those of a treatise, of something discursive. The parts of a treatise, most simply stated, are introduction, body, and conclusion; these correspond to the Averroistic beginning, middle, and end. Each may be further divided, of course, and the logic by which material may be ordered and presented covers and rationalizes the various material possibilities which the medieval arts of rhetoric and poetic, and the medieval commentators on poems, recommend, explain, or presume.

In medieval doctrine and practice, there are three primary ways of dealing with the parts of things: dispositio, divisio, and distinctio – arrangement, division, and distinction. I begin with dispositio. This is one of the six outlining topics which define the content of the *Poetria nova*; one of Geoffrey's commentators defines dispositio as 'ordo et distributio rerum que demonstrat quid quibus locis sit ponendum. / the order and distribution of things which shows what should be put in which places.'[19] It derives, of course, along with the other five, from Cicero. In practice, in the manuals, dispositio is more recommended than treated. Such treatment as there is deals primarily with various types of beginning, or reflects the division commonly made by commentaries into 'proponit, invocat, narrat,' or recommends the outline of dictamen.

Geoffrey of Vinsauf's treatment of dispositio is both popular and representative. After contrasting natural and artificial ordering, which differ in terms of whether or not the natural chronology of the material is followed or rearranged, Geoffrey concentrates wholly on beginnings. Artificial order is more interesting than natural order because it permits eight, rather than only one, different possible beginnings. One may begin at the middle, or at the end, or one may begin with either a proverb or an exemplum drawn from beginning, middle, or end. All these are elaborately explained and illustrated, and the commentaries repeat Geoffrey's emphasis. Nowhere, however, is there any serious discussion of whole outlines. Geoffrey assumes without argument that material has a natural shape, that this shape is based on chronology, and that the only problem complex enough to need discussion is the problem of choosing which part of this whole material should serve for a beginning, and in what way. The trust of proverbs and exempla, which is of course widely reflected in medieval theory and practice, affirms the relationship which must exist between any given material and some universal, or some illuminating comparison.[20] Doctrinally, this manual material is familiar to the point of banality; the question which one must answer is why Geoffrey is satisfied with saying it.

The Assisi commentary on the *Poetria nova* permits us to begin to find this answer. Discussing this part of Geoffrey's doctrine, which begins at 'Ordo bifurcat ...' (line 87), the commentator says:

Postquam auctor de specie materie in generali communiter, hic determinat de dispositione materie in speciali. Et quia ut dicit commentator in poetria Aristotelis, bonitas in composito est ex parte duorum, quorum unum est ordo et alterum quantitas. Ideo cum materia sit quodam compositum ex partibus que sunt principium, medium, et finis, duplex est eius bonitas: et dispositio [est] una que attenditur in ingressu materie, penes quantitatem que attenditur in progressu materie ... In quarum prima sciendum est quod quia materie specialis dispositio quantum ad ingressum consistit in ordine et ut dicit commentator poetrie Aristotelis, res quarum consistencia penes ordinem est et bonitas sue operationis penes debitum ordinationis si privetur debito ordine non consecuntur debitam sibi operationem, et huic consonat boecius in primo de consolatione dicens: quicquid precipiti via rectum deserit ordinem letos non habet exitus, ideo auctor volens ostendere quomodo penes ordinem sit materia disponenda, dividit ordinem dicens quod ordo est duplex scilicet naturalis et artificialis.

After the author [deals] with the kind of material in general as is commonly understood, here he decides about the disposition of material in particular cases. And because, as the commentator on Aristotle's *Poetics* says, the quality of composition exists in terms of two things, of which one is the order and the other is the quantity. Thus since material should be understood as something composed of parts which are the beginning, the middle, and the end, its quality is double, and the disposition [is] the one which is expected when one begins the material, in terms of the quantity one expects as the material unfolds ... With regard to the first of these it should be known that because the special disposition of the material with regard to beginning it consists of its order, therefore the author wishing to show how material should be disposed with regard to order, divides order saying that order is twofold, that is, natural and artificial – for as the commentator on Aristotle's *Poetics* says, things whose integrity depends on ordering, and whose excellence of effect depends on fitness of order, if they are deprived of their right order they will not have their proper effect, and Boethius agrees with this in the first book of the Consolation saying, whoever in haste deserts the right order will not have a happy end.[21]

From the comment as a whole it is clear that ordering is most important, that a text whose parts are out of order is seriously discomposed, and that right ordering seems above all to consist in beginning correctly, in the light of all that is to follow: the twofold goodness of a piece that has a beginning, a middle, and an end consists of order and quantity. The order, or disposition, is that which one notices at the beginning of the text – I might almost say *as* the beginning of the text – considered with regard to the quantity of material which is to follow.

This same emphasis on correct beginnings is reflected in commentary divisions of poetic texts. A common formula explains that the author 'proposes, invokes, and narrates.' Giovanni del Virgilio's version of it, in his commentary on the *Metamorphoses*, is the statement that 'liber iste more poetico dividitur in partes tres, quia primo proponit, secundo invocat, tercio narrat. / this book is divided in the poetic manner into three parts, because first it proposes, second it invokes, and third it narrates.'[22] This is a formula often repeated;[23] it also occurs in connection with other texts, such as the *Thebaid* of Statius.[24] In terms of this formula, the *Metamorphoses* is to be divided into three grossly unequal parts, with narratio occupying all but five lines of the whole poem.[25] Such an unbalanced outline reflects the strategy of dispositio, which radically emphasizes good beginning. This strategy Giovanni labels a 'mos poeticus'; presumably, since he also mentions in his accessus the forma tractandi and the forma tractatus, with explicit reference to logic, he believes that the poem is so organized as to achieve effectiveness both 'more poetice' and as a discursive treatment of its material – that is, that the poem is both rhetorically and logically effective. In addition to making sense, the parts of the poem are defined and ordered attractively. As we shall see, a part of the attractiveness which makes the 'captatio benevolentiae' possible is that the piece makes sense; at the same time, there is an attractiveness which dispositio achieves as such, and to which this formula, 'proponit, invocat, narrat,' refers. Dispositio may, of course, include other formulae. In the largest sense, it includes all artful orderings, including both the conventional artificial ones, as well as, occasionally, the natural. But whatever these orderings, they will, under medieval expectations, have beginnings which fully fit the whole, and outlines which make both discursive and rhetorical sense.

What we must define, therefore, is this kind of making sense which a text achieves primarily by right beginning, after which its parts are defined, like the commutative parts of an addition, by their correct quantity, or by their arrayed relation to that beginning. This sense is so important, so pervasive, that it is axiomatic. The critics (and the poets, of course) presume it more than they define it, and we must for its definition be largely satisfied with indirect statements and betrayals. It is a sense which the *Romance of the Rose* makes, or a series of romance adventures makes, when we find each merely miscellaneous. In their own terms, medieval critics discuss this sense by presuming that the same text may have both a forma tractandi and a forma tractatus, and be the result of a conscious poetic act of dispositio, all at the same time. But presumption is not, for a later time, explanation.

The best explanation, as such, treats an analogous case – a twelfth-century situation in which a text's meaning, its literally artificial order, and the nature of its materials are all considered together. This is Bernardus Silvestris' commentary on the *Aeneid*, to which I have already referred.[26] What Bernardus says could have been more efficiently said, if he had had the terminology which developed later. Doubtless he would have still wished to distinguish between the allegorization which he was expounding, and the exemplification which would have been normal later, but both would have been, in his terms, philosophical. The example is further complicated by the fact that Bernardus is abusing a poem which we find, on aesthetic grounds, excellently ordered and intelligible, while late medieval terminology presumes order for poems we find incoherent. But our point of view is not a part of the evidence. Once we allow for the difference between twelfth-century allegorization and later exemplary modes, we should see that Bernardus is explaining a relation between material, ordering, and meaning which is typical of most medieval texts, whether they are allegorized or not.

After explaining that the order of the *Aeneid* is artificial, Bernardus explains that it has a philosophical meaning:

Scribit ergo [Virgilius] in quantum est philosophus humane vite naturam. Modus agendi talis est: in integumento describit quid agat vel quid paciatur humanus spiritus in humano corpore temporaliter positus. Atque in hoc describendo naturali utitur ordine, atque ita utrumque ordinem narrationis observat, artificialem poeta, naturalem philosophus.

In so far as he is a philosopher, Virgil writes about the nature of human life. His mode of doing is thus: under an integument he describes what the human spirit, temporally placed in a human body, does and suffers. And in this he uses the natural order of describing, and thus he observes both orders of narration, the artificial as a poet, and the natural as a philosopher.[27]

As an allegory of the ages of man, the *Aeneid* is arranged in natural order, with the first book corresponding to the first age, the sixth to the last. I have already claimed that this relation between the literal history of Aeneas, artificially ordered, and the allegory of human life, naturally ordered, expresses the relation between modus tractandi and forma tractatus. Textually, of course, the material stays in the same order, no matter whether read literally or allegorically, but that same order is being subjected to three different and as it were contrapuntal readings – the allegory of the ages of man, and the history of the wanderings of Aeneas, and the narratio which juxtaposes the fall of Troy as told and the court of Dido as audience, and implicit equivalent. What gets all this to happen at the same time, of course, is dispositio. The manuals presume this dispositio, and implicitly define it, in their discussion of it almost entirely in terms of beginnings; the commentaries do the same when they divide poems so unevenly into proposition, invocation, and narration. In both cases what they are really presuming is a beginning which will make one expect, in the material to follow, all of the discursive discussion of theme and distinctio of parts of theme which the material is intended to convey, and of which it is in quantity a sufficient treatment. What Bernardus' comment really claims, behind and beyond the specific claim that the *Aeneid* is allegorical, is that all meaningful texts are, at the level of meaning, naturally ordered. They have beginnings, middles, and ends – and their beginnings create the expectations in terms of which their great middles (since medieval endings are usually nothing but stoppings) are adequate in size and content. This claim presumes, of course, that the texts involved are of a character which can be thus taken as naturally ordered, as sententiously begun, and as consummated by an adequate middle. Once again, the implicit, and in Bernardus' case, explicit, presumption is that the text under consideration is essentially a treatise, a discursive thing, treating a discursive subject whose sentence can be expressed by a proverb or exemplified in the comparison of an exemplum.

In saying all this, and in using Bernardus' most telling comment as my defining exemplum, I am in no sense claiming that all medieval literature must be allegorized or must be reduced to some merely abstract sententia. What I am claiming is rather that the relation between a poem and its universality, which exists for all great poetry in some manner, no matter when that poetry is written or read, is for medieval poetry a relation which exists in a particularly explicit way, and which both can and must be seen in terms which can be stated discursively. The literal material of most poetry is concrete, in all eras. But it makes a great deal of difference to our understanding of Hamlet whether we begin by taking the concrete details of his life as data composing the clinical description of an Oedipus complex, as the narratio of an Aristotelian tragedy, as an exemplum of a prince's revenge, or as the biographical excuse for great poetic soliloquy. None of these choices, except perhaps the Oedipal one, either suggests or requires an allegorization. None of them rejects, though each in its way may distort, the passionate concreteness of Hamlet himself. But each of them, once accepted, does determine a great many things about our sense of the play, its parts, its logic, its ordering, and the kinds of critical generalizations we are willing to admit as intelligible statements about it. Thus, I am claiming that the medieval critics' discussion and practice of dispositio, in the light of all the other definitions which logically precede and give context to this dispositio, suggest that late medieval poetry, which can be expected to be in general about ethics, will be so in terms of relations between concrete exemplary materials and the ethical definitions and generalizations to which one is guided by that material's beginnings and the orderings of its parts. Thus, after an elaborate statement, in his accessus to the *Metamorphoses*, defining changes as the subject and material of the poem, Arnulf of Orléans is careful to emphasize the same concept in his discussion of its opening lines.[28] Thus Chaucer begins his *Canterbury Tales* with a long, periodic proverb ('What that April ... than longen ...'), a knight, and a knight's tale; these introduce, predict, and outline a collection of tales whose explicit concern is the working out of structures in this interim life of pilgrimage, whose best philosopher of tale collections is the knight himself, and whose implicit foundation is that life of promised love named marriage – a love which Chaucer's initial lines make us expect instead of pilgrimage, and which his collection of tales gives us as the meaning and achievement of this pilgrimage. The Wife of Bath begins her talk with a promise to speak of 'wo that is in marryage'; all that she says will, in fact, outline most coherently in terms of this announced theme. In each of these cases the work begins with some kind of explicit or implicit announcement of overall subject; in each case the subject is some truth involving human behaviour; in each case the material which follows best outlines itself in terms of a logical and discursive treatment of that truth of human behaviour. Dispositio, therefore, most properly preoccupies itself with beginnings, because it is from the beginning that all else hangs – medieval poems, like modern newspaper articles, depend on their headlines.

Commentary analysis of these matters, as distinguished from the mere announcement of them, is rare. We have to do, as I have said, with something more axiomatic and presumed than merely possible and to be argued for. There are, however, a few hints. A commentary on the *Thebaid* of Statius, for instance, in announcing the conventional dispositio in terms of proposition, invocation, and narration, makes a connection between this schema and the forma tractandi:

Et notandum quod satis ydonee quasi quadam prefatione prescribitur breviter partiendo in tria, scilicet in propositionem, invocationem, et narrationem, prohemiorum officia eleganter exequendo. Nam lectores benivolos, dociles, et attentos facit. Proponit ubi dicit *Fraternas acies* et ibi reddit dociles. Invocat ubi dicit *Unde iubetis* etc., et tunc attentos facit. Narrat ibi *Impia iam merita* et ibi facit benivolos. Vel ubi [cod ibi] proponit de qua re dicturus est, ibi attentos; ubi invocat, benivolos. Nam tunc quoddammodo manifestatur modus tractandi, et in modo tractandi sunt semper lectores benivoli. In narratione vero dociles.

And it should be noted that it is begun, fitly enough by way of preface, by briefly dividing into three, that is, into a proposal, an invocation, and a narration, elegantly accomplishing the office of prologue. For it makes the readers benevolent, teachable, and attentive. He proposes where he says *fraternal war* and there he renders his audience teachable. He invokes where he says *whence you command*, and then he makes them attentive. He narrates at *now impious merit* and there he makes them benevolent. Or, where he proposes what he is going to tell, there he makes the audience attentive; where he invokes, he makes them benevolent. For then in a certain manner the mode of the treatment is manifested, and in the mode of the treatment readers are always benevolent; and in narration they are teachable.[29]

It is immediately clear, as one compares this gloss with the passage it explains, that the commentator confronts in all this an elaborate and repeated statement of the subject and intention of the whole book. The *Thebaid* will treat a part of a canonical body of material,[30] and will treat it in a certain way. This introductory material renders the hearer teachable, receptive, and attentive – the three emotional postures constitute a rhetorical commonplace; by the principle of parallel systems, the commentator feels obligated to equate these three with the three parts of the poem's beginning. It is not, I think nearly so important which of the three emotional postures corresponds to which of the three parts of the introduction, as it is that the two triads must correspond. The commentator argues the relationship in two different ways, as an allegorist will give multiple interpretations of the same passage.

It is important, however, to try to understand how the manifestation of the modus tractandi, in that part of the poem which 'invocat,' renders readers 'benivoli.' What the invocation in fact does is distinguish the book which Statius intends to write both from the whole body of material of which it is a part, and from the praise of Domitian which is alternative to it, and which Statius promises to perform later. The irony of his reference to Domitian was not entirely lost on medieval readers, but the mode of praise is as much posited by irony as by direct statement. In addition, the description of content which is the material of Statius' distinction is itself a list, or a series of lists, of topics, events, and themes. Causal, and even chronological, connections tend to disappear, and we are left with sets of homologous parts, allusively specified. The commentator nowhere defines the modus tractandi as such, though he does say that the *Thebaid* is a heroic poem, written in imitation of Virgil.[31]

Obviously, Statius' invocation includes, by implication, promise of various modi: of praise, of heroic metre, of division, perhaps even of definition, by virtue of the abstract reference to 'geminis tyrannis' (line 34). This introduction promises what in fact occurs – a series of rather static, oratorically elaborated set pieces, each of which could be analysed as one element in a distinctio under the title 'Fraternas acies alternaque regna.' It promises material, subject matter, themes, certainly – but more, it promises these things, as it were, as treated in a certain way, and related (or strung together) in a certain way. The reader is made to expect both content and modality – they are probably two faces of the same thing, but the critics distinguish them, and so should we. What makes the reader 'benivolus' is that all his expectations are taken care of at once – generic ones, content ones, even the occasional one which involved awareness of the existence of Domitian, though this, for the medieval reader, would have been generalized into an ethical occasionality, more than an immediately political one.

Medieval poems, one must admit, do not always begin in the exercise of these precise, literal formulae. We have instead the dream vision; we have Chrétien's autobiographical and occasional introductions, we have Chaucer's springtime, we have Arthur's father's love affair. But these formulae must be expected to remain in mind, especially because they continue so explicitly important for dictamen.[32] They must be expected to be implicit, at the level of forma tractandi, and therefore present in the forma tractatus even when that is complicated by multiple strategies, as in the *Aeneid* for Bernardus.

The second medieval strategy, through which one may understand the full shape and significance of the forma tractatus of any medieval literary text, is the strategy of divisio. I have already noted several times how pervasive divisio is, as an instrument of analysis. One understands something in the naming of its parts, and in specifying just where one part stops and another part begins. This habit of analysis, and answeringly of composition, appears in all aspects of medieval culture, from initial letters in medieval manuscripts to the additive articulation of gothic architecture to the strip farming of medieval manors. In preaching, and in the exegetical and exemplum traditions which relate to preaching, the strategy of divisio was, in fact, elaborated into something with elegances of its own, based on intricate rhymes.[33] All this is much too well known, and much too well understood, to need more than the most cursory illustration here, and I shall limit myself to a few examples in which the meaning of divisio for medieval critics and poets seems especially telling. A few principles seem to stand out.

First, at least grossly, division demarcates and distinguishes parts whose character and nature fit the overall character of the book. The commentaries on the *Metamorphoses* of Arnulf and Giovanni, both of whom emphasize mutationes in their accessus, do divide the poem into its changes, totally ignoring changes in level which might be implied by framing devices, that is, by the inclusion of one tale in another by virtue of its being told by one of Ovid's characters, instead of by Ovid himself. Bersuire, who begins his accessus talking of fables, proceeds similarly to divide the text into fables.

Second, division tends to distinguish parts which are themselves whole, in a way which, as named and distinguished, is quite static. Medieval parts relate additively, not dynamically; therefore medieval distinction and definition of parts tends quite naturally to identify parts appropriate to this additive kind of relationship. A particularly neat example of this tendency is Bersuire's way of dividing Ovid's fables for allegorization – the result of his analysis is a set of discrete parts of a narrative plot, which exist as more or less independent events, each having its meaning.[34] Again, a commentary on the *Metamorphoses* divides the opening lines of book II, which deal with the palace of the Sun, by dividing: 'primo describit eam materialiter, secundo formaliter. / first he describes it in terms of material, second in terms of form.'[35] This distinction depends on Ovid's phrase, 'materiam superabat opus / the work outdoes its material' (II.5), of course, but it strengthens it by naming the separate categories, and transforms a mere transition from doors to their iconography into two separable modalities.

Occasionally, there is disagreement about divisio; it is clear that division is, for the medieval critic, a serious instrument of analysis, existing in a self-conscious tradition. One could illustrate this fact virtually at random in the commentaries on any medieval work which was popular enough to attract attention; I have chosen for example a brief array of glosses on book V of the *Thebaid* of Statius. Disagreement is most clearly put by a commentary now at Yale:

Iste est quintus [cod quartus] liber in quod proponuntur quedam carmina qui secundum quosdam duobus capitulis consumatur sed secundum magistrum meum preceptorem quinque capitulis consumatur.

This is the fifth book in which are presented certain songs, which according to some is divided into two chapters, but according to my teacher is divided into five.[36]

The 'quosdam' to whom the commentator refers could be people directly, or glossed or rubricated books, but the reference to 'magistrum meum' is clear evidence of a school tradition, to which presumably this commentator belongs. Other glosses divide the fifth book of the *Thebaid* into two, three, and five parts, reflecting and expanding on the disagreement which my first commentator reports. The five-part division is as follows:

Pulsa sitis: Huius quintem [sic] distinctionis quinque sunt capitula. In primo ysiph' adrasto suam commemorat originem et patriam et scelus lempniad'. In secundo qualiter regni regnum recepit et qualiter iason ex ea duos filios genuit. In tertio qualiter exulavit divulgato quod pater suus regnaret. In quarto qualiter archemorum a serpente interfectum invenerit et planxerit. In quinto qualiter sui eam cognoverunt filii et ipsa eos et qualiter greci ligurgum planxerunt.

There are five chapters in this fifth distinction. In the first part Hypsipyle tells Adrastus about her origin and homeland and the treason of Lemnos; in the second how she took command of the kingdom and how Jason got two sons from her; in the third, how she was exiled when it became known that her father was reigning; in the fourth, how she found Archemorus killed by the serpent and mourned for him; in the fifth, how she and her sons recognized each other and how the Greeks mourned Lycurgus.[37]

In this divisio, there is at least a slight notice given to what I might call dramatic enclosure – that is, the fact that some of this material is narrated by the author, and other of it within the book by Hypsiphile – but this notice is neither consistent nor fully adequate. The first chapter clearly is something 'commemoratur.' But the rest may not be; they are all mentioned in the same way, with the same formula 'qualiter,' even though some are dramatically enclosed and others are not. Moreover, the five chapters are rhetorically separated. The commentator gives no notice to the fact that these events are a part of the same story, but divides into essentially additive bits. In so doing he is consistent with what usually happens in commentary.

There are, however, rare exceptions. The additive character of the parts of a medieval division is dominant, but occasionally quite sequential divisiones occur. This is true of a gloss which divides book V of the *Thebaid* into three parts:

Pulsa sitis: Hic est quintus liber huius voluminis que quamquam habeat nobilem materiam tamen distinctus est in tria capitula. In quorum primo ponit interrogationem Adrasti at ysiphylem ut narraret sua infortunia, suos casus, et eius originem et patriam. Ac et etiam responsum ysiphylos et suam narrationem ad petitionem Adrasti. In secundo autem capitulo describitur mors archemori quem ysiphile reliquerat inter flores ut monstraret grecis langiam fontem. In tertio vero et ultimo ponitur trena et lamentatio facta de morte Archimori.

This is the fifth book of this volume, which, although it has noble material, nevertheless it is divided into three chapters. In which first it puts the questioning of Adrastus to Hypsipyle, that she should tell about her bad luck, her misfortunes, her origin and her homeland. In the second chapter is described the death of Archemorus, whom Hypsipyle left among the flowers to show the Greeks the fountain of Langia. In the third and last is put the mourning and lamentation made for the death of Archemorus.[38]

This I take to be the exception that proves the rule. Medieval authors were capable of sequential narrative, and medieval commentators were capable of noticing its existence. But neither medieval poetry nor medieval commentary, generally considered, held such a thing as of first importance.

Division into two parts occurs in a manuscript now in Florence; it is not given all in one place, but is clear from two separate glosses:

Pulsa: Iste liber in 2o capitula dividitur. In primo continetur orationem quam ista fecit ad regem adrastum.

This book is divided into two chapters. In the first is contained the speech which she made to King Adrastus.

This gloss occurs at the beginning of the book. Later, at 'Talia Lerneis' (line 499), we have the second one:

In iste capitulo continetur qualiter puer ille alpheltes est sopitus in herbis, ista stante cum ista gentis [sic], mortuus est et interitum serpentis, etc.

In this chapter is contained [the story of] how that child Opheltes, who was laid down in the grass, while Hypsipyle was standing with the people of Adrastus, died, and how the serpent was killed, etc.[39]

Of these divisions, the one into two, which separates Hypsiphile's story from the events which follow, is the most plausible to the modern mind, because it is a division which most respects the formal character of the text, considered as a piece of writing, and distinguishing reported speech from reported action. But the fundamental medieval principle of division, as we have seen, is not textual but sentential, and in these terms the division into five separate bits of action, each single in that each is susceptible to a very particular and singular ethical judgment, is probably the one most typical in general of medieval analysis by division. It is difficult, of course, to be absolutely sure. Critics universally made divisions, even when they did not always make the same ones. When they discussed the question at all, they claimed that their divisions were based on, and separated, sententia or distinct meanings. These meanings they sometimes named, defined, discussed, or allegorized; more often, they simply presumed them. In attempting to get behind all this to the fundamental reason of it all, one must necessarily act inductively. In these terms, I conclude that the most important principle one must see in this habit of analysis by division is that there must have existed, in the medieval awareness of the material of their poetry, a firm conviction that the material involved had a unity, an integrity, an essence, a stability, so strong that analysis by mere division would reveal and not obscure its essence.

I gain support for this conclusion from my third topic of division, that is, the distinctio. Already in this material presenting medieval analysis by division, the word has appeared. Parts of things may be called their distinctiones. The distinctio, I would suggest, is both structurally and as an actual tradition of medieval text the single most powerful aid to criticism that we have, as we attempt to understand medieval texts in medieval fashion. I have already had a good deal to say about the distinctio, in a number of places – most to the point here, I suggested that its structure significantly informs a proper understanding of the forma tractandi, or the complex and multifold manner of thinking which precedes and determines the actual textuality, or forma tractatus, of a medieval poem. I further suggested that the way of thinking which the distinctio prescribes, that is, in terms of an array of parts or topics under a single name, topic, concept, or thing, is a way of thinking that plausibly can conceive of definition in terms of a normative array of parts or topics.

In a way, it might seem more plausible to argue that the distinctio is essentially a device of the forma tractatus, and not of the forma tractandi. A distinctio is, after all, textually a list of topics, and therefore more or less explicitly an outline. Many of them even look, as they are preserved particularly in twelfth- and thirteenth-century manuscripts, like outlines, with their topics and sub-topics drawn schematically across the page. One might therefore suppose that the distinctio is simply the other side of, or the result of, divisio, and thus that it merely names the parts of a poem's actual text. This is sometimes, and to some extent, true; the most obvious large vernacular example is the *Confessio amantis*, whose outline (or rather, most of whose outline) is a distinctio on the seven capital sins. All divisiones of medieval texts discriminate an array of parts of a whole. In terms of the usual medieval sensibility, these parts can be expected to form an array, rather than, for example, a process. They are likely to be nameable, either modally, as in the example 'materialiter-formaliter' given above, or in terms of substantives. Thus divisiones are implicit, or explicit, distinctiones, which come into existence as we give names to the parts and to the whole which they compose. I shall eventually argue that the most promising way to deal with a medieval text is to do precisely this – determine its parts and their names, and the name of the whole of which they are the arrayed parts. Criticism and interpretation can then proceed in a way fair both to the medieval sensibility and to modern needs for explanation by rationalizing the relationships which this naming of parts makes visible. One might say, therefore, that what I recommend is essentially an analysis of outlines, and therefore an analysis of forma tractatus.

In a way, I do. An analysis by division, and thus necessarily an analysis of outline (and therefore forma tractatus), is the point at which all medieval analysis of texts must begin. But this dividing is only the first step. More is distinguished by a medieval poem than the parts of its outline – the parts which define the forma tractatus exist to permit one to discover as well the forma tractandi. I discussed the distinctio in chapter two, under the topic of the forma tractandi, because the distinctio clearly had to do both with the mode definitivus and the mode divisivus. Both these modes, according to the medieval critics, are features of the forma tractandi, and are therefore pre-textual and logically prior to and separate from the forma tractatus. At the same time, I discuss the distinctio here, in connection with discussion of the forma tractatus, because it is clearly and literally the result of division, and exists as an outline. It specifies parts, which may indeed be literal parts. When they are, then textuality is implicated, and the distinctio may indeed define, or name, the parts of a poem's forma tractatus.

To admit that the distinctio is significant both for the mode divisivus of the forma tractandi and for the divisions of the forma tractatus would seem to betray my distinction as one without a difference. It does not. There is indeed a difference, and a crucially important one. But it is a medieval one, which is not easy to explain. I begin to try to do so by introducing and discussing a few representative distinctiones. In so doing, I respect the medieval usage of the word, and include examples involving a larger range than merely the distinguished meanings of a biblical word or thing, but I think I remain completely fair to the essential meaning of the thing, which is rooted in the concept of an array, or more particularly a normative array, of parts, aspects, or items, which constitute a whole, whether material or conceptual.

At the simplest and historically most primitive level, distinctiones were indeed lists which distinguished the meanings of biblical things or concepts. They tended first to occur in connection with commentaries on the Psalms. Thus, in the Psalter commentary of Hugh of St Cher, which is a compilation made between about 1230 and 1235,[40] there are eight kinds of good kisses and four kinds of bad kisses.[41] 'Comparatur justus palmae, propter multas proprietates / The just are compared to a palm, because of many properties' (f 245r). There are seven kinds of law (f 41v); eleven kinds of good flowers and three kinds of bad flowers (f 65v). There are few surprises in any of this; to the modern sensibility, these lists are simply quaint lists. They become interesting, however, as soon as they are taken seriously. The kinds of law, for instance, are based on a biblical concordance. If the Bible contains the phrase 'lex peccati,' or the phrase 'lex membrorum,' then the list will contain both the law of sin and the law of one's members which is the tinder or kindling of sin. But once the Bible verses are collected and arrayed, the list of kinds exist, and we have the laws of charity, truth, sin, the kindling of sin, Moses, nature, and the New Testament. In philosophical terms, these might seem too many, but here they are, and they must be taken as both distinct and exhaustive.

The list of the kinds of rule is similarly significant:

Rex regnum, nauta navem, sessor equum, dux bellum, paterfamilias familiam, magister scholares, ductor caecum, pastor oves, abbas vel prior claustrum, anima membra, ratio cor.

The king [rules] the kingdom, the sailor his ship, the rider his horse, the captain the battle, the father his family, the teacher his students, the guide the blind man, the shepherd his sheep, the abbot his cloister, the soul the body's members, and reason the heart. (f 211r)

Again, as in the case of the law, this list is based on a collection of Bible verses, in which some kind of activity of directing or rule is mentioned. But the list, as a distinctio, has significance as definition. One should properly consider, thus, just what definition of sovereignty would result, as an essay in political science, from accepting it as the unitary power which exercises these, precisely these, and only these functions. Inversely, one can consider just what definition of obedience results from attempting to combine, in a single conceptualization, the submission of emotions, parts of the body, individual people and groups of people, animals, and that semi-inanimate object, a ship. Implicitly, the distinctio asserts precisely these definitions, and by asserting them insists upon the combinative and at least conceptualist philosophy capable of entertaining them.

In the same way, one gains a vivid sense of the grimness of certain religious sensibilities from a joyless distinctio on joy:

Gaudium: Aliud est gaudium corporale aliud spirituale. Gaudium corporale est risus, iocus, et cetere delectationes carnales. Gaudium spirituale est spes sicut ait apostolus: Spe gaudentes, in tribulatione pacientes. Vides quia potest fieri ut tristantes carnaliter spiritualiter gaudeamus in spe.

Joy: Corporeal joy is one thing, spiritual joy is another. Corporeal joy is laughter, joking, and other carnal delights. Spiritual joy is hope, as the apostle said: Rejoicing in hope, patient in tribulation. You see that it can happen that we rejoice in hope, sorrowing carnally.[42]

Similarly, one learns that beauty may be something quite other than the aesthetic from a distinctio on pulcritudo:

Pulcritudo multiplex est, una moralis que est ipsa morum reverencia [cod rᵃ] vel honestas, qua ad bonum rectificantur, alia spiritualis que est anime puritas, tertia intellectualis que est angelica sanctitas, 4ᵃ celestis que est beatitudo in patria, 5 supersubstantialis que est divina. Moralis namque est in vite honestate, spiritualis in virtutum varietate, intellectualis in excellente puritate, celestis in superne contemplacionis aviditate, supersubstantialis vero in ardenti dei caritate etc.

Beauty is multiple: the moral one is respectability of behaviour or honesty, by which people are reconciled to the good; another is the spiritual which is purity of soul; the third is intellectual which is angelic holiness; the fourth is celestial which is blessedness in the fatherland; the fifth is supersubstantial which is divine. The moral consists of honesty of life, the spiritual in the variety of virtues, the intellectual in excellent purity, the celestial in longing for supernal contemplation, the supersubstantial in the ardent love of God, etc. (f 274v)

All these distinctiones are formally of the simplest kind. Each simply arrays the parts of some whole.

More elaborately, distinctiones make comparisons. I give two examples: one rather simple one from Hugh's commentary; and one considerably more elaborate one from the commentary of Raoul on the *Anticlaudianus*. Hugh is explaining that 'apostoli et viri spirituales dicuntur coeli' for the following reasons:

Quia sunt alti: Philip. 3d. Nostra conversatio in coelis est. Job 7c. Suspendium elegit anima mea.
Quia semper volvuntur, et nunquam retrocedunt. Philip 3c. Posteriorum oblitus, ad anteriora me extendo. Ezech. 1d. Animalia ibant, et non revertebantur. Econtrario mali facti sunt retrorsum, et non in ante. Jerem. 7c.
Quia licet moveantur, nunquam tamen lassantur ...
Quia moventur ordinate ...
Quia ab eis descendit pluvia doctrinae ...

Apostles and spiritual men are said to be of the sky ... because they are high. Philippians 3: Our conversation is in the heavens. Job 7: My soul chooses hanging.

Because they always turn, and never go back. Philippians 3: Forgetful of those things which are behind, I press forward to what is before. Ezekiel 1: The living creatures went, and did not turn back. On the contrary the evil are made backward, and not forward, Jeremiah 7.
Because though they are moved, yet they are never tired ...
Because they move regularly ...
Because from them descends the rain of doctrine.[43]

There are a great many distinctiones of this type; in literary terms it is straightforwardly an analysis of a metaphor. Considered as representative of its type, it makes one see the intimate and wholly natural relationship which obtained between thinking which is formally analogical, and the discursive, analytical, logical presumptions because of which distinctiones were made and collected. Structurally, the pictures of gods and goddesses in the *Fulgentius metaforalis* are nothing more than distinctiones of this type, with the difference that the distinctio has one extra name, and the use of rhyme in these pictures, and the citation of confirming quotations, strengthen the resemblance.[44] One step further than this kind of comparison is that based on what I call the principle of parallel systems. This I can illustrate with a distinctio on 'artifex' from the commentary of Raoul de Longchamp on the *Anticlaudianus*.

Materia huius libri sunt quattuor artifices et quattuor artificum opera. Est enim artifex Deus, artifex natura, artifex fortuna, artifex culpa.

   Deus autem specialiter dicitur artifex eorum, quae facit de nihilo, ut sunt spiritus et animae; unde Deus dicitur proprie creare et eius operatio dicitur creatio.

   Natura autem proprie dicitur artifex eorum, quae sunt ex praeiacente materia ...

   Fortuna sive casus, quia pro eodem hic accipitur, est artifex eorum, quae casualiter fiunt vel eveniunt, ut si rusticus fodiens agrum inveniat thesaurum. Est autem fortuna sive casus inopinatus rei eventus ex causis confluentibus, uti patet in praemisso exemplo. Inventio enim thesauri est inopinatus rei eventus. Causae confluentes sunt ea, quae ad hoc concurrunt, ut accessus rustici ad thesaurum, terrae fossio et similia. Huius artificis opera sunt libertas, servitus, divitiae, adversitas, prosperitas.

   Artifex culpa malus artifex est, cuius opera sunt diversa vitiorum genera.

   Hos quattuor artifices et eorum operationes intellexerunt auctores per quattuor Saturni filios: Jovem, Junonem, Neptunium, Plutonem. Per Jovem intelligitur Deus et eius opera. Jupiter enim 'iuvans pater' interpretatur, vel 'ẏa' – pater' id est universalis pater; 'ya' graece, universale latine. Universa autem fiunt auctoritate Dei. Per Junonem intelligitur natura. Juno enim interpretatur 'iuvans monos,' quidquid enim in novitate essentiae procreatur, mediante natura fit. Per Neptunum, qui 'nube tonans' interpretatur et 'deus maris' dicitur, artifex fortuna intelligitur et eius opera.

Fortuna enim per prospera blanditur et amicatur, per adversa inimicatur et adversatur. Pluto dicitur a polis, quod est pluralitas. Per Plutonem ergo, qui pluralitas interpretatur, artifex culpa intelligitur et eius opera. Quia, ut dicit Boethius, omne malum infinitum, bonum vero finitum, et vitiorum est infinitas et diversitas, virtutum vero est identitas.

Haec autem quattuor operum genera a Saturno, id est a summo Deo procedunt, primum per creationem, secundum per generationem, tertium per gubernationem, quartum per permissionem.

The material of this book consists of four artificers, and four works of artificers. For there is the artificer God, the artificer nature, the artificer fortune, and the artificer guilt. God is said especially to be the artificer of those things which he made from nothing, such as the spirit and the soul, whence God is properly said to create and his work is called creation. Nature is properly called the artificer of those things which are made from pre-existent material. Fortune or accident, since these two are taken as the same, is the artificer of things which are made or happen by chance, as if a peasant digging in a field might find a treasure. Thus fortune or accident is the unexpected occurrence of a thing from confluent causes, as is shown in the above example. For the finding of the treasure is an unexpected occurrence of a thing. The confluent causes are those things which happen together at the right time, as the coming of the peasant to the treasure, the digging in the ground, and the rest. The works of this artificer are liberty, servitude, riches, adversity, prosperity. The artificer guilt is a bad artificer, whose works are the diverse kinds of vices. The authors understood these four artificers and their operations in terms of the four children of Saturn: Jupiter, Juno, Neptune, and Pluto. By Jupiter is understood God and his works. For Jupiter means helping father or *ya pater* that is universal father – *ya* in Greek is universal in Latin; for everything is made by the authority of God. By Juno is understood nature. Juno means helping new things; whatever is procreated in newness of essence is made by mediating Nature. By Neptune, who means thundering in cloud and who is called god of the sea is understood the artificer of fortune and its works. For Fortune soothes and gains friendship with prosperity, but creates dejection and hostility with adversity. Pluto derives from *polis*, that is plurality. Therefore by Pluto who means plurality is understood the artificer of guilt and its works, because, as Boethius says, all evil is without limit, but the good is definite. There is an infinity and diversity of vices, but identity of virtues. Thus these four kinds of works proceed from Saturn, that is, from the highest God – first by creation, second by generation, third by governance, and fourth by permission.[45]

The first part of this example is purely a distinctio on artifex – a list of kinds, perhaps more elaborately explained than some, but thoroughly conventional. It becomes unusual because the author goes on to make a seriatim parallel with another received system, that is, with the list of the children of Saturn, in their usual order. This same analogical procedure, worked in the other direction, is the basis of the *Fulgentius metaforalis* – the Fulgentius 'metaphored' of John Ridewall. There one began with the pagan gods, in their normal order, and applied to them the parts of the virtue of prudence. In both cases what has happened is that one organized system of information, taken as a whole system, is placed in parallel with another, as its equivalent and its interpretation. This placing in parallel is one kind of the general poetic procedure of assimilatio, which is the chief subject of the chapter to follow. Here, I am not concerned with the parallel placing as such, but rather with the fact that two systems are involved in it, because the difference that obtains between these two systems, or any two analogous ones, is the difference that distinguishes between the distinctio of the forma tractandi and the divisio-distinctio of the forma tractatus. Any text which contains parts, obviously, may have these parts named by an outline, and the topics of this outline will name a distinctio of the forma tractatus. But this outline, as such, may be a system in parallel to another system – that external system, parallel from the outside, will contain the distinctio of the forma tractandi. The medieval sense of poetic form – that is, that a text has both a forma tractatus and a forma tractandi – necessarily implies that it also has two outlines, one internal and intrinsic, and one external and parallel.

I shall eventually argue that the unity of Malory's eight-part chronicle of the rise and fall of the society of the Arthurian Round Table is not based on its own plot, but rather on the fact that its eight parts operate in parallel to a larger distinctio of universal history, which itself has eight parts. I have already argued, in another place, that the unity of the *Canterbury Tales* is similarly based on a parallel which operates between its parts and an external distinctio, in this case a distinctio of the kinds of changes which stories can sententially express. In neither case do I deny, in any way, the primacy of the concrete particularity of Malory's or Chaucer's narrative; I rather affirm that it is, as particular, exemplary, and that its exemplary character is defined by a name which is contained in an independently existing distinctio. Of this relation between a text and an external distinctio, the discussion of artifex just quoted is an example which might properly be labelled allegorizing, in that the equations asserted are to the modern mind arbitrary, and can be classified as symbolic. The relationship between the last book of Malory's *Morte* and the apocalyptic end of the world is not arbitrary at all – the one is certainly a microcosm of the other, and an analogous example. But in both cases what is important, for my purposes here, is the parallel itself, and not the basis of it. What is important is the fact that two layers exist; one of the textuality of a story, or in the conventional textuality of the received medieval image of the pagan gods, and the other in some essential distinctio, whether it be that of kinds of change, kinds of artificer, or ages in world history.

Distinctiones, therefore, may indeed be found both at the level of the forma tractandi and at the level of forma tractatus, though because they are schematic, often abstract, and always in some way definitive, they tend more properly to be associated with the forma tractandi. In a very few cases, as I have said, the two levels are merged. Both are assimilated into the forma tractandi in the case of Canticles as Aegidius Romanus argued it, and in the case of *Piers Plowman* as I suppose it. Both are assimilated into the forma tractatus in the case of the *Confessio amantis*, which wears its sentential outline ostentatiously as its textual outline.[46] On the other hand, the two are argued as separate, in an overt and unmistakable manner, by Bernardus Silvestris in his commentary on the *Aeneid*, in his discussion of natural and artificial orderings, and in connection with his assertion of an allegorical interpretation of the poem. This separateness, I think, is the normative case, though it does not often in the later Middle Ages include the allegoresis normal for twelfth-century commentators. What it does require is merely that a text have, as I have said, two outlines. The repeated usefulness of both the concept and the material of distinctio, in understanding the related procedures and modes such as dispositio, divisio, and the mental act divisivus, is testimony to this persistent doubleness of outline. At one level an outline names literal parts, and them only, and constitutes the forma tractatus; at the other, the outline gives names to those parts which understand them as exemplary, and as related to one another under some single general topic, trope, or thing – this constitutes the forma tractandi. This second outline always takes the form of a distinctio. The first may, or it may be merely a miscellaneous list – the fact that such a miscellaneous list is possible, as the outline 'per divisionem' of a medieval poem, is the basis of our modern problems with the unification of medieval poems. The distinctio which constitutes the forma tractandi is logically pre-textual. In terms of the literal existence of medieval manuscripts, this distinctio should, and very often does, have an existence apart from the poetic text to which it is parallel. As a text itself, it has a unity, a coherence, and a significance, which are obviously logical, sentential, reasonable. Distinctiones are not plots; they do not express (though they may analyse) processes. They rather array the parts of wholes, and in so doing have normative power to express definitions. The connection between the distinctio which constitutes a text's forma tractandi, and the divisio which names a text's literal parts, is ideally, if often only implicitly, achieved by dispositio, which arranges for a text's beginning that it shall name the governing distinctio.

It is vitally important that we not collapse these levels. In a sense, it is true that a poem's meaning is also a part of the text; in medieval terms, it is true that all the kinds of causality are real – formal, final, material, and efficient – and that a poem which is classifiable under ethics should in a manner be philosophical, textually as well as by implication. Nevertheless the principle of parallel is most important. Just as the universe of a poem is composed of parts, so the universe to which the poem belongs is composed of parts, and all these parts must first be separate and whole in themselves before they can be assembled into a universe. The medieval logic of commentary operates by a continual process of looking in and looking back – looking at a text itself, and then looking for some external similar which will furnish the explanation. The fact that the distinctio of a poem's forma tractandi has existence independent of the poem itself is what gives it the right and the power to interpret and unify the poem; it is this dialectic between a poem's textuality and an independent outline of its meaning which makes medieval literature so baffling to a new critical or merely aesthetic sensibility. It is the same dialectic, on the other hand, which tempts merely philosophical or theological critics to affirm only the distinctio or the definition, and throw the poem away. But it is the dialectic, once accepted as itself, which explains the fact that the particulars of medieval poetry seem to have, in themselves, far more normative power than most. It is this dialectic which explains, for instance, the valid moral delight which one gains in putting one's own contemporaries in their fit places in Dante's *Commedia*; it is a delight which exists in recognition of a world in which one has, not only such truths as one can believe, but also dependable relationships between systems.

Thus the primal act of criticism is the relating of separate things, rather than the search for something limited to the integrity of a single text. I can perhaps make this critical necessity most clear by means of an analogy. In Shakespeare's *King Lear*, as we all know, the main plot of Lear and the sub-plot of the Duke of Gloucester are analogous. In addition, the storm which batters Lear's body and the insanity which racks his mind are, by the very power of the lines he utters, made equivalent. Both in the relation between Lear and the storm, and in the relation between Lear and Gloucester, we can find almost infinite complexity. When we say that one 'is' or means the other, we say nothing which compromises the existence of either; rather, we enrich both by connecting each to the other, in a relationship of mutual interpretation. In so doing, we are trusting to a fundamental organizing feature which is true in the microcosm of the play's world – a feature which we rightly honour as one of the bases of the greatness of Shakespearean drama.

The difference between *Lear* and most late medieval poetry is that the cosmos is larger. For *Lear*, the analogies work within the world of the play; for medieval poetry, they work for the world as a whole. Thus, for any given late medieval poem, one must expect parallels which exist outside the poem but are no less present to it than Gloucester is to Lear. For the medieval situation, one must imagine a play of Lear which contains only the sub-plot or only the main plot, but not both – but which nevertheless has both by being in parallel with something outside the play. Outside, of course, there is the whole world of beasts, and histories, and other books, and philosophy, and God. Outside, there are the distinctiones of the forma tractandi.

Renaissance criticism makes much of the poet as vates, and even as creator; the poems made by Renaissance poets are whole microcosms, which explicate in terms of the same complex intricacies of parallelism which medieval thinkers applied to their ethics, their natural history, their astronomy, their Bible, and their classical heritage. The crucial difference between the Middle Ages and the Renaissance, however, is one which has made us much more willing to accept these structured parallelisms from the one than from the other. Renaissance poems, even unfinished ones like the *Faerie Queene*, explicate in terms of coherences and parallels expressed internally. One may need information about various occasional matters in order to understand the literal sense of the Red Crosse Knight's adventures, but everything past the literal sense is in the poem, explicit in the shape of event or implicit in the coherences and parallels which the poem itself creates. The poem is its own commentary, and critics who attempt too rigorously to apply their own usually find that they have been reductionist, or partial. The same is even more true of a play like *Lear*, with its two plots, or like *Hamlet*, with its Chinese-box-like series of enclosed revenges, or of the poetic cosmos of *Paradise Lost*. Modern critics find it wholly natural that the poems submit to being read as poems – that is, as a species of thing separable from such other possibilities as science, theology, and politics – and can follow their complex internal workings with no axiomatic trouble.

Medieval poetry is much less self-contained. Whereas even unfinished poems like the *Faerie Queene* operate as if they were complete, medieval poems tend to operate as if incomplete – or rather, as chapters or books in the whole poem made of ethics – the whole poem of the real world. The *Commedia* is one of the most intricately finished poetic organisms ever created in any language, and yet ultimately it is but a beautiful descant played solo, presuming the melody of Florentine politics and the figured bass of divine reality. *Beowulf*, similarly, parallels both Virgil and Christ. The *Romance of the Rose*, being ironic, is even less autonomous. Once the character of Reason is introduced, it is impossible to avoid the parallel of the *Consolation of Philosophy*. With this parallel in mind, the striking fact that the *Romance* discusses most of the topics treated in the *Consolation*, and in roughly the same order, but absolutely omits any material to correspond with the crucial Platonic prayer of book III, metre 9, becomes most important. The outline of the *Consolation* is the distinctio constituting ironically the forma tractandi of the *Romance*; the most important evidence for the interpretation of the poem is something ostentatiously absent. The same kinds of irony relate the *Romance* to the *Complaint of Nature*. The character of this relationship is not always the same, of course, throughout the Middle Ages. For *Beowulf* and the stories of the Old Testament, it tends to be typological. For twelfth-century poetry, it tends to be allegorical. For later poetry, it may be ironic, or it may be logical and exemplary in the way defined by the strategies of distinctio and forma tractandi. But whatever its mode, it is the crucial strategy of medieval poetry.

For the sake of clarity, I will abuse the *Lear* analogy one step further, and make some one-to-one equations. If the *Romance*, as I understand it, is the bastard Edmund, the *Complaint of Nature* is Edgar, and the *Consolation of Philosophy* is Gloucester himself, whose unfortunate suffering is the beginning of a higher wisdom. Lear has withdrawn himself. A medieval preacher would doubtless have been able to find him, in some allegorization or other, but I have no need to abuse the point that far. It must simply be affirmed that one always understands medieval poetry best by going outside and looking back. My going outside to *Lear* in order to look back at possible interrelationships in the Middle Ages is, I hope, perverse enough to be striking, and striking enough to make the point. The point, at least, is completely serious. The existence, in medieval criticism, of both the forma tractandi and the forma tractatus, and of the double intellectual strategy of divisio and distinctio, demands that medieval poems explicate in terms of external relationships. Structurally, these relationships are remarkably like those that in later periods exist within the textual confines of single great poems, and this likeness keeps my *Lear* analogy from being totally fanciful or perverse.

One may illustrate this relationship between forma tractandi and forma tractatus, which the strategy of distinctio achieves, in many ways. I choose four, which are I hope of representative kinds. The first is a subject index to the *Aeneid*; the second, one of the passages in the *Commedia* in which Dante makes what amounts to a distinctio; the third, a fabricated outline for the

Wife of Bath's Tale which makes clear its divisio: and the fourth, an interpretation of one of the books of Malory's *Morte Darthur* which the strategy of distinctio makes possible.

The subject index to the *Aeneid* is preserved in Vatican Library, ms Barberini lat 128, as one of a collection of such indexes. To a considerable extent, it is an index in the simple modern sense, but the subject headings tend to be more moral, less merely factual, than they would be now. Occasionally an important subject heading will have subdivisions, which, when they occur, are written in the tabular form of an early manuscript distinctio. In content, these subdivisions are often simply that. But sometimes they are of a form and character which proves the influence of the distinctio. The best example is a distinctio of distinctions; the arrayed material is as follows:

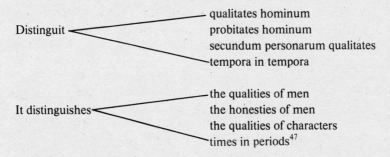

Distinguit
- qualitates hominum
- probitates hominum
- secundum personarum qualitates
- tempora in tempora

It distinguishes
- the qualities of men
- the honesties of men
- the qualities of characters
- times in periods[47]

By contrast, an obvious list of mere subheadings is the following:

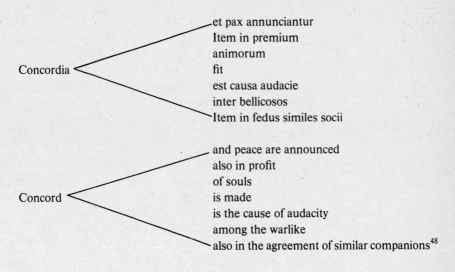

Concordia
- et pax annunciantur
- Item in premium
- animorum
- fit
- est causa audacie
- inter bellicosos
- Item in fedus similes socii

Concord
- and peace are announced
- also in profit
- of souls
- is made
- is the cause of audacity
- among the warlike
- also in the agreement of similar companions[48]

In the manuscript as a whole, which contains also indices of Seneca's letters to Lucilius and of Lucan's *Bellum civile*, the number of genuine *distinctiones* is, of course, smaller than the number of mere groups of subheadings. The fact that they occur at all is, I think, accidental in a manner which permits one to sense the profoundest kind of intellectual self-betrayal. The habit of arraying by distinguishing parts is so strong that it has some influence even on miscellaneous lists.

Consciously used, of course, the *distinctio* is supremely elegant and powerful. It is the literal governing strategy, for Dante, of the whole, as well as of the most detailed of the parts, of the *Commedia*. Dante does not, of course, always specify in detail the *distinctio* which governs and interprets the arrays in which we find his exemplary sinners and saints, and when he does so, the rhetoric of the *distinctio*, its dramatic use as a part of the poem as distinguished from its glossing use as an explanation of the poem, may well be as complex as that of Dante's exemplary material. It is, nevertheless, possible to discern with absolute clarity the strategy as such, however complex it is in practice and in application. In these terms, for instance, canto XI of the *Inferno* is a *distinctio* on the kinds of sin. Sins are of three kinds: incontinence, violence, and fraud. Sins of incontinence are further subdivided into sins of violence against self, against neighbour, and against God. Medieval commentators, of course, understood what Dante was doing; Benvenuto da Imola, for instance, says that Dante 'facit unam distinctionem perutilem et necessarium omnium circulorum istius civitatis. / makes a most useful and necessary distinction of all the circles of this city.'[49]

Something very like Dante's use of *distinctio* strategy, complex as it is, predictably occurs in real *distinctio* collections. For instance, in the one made by Nicholas Gorham, under the heading 'Maculare,' we find the following:

Dyabolus maculat homines sibi consencientem multipliciter: quandoque fumo superbie ... quandoque albugine ignorancie. Albugo enim maculans oculum excecat eum ... quandoque sanguine iracundie ... quandoque pice avaricie, tenacitas enim in pice maculat manum contigentem, sic et plumbum ... Carnalis concupiscencia maculat hominem ipsam sequentem multipliciter, quandoque luto gule. Lutum enim maculat viam, sic gula vitam ... quandoque lepra luxurie, lepra enim maculat pellem propriam et inficit alienam ... quandoque rubigine accidie, rubigo enim maculat ferrum ociosum.

The Devil defiles in many ways men who consent to him, sometimes with the smoke of pride ... sometimes with the film of ignorance. For a film defiling the eye blinds it ... sometimes with the blood of wrath ... sometimes with the pitch of avarice – the stickiness of pitch soils the hand that touches, and likewise lead. Carnal concu-

piscence defiles in many ways the man who follows it. Sometimes the mud of gluttony. For mud defiles the road, and gluttony the life ... sometimes the leprosy of lust,
for leprosy pollutes one's own skin and infects another's ... sometimes the rust of
sloth, for rust defiles steel that is not used.[50]

This array of sins, stains, staining agents, and human conditions in parallel
works precisely as does Dante's *Purgatorio*; the difference in eloquence
between a great artist and a popular compiler should not obscure the fact that
the same structural habit of mind governs them both. In these terms, and
following the example of Virgil in canto XI of *Inferno*, one could outline the
whole of the *Commedia*. Most of the charts of otherworldly geography which
one finds in old and modern editions of the *Commedia*, in fact, do just this.
In the naming of the parts – that is, in specifying the fully complex manner in
which the distinctio should be named, one finds Dante most demanding, as
did Pézard in the case of Brunetto Latini, and as I did above in trying to
explain Farinata as a 'heretic.' But though he is subtle, Dante is at the same
time obvious. Distinctio is his literal strategy, and the poem often wears in its
very words the names of the distinguishable parts of ethical and theological
wholes. What I wish to claim, in this set of examples, is that the strategy of
distinctio, carrying with it the implicit claim to constitute a normative array,
is in fact what defines the choice, arraying, and ordering of the parts of medieval poems, even when these parts are not literally named by abstractions.
This claim I can illustrate by reference to the Wife of Bath, and to parts of the
Morte Darthur of Malory.

I have claimed, in another place,[51] that the Wife of Bath's *Prologue* and
Tale, in the light of surrounding material, make sense best when taken as a
four-part treatise whose subject the Wife defines in her opening sentence:
'Experience, though noon auctoritee were in this world, is right ynogh for
me to speke of wo that is in mariage.'[52] Literally the four parts of this material are: a defence of sex and marriage, an autobiography, the tale of the
loathly lady, and an enclosed sermon on 'gentilesse.' One may easily enough
see how these four parts treat four woes of marriage; with a little more
thought, one can even state these four woes by fabricating a rhyming Latin
outline, of a type fashionable in Chaucer's time: Connubium est virginitatis
refutativum, tranquilitatis destructivum, quasi poenum mortis impositum,
non nobilitatis generativum.'[53] Such a sober outline, of course, does not
deny that the usual Chaucerian ironies can work their usual high comedy; it
merely suggests that whatever Chaucer means by the Wife of Bath, he
intends for us to understand it in terms of the opening aphorism, whose
importance the whole weight of medieval dispositio affirms, and in terms of

four arrayed and parallel parts into which his text so clearly and literally divides itself. To do so is to understand it as a developed distinctio.

In its literal content, this distinctio is a modern fabrication, though it seems to be at least both fair to what the Wife announces that she will say, and of some use as a catalyst for interpretation. It may well be that further study of distinctiones will turn up an actual medieval one, plausibly available to Chaucer, which defines the four woes of marriage in a way far more useful to criticism than this invented one. A vast number of collections survives, most of them only in manuscript, containing a quantity of material too large to be assimilated for literary criticism except by the concerted labour of many scholars. Even when this is done, it may still be that some given poem or story will obey an implicit distinctio not literally preserved anywhere – the mind of a poet can distinguish just as neatly as the mind of a theologian or preacher. Criticism may always need to depend, from time to time, on plausible fabrication.

It is, however, more satisfying when one does have independent documentation for the distinctiones in terms of which one reads. In the case of Malory's *Morte Darthur*, one does. A full analysis of the work and the distinctiones which inform the ordering and unity of its stories is beyond the scope of this book. It is, however, appropriate to indicate the direction this analysis might take, for the sake of showing just how powerful the distinctio is as an instrument of criticism, and how effectively it protects the modern critic both from false expectations and from false starts. In order to show these things, I apply to the *Morte* two medieval distinctiones, one of which justifies and comments upon its most pervasive themes, and the other of which explains how the eight books of Malory's 'works,' which of course do not have the unity of Aristotelian plot, or any other unity under definitions normal to modern literary criticism, are in medieval terms a complete and unified series of eight.

I am confident that this use of the distinctio as an external outline, by which to rationalize the content of a seemingly miscellaneous work such as Malory's, is critically appropriate. The whole of this book is a defence of such a procedure. At the same time I must admit that my work on the *Morte* is just beginning. Though I have no doubts whatsoever about my critical procedure, I present the specific distinctiones which I am applying merely as speculative illustration. It may well be that further research will turn up others, presumably of similar general character, which will explain the *Morte* more precisely, and in greater detail. The ones which I present here do have a certain a priori authority, and will I hope be at least tentatively persuasive.

But I am here far more concerned to show that the distinctio is a promising tool of analysis than to say anything final about Malory.

The two most sustained concerns of scholarship on the *Morte Darthur* have been to establish the biography of the author, and to argue the question of the book's unity. With regard to unity, Vinaver's edition of the *Works* argues in its very title that the Winchester manuscript's divisions prove that the *Morte* is an assembly, not a book. Arguments to the contrary have tended to see in these 'works' a kind of thematic continuity, which, if it were tighter, could be called the 'plot' of the rise and fall of Arthur's Round Table kingdom.[54] The result, I think, has been a stand-off; because both Vinaver and his opponents have been trying to argue for the *Morte* a unity foreign to medieval literary theory, neither side has made a convincing case. With regard to authorship, research has by now discovered so much hard information about the sordid career of Sir Thomas Malory of Newbold Revel that he has become a complete embarrassment to the book with which he is credited, even while the likelihood that he was not too brilliant has buttressed arguments against complex schemes of architectonic unity for his book. William Matthews has, I think, cleared the ground by demolishing this man's claim, and has constructed a hypothetical description of the likely author from the kind of evidence that we would still have even if we lacked the specific name, 'Malory.'[55] On the basis of his work, we are now permitted to conceive of Malory as a person of some cultivation, literate in two languages and possibly in three, worth holding for ransom, and well acquainted, presumably as a participant, with the international society of fifteenth-century chivalry.[56] What kind of book would such a man write? Obviously, the *Morte* is the answer to such a question. But there is also some valuable external evidence, which will suggest in general how books of chivalric romances were regarded, and what kind of book they were taken to be, in the light of which we can approach the *Morte* with the proper expectations. This evidence is the library of Jacques d'Armagnac, of which eighty-six surviving volumes have been identified,[57] and in which Malory may well have written his book. It does, at least, contain the books Malory had to have; if Malory did not use them, then he had to have worked in one of the very few other libraries of similar character, all of them the private collections of great magnates. Jacques' library therefore has exemplary significance. It was the kind of library in which romances were to be found; the other books which were also there are a powerful indication of the significance of the romances themselves, and of what their meaning must have been to the noble gentlemen who paid so handsomely to have them compiled and copied.[58]

Taken as a whole, the library is a remarkably coherent and intelligible collection, which reveals a developed and distinctively medieval interest in statecraft. In this collection, three categories of books stand out: histories, romances, and theoretical books of ethics – many of them especially useful to a ruler. Among the histories are two partial copies of the *City of God*,[59] three Livys,[60] Valerius Maximus,[61] a French version of the *Speculum historiale* of Vincent of Beauvais,[62] the chronicles of England by Jean de Wavrin,[63] a book of the chronicles of France, from Phillipe le Bel to the coronation of Charles VI,[64] a compilation of universal history from the time of creation, and including translations from Lucan and Sallust,[65] the *Recueil des histoires de Troie*,[66] romances of Troy, Thebes, Aeneas, and Alexander,[67] and part of Froissart.[68] There is also probably a copy of the *Metamorphoses* of Ovid.[69] All these books are in French.

Alongside these histories are the romances, enough of them, according to Matthews, to account for Malory's French book,[70] and including the *Lancelot* by Micheau Gonnot which in narrative technique and method of compilation resembles Malory's work more than does any other medieval book of romances.[71] Probably for medieval readers the borderline between history and romance was less marked than it is for us, and it is therefore likely more our convention than theirs which leads me to put the romances of Troy, Alexander, and the rest with the histories, and these Arthurian ones to themselves. Logically, these two classes are either continuous, or closely analogous, and either relationship will make the point that Jacques' library takes romances, along with history, as something seriously capable of informing the moral and political life of the ruler who reads them. Gonnot, at least, make both his classification and his moral purpose explicitly clear:

Mais aux bons et vrais hystoriens [je] prie de bon cueur que silz y treuvent faulte ne prolixite de langage leur plaise que par doulces et amyables paroles le veullent amender et corriger. Car selon mon petit entendement les jeunes chevaliers et excuiers y pourront aprendre moult de beux faitz darmes, et quant ils trouveront chose villaine ne de reprouche je leur conseille quilz ne ne facent mie. Car les choses malfautes sont escriptes aux livres pour les fouir et eviter. Et les bonnes pour les ensuyvre et les accomplir chaque homme de bon voloir.

But I ask the favour of good and true historians that if they find here a fault or prolixity of language that they will emend and correct it with sweet and amiable language. For according to my little understanding the young knights and squires can learn here much of beautiful deeds of arms, and when they find vulgar or wicked things I advise them that they don't do any of them, for evil things are written in books that they might be avoided and fled, and good things that they might be followed and accomplished by every man of good will.[72]

In addition to the histories and the romances, Jacques' library included books on ethics or personal behaviour. Among these were the ethics, politics and economics of Aristotle,[73] a French version of the *De regimine principum* of Aegidius Romanus,[74] as well as devotional and moral books of a more popular character, such as the *Somme le roi*,[75] and de Guilleville's *Pèlerinage*.[76] A work catalogued as the 'Lamentations de Saint Bernard' includes also the *Dicts of the Philosophers* and the proverbs of Seneca.[77] A French version of the book of monastic devotion, the *Collations* of Cassian, may well have appealed to its noble owner for metaphoric reasons; after an introduction referring to King David, it says:

Cy commence le premier chappitre que traicte de labbit des moynes. Le moyne doit estre nomme ung chevalier de dieu tousiours arme et doit avoir habit clox pardevant et tousiours estre appareille a combattre et entre en battaille contre lennemy.

Here begins the first chapter, which treats of the habit of monks. The monk ought to be called a knight of God, always armed, ought to have his habit gathered in front, and ought to be always dressed to combat and enter into battle with the enemy.[78]

As an indication, both of the characters of its owner and of the political mentality of the last of the feudal ruling class, this library would repay detailed study; even this most preliminary survey makes both clear and important the kind of bibliographic and therefore ideological context in which Arthurian romances existed, and must now be read. When written, they were obviously taken seriously as a part of the paideia of the statesman; they were read along side of it, if not simply as a part of, world history. They were books relevant to a person who wished to know how to rule wisely, virtuously, and well. There is every reason to expect that Malory, though he had less responsibility for the exercise of power than Jacques d'Armagnac, would have had the same attitude toward his material.[79]

If, then, Malory's book can be expected to be about good government in the broadest sense, and about the human predicament in history which makes good government both possible and desirable, how can it be said to be so, and what is the nature of its particular relationship to this general theme? Most obviously, we can expect Malory's book to be exemplary – to contain an exemplum, or exempla, illustrating the works of good and bad government, and presenting the typical deeds of people in the act of history. As exemplum its narratio exists in parallel to history, stands for it, and represents it. The parts of Malory's *Morte*, therefore, can be expected to reflect, to be named by, the distinctiones which obtain generally for history and politics. Thus named, its parts, which are its forma tractatus, will also serve a forma tractandi. The story of a single kingdom, the Kingdom of Arthur, will then stand for all kingdoms – the collected deeds of the history of that kingdom will stand for, exemplify, all of history.

Whenever medieval people considered history as a whole, they did so in terms of a single pervasively popular schema – that of the six ages. This schema of course varied, but its basic structure, whereby one related the days of the week of creation, the stages in the life of the human individual, and the periods of world history as defined by the Bible, was so generally accepted and so often repeated that one can safely take it as normative. Unless we have explicit evidence for some particular case, we can safely presume that any medieval writer, thinking of making an example of history in the large sense, will have in mind in some way the schema of the six ages. Further, we may presume that the political behaviour which is represented in any such exemplum of history will reflect, in some measure, the concerns and themes which medieval political scientists had established as definitive, and therefore as possible. We are led by Jacques d'Armagnac's library to expect that a compiler of Arthurian romances will indeed be concerned for these things, and we can therefore approach Malory's *Morte* with expectations properly defined.

The text fulfils these expectations; Malory gives us clear indication of his intentions. First, there is his careful emphasis on days and dates – on Pentecost as a time of beginning, and Trinity Monday as the day of the calamitous end. Allowing for the ambiguity of the Judeo-Christian tradition, in which the holy day is both first and last, it is obvious that Malory intends his whole work to be seen as extending through the pattern of a week and its octave – the whole of a single week, and the beginning day of the next. Second, there is in Malory's book a constant literal interplay of three great concerns – the concern for personal virtue, the concern for the love of woman, and the concern for civic order symbolized by the society of the Round Table. His first emphasis, on the pattern of the week, obviously evokes the schema of world history of which his Arthurian history is intended to be sufficient exemplum. His second, upon these three great themes, happens not coincidentally to correspond to the fundamental distinctio under which is organized one of the most important and popular 'guide for princes' books of the later Middle Ages – the *De regimine principum* of Aegidius Romanus, of which there was a French version in the library of Jacques d'Armagnac.

A full analysis of the *Morte*, in these terms, must wait for another opportunity. What I wish to do here is make no more than a suggestive beginning, by showing, first, how an awareness of the distinctio of Aegidius sharpens our sense of what the *Morte* means in part because of what it omits, and second, how an awareness of the hexameral distinctio of world history defines for the *Morte* a unity which perfectly fits the eight 'works,' but which depends upon none of the features of plot and theme which previous believers in unity had to force from materials at times recalcitrant.

According to Aegidius, the good prince is the one who rightly rules himself, his family, and his kingdom. Such a distinctio is in one sense merely obvious – self, family, and society are a triad significant in every conceivable sociology. But it does help us see what is missing from Malory – that enactment of marriage and family without which virtuous men and knightly deeds cannot permanently give peace and justice to society. In Malory's work, love refuses marriage, and marriage is sterile. What is engendered is disorder – Mordred on the one hand and Galahad on the other. The distinctio of Aegidius, developed into a detailed analysis of personal virtue, of the family, its members, and their relations, and of society at large, including war, constantly informs Malory's work – or more properly, the particulars of Malory's stories constantly exemplify, both literally and by significant omission, the truths which Aegidius defines. What the relationship – a kind of assimilatio – means, is that we may, indeed must, see that Malory is continuously concerned for political truth – even, or especially, when he is talking specifically about the analogous cases of personal virtue or the right rule of self, and the love of woman and the right (or in most cases wrong) rule of family.

Malory's emphasis upon his framing week – Pentecost and Trinity Monday, the first day of the week, the day of beginnings, and the Monday of the next week, the day of final calamity – only underscores what would have been obvious anyway. If the whole of world history presents itself normally as organized by a hexameral distinctio, and if Malory's work, which is the whole history of Arthur, is an exemplum of that history, then the exemplum must represent by existing in parallel to the whole which it exemplifies. Forma tractandi must rule and explain forma tractatus. The history of Arthur must necessarily have, as history, the form of history – that Malory knows this consciously as well as merely archetypally he betrays by his use of the week as framing device.

The proper response of the critic is to apply the distinctio. For it the glosa ordinaria is a convenient and obvious authority,[80] which seems to fit quite neatly. There are eight books in the Malory; there are eight days in the glosa.

Putting the two eights in isometric parallel neatly names the parts of Malory's great work, and gives them sequence and coherence. Moreover, the allegories attached to the exegesis of the days of creation echo and reinforce Malory's other distinctio, as defined by Aegidius. The literal history of the world, the specific history of the family of Israel, and the stages in the life of a single individual are the themes in terms of which the interpretation develops.

The first day, according to the glosa, represents the time from Adam to Noah in world history, or the period of infancy in human life. In this day was made light – the light of faith. When at first one believes in invisible things, God deigns to appear because of that faith.[81] In Malory, this is the book of the appearance of the king, of the invisible knight, and of the slaughter of the innocents. Arthur appears, is identified, is crowned, and establishes his kingdom in Britain. Of the themes and notions which the glosa establishes, Malory's first book is a rich and complex mixture of direct and parodic echoes. Instead of God, there is the invisible knight; instead of the baby Jesus, Mordred escapes the slaughter of the innocents.

The second day is the time between Noah and Abraham, the time of childhood, between the infancy which is forgotten and the time of the beginning of puberty. Biblically, it is concerned mostly with genealogies, and with the roll calls of heroes. On this day was made 'the firmanent, that it, of discipline, which discerns between the carnal and the spiritual, as between the inferior and superior waters.'[82] In Malory, this is the book of the constitution of the political firmament. In this book the fundamental polarity between the Saracens and the Christians is expressed; it is structured by a series of embassies; much of its content is given over to lists of heroes and their armies. For this day only, the relationship between Malory's concerns and the hexameral distinctio can also be glossed from Denis the Carthusian, who makes explicit what was implicit in the glosa, in a way which precisely fits Malory:

et dividat aquas ab aquis. Firmamentum istud est Ecclesia electorum, quae, teste Gregorio, ab Abel justo coepit, quae divisit inter aquas et aquas, videlicet inter diversas nationes et gentes, quas dijudicavit et separavit ab invicem, et quosdam convertit, incorporatque sibi. Divisit quoque inter aquas quae supra se sunt, et eas quae infra se sunt, id est inter divinam scripturam et supernaturalem sapientiam atque angelicam illuminationem, et inter saeculares philosophicasque scientias, seu haereticorum documenta nefaria, et superstitiosas ac falsas doctrinas. In quibus omnibus separavit pretiosum a vili, verum a falso, amplectens vera atque salubria et reprobans falsa itemque inania.

This firmament is the Church of the elect, which, as Gregory says, began from just Abel, which made a division between waters, that is between diverse nations and peoples, which it distinguished and separated from one another, and some it converts and incorporates into itself. It divided also between the waters which were over it and the waters which were under it, that is, between holy scripture and supernatural wisdom and angelic illumination, and secular philosophic sciences and wicked testimony of heretics and superstitious and false teachings. In all this it separated the precious from the vile, the true from the false, embracing the true and beneficial and rejecting the false and worthless.[83]

The third day is the day of youth – from Abraham to David, a youth capable of childbearing. Biblically, it is the time of the patriarchs and judges, when every man did right in his own eyes. Allegorically, it is the day of the appearance of dry land, that is, of the preparation of the mind for the bearing of good works, having separated itself from the waves of carnal temptation.[84] In Malory, this is the book of Lancelot. The first half of it is preparatory – it begins with Lancelot asleep under an apple tree in the posture of a tomb effigy and ends with the refusal of paramours and marriage. The second half is a quite varied array of good works.

The fourth day is the day of heavenly bodies; on that day the mind of discipline deals with and distinguishes the spiritual intelligences. It sees what is the unchangeable truth, which like the sun shines in the soul, and how the soul participates in it, and attributes to the body its order and beauty, like the moon lighting the night. It is the age of full adulthood, and in Israel the time of the Kingdom of David.[85] In Malory, this is the book of Gareth, for which we have identified no proper source. Though like the book of Lancelot it is full of knightly deeds, there seems to be a fundamental difference. In the Lancelot, clearly, we are shown 'the bearing of good works' – we are shown what a knight can do. In the Gareth, on the other hand, we are shown who it is who can behave so. The questions asked and answered in this book have to do with the problem of identity. Gareth, as the episodes progress, proves himself one right in birth, in relation to a lord, in relation to subjects and vassals (whom he conquers himself), in relation to women, and in relationship to the worship of men and women (he wins a tournament, and he marries). In this contrast, it must be emphasized that the order of the glosa, which puts 'good works' before the act of understanding which clearly seems to be more definitive than merely active, though it is logically puzzling, is an example of that kind of medieval fact which makes criticism both so unpredictable and so finally satisfying. Without this order which the ordering of the glosa's interpretations defines, the order and relation of these two books of Malory, and the basis of their difference one from the other, remain obscure. With it, and everything makes sense – two different books are needed, centring on different single heroes, whose careers have to do, respectively, with good works and with the achievement of identity.

The fifth day, the day of sea beasts and birds, is, briefly, the active life in this world. Biblically, it is the time of the Babylonian captivity.[86] In Malory, it is the long book of Tristram – the book concerned with the analogous bad kingdom of Mark, with the consummation of the Lot-Pellinore feud, with successful adultery, and, at the end, with the parody of family by which Lancelot engenders Galahad, and wanders mad like Nebuchadnezzar.

The sixth day, the day of the creation of man, is the day when the Old Man descends into old age and becomes the new man who lives spiritually. Biblically, it is the time of the preaching of Christ.[87] In Malory, this is the book of the achivement of the Grail.

The seventh day, the day of the Sabbath, is the day when God's work is ended and man's must begin. Curiously, the glosa makes it very clear at this point that the Sabbath is not, allegorically, a day of rest – rather, it is the day of man's chance to follow up God's creative work with works of his own doing. The new regime of the steward, as it were, takes over.[88] In Malory, the seventh book is concerned primarily with the works of love – inner and outer, truth and falsity – through which Lancelot and Guinevere move toward the eighth day, which is the day of judgment,[89] and in Malory, the day of the death of Arthur.

In this analysis, three theoretical principles are involved. The first is that of isometric, or one-to-one, equivalences. The second is the principle of ordering by distinctio. The third is the principle of discursive unity. The first of these principles must not be mistaken for mere allegorization. The relationships between the items in series defined by the glosa, and the narratives in series contained in Malory's Morte, are, as I have stated them, ostentatiously neat. But this is no reductionist neatness. To put the label: 'appearance of things invisible' on Malory's first book is not to allegorize it, or reduce it to anything other than itself – it is merely to name it. To compare the Tristram material with the Babylonian captivity is only to underline the literal fact that King Mark's kingdom is different from Arthur's, alongside it, and in a state of comparison with it – the comparison literally names the material as it is. To relate the book of the Grail to the achievement of the spiritual life is no relationship at all – it is only and obviously what happens in the book. In short, the one-to-one neatness of the fit between Malory's material and the glosa's interpretation of the days of creation is nothing more or less than the appropriate neatness by which a discursive outline fits its material development.

What is distinctive about the medieval procedure is that this neat fit between outline and material is a fit between two entities essentially distinguishable from one another, and capable of existing independently. Any given distinctio may find development by means of a wide variety of exemplary and particular material, and a given array of material, already compiled, presumes for its full understanding an outline logically external to it. This is why all merely intrinsic analysis of medieval narrative material tends to be unsatisfying, because intrinsic analysis makes too much of narrative as such, and therefore of the causalities which we understand as plot. Only after one has named the parts can one make sense of their having been compiled. When one has named the parts, of course, a unity appears. It is the discursive unity, defined by Averroes' discursive version of the beginning, middle, and end of a piece of praise, which makes sense both of the assembly and the ordering of medieval parts of works. Under any other critical presumption, they all too often seem merely miscellaneous.

What the *Morte Darthur* is about is politics. It is an exemplum of the history of the world. In telling of one kingdom, the Kingdom of Arthur, it is an exemplum of all earthly kingdoms. As such, its parts must be arrayed in exemplary fashion. When we ask, 'What are the parts, and what is the arraying, given for the whole of world history, of which Arthur is the exemplum?' we find both the right number of parts and a plausible set of names for those parts. These names do not distract us from Malory's Arthur into theology, or contemplation of creation or Hebrew history. Rather, they sharpen our insight into Malory's own concern for politics – for the good kingdom and its ordering. They help us see how he can talk of love and virtue and adventure, and feastings and enchantments, and all the apparently miscellaneous actions of his stories, and even about two different and only casually related kingdoms, without ever losing the fundamental focus or the fundamental point. But they can help us only if we accept them – if we will grant that Malory's fundamental focus, point, and attitude toward stories are medieval. Malory, and Chaucer as well, are not the first great novelists in English, fumbling toward a form which Conrad and James and Joyce were to perfect. Rather, in a very precise sense, they were the last great moralists, because their fundamental presumption about the stories in which we remember all the particularities of life was that these stories would connect to universal names.

The fascination which Malory's great stories have for us, as for all the ages that have attended him and them, is that they are dealers in truth, from an age when stories had access to a quality of truth which we have since lost. Medieval literary theory, by which the stories which so miscellaneously compose so much of our medieval inheritance can be ordered and named, explains the power we still feel in Malory and his coevals. Even in that late nominalist world, the universals were there, still within reach, if only one would tell enough stories. In Malory, obviously, there are enough.

NOTES

1 'Vel pro reverentia Trinitatis, vel quia funiculus triplex difficile rumpitur, vel quia hic modus a Bernardo maxime frequentatur, vel, quod credo verius, tempori sermonis requisito convenientius.' Robert Basevorn *'Forma praedicandi'* in Th.-M. Charland OP *Artes Praedicandi: Contribution à l'histoire de la rhétorique au moyen âge* (Paris 1936) p 254.

2 Otto von Simson *The Gothic Cathedral: Origins of Gothic Architecture and the Medieval Concept of Order* (New York 1956); and the study of Chaucer which depends on Simson: Robert Jordan *Chaucer and the Shape of Creation: The Aesthetic Possibilities of Inorganic Structure* (Cambridge MA 1967)

3 From a commentary on the *De consolatione* of Boethius, Assisi, Biblioteca communale, ms 555, f 3r

4 On the hymns: 'Forma tractatus consistit in divisione libri / The form of the treatise consists of the division of the book,' Leiden, Bibliotheek der Rijksuniversiteit, ms BPL 191D, 25r; 'Forma tractatus consistit in ordinatione partium illius libri / The form of the treatise consists of the ordering of the parts of that book,' Munich, ms Clm 13439, f 160v-1r; on Aesop's *Fables*: 'Forma tractatus est distinctio libri per fabulas vel per flores et fructus / The form of the treatise is the distinguishing of the [content of the] book into stories, or into flowers and fruits,' Brussels, Bibliothèque royale, ms 2519, f 89r; on the *Doctrinale* of Alexander of Villa Dei: 'Forma tractatus est divisio libri per capitula et capitulorum per partes et partium per particula / The form of the treatise is the division of the book into chapters and of the chapters into parts and of the parts into bits,' Oxford, University College, ms 53, f 23r; on Valerius Maximus' *Facta et dicta*: 'Sed forma tractatus est divisio libri in partes et in parciales libros, et libros dividere in capitula et hec in partes / But the form of the treatise is the division of the book into parts and into partial books, and to divide the books into chapters and these into parts,' Yale University, ms Marston 37, f 5r; on the *Commedia*, from Dante's letter to Cangrande: 'Forma tractatus est triplex, secundum triplicem divisionem. Prima divisio est, qua totum opus dividitur in tres canticas. Secunda, qua quaelibet cantica dividitur in cantus. Tertia, qua quilibet cantus dividitur in rithimos / The form of the

treatise is triple, according to its triple division. The first division is that by which the whole work is divided into three canticles. The second, that by which each canticle is divided into cantos. The third, that by which each canto is divided into verses.' (p 416).

5 Bibliothèque nationale, ms lat 16089, f 146r

6 Sic: Bodleian Library, ms Canonici misc 457, 2r; Ghisalberti, 'ordinario.'

7 'Giovanni del Virgilio' 18. Given Giovanni's clear emphasis on *sententia*, I think one must believe that his last sentence wishes to say that by dividing a text we find parts which, by coming one after the other, imply or suggest a logical sequence. That is, the parts we get by dividing make sense together. But comparison with the *Elenchorum* indicates that something has gone seriously wrong. Averroes translates the passage which corresponds: 'appositis enim iuxta se contrariis, minora et maiora apparent, et peiora et meliora hominibus' (*Aristotelis opera cum Averrois commentariis* I.iii [Venice 1562, rpr Frankfurt 1962] 159r). This is precisely what Aristotle meant, according to the translation of W.A. Pickard-Cambridge: 'for the placing of their contraries close beside them makes things look big to men, both relatively and absolutely, and worse and better' (*The Works of Aristotle translated into English* ed W.D. Ross, vol I [London 1928] 174b.5). I have verified Ghisalberti's transcription by Oxford, Bodleian Library, ms Canon, misc 457; it is easy enough to see how Aristotle's text could acquire the errors Giovanni must have read, to put his reference as he did, but it is less easy to see how he could have thought the quotation relevant to his point if he knew its context.

As a rule, I have not traced my critics' quotations to their sources, since my point has been what they meant, and not how they knew. Cruxes such as this one, however, suggest that finally accurate maps of this wilderness of glosses will be some time in the making.

8 Paris, Bibliothèque nationale, ms lat 6459, f 1r

9 Boggess pp 23–7. I have quoted here the substance of what Bartholomew of Bruges, in his commentary on Averroes' text, defines as one of the 'documenta' (characteristics) by which poetry attains what it should attain 'secundum naturam. / according to nature.' Thus I deal with what is, in terms of medieval *divisio*, a complete section. See Paris, Bibliothèque nationale, ms lat 16089, 149r.

10 Paris, Bibliothèque nationale ms lat 16089, f 149r. All subsequent quotations from Bartholomew of Bruges are from this manuscript.

11 I omit full discussion of this contrast with rhetoric, because it raises the question of audience, which will be dealt with in chapter six.

12 Unless, of course, it is unfinished. But even here, the practice of medieval writers raises difficulties. *The Romance of the Rose* by Guillaume is unfinished;

as adapted by Jean de Meun, it is complete. Chaucer's *Canterbury Tales* lacks a great deal of what Chaucer announced that he would do, but he did put an end to what we have of it, and it is complete. But Lydgate added to it the tale of Thebes, and made of the *Canterbury Tales* another complete book, just as validly, if not as valuably, as Jean de Meun did with the *Rose*. Generally and roughly speaking every Arthurian tale is complete, and so are all intentional collections – every addition or continuation makes the whole a different but still complete, book. When T.S. Eliot, in his essay 'Tradition and the Individual Talent,' suggested that every new poet not only writes in the light of the accumulated body of past poetry, but also, by his writing, adds to it so as to change its character as a whole body defining tradition, he was describing the process by which individual medieval poems often attain their wholeness and character as a unity. The medieval principle is, however, more powerful than Eliot's, because, in addition to affirming the notion that whatever one has is enough, it is willing to take normative attitudes toward the result.

13 *In Anticlaudianum* ed Sulowski, pp 127–8. The comment is in explanation of *Anticlaudianus* III.63–4. The whole passage is telling witness to the importance of division among the procedures of logic, which in this context according to Alanus 'open the secrets of Sophia.'

14 As I shall try to show in chapters four and five, this likeness or 'convenientia' which Raoul specifies as one half of fit division is one of the key constituents of assimilatio, and therefore includes metaphoric as well as substantial likeness – or, in more medieval terms, presumes substantial likeness that is both materially and metaphorically based.

15 Eg, 'Tunc sequitur illa pars "et sermones poetici" in qua Aristoteles dividit de poemata penes suam formam que quidem est ymaginatio vel assimilatio. / Then follows that part, "and poetic language" in which Aristotle divides concerning poetry with regard to its form, which clearly is imagination or assimilation.' Paris, Bibliothèque nationale, ms lat 16089, f 146v.

16 Allen and Moritz *A Distinction of Stories.*

17 *The 'Parisiana Poetria' of John of Garland* ed Traugott Lawler (New Haven 1974) pp 2–3

18 Assisi, Biblioteca communale, ms 309, f 28r. This is the fullest commentary on the *Poetria nova* that I know; a fragment of the same full treatment is preserved in Munich, ms Clm 14482, ff 93v ff. (The Assisi accessus contains citations of Hermann the German.)

19 Oxford, Corpus Christi College, ms 144, f 18v. By virtue of its having been a gift, this manuscript can be dated before 1438.

20 The commentary preserved in Assisi explains Geoffrey's reference to proverbs and exempla thus: 'Notandum autem hic quod proverbium et exemplum, licet in predictis conveniant, differunt tamen esse [sic, cod ee] naturaliter, quia pro-

verbium nihil aliud est quam parabola vel similitudo per quam aliud dicitur et aliud intelligitur, ut dicit uguccio. Sed secundum Tullium et autorem istum proverbium est idem quod sententia, prout sententia est color rethoricus. Quem sic diffinit Tullius in 5o nove rethorice: sententia est oratio sumpta de vita que aut quid sit aut esse oporteat in vita breviter ostenditur, cui consonat aristoteles: sic diffiniens sententiam in 2o rethoricorum: Sententia est enuncia-tio non de singularibus sed de universalibus. Nec de omnibus universalibus, puta: rectum curvo est contrarium, sed de quibuscumque actiones sunt et eli-genda sunt aut fugienda sunt ad operari. Ysidorus vero libro ethymologiarum [cod rethoricarum] 2o in tractatu de rethorica dicit quod sententia est dictum inpersonale idest sine persona ut obsequium amicos, veritas odium parit parit [sic]. Exemplum autem etsi sit color rethoricus non tamen hic ita sumitur, prout diffinitur a tulio cum dicit quod exemplum est alicuius determinati aut facti cum certi auctoris nomine proprio. Sed sumitur large pro omni simili quod potest adduci ad propositum. / It should be noted here that the proverb and the exemplum, though they are related in what has just been said, are naturally different, because a proverb is nothing other than a parable or a similitude by which something is said and something else is meant, as Huguccio says. But according to Cicero and this author a proverb is the same as a maxim, in so far as a maxim is a rhetorical colour. Cicero defines it thus in the fifth book of the new rhetoric: A maxim is a saying taken from life, which briefly shows what may be or what should be in life; Aristotle agrees, defining maxim thus in the second book of the rhetoric: A maxim is a statement not of singulars but of universals. But not every universal statement is a maxim – for instance, "A straight curve is a contradiction," but only a statement about some kind of action, and whether it should or should not be done. Isidore indeed in the second book of the etymologies in the treatment of rhetoric says that a maxim is an impersonal saying, that is, one that has no point of view, as "Loyalty makes friends, the truth makes hatred." Although an exemplum is a rhetorical colour, it is not taken as such here, as it is defined by Cicero when he says that an exemplum is of something determinate or done with the proper name of a certain author. Rather, it is taken generally for any illustra-tion which may be applied to a proposition.' Assisi, Biblioteca communale, ms 309, f 9v.

21 Assisi, Biblioteca communale, ms 309, f 7v. The 'Commentator in poetria aristotelis' here cited is, of course, Averroes.
22 Ghisalberti, 'Giovanni del Virgilio,' p 19
23 Ghisalberti, 'Arnulf,' p 181. Cf also Munich, ms Clm 14748, f 38v; ms Clm 14809, f 66v; Paris, Bibliothèque nationale, ms lat 8253, f 1v; Vatican Library, ms Vat lat 2781, f 187v.
24 Leiden, Bibliotheek der Rijksuniversiteit, ms BPL 191A, f 214r

25 'Proponit' includes line 1, and the first word of line 2; 'invocat' begins at 'di, coeptis' in line 2 and continues through line 4; 'narrat' begins with 'ante mare' of line 5 and includes the rest of the book.

26 Chapter two, note 38

27 Bernardus Silvestris, ed Jones, p 3

28 Ghisalberti 'Arnulf,' p 181–2

29 Venice, Biblioteca Marciana, ms lat XII.61 (4097), f 2r

30 The poem is in artificial order, says the commentator, because Statius begins his story with Oedipus already blind: 'ab hoc puncto Statius incipit, quod fere ultimo loco gestum erat. / Statius begins at this point, with an event done almost last.' f 2r.

31 'Et nota quod in statio achilleidos imitatur Homerum, in hoc autem opere imitatur Virgilium secundum tractatum eneydos. Utitur igitur carmine heroyco grandiloqui stylo, ordine artificiali. Carmen autem heroycum constat ex divinis humanisque personis continens vera cum fictis. / And note that in the Statian Achilleid he imitates Homer, but in this book he imitates Virgil, following the treatise of the Aeneid. Therefore he uses heroic verse in the grand style, and artificial order. Heroic verse deals with divine and human characters and contains truth and fiction.' f 1r–v.

32 See, for instance, the *Parisiana poetria* of John of Garland, pp 58ff. I have already noted the manual presumption of relation between poetic and dictamen.

33 For examples, see Allen *The Friar as Critic* pp 69ff.

34 Ibid p 73

35 Oxford, Bodleian Library, ms Canon, misc 457, f 10v

36 Yale University, Beinecke Library, ms 166, f [E6v]. Numbering is frequently off in medieval manuscripts; the gloss in fact refers to the fifth book.

37 Leiden, Bibliotheek der Rijksuniversiteit, ms BPL 191A, f 223r

38 Vatican Library, ms Palat 1at 1690, f 46v. This is a fifteenth-century commentary from north Italy. In addition to the sequential atmosphere of its divisiones, it is unusual in that it expresses frequent and ostentatious admiration for Statius' poetic skill, in such language as: 'Hoc est secundum capitulum in quo est intentio autoris discriminare et valde bene enucleare mortem archemori. / This is the second chapter in which it is the intention of the author to distinguish and to explain very well the death of Archemorus.' f 54r. The implication of the division, that is, that the nobility of some material is compromised by its having parts, is curious; I have not seen it elsewhere.

39 Florence, Biblioteca nazionale, ms II.II.55, ff 157r, 162r

40 For a discussion of Hugh's work, see Smalley *The Study of the Bible* pp 269–72.

41 Hugh of St Cher *Opera omnia* (Venice 1732), vol II, f 223v
42 *Rosarium theologicum*, Oxford, Bodleian Library, ms Bodl 448, f 86r
43 Hugh of St Cher *Opera*, vol II, f 16r
44 John Ridewall *Fulgentius Metaforalis* ed Hans Liebeschütz (Leipzig 1926)
45 Raoul de Longchamp *In Anticlaudianum*, ed Sulowski, pp 19–20
46 Even here there are problems. The outline of the seven capital sins accounts for seven of Gower's eight books, but the presence of a book 'de regimine principum' as his book seven makes the forma tractatus of the seven sins not quite completely satisfactory as a distinctio of forma tractandi. What is needed to rationalize the form of the *Confessio* properly is a set of eight which will relate sin and its remedy with both love and good government.
47 Vatican Library, ms Barb lat 128, f 48r
48 Ibid f 39v. For the sake of comparison, I include also a pair of examples to the same point from that part of the index covering Seneca's letters:

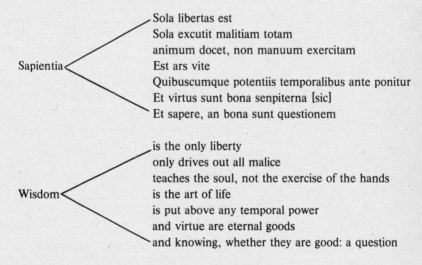

Sapientia
- Sola libertas est
- Sola excutit malitiam totam
- animum docet, non manuum exercitam
- Est ars vite
- Quibuscumque potentiis temporalibus ante ponitur
- Et virtus sunt bona senpiterna [sic]
- Et sapere, an bona sunt questionem

Wisdom
- is the only liberty
- only drives out all malice
- teaches the soul, not the exercise of the hands
- is the art of life
- is put above any temporal power
- and virtue are eternal goods
- and knowing, whether they are good: a question

Further, on an oblique case of the same Wisdom:

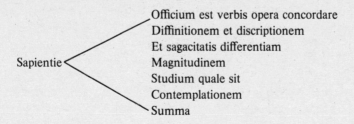

Sapientie
- Officium est verbis opera concordare
- Diffinitionem et discriptionem
- Et sagacitatis differentiam
- Magnitudinem
- Studium quale sit
- Contemplationem
- Summa

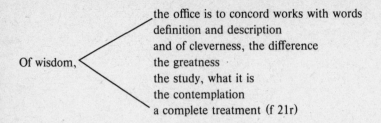

Of wisdom,
- the office is to concord works with words
- definition and description
- and of cleverness, the difference
- the greatness
- the study, what it is
- the contemplation
- a complete treatment (f 21r)

If any single sentence could define the essence of late medieval literature, it would be this one: 'Sapientie officium est verbis opera concordare.' It preserves, in a triad of coordinate value, words and things and the wisdom or meaning which is at once their relation and their truth.

49 Benvenuto da lmola, ed Lacaita, vol I, p 360. To Benvenuto's testimony may be added: '*Dogni malitia*: Nunc Virgilius ad declarationem distinctionis facte incipit modicum a longe et premittit unam divisionem bimembrem. / Now Virgil, to explain the distinction he has made, begins at a certain distance and puts first a division with two parts.' Florence, Biblioteca Laurenziana, ms 42.14, f 62r 'Qui commincia sua distinctione et dice dogni malitia cioe dogni inganno ... De violenti, etc. Procede alla distinctione de circuli, et collocare in essi li peccatori in cio viciati come appare nel testo, et nella chiosa generale di questo capitulo. / Here he begins his distinctio and he speaks of every malice, that is of every fraud ... of the violent, etc. He proceeds to the distinctio of the circles, and to locate the sinners inhabiting each as appears in the text, and in the general matter of this chapter.' Vatican Library, ms Barb lat 4103, ff 54, 55. In a commentary on the *Thebaid* of Statius, one may find reference to the distinctio quite self-consciously elaborated: '*Interea*: Hic incipit secundus liber. Distinctiones ideo fiunt ab actoribus ut priori parte bene collecta et memorie commendata possit aliquid in mente edificari. In superiori libro habuistis quomodo pollinices in exilium profectus secundum conditionem alterni exilii ad Larissam civitatem Adrasti venit. Similiter et thideus fratricidii reus fugiens calidonem venit eodem ibique in cenobio adrasti rixabantur. Rex vero accensis luminibus ad eos descendens separavit litigantes [cod litigate*n*s] et utriusque habitum diligenter considerans, quod diu latuerat oraculum deprehendit. / Here begins the second book. Distinctions are made by authors so that, when a prior part has been well considered and commended to memory, he might build up something in the mind. In the preceeding book you have now Polynices, who had set out in exile in accordance with the agreement of alternate exile, came to Larissa the city of Adrastus. Similarly Tydeus, fleeing Calydon guilty of fratricide, came to the same place and there in the courtyard of Adrastus they brawled. But the king, when he had lit the lights and descended to them, separated them, and, considering carefully the appearance of each of

them, understood what the oracle had long concealed.' There follows in this gloss a similar summary of the second book. Venice, Biblioteca Marciana, ms XII.61 (4097), f 28v.

50 Assisi, Biblioteca communale, ms 396, f 120v
51 Allen and Moritz *A Distinction of Stories*
52 Robinson p 76, lines III (D), 1–3
53 For an extended treatment of the whole subject of rhyming prose, of which this rhyming outlining is from one point of view a part, see Karl Polheim *Die lateinische Reimprosa* (Berlin 1925). I treat the matter briefly in *The Friar as Critic*, pp 70–1. In a literary context, one of the best known examples of this kind of rhyming *distinctio*, used as the outline of exposition, is the collection of mythographic pictures in John Ridewall's *Fulgentius Metaforalis*.
54 The most important work along these lines is collected in Robert Lumiansky ed *Malory's Originality: A Critical Study of Le Morte Darthur* (Baltimore 1964).
55 William Matthews *The Ill-framed Knight: A Skeptical Inquiry into the Identity of Sir Thomas Malory* (Berkeley 1966)
56 For a study which relates the *Morte* to fifteenth-century chivalric practice, see Larry D. Benson *Malory's Morte Darthur*. Federigo di Montefeltro, Duke of Urbino, was made knight of the Garter in 1474; what was true of chivalry at that eminence was relatively true at all levels – the society in which Malory participated and for which he wrote was international, self-conscious, and idealistically at least unified.
57 The bulk of the library is listed in Leopold Delisle *Le Cabinet des Manuscrits de la Bibliothèque Impériale: Étude sur la formation de ce dépôt comprenant les éléments d'une histoire de la calligraphie, de la miniature, de la reliure, et du commerce des livres à Paris avant l'invention de l'imprimerie* (Paris 1868) vol I, pp 86ff. Others are listed by Delisle 'Note complémentaire sur les mss de Jacques d'Armagnac' *Bibliothèque de l'École des Chartes* 66 (1905) 255–60.
58 For a discussion of some of these noble collectors, see Cedric Edward Pickford *L'Évolution du roman arthurien en prose vers la fin du moyen âge* (Paris 1960).
59 Paris, Bibliothèque nationale, mss fr 22, 25, and 26
60 Paris, Bibliothèque nationale, mss fr 37, 268, and 9186. This last manuscript also contains excerpts from the *City of God*.
61 Paris, Bibliothèque nationale, ms fr 41
62 Paris, Bibliothèque nationale, ms fr 50–1
63 Paris, Bibliothèque nationale, ms fr 71–2
64 This was a Hamilton manuscript, sold in London in 1889, on which Delisle had made notes at Strasbourg. See his 'Notes complémentaire.'
65 Paris, Bibliothèque nationale, ms fr 256
66 Paris, Bibliothèque nationale, ms fr 253

67 Paris, Bibliothèque nationale, ms fr 783, 784, and 790
68 Paris, Bibliothèque nationale, ms fr 2660–1
69 Delisle lists Paris, Bibliothèque nationale, ms fr 869, which is not a copy of the *Metamorphoses*. This is probably a mistake for ms fr 870.
70 Matthews p 145. Cf Paris, Bibliothèque nationale, mss fr 99, 106–9, 112, 113–16, and 117–20.
71 Paris, Bibliothèque nationale, ms fr 112. For a discussion of Gonnot, see Matthews pp 146–7 and Pickford, pp 18–24. Though Gonnot's narratives are less interlaced than those from which he must have compiled his book, the decoration of the manuscript makes clear that the essential unit of romance is still a single short episode – a single bit of action, which must be taken to relate to those which precede and follow in ways more important than mere narrative continuity.
72 Paris, Bibliothèque nationale, ms fr 112, book IV, f 1r–v. Caxton's introduction to his Malory, of course, has similar sentiments.
73 The *Politics* and *Economics* are Paris, Bibliothèque nationale, ms fr 125; the *Ethics*, ms fr 207.
74 Paris, Bibliothèque nationale, ms fr 579
75 Paris, Bibliothèque de l'Arsenal, ms 6329
76 Paris, Bibliothèque nationale, ms fr 602
77 Paris, Bibliothèque nationale, ms fr 916
78 Paris, Bibliothèque nationale, ms fr 175, 4v
79 Benson, *Malory's Morte Darthur*, makes the analogous point about chivalry – that in Malory's time, life could be as much expected to be imitating romances as could romances be expected to describe, either realistically or idealistically, the knightly activities of real life.
80 It is not necessary to claim that Malory read the glosa – the notion is, as I have said, commonplace. It may well be that further research will turn up a medieval gloss as perfectly connected to Malory as the one Siegfried Wenzel found for the Moor Maiden ('The Moor Maiden, A Contemporary View' *Speculum* 44 (January 1974) 69–74); the distinctiones and sermon collections surviving from the later Middle Ages are an enormous body of still largely unmined evidence, whose arrayed outlines will establish the discursive patterns in terms of which late medieval poetry is likely to unify itself. Lacking the kind of broad access to that evidence which modern indexes and editions will eventually give us, explications of late medieval literature must remain speculative – but not, I think, seriously doubtful.
81 'Primo die lucem fidei, quando primo invisibilibus credit, propter quam fidem dominus apparere dignatus est.' *Biblia sacra, cum glosa ordinaria* (Lyons 1520), vol I, f 24v.

82 'Secundo die factum est tanquam firmamentum discipline, quod discernit inter carnalia et spiritualia, sicut inter inferiores et superiores aquas.' *Biblia sacra* vol I, f 25r.

83 *Doctoris ecstatici D. Dionysii cartusiani opera omnia* vol I (Monstroli 1896) p 61

84 'Tertio die, quo mentem suam ad ferendos bonorum operum fructus preparat homo, separata labe ac fluctibus carnalium tentationum: tanquam aridam habet terram tentationibus separatis.' *Biblia sacra* vol I, f 25v.

85 'Quarto die quo in illo firmamento discipline mens spirituales intelligentias operatur atque distinguit; videt que sit incommutabilis veritas, que sicut sol fulgeat in anima et quomodo anima ipsius particeps fiat; et corpori ordinem et pulcritudinem tribuat, tanquam luna illuminans noctem. Et quomodo stelle omnes idest intelligentie spirituales in huius vite obscuritate, tanquam in nocte fulgeant' vol I, f 26v.

86 'Incipit provecta mens quinto die in actionibus turbulenti seculi, tanquam in aquis maris operari, propter utilitatem fraterne societatis, et de corporalibus agnitionibus, que ad mare, idest ad hanc vitam pertinent, producere animarum vivarum reptilia, idest opera que prosunt animis vivis, et cetos magnos, idest fortissimas agnitiones, quibus fluctus seculi dirumpuntur et contemnuntur, et volatilia celi, idest voces celestia predicantes.

'Et factum est vespere et mane. Isi.mystice; Mane transmigratio in babyloniam, cum ea captivitate populus leviter in peregrino ocio est collocatus, et porrigitur hec etas usque ad adventum christi, idest quinta declinatio, scilicet de iuventute usque ad senectutem; nondum senectus, nec iam iuventus, sed senioris etas, quam greci presbyten vocant. Nam senex apud eos non presbyten, sed geron dicitur. Et revera sic ista etas a regni robore est inclinata et fracta in populo iudeorum, ut homo a iuventute senior fit. Que bene comparatur diei quinto, quo facta sunt animalia in aquis et volatilia celi, postquam inter gentes tanquam in mari vivere ceperunt, sedem incertam et instabilem habentes, sicut aves volantes. Ibi ceti, idest homines magni, qui magis dominari fluctibus seculi, quam in captivitate servire potuerunt, nullo enim terrore ad idolatriam depravati sunt. Ubi advertendum quod benedixit deus animalia dicens, Crescite et multi., quia gens iudeorum per gentes dispersa valde multiplicata est. Huius diei idest huius etatis quasi vespera est, multiplicatio peccatorum in populo iudeorum, quia sic excecati sunt, ut nec possent christum cognoscere.'

'On the fifth day the advanced mind begins the action of the busy world, as if it were active in the waters of the sea, for the sake of usefulness to brotherly society, and physical perceptions, which pertain to the sea, that is, this life, to produce the reptiles of living souls, that is, the works which are helpful to living souls, and great whales, that is, strong perceptions, by which the waves of this world are broken and defied, and the flying things of the sky, that is, voices preaching celestial things.

'And it was made the evening and morning. Isidore mystically: In the morning the migration into Babylon, when by captivity the people were set lightly in foreign idleness, and this age extends to the advent of Christ, that is the fifth declining, from youth toward age – not yet aged, nor yet young, but of mature age, which the Greeks call *presbyten*. For the aged among them are not called *presbyten*, but *geron*. And in truth this age in the people of Israel is declined and broken from the strength of the kingdom, as a man grows mature from youth. This age is well compared to the fifth day, in which were made the sea animals and the flying things of the sky; after they began to live among the gentiles as if in the sea, they had an uncertain and unstable seat, as do flying birds. There [are] the whales, that is great men, who are more able to govern the waves of this world than serve in captivity, for by no terror are they depraved into idolatry. So we must notice that God blessed the animals, saying, grow and multiply, because the people of the Jews, dispersed among the gentiles, multiplied greatly. What stands for the evening of this day, that is, of this age, is the multiplication of sins among the people of the Jews, because they were so blinded that they could not recognize Christ.' *Biblia sacra* vol I, f 27v.

87 'Isi. Mane sexti diei fit predicatio evangelii per Christum. Finito vero quinto, incipit sextus, in quo veteris hominis apparet senectus. Hac enim etate vehementer attritum est illud regnum, quando templum deiectum est, et sacrificia cessaverunt, et nunc gens illa quantum ad vires regni quasi vitam extremam trahit. In hac tamen etate tanquam in veteris hominis senectute nascitur novus homo qui spiritualiter vivit ... Et sicut in illa die masculus et femina, sic in ista etate Christus et ecclesia. In illa die preponitur homo pecoribus et serpentibus et volatibilibus celi, et in hac etate Christus regit animas sibi obtemperantes, que partim de gentibus, partim de iudeis venerunt, ut ab eo domite mansuescerent, carnali scilicet concupiscentie dediti, sicut pecora, vel tenebrosa curiositate obtenebrati, quasi serpentes, vel superbia elati quasi aves. In illa die pascitur homo et animalia que cum ipso sunt, herbis seminalibus, lignis fructiferis, et viridibus herbis. In ista quoque etate homo spiritualis quicumque bonus minister est Christi, et eum pro posse imitatur, cum ipso populo spiritualiter pascitur, scripture alimentis et divine legis, partim ad concupiscendam fecunditatem rationum atque sermonum tanquam herbis seminalibus, partim ad utilitatem morum et humane conversationis, tamquam lignis fructiferis, partim ad vigorem fidei, spei et charitatis in vitam eternam,

tanquam herbis viridibus, idest virentibus, que nullo estu tribulationum arescant. Sed spiritualis sic pascitur, ut multa intelligat ...

Moraliter: Sexto die producit terra animam vivam, idest homo de stabilitate sue mentis ubi habet fructus spirituales, idest bonas cogitationes: omnes motus animi sui regit, ut sit in illo anima viva, idest rationi et iusticie serviens non terrentitati et peccato. Ita fit homo ad imaginem et similitudinem dei masculus et femina, idest intellectus et actio, quorum copulatione spiritualis fetus terram impleat, idest carnem subiiciat et cetera que iam in hominis perfectione dicta sunt. In istis namque diebus, vespera est ipsa perfectio singulorum operum, et mane, inchoatio sequentium.'

'Isidore: On the morning of the sixth day there is made the preaching of the Gospel by Christ. When the fifth is done, the sixth begins, in which the old man appears aged. For in this age that kingdom is very much wasted away, when the temple is thrown down, and the sacrifices have ceased, and now the people go down into extreme old age, as far as the strength of their realm is concerned. But in this age, as if in the old age of the old man, the new man is born who lives spiritually ... And as in that day male and female, so in this age Christ and the Church. In that day man was preferred above the beasts and serpents and flying things of the sky, and in this age Christ rules the spirits obedient to him, who come partly from the Jews and partly from the gentiles, that tamed by him they might be meek – that is, those who were given to carnal concupiscence like beasts, or darkened with shadowy curiosity like serpents, or elated in pride like birds. In that day man and the animals who are with him feed on seed-bearing herbs, and fruit-bearing trees, and green herbs. In this age also any spiritual man is a good minister of Christ, and imitates him as much as possible, and is fed spiritually with the people, on the nourishment of scripture and holy law, partly as if on seed-bearing herbs for the sake of the desire of fertile reason and speech, partly as if on fruit-bearing trees for the sake of usefulness in behaviour and human conversation, partly as if on green herbs, that is, on flourishing ones, which dry up from no heat of tribulation, for the sake of strength of faith, hope, and love in eternal life. The spiritual are nourished, thus, that they might understand much.

'Morally: On the sixth day the earth produced a living soul, that is, a man with stability of mind, from which he has spiritual fruits, that is good thoughts; he rules every motion of his soul, that there might be in him a living soul, that is, one serving reason and justice, not sin and earthly concerns. Thus man is made in the image and similitude of God male and female, that is, intellect and action, by whose intercourse a spiritual offspring fills the earth, that is, subdues the flesh, etc., which is what happens when men become perfect. And in these days, the evening is the perfection of every single work, and the morning, the beginning of the next ones.' *Biblia sacra* vol I, f 29r.

88 'Allegorice. Post illorum quasi sex dierum opera valde bona, speret homo requiem perpetuam, et intelligat quid sit, requievit deus die septimo ab operibus suis, quia et ipse in nobis hec bona operatur, qui iubet ut operemur, et recte quiescere dicitur, quia post hec omnia opera requiem nobis prestabit, quomodo paterfamilias domum edificat, cum servientibus facere imperat, et post ab operibus requiescere, cum perfecta fabrica, iubet quiescere. / After the very good works of those, as it were, six days, man hopes for perpetual rest, and he should understand what it means that God rested on the seventh day from all his works, because he also does these good works in us, who orders that we work, and rightly to rest is said, because after all these works he will offer us rest, as the head of a household builds a house, when he orders his servants to build it, and afterwards rests when, after the building is finished, he orders rest.' *Biblia sacra* vol I, f 34r.

89 'Nam in revolutione idem est octavus qui et primus ... Unde et dies iudicii, quia post septimam sabbati ventura est, octava in scripturis dicta est, quasi septem tantum precesserint, dies quoque resurrectionis domini, cum post tot dierum milia ventura esset, octava dicta est. Potest autem dici complevisse deum die septima opus suum, quia ipsum benedixit et sanctificavit; opus enim est benedictio et sanctificatio. Aliquid enim operis fecit salomon, cum templum dedicavit. / For in revolving the eighth and the first are the same ... so also the day of judgment, because it is going to come after the seventh of the Sabbath, is called the octave in scripture, as if just seven had gone before. Also the day of the resurrection of the Lord, when it comes after all the thousands of days, is called the octave. And it can be said that God completed his work on the seventh day, because he blessed and sanctified it, for benediction and sanctification are a work. For Solomon did a kind of work, when he dedicated the temple.' *Biblia sacra* vol I, f 34r.

4

Assimilatio and the material of poetry

When Archibald MacLeish proclaimed that 'a poem must not mean, but be,' he gave a defining slogan to a generation of literary criticism. As a slogan, it was useful enough; as a serious statement about the nature of poetic language, it is hopelessly silly, because it polarizes as opposites the two features of language whose identity is the basis of all the value language has. Words exist as the achievement of relationships, not as their rival. Nevertheless, MacLeish is right in honouring the fact that in poetry, something is – the words evoke a species of existence. For this species of existence, the Middle Ages had many names, which it is the business of this chapter to array and define. Of them all, the most fundamental, the most able to take centre place and give meaning to all the rest, is the word 'assimilatio.' This is the word which, in the Averroistic version of Aristotle's *Poetics*, replaces the key concept of mimesis. It is associated with, and even equated with, other key terms such as 'ymaginatio' and 'representatio.' To translate it, Hardison adopts the neutral term, 'likening,' which can permit, though it cannot evoke, the extremely complex array of cases which the term covers, includes, and synthesizes.

Before presenting the medieval material which defines and depends on the word 'assimilatio,' I must admit two things, by way of a heuristic introduction. The first is that I take this term, in the strongest possible sense, as a betrayal of the medieval doctrine more even than as an intentional exposition of it. Other words are more popular; the conscious and habitual concerns of medieval critics do not so much refer to or gesture with the term 'assimilatio' as presume it. In the second place, I recognize in this term, which denotes not the state of the existence of an entity but the result of the achievement of a relation, the same demand which I have repeatedly emphasized throughout this book – that is, that what we call poetry exists in the

Middle Ages only because of and in terms of some larger complex of relationships and significances. The very stuff of which poetry is made – the stories and descriptions which are, literally, the words which poems are – cannot be taken as merely and in isolation themselves. The key definition of the words, stories, figures, and statements of which poems compose themselves is a definition, not of a thing, but of an act – an act, moreover, whose actors and objects inhabit a larger world than that of the poem itself. Considered as texts, poems are, as it were, locations in a tissue of assimilatio larger than themselves.

In calling the word 'assimilatio' a betrayal, I in no sense wish to suggest that medieval critics were themselves unconscious of the fact that, as Michel Foucault puts it, 'resemblance played a constructive role in the knowledge of Western culture ... representation – whether in the service of pleasure or of knowledge – was posited as a form of repetition: the theater of life or the mirror of nature, that was the claim made by all language, its manner of declaring its existence and of formulating its right of speech.'[1] The role and power of analogical thinking was obvious. At the same time, analogy or resemblance was, as a mental procedure, itself the subject of discussion. As Sheila Delany has shown, the validity of analogical thinking in the later Middle Ages was itself discussed, and advanced thinkers began to express doubts about it. In spite of and in the midst of these movements of thought, however, the persistent use of the term 'assimilatio,' that is, the persistent creation of poetry which patently assumes and reflects it, betrays two things. First, it betrays the fact that analogical structures persisted even in the thought of persons who were, as philosophers, at some pains to deny or limit their conscious affirmation of analogy as an instrument of thought.[2] Second, and even more important, the term 'assimilatio,' used to designate that of which poetry is made – that is, used to designate something taken as material even while it is actually a term of relationship – betrays a medieval sense of the ontology of poetry as something neither material nor verbal, but rather structural. Like certain subatomic particles, which do not exist in any sense readily intelligible to human beings who inhabit solid worlds, but which are nevertheless implicated by certain relationships and processes in the atom, the assimilationes of poetry exist as dynamic structures rather than as static things.

These betrayals have a more than merely historical significance. It would be intellectually irresponsible to presume from them an easy equivalence between medieval poetic and modern structuralism. Assimilatio is a feature of medieval culture, and so has its own irretrievably historical integrity. At the same time, the modern willingness to think in structural terms, rather than in (or in addition to) materially atomist or merely mechanical terms, does prepare us to understand and profit from the analogous existence, in medieval culture, of such structures as assimilatio. We are prepared first of all to understand a cultural universe which has poems, but no category for literature; we are prepared to understand a cultural universe which has words and grammar and language, but no sense of the solipsism except as a theo-logical and so redeemable condition; we are prepared for a universe in which fact and significance are radically related, rather than radically separated from one another. In purely and narrowly critical terms, the medieval fact of assimilatio permits one to deal with the question of occasionally, the prob-lem of the relation among parts of a text, and the problem of the relation between a text and its external 'distinctio' outline, in terms whose very inter-relationship solves most problems. In addition, in making allegory, commen-tary, metaphor, and 'conjointure' versions of one another, assimilatio not only provides criticism with a powerful resource of definition, but also per-mits a richer and more fruitful understanding of audience, and therefore of the act of interpretation itself. At the other extreme, in the largest possible sense, the medieval notion of assimilatio permits certain assertions about language which should be of great benefit to a modern structuralism which is too much under the influence of merely formalist linguistics.

In my analysis of assimilatio I have two purposes – first, to make the notion itself clear, and second, to show that it is a structure or a critical presumption in terms of which literary texts may be profitably analysed and understood. In the service of these two purposes, my treatment will neces-sarily oscillate between expository definition on the one hand, and pre-sentation of a variety of medieval examples on the other. Assimilatio is a complex structure, which assumes identity or at least coherence among various entities we are now disposed to know as different, or incoherent; only by a variety of examples can I begin to do it full justice. But these examples, in their variety, obscure the track of the argument. I therefore predict it here.

I begin with a medieval analysis of the term, which permits one to posit three kinds of assimilatio – that which most generally involves a comparison of some sort, and more specifically, that which relates a description to the thing described, and that which evokes a universal. This range of kinds, which logically should be ordered as description, comparison, and relation to universal, then furnishes an outline to the rest of the chapter. Description raises the whole problem of language, and of its truth value – assimilatio relates to imagination, or conceptualization, as a verification. Further, under medieval presumptions, descriptions are not mere signs of an empirical reality, but rather shape particulars in part according to what language presumes as itself. All these relationships, and their relation to the general notion of comparison which is what 'assimilatio' most broadly means, are illustrated, by presenting medieval texts which enact or explain them. In the second place, comparison narrowly understood, which is by medieval understanding the basic device of poetry, raises the question of metaphor. Illustrations will be presented which show that metaphors must be based on real similitudes, that some metaphors, in these terms, are impossible, and that commentary often reacts to metaphoric language by showing that it can be seen as literally true. In all this material, we have very clearly betrayed the medieval presumption that metaphoric structures are more than arbitrary, linguistic, or personal creations, but rather reflect, or enact, something materially true of the universe. In the third place, the power of assimilatio to evoke the universal is explained in terms of a larger medieval habit, that of understanding systems by placing them in parallel with other systems. This strategy of parallel systems, which is both the most complex and the most powerful mode of existence of assimilatio, is illustrated by a number of medieval texts and structural acts, ranging from the very brief and simple to the cosmically large – from a double distinctio in a commentary margin and a brief speech from Malory to the systems defined by exegetical commentary and by Dante's *Commedia*.

My initial analysis of the term comes from a commentary, the lecture on the Averroistic *Poetics* made by Bartholomew of Bruges in 1307, to which I have several times already referred. Bartholomew is making a fundamental distinction, dealing with material very near the beginning of Averroes' text.[3] Averroes, he says

primo dividit contextionem poeticam penes finem eius, secundo penes formam ... In prima dicit quod omne poema aut est laudatio aut vituperatio ... Tunc sequitur illa pars 'et sermones poetici' in qua Aristoteles dividit de poemata penes suam formam que quidem est ymaginatio vel assimilatio, et dividitur in duas partes quia in prima parte dividit sermonem poeticam penes assimilationem que est eius forma, et secundo ostendit ex quibus habentibus fit assimilatio. Secunda ibi, 'et quemadmodum quidam hominum.' Vel possit dici quod his distinguit artem poeticam ab aliis artibus ymaginativis et patebit isti divisio. Et nota quia sermo poeticus est sermo assimilativus et ymaginativus, ideo dividit ipsum penes modos assimilandi et ymaginandi. Item notandum quod hec divisio potest dici formalis rationabiliter quia est ex ratione eius. Est enim ratio eius quod est sermo assimilativus et ymaginativus. Ratio autem accepit partes forma idest metaphysice. Primo nota quod dicit sermones poeticos esse ymaginativos assimilativos eo quod non directe exprimunt rem sed in suo simili vel proportionali vel quia utuntur similitudinibus et proportionibus; econtrario sermonibus demonstrativis qui directe exprimunt rem. Item vel dicit hec quia procedit ex assimilationibus ut patet in littera. Item dicit eos ymaginationes vel quia exprimunt rem in sua ymagine idest similitudine, vel quia non semper procedunt ex hiis que sunt sed que sunt possibilia ymaginari ut patet in principio secundi, vel quia faciunt estimationem et ymaginationem quod res ita sic se habeat sicut dicit, et istud et primum videtur melius et concordat cum sequentibus et cum averroe versus finem super illa parte 'et species signaculorum.' Item nota quod assimilatio et ymaginatio se haberet per ordinem quia primo poeta versatur circa assimilationem scilicet assimilans rem cum re et secundo circa ymaginationem scilicet faciendo estimare rem sic esse per talem assimilationem. Item notandum quod ex dictis apparent due descriptiones sermonis poetici vel orationis poetice. Prima est quod est sermo laudativus aut vituperativus. Secunda est quod est sermo assimilativus et ymaginativus.

first divides poetic composition with regard to its end, second with regard to its form ... On the first he says that every poem is either praise or blame ... then follows that part 'et sermones poetici' in which Aristotle divides concerning poetry with regard to its form, which clearly is imagination or likening, and it is divided into two parts since in the first part he divides poetic speech with regard to likening which is its form, and second he shows what must be had to make a likening. The second part begins at 'et quemadmodum quidam hominum.' Or it can be said that in these [divisions] he distinguishes poetic language from other imaginative arts – now the division of this is clear. And note that since poetic language is the language of likening and imagination, he divides it in terms of the modes of likening and imagining. Also it should be noted that this division can be said to be formal rationally because it comes from the theme[4] of the material. The theme or essence of it is that it is the language of likening and imagining, and theme gets its parts from form, that is, metaphysically. First note that he says poetic sentences are imaginative [and] likening because they do not express a thing directly, but in its similar or its proportionate, or because they use similitudes and proportions; on the contrary in demonstrative sentences there is direct expression of the thing. Or he says this because his content consists of likenings, as is obvious in the letter. He calls these expressions imaginations either because they express a thing in its image, that is, in its similitude, or because they do not always proceed in terms of things which exist, but in terms of things which are possible to imagine, as is clear in the premise of the second part; or because they make an estimate and an imagination that the thing is as he says. This alternative and the first one seem better and agree with what follows, and with Averroes near the end, when he comments on that part 'et species signaculorum.' Note also that he puts likening and imagination in the right order, because first the poet works with likening by likening a thing with a thing, and then he works with imagination by verifying that the thing is itself, and the likening is right. Also it should be noted from this passage there arise two descriptions of poetic statements or poetic language. The first is that it is language which praises or blames. The second is that it is language which likens and imagines.[5]

This is a very rich, complex, and dense piece of criticism. I shall deal with it first of all by relating it to the text of Averroes, since Bartholomew does not deal quite with the array of topics which one might expect. Second, I shall try to unpack Bartholomew's assumptions. Only then can we begin to get at what he thinks Averroes means by the term 'assimilatio.'

In the text of Averroes, the passage which Bartholomew treats contains a classification of similes, several metaphors adduced in illustration, and the specification of melody and rhythm as well as assimilatio as elements which can make a representation. In his comment, Bartholomew refuses all subtopics. He makes it absolutely clear what he considers most important, by refusing to discuss anything else. The form of poetry is assimilatio or ymaginatio; the passage deals with this fact, and with the modes in which it occurs. Bartholomew does not discuss the kinds of simile; he does not treat the content of any of the illustrations; he does not deal with the representative power of melody or rhythm. Rather, he tries to account for assimilatio itself, by telling what it is, what its metaphysical basis is, and how it is achieved and believed.

In his analysis, he presumes first of all that analysis consists of division: Averroes 'primo dividit ... penes finem eius, secundo penes formam.' Correspondingly, he uses the word 'contextio' to designate that act by which poetry is made – obviously, it is a contextio or an assembly or interweaving for which the appropriate act of analysis is division. This contextio may be taken, I think, as a synonym for the French term 'conjointure,'[6] and as a close relation of the Latin 'compilatio.'[7] It is also, as we shall see, an appropriate name for what exists as a result of, or as the presence of, assimilatio.

What Bartholomew divides, or rather what Averroes divides, is praise and blame from assimilatio. Bartholomew's contribution here is the generic specification – praise and blame are related to the end of poetry, and assimilatio and ymaginatio to its form. Without this specification, one might read Averroes and think that both praise and blame, and assimilatio, were descriptions of the content of poetry, as indeed, literally, they are. Bartholomew's specification of end makes the rhetorical dimension of poetry radically essential to it; his specification of form gives assimilatio and ymaginatio a high metaphysical importance – they are the 'ratio' of poetry. But ratio, as we have already seen, may be what we would call subject matter, or theme.

It is in no sense legitimate to take either of these texts as a commentary on the genuine Aristotle; the misunderstanding which divides Averroes from Aristotle is so large as to make the texts incommensurable. At the same time, it is appropriate to remind ourselves of the genuine concept of mimesis, if only to emphasize what a different kind of thing we confront in Averroes, and to define in a theoretically absolute sense the consequences of defining poetry in terms of assimilatio rather than in terms of mimesis. For Aristotle, tragedy is the imitation (mimesis) of an action of determinate size, having beginning, middle, and end, whose constituent parts are plot, character, thought, etc. Aristotelian mimesis, according to Hardison, has been taken to be a superior kind of copying, by which the artist achieves, not a copy of a copy, but something close to the divine form itself. Hardison prefers to interpret it as a process, variable according to artistic genre, by which the chaotic particulars of experience are universalized by being processed according to the rules and procedures of an art of making – in this case, the verbal art we call poetry. Both the process and the result, obviously, are properly classified as aesthetic.[8] That is, both the process and the result achieve, ideally, an imitation which is like, but separate from, that which is imitated. An imitation is something single, whole, self-existent, whose existence demands to be appreciated for its own sake, as the result of the exercise of an art, and apart from all reference, both of verification and of application. The art of making itself is something special, as well – in fact, the *Poetics* may be validly seen not as an empirical examination of what happened to exist as Greek tragedy, but rather as a deductive analysis of the kinds of makings, whose achievement is the definition of the one appropriate to mimesis. the universalization which mimesis achieves transforms the chaotic particulars of experience into language. Taken from every angle, the genuine doctrine of Aristotle distinguishes poetry from, rather than relates it to, defines it as itself, rather than as an organic part of a larger system.

By contrast, Bartholomew seems to be implying that assimilatio, whatever it is, is neither single nor isolable. His references to metaphysical form and ratio on the one hand, to things on the other, and his reiteration of the combinative, comparative force of assimilatio all lead to the opposite conclusion. Beyond this, his comments seem paradoxical. Assimilatio seems to be at once a way of analogizing ('non directe exprimunt') and a way of making a univocal reference ('res ita sic se habeat sicut dicit'). Moreover, assimilatio and ymaginatio seem sometimes to be the same operation ('sermones poeticos esse ymaginativos [et] assimilativos'); but when they are ordered they seem reciprocal. The poet first 'works on likening by likening a thing with a thing, and then he works on imagination by verifying that the thing is itself, and the likening is right.'[9] Unequivocally, however, we have doubleness, comparison. Assimilatio would seem to involve two terms, and never one. In this, it is to be distinguished from demonstrative speech, which 'directe exprimit rem.' Yet here we must not be misled. This difference between direct and indirect speech involves a difference in subject matter as well. Demonstrative speech deals with universals; poetry is ethics, and therefore deals largely with particulars. 'Directe exprimere rem,' therefore, must be taken to mean an act of naming, while 'non directe exprimere rem' may mean a comparison or a simile, but must be permitted also to mean a description. But in both cases the referential quality of poetic language is radically involved – language 'must not be but mean.' Yet this is a meaning which is subject to imaginative verification – almost empirical, I think, but not quite.

Our problem with this concept of assimilatio is not, I think, that its meaning is unclear. 'Likening' translates it excellently. Our problem is that the notion of likening fails to distinguish what we are accustomed to accept as the two-term relationships which poetry generates and contains, such as simile, metaphor, and comparison, and other two-term relationships in which we are accustomed to find only one real term, or which we are accustomed to distinguish from things 'poetic.' This failure to distinguish is precisely the point. The medieval assimilatio imposes on poetic theory an array of operations which must be taken as essentially identical, even though taking them as such requires large adjustments in our notion of the customary boundaries between areas and layers of the real.

Averroes uses the term constantly, throughout the *Poetics*. From his usage, it is possible clearly to establish the array of meanings which the term 'assimilatio' must have – all of which must be taken as equally illustrations of these definitions of Bartholomew with which we have begun, that is, that assimilatio involves indirect reference, it is verified by the imagination, it expresses the metaphysical form or ratio of that species of language whose end is praise and blame, it uses similitudes and even fictions, and it is different from 'sermo demonstrativus.' Three classes of meaning seem most important. First and most basic is the notion of comparison – an assimilatio is a comparison.

Et sermones poetici sermones sunt ymaginativi. Modi autem ymaginationis et assimilationis tres sunt: duo simplices et tertius compositus ex illis. Unus duorum simplicium est assimilatio rei ad rem et exemplatio eius ad ipsam. Et hoc fit in qualibet lingua aut per dictiones proprias illi lingue ut est hec dictio 'quasi' vel 'sicut' et que istis similantur que nominantur sinkategoreumata similitudinis aut per sumptionem ipsius cum suo assimilabili vel loco suo assimilabilis. Et istud nominatur in hac arte concambium. Et est ut dixit poeta quidam de quodam valde liberali: ipse est mare inundans undecumque venientium indigentias replens copiose et effluenter.

And poetic language is imaginative language. The modes of imagination and likening are three: two simple and the third composed of these. One of the two simple ones is the likening of a thing to a thing and the exemplification of this as that. And this is made in any language either by the use of words proper to that language, such as the words 'like' or 'as' and other words like these which are called particles of similitude, or by the use of something with what it is like or in place of what it is like. And this procedure is called in this art exchange. As a certain poet said of a very liberal person, exchange is: he is a flooding sea, filling copiously and overflowingly the needs of all comers. (pp 3–4)

But this comparison does not necessarily have to be one contained within the text of the poem; one of its terms may be outside. Assimilatio, in other words, may mean simple description, with univocal reference.[10] Averroes puts the matter thus:

Et in assimilatione que fit per sermonem inveniuntur tres differentie. Et est assimilatio per quam intenditur convenientia assimilati cum suo assimilibili preter ostensionem aliquam decentis aut turpis, sed solum intenditur ipsamet convenientia. Et hec assimilationis species est quasi materia apta ad hoc ut alteretur seu permutetur ad utramquam duarum extremitatum, scilicet assumitur interdum ad ostensionem decentie valde exprimendo ipsam et interdum permutatur ad ostensionem alicuius turpitudinis similiter valde exprimendo illam ... Et ista fuit via homeri videlicet quod ipse procedebat in suis assimilationibus per convenientiam exprimens decentiam et turpitudinem. Et quorundam poetarum bona operatio consistit penes convenientiam tantum et quorundam penes ostensionem decentie et turpitudinis et quorundam penes coniunctionem utrorumque simul ut Homeri.

And in likening which is made by language there are three possibilities. There is likening in which is intended a relationship between what is likened and what it is like without meaning anything decent or shameful, but simply meaning the likeness. And this kind of likening is a kind of material, suitable for being altered or changed into either of two extremes – sometimes it is used to show something decent, expressing it very strongly, and sometimes it is changed to meaning something shameful, expressing it with similar strength ... And this was the way Homer, who in his likenings expressed decent and shabby values by apt comparison. Some poets do well simply by making good comparisons, and others by expressing the decent or the shabby, and others by doing both at the same time as did Homer. (pp 8–9)

Whether with or without expression of the decent or admirable or the base, the subject of this language seems to be description. Certainly it may be. In another place, Averroes makes it completely clear that the relation between that which assimilates and that which is assimilated is simply the relation that obtains between words and their referent. His subject is exempla:

Et signum huius scilicet quod homo naturaliter letatur et gaudet ex assimilatione est quod delectamur et gaudemus in representatione aliquarum rerum in quarum sensu non delectamur. Et precipue quando representatio valde subtiliter exprimit rem representatam ut contingit in formatione multorum animalium que periti exprimunt sculptores aut pictores. Et propter hanc causam utimur in docendo exemplis ut facilius intelligatur quod dicitur propter hoc quod in eis est de motivo imaginative ... Et ex quo imitationes exemplares non sunt nisi quedam assimilationes ad res que iam ceciderunt in sensum, patet quod non assumuntur nisi ut citius et facilius intelligatur quod dicitur.

And the sign of this, that is that man naturally is pleased and made happy by likening is that we are pleased and made happy by the representation of some things in which we are not delighted by sense experience. And above all this is true when the representation expresses the thing represented very subtly, as happens in the formation of many animals which skilled sculptors and painters make. For this reason we use examples in teaching, that what is said may be more easily understood, because of the imaginative element in our examples ... And since exemplary imitations are nothing but certain likenings of things already known by sense experience, it is clear that they are not used except that one may more quickly and easily understand what is being said. (pp 11–12)

In addition to comparison and description, assimilatio also presumes and generates a relationship to the universal:

Et terminus substantialis sive intelligere faciens substantiam artis laudandi est quoniam ipsa est assimilatio et representatio operationis voluntarie virtuose complete que habet potentiam universalem in rebus virtuosis, non potentiam particularem in unaquaque rerum virtuosarum.

And the substantial end, or what makes the content of the art of praising intelligible, is that the likening and representation is of a whole voluntary virtuous deed which has universal ethical significance, and not particular significance for some particular act of virtue. (p 16)[11]

Of these three classes of meaning, comparison or 'likening' is of course the fundamental and most important one. Here, obviously, one may range the various kinds of conventional poetic comparisons or likenings – simile, metaphor, and allegory. Here also, because allegory in the Middle Ages presumes and includes texts on which allegory was imposed, one must include that most medieval of all likenings – that which relates a text to a commentary. Surrounding these comparisons or likenings, and defining them, are the other two classes of meaning which Averroes clearly intends – first, that likening which relates a description to the thing described, or more generally language to its referent; and, at the opposite extreme in linguistic space, that likening by which descriptions of particulars are connected to their universal names and significance. This is a range of meanings which obviously implies a theory of language. More important, here, however, is the fact that this range of meanings requires that the operations and relationships internal to the textuality of poetry, such as, for instance, simile and metaphor; and those relationships and operations which are intrinsic but not entirely internal, such as allegory; and finally, those relationships and operations which are extrinsic, by which poems are attached to real particulars of life and history, and to the universal sententia which they argue; are all the same. Further, this range of meanings requires us to conclude that the structures by which poetic texts are to be related to real particulars and to universals – that is, the structures of ordinary reality because of which language works and thinking is possible at all, are those metaphoric and comparative structures which are conventionally considered as especially poetic. As in the classification of poetry as ethics, so here – that which is in fact empirically characteristic of poetry enters into the definition of the ethics into which poetry is assimilated; and likewise that strategy of assimilatio obviously characteristic of the internal workings of poetic texts is expanded in application, and now defines other relationships as well. One of these relationships, that involving real particulars, was one conventionally confirmed in medieval culture – the world did in fact operate very much as did a poem, and the phrase 'book of the creatures' was more than mere metaphor. This relationship, as we shall see, permits one to make much of the fact that moral and metaphoric structures were defined by commentaries with the same formulae; it permits one to relate memory to history on the one hand, and imagery on the other, so as to minimize the difference between fact and fiction to the advantage of poetry, and reciprocally permits one to deal with the occasionality of poetry even when one does not know for sure the specific occasion. The other relation, the one which assimilates poetry to universals, was, as we have seen, axiomatically denigrated or doubted by medieval philosophy; I shall eventually try to argue that the very doubleness which the term 'assimilatio' always asserts is in fact an implicit solution for this doubt, and permits one to be nominalist without having to be at the same time radically sceptical. Both relations tend to minimize, if not erase, the border of distinction between the poetic and the non-poetic, and thus to make meaningless, as have so many features of this medieval poetic already treated, the antonomous moden category of the aesthetic.

The whole range of meanings which Averroes implies under assimilatio can, of course, be independently confirmed from other medieval commentaries and discussions of poetic. The most important point which all this material makes, as I have said, is that it defines as structurally identical those comparative structures internal to poetry and those structures by which poetry relates to particulars and to universals. In tems of bulk of material, the largest part is that which tells us what assimilatio is and how it works in those contexts in which it functions for the most part in a way internal to poetry. What is said about assimilatio as the name of the act of description, on the other hand, simply affirms that the name is in fact appropriate – description, or more broadly reference, is an assimilatio, leaving largely implicit *what* it is. Because all these structures are essentially the same, all instances of them are mutually informing, and there is no way to talk about simile without implicating description, or allegory without implicating commentary and occasion. Still, one must distinguish. I shall therefore begin with a discussion of the broad question of assimilatio as description or reference – that which defines the relation between words and the worlds words relate to, describe, and define. After this discussion, and as a refinement and further definition of it, I shall present each of the other modes of assimilatio in turn – comparison or simile, then metaphor or more generally 'translatio,' and finally those more radical parallelisms we call commentary and allegory. We are accustomed to distinguish these things; the burden of my analysis will be to show that in spite of obvious but essentially trivial differences, all these things are really the same, and it is in their sameness that the true distinctiveness of the medieval poetic defines itself.

It is impossible here even to summarize medieval doctrines of language. As general background I presume Dante's *De vulgari eloquentia* and Dragonetti's excellent analysis of it, along with Mazzotta's more comprehensive study of the *Commedia*,[12] the tradition of discussion of interpretation that includes Augustine's *De doctrina christiana* and Hugh of St Victor's *Didascalicon*,[13] and such modern treatments of language as base themselves in medieval philosophy or exist as analysis of medieval texts.[14] For my purposes here, there are three commonplace medieval beliefs about language which must be emphasized – the medieval belief that language was perfect in paradise, that though because of sin language lost its perfection it still retained, as it were, a certain natural resemblance of the reality it described, and, third, that grammatical, linguistic, and etymological structures which one might discover by the analysis of language could inform one's analysis or understanding of reality. Assimilatio presumes all three beliefs. If language had not been perfect, there would be no need to strive to achieve the convenientia which might point toward the recovery of that perfection. If there were no resemblance involving, obviously, two terms, then assimilatio would not be a structure of doubleness. Finally, if one could not get behind the errors of specific uses of language, specific dialects, versions, words, etc, to that common ground of linguistic essence which is presumably closer to Edenic perfection that is any living language, then there would be no reason to be preoccupied with assimilatio as such – as a structure which, apart from any use or application of it, echoes or resembles the operation of reality.

The first and most important feature of assimilation, then, is that it is a structure in which one becomes aware of the fact, or possibility, of truth. As Bartholomew says: 'Primo poeta versatur circa assimilationem scilicet assimilans rem cum re et secundo circa ymaginationem scilicet faciendo estimare rem sic esse per talem assimilationem.'[15] An assimilatio asserts that a certain formula of language resembles in some way something else – either a meaning, or a thing capable of being described, or another formula of language. This resemblance, as many passages in Bartholomew and Averroes make clear, is based upon some kind of similitude – and though in one sense this language merely asserts that 'a resemblance is a resemblance,' it is still important to make it becuase, more seriously, it asserts that a verb is a noun – 'to resemble' equals 'similitudo.' It is this similitudo which the imagination verifies by 'estimando rem sic esse per talem assimilationem.' In this context, of course, the imagination must be taken as more than merely the mental ability to form images of sensibilia, or of fantasies, but rather as a faculty of conceptualization, in that it organizes sensibilia into the discrete objects of thought to which descriptions can be assimilated. Imagination itself is thus an active, not merely passive, faculty – it makes images and concepts, and does not simply receive them from an imprinting world.[16] But Bartholomew's ordering would seem to imply that assimilatio is still more powerful, still more active, and that it is in the light of and under the guidance of this prior activity that imagination can 'estimare.'

The truth which assimilatio by description generates is, of course, rooted in and related to particulars, for which it generates some connection with the universal. To some extent, of course, this involves the manipulation of the particulars themselves. Of this manipulation, the most radical examples occur in the religious and devotional tradition, as facts are mythologized, revised, and allegorized to make their descriptions convenient to the faith. In illustration, I have chosen a very simple and material distinctio from a medieval sermon on the cross:

Quattuor sunt cruces, diversa meritorum stipendia expectantes. Prima est crux Christi, unde lignae illa in qua pependit, scilicet crux caritatis, in qua ... extensus, quasi ad amplexandos nos amoris brachiis ... Post hanc secunda est crux penitentie, crux latronis illius qui ad dexteram domini pependit ... Est alia crux latronis scilicet sinistri, sine penitentia, sine spe, sine consolatione in qua pendens ille totus sinister ... Est crux alia in angaria quam portat ille cuius nomen symon idest obediens, qui vere omnis obedientie labores instantissime portans quasi crucem domini.

There are four crosses, anticipating the diverse rewards of merits. The first is the cross of Christ, that wooden cross on which he hung, that is the cross of charity, in which (he hung) with the arms of love outstretched as if for embracing us ... After this the second cross is the cross of penance, the cross of that thief who hung on the right side of the Lord. There is another cross of a thief, that is, of the left, without penance, without hope, without consolation in which he (was) hanging all sinister ... There is another cross in service which the person named Simon carried, who means obedience, ready to bear the labours of all obedience as if they were the cross of the Lord.[17]

In the only sense which matters to a modern mind, there were only three crosses, not four – the preacher has used Christ's cross twice. This medieval willingness to make four crosses out of three specifically illustrates that monadic, bit-by-bit approach to reality which was not careful to distinguish between material and temporal separations or to treat one as more substantial than the other; more generally, it betrays the pervasive medieval willingness to submit empirical to devotional or interpretative necessities. In a more poetic context, a fifteenth-century commentator on the *Poetria nova* of Geoffrey of Vinsauf tells us how a man may be praised in a way which betrays an interesting manipulation, both of the concept of a human being and of the notion of his virtue. The commentator's lemma is 'Lex publica mundi; digneris lucere mihi. / General light of the world, deign to light me' (lines 33–4).

Et auctor volens esse rhethor et poeta utitur vera parte poetica que dicitur laudatio. Laus autem secundum Aristotelem primo 22° rethorice sermo elucidans magnitudinem virtutis.[18] Sed quia virtus potest esse multiplex, multipliciter potest quisquis [cod q's] laudari ex virtute scilicet v modis: uno modo ex nomine, 2⁰ ex dispositione corporis seu forma, 3⁰ ex ipsius eloquencia, 4⁰ ex ipsius potentia, 5⁰ ex loco sue habitationis, et illud patet in hiis versibus: Nomen cum forma virtus sapiencia posse / Et loca sunt norma quam laudem scis bene nosse.

This author, desiring to be a rhetorician and a poet, uses that true poetic part called praise. Praise, according to Aristotle in the first part of the twenty-second book of the Rhetoric, is speech making clear the greatness of virtue. But because virtue can be multiple, one may be praised for his virtue in many ways, that is, five modes: in one mode in terms of one's name, second in terms of the disposition of one's body or one's form, third in terms of one's eloquence, fourth in terms of one's power, fifth in terms of the place of one's habitation, and this is clear from these verses: Name with form, and virtue, place, and wisdom / These are the norms by which praising is done.[19]

The specification of the topics of praise, of which this is an example, is a medieval commonplace, of which this commentator was himself aware because he had a mnemonic formula for it. I cite this example not because it is any way unusual, but because even in its very conventionality it represents a considerable manipulation of the world – it defines the praiseworthiness of a man in terms which are a mixture of the intrinsic and the extrinsic, and within which such items as the habitation, the eloquence, and even the bodily beauty, are possible to the Christian sensibility only because of the very powerful influence of an essentially non-Christian rhetoric. The difference between the extrinsic and the intrinsic, of course, is much more felt by the modern sensibility than by the medieval one – though we might still praise a man by praising his house, there are more people now than in the Middle Ages who would think that praise either irrelevant or perversely elitist or capitalist. The point of the difference is that the medieval topics of praise presume, for the real definition of the real world, a greater diffusion of human and ethical value into things, places, and skills than is absolutely necessary or than would be today normally presumed. This dispersion answers to and corresponds to those areas which assimilatio also covers.

Both these examples have to do with objects of possible perception – one, a material object called a cross, and the other, an objective human being deemed praiseworthy. What is true of objects is also true of perception or interpretation, that is, of acts now usually located more in or generated more by perceiver than perceived. The best illustration of this fact is the whole medieval category of the aesthetic, which, far from being in the eye of the beholder, was taken to be a real part of the description of the world and its operations.[20] Bernardus Silvestris might, I suppose, be taken to be an extreme witness to this fact of medieval sensibility; in his commentary on Martianus Capella's *De nuptiis*, at 'pugillo iam asseverante,' he repeats the twelfth-century commonplace to which this aesthetic can be most profoundly related:

Mundus hic sensibilis liber quidam est habens in se divinitatem in se scriptam. Singule vero creature littere sunt, et note alicuius quod in divinitate est. Immensitas enim mundi nota est divine potencie, pulcritudo mundi divine sapientie, utilitas mundi divine bonitatis.

This sensible world is a certain book having divinity intrinsically written in it. The single creatures are letters and notes of something which is in divinity. The immensity of the world is a note of the divine wisdom; the usefulness of the world, of the divine goodness.[21]

Bernardus reduces all this, with its development, to a chart, from which I reproduce only that part dealing with 'pulcritudo' (f 9r):

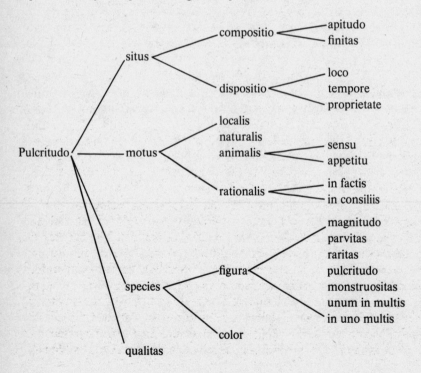

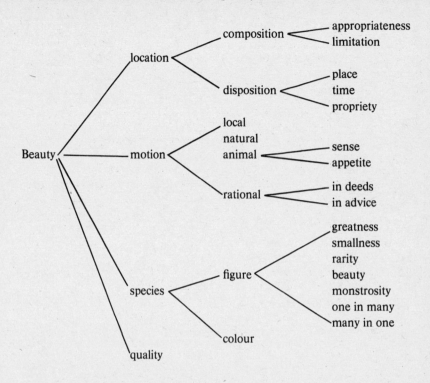

What is important about this chart is that it utterly ignores what we would consider important distinctions between material, formal, and mental realities. In ignoring these distinctions, of course, Bernardus is being conventionally medieval. His world is a world, which, as such, ontologically contains, dispersed in its being, a great deal of what we would call the mental. When we presume his world, we find that the aesthetic dimension is merely a feature of objective analysis, rather than a result of a particular kind of subjective judgment. Because his world is one into whose being so much of thought is already dispersed, the assimilatio by which the world is aligned with significant descriptions of it is a wholly natural act. The language of Aegidius Romanus, which I have already cited, explains the relation between particulars (as it happens, biblical ones) and universals in a more Aristotelian way: 'singulares personas in sacra pagine memoratas, per quandam signationem, universalis rationem habere. / single persons mentioned in the Bible have a universal significance by virtue of a certain signing.'[22] But whether Platonist or Aristotelian, the connection is real. For the purposes of poetry, of assimilatio, the world is an array of particulars already so conceptualized, already so imagined, as to make the still more combinative, more synthetic act of assimilatio entirely appropriate. The word which Averroes uses repeatedly to mean that an assimilatio is well made, that the relation constructed between a description and what is described, between a res and its representatio, is the word 'convenientia,' which it is easiest in most cases to translate as 'accuracy' – though the Latin word implies, I think, a more active reciprocity than does accuracy. Thus thought and the world are convenient to one another, both because the world organizes itself in a physical manner convenient to thought, and because the things thus organized behave toward one another in an assimilative way.

It is because thought and the world are convenient to one another that description is possible. This is the act of assimilatio which, according to Bartholomew of Bruges, 'indirecte exprimit rem.'[23] Literally, of course, description is made of words, and that which is expressed is some material or ideal thing. Gervaise of Melkley, in his *Ars poetica*, literally expresses the Averroistic implication by saying: 'Comparatio: tum fit per comparationem, tum per descriptionem. / Comparison: sometimes it is made by comparison, sometimes by description.'[24] Probably he does not quite mean it, since this sentence occurs in the section of his poetic which treats of 'idemptitas,' and he postpones his treatment of comparatio with and without such particles as 'like' or 'as' for the section on similitudo. But it is difficult to be sure just how much difference can be comprehended under idemptitas, since the topic treated just before this comparatio, for example, is digressio. In any case, something like assimilatio must be very important to him conceptually, since, though he does not deal with the term as such, he does organize his whole *Ars poetica* in terms of identity, similitude, and contrariety, that is, according to the different possibilities for the relation between two terms. In any case, he defines description in such a way as to require of it both a relation to particulars and a relation to significance:

Descriptio est demonstratio proprietatis alicuius rei, puta vel hominis, vel loci, vel temporis vel huiusmodi. Descriptio autem in nulla materia fieri debet, nisi talis ut auctor ex ipsa eliciat aliquod argumentum.

Description is demonstration of the property of some thing, such as a man, a place, a time, or something of this sort. Description ought to be made of no material, unless it be such that an author may elicit from it some evidence. (Ibid)

Further, Gervais, in his book as a whole, treats various features of the behaviour of language, and various features of the use of the content of language, without real distinction, and thus reflects, in his way, the same inter-dispersal of linguistic and material reality which medieval discussion of language so consistently presumes.

Beyond the mode of assimilation which names the relation between descriptions and that which descriptions represent, there is comparison in the common modern sense of the word. This, as I have said, is the relation central to the meaning of assimilatio; this is the relation which the whole range of meanings of assimilatio expresses by virtue of having that meaning. Comparison of course, or the exploitation of similitudes, is the 'basic device' of poetry.[25] It is so if we think of comparison as a word that refers to the whole range of possibilities for assimilatio, extending from description to allegory. Some such large significance is certainly what Hardison means by his use of the term, and is probably also what Thomas meant. The word, however, involves an ambiguity – in literary contexts, it also and quite narrowly means 'simile' or, slightly more broadly, the kind of metaphor which is nothing but a simile with the particle of comparison missing.

This narrower meaning of 'comparatio' is apparently what some medieval writers mean. Even thus restricted, it is of capital importance. Geoffrey of Vinsauf, for instance, treats much this kind of comparison under 'digressio' in his prose *Documentum*. After giving two examples, he generalizes: 'Infinita inveniuntur exempla comparationum in auctoribus et precipue in Statio. / One may find an infinite number of examples of comparison in the authors, and above all in Statius.'[26] This opinion of Statius must have been commonly held, since a number of manuscripts of the *Thebaid* have their similes marked, either regularly or occasionally, by the marginal note, 'comparatio.'[27] In one manuscript, the commentator goes beyond simply noting the comparisons. For instance, at *Thebaid* III.46, where the lone survivor of the failed ambush of Tydeus is compared to a herdsman, the commentator says: 'Facit comparationem valde decentem ad mercurium ostendendum cuiusdam pastoris cui lupus interfecerat animantia sui taurorum vel pecudum. / He makes a very nice comparison of a certain shepherd whose herd of cattle and bulls a wolf had killed, in order to describe Mercury.'[28] Again at III.317, where Mars' driving speed is compared to Jupiter's thunderbolt, the commentator says: 'Comparat valde eleganter ut melius ostendat velocitatem equorum Martis. / He compares very elegantly that he may better show the velocity of the horses of Mars.'[29] Gervais of Melkley disagrees. In his discussion of comparatio, he defines the device as 'rerum dissimilium collatio / the bringing together of dissimilar things'; adds that 'consilium est talibus parcius uti / it is advised that such things be used sparingly'; and denounces the *Thebaid*: 'Fama enim nobilissime *Thebaidos* ob comparationum frequentiam vix permansit illesa. / the great fame of the *Thebaid* scarcely remains undamaged on account of the frequency of comparisons.'[30] Either way, there are indeed a great many heroic similes in the *Thebaid*, and the consensus of the commentaries gives every indication that most people liked it that way.

The basis of this liking was that comparison worked. 'Comparat valde eleganter ut melius ostendat.' Medieval speakers and hearers, writers and readers, were disposed to accept comparison, or assimilatio based on convenientia, in all its modes, as a very superior resource of exposition and explanation. They were so disposed, I think, because they believed that their world really operated in structures of parallel, and in so operating included everything from the merely material to the moral and the spiritual. These structures are analogical, but they are far more profound and pervasive than conscious analogical logic. The medieval critics reveal this deeper trust of comparison in many ways, three of which are most appropriate for my purpose here. The first of these has to do with discussions of metaphor, or translatio; the second derives from the fact, and intellectual structure, of commentary; and the third can be developed from the tradition of allegorical exegesis of the Bible, as it came in the later Middle Ages to govern the interpretation of fictions.

Late medieval discussions of metaphor are of two sorts: theoretical and definitional treatment, and commentary explanations of actual passages of poetry. Superficially, these seem to conflict, but when properly understood they presume the same thing. Actual commentaries, in the earlier centuries of the Middle Ages, through the twelfth century, tended to deal with the indirect and figurative language of poems by making some etymological or allegorical reduction of it – that is, by explaining that this language really says something else capable of being taken literally as truth. The usual formula of commentaries on Ovid's *Metamorphoses* is, 'Veritas huius est / the truth of this is.' Later commentaries, in addition, of course, to continuing this procedure, usually added other features. Either they allegorized as if they were dealing with the Bible, or they read with an almost relentless literalism. Theoretical discussions of metaphor, or course, actually treat metaphors – that is, formulae in language involving reference to a tenor and a vehicle. Commentaries, on the other hand, tend to obscure the difference between literal poetic statement and poetic statement involving a translatio literally put, by dealing with both in the same way. Explicit internal assimilationes and implicit ones involving some element external to the poem, which the commentator can supply, are essentially the same. But theoretical discussions relate metaphor to real similitudes, and thus to the real world, in a way which implicitly affirms what the commentaries actually practice.

In the *Poetria nova* of Geoffrey of Vinsauf there is a discussion of metaphor which seems to say the familiar things in the familiar ways. Style should fit content; metaphors are made by transferring the meaning of a word from its proper referent to another in some way similar. We have the familiar examples: snowy teeth, rosy face, golden hair.[31] Yet there is nothing here which would prohibit our continuing to think of metaphor as a fundamentally arbitrary or creative mental procedure, based on merely accidental similarities, tending in the extreme to 'the most heterogeneous ideas ... yoked by violence together.'[32] Yet our so thinking misunderstands Geoffrey's doctrine and wrongs the Middle Ages. A fragment of a commentary, obviously reflecting the lecture hall and copied out in a form well on the way to a glosa ordinaria, lets us know quite precisely what the Middle Ages understood in Geoffrey's words. The line which begins Geoffrey's discussion, 'Instruit iste modus transumere verba modeste, / this mode shows how temperately to make metaphors,'[33] is glossed at 'modeste' by the word 'rationabiliter,' and in the extended comment, by the phrase 'debito modo. / in the proper way.'[34] Metaphoric language is clearly what makes poetry most worth taking seriously:

Et quia exornatio verborum duplex est, quedam fit in eo quod verba in propria significatione ponuntur et hec pertinet ad levitatem, quedam vero fit transumendo verba a propria significatione ad aliam et hec inducit gravitatem.

Verbal ornament is of two kinds: sometimes it is made when words in their proper meaning are used as occasions of wit; sometimes it is made by changing a word from its proper meaning to another. This procedure suggests seriousness. (f 94r)

The commentator goes on to explain just why metaphors work. Referring to the examples Geoffrey gives, he says:

Ratio autem propter quam predicta bene aptantur ad invicem est similitudo que reperitur inter ipsam. Nam sicut dicit Aristoteles: Omnes transferentes propter aliquam similitudinem transferunt.

The reason why these two things just mentioned relate well to one another is the similitude which exists between them. For as Aristotle said, all metaphors are based on some similitude. (f 94v)

This is at once obvious, because it is no more than common knowledge that metaphors depend on some kind of similarity between the things joined, and at the same time most important, because the commentator's attitude, as revealed in the very length and straight-faced seriousness of his glosses, can only be explained by seeing similitude as something both real and fundamental. In justifying Geoffrey's examples, the commentator identifies each similitude and belabours it with commentary.[35] That both the accident being transferred and the transfer itself, which are involved in the making of metaphor, are to be taken as real, the commentator makes clear by saying, of metaphors which transfer a human characteristic to something non-human:

Et ultima parte commendat istum secundum modum methaphorice transumptionis et ostendit eius preeminentiam ad primum modum, dicens quod pulcrior et delectabilior est transumptio facta ab homine ad non hominem quam econverso, et hoc ideo quia per talem transumptionem quasi per speculum potest homo videre *suas oves* idest proprietates in *alieno rure* idest alieno subiecto ... nota hic quod ratio propter quam iste secundus modus est pulcrior quam primus potest esse quia proprietates hominis cum sint nobiliores magis exornant rem inanimatam quam rei inanimate proprietates exornent hominem.

And in the last section he commends this second kind of metaphor and shows its pre-eminence over the first kind, saying that it is prettier and more delightful to make a metaphor by linking the human to the non-human than the reverse; this is because by such a metaphor one may see as if in a mirror *his sheep*, that is, his properties, in an *alien pasture*, that is, in an alien subject. Note this, that the reason why this second kind is prettier than the first is that human properties, since they are nobler, are a greater ornament to inanimate things than their properties can be to men. (f 95r)

John Balbus, in the grammatical introduction to his *Catholicon*, puts the matter at its simplest and bluntest: 'Metaphora est rerum verborumque translatio. / Metaphor is the translation of things and of words.'[36] The material implications of his statement must, I think, be taken quite seriously. The transfer effected by translatio is a real one; the similitude upon which it is based represents a link in being as well as in thought; the distances which metaphors traverse are real. Geoffrey's commentator underlines this last fact when he justifies Geoffrey's treating only two of the four modes of metaphor, that is, from animate to inanimate and conversely, by saying that these are the extreme modes, involving the greatest artifice and distance between terms. Thus, 'if one can make a metaphor from animate to inanimate, no one doubts that one can make one from animate ... the smaller the distance between extremes, and the greater the similitude, then the easier it is to make the transfer.'[37] There are also, in addition to these more or less difficult

distances which translatio must traverse, certain absolute limits. Some metaphors are possible, and others are impossible.

The best illustration of this fact that I know is a statement about metaphor,
found in Isidore's *Etymologies* and in the grammar of Donatus, as well as in
such dictionaries as the *Catholicon*. Isidore's version is economical:

Metaphor autem aut partis unius est, ut 'fluctuare segetes' (non potest dicere 'sege-
tare fluctus'), aut antistropha est, idest reciproca, ut 'remigium alarum.' Nam et alae
navium et alarum remigia dicuntur.

Metaphor is either one-way, as 'wavy grain' (one does not say 'grainy wave') or
two-way, that is reciprocal, as 'oarage of wings.' For wings are used of boats and oars
of wings.[38]

That this is true is obvious, as soon as one thinks the absurdity, 'a grain-
field-y sea.' The precise and adequate reason why it is true is more difficult. I
speculate, without much confidence, that what this means in general is that
accidents may be transferred from an entity of which they are relatively more
intrinsic to another of which they are less intrinsic, but not the other way
around. The reciprocal metaphor, on the other hand, involves not the transfer of an accident, but rather a proportional analogy.[39] A is to B as C is to D;
therefore necessarily AD equals BC and vice versa. But it is really less important to know why this is true than it is to appreciate that it is true, and that
therefore there is an intimate and necessary connection between the logic of
metaphor, the possibility of some connections and the impossibility of
others, and on the other hand the logic of the operation and organization of
the real world. As in grammar one can identify a solecism, and in music a
discord, so in poetry one can invalidate a metaphor. In all cases we confront
cosmic structures, as expressed for instance by Bonaventure: 'Divinae autem
dispositioni placuit, mundum quasi carmen pulcherrimum quodam discursu
temporum venustare / It was pleasing to the divine will to beautify the world
in a certain discourse of time like a beautiful song.'[40] 'Musica mundana,' and
the pervasive medieval conceptualization of the world as a divine book,
require that all structures integrate, and that the range of all possibles in all
systems be accountable to one another. Metaphor is true. Assimilatio only
makes what is already possible – in a sense, only repeats or actualizes the
real.

Poeticized twelfth-century descriptions of the universe are the most obvious medieval illustration of this fact, as well as the most philosophically
impressive. There is no need to describe them here, since the description has

already been so well made.[41] It is probably fairer to the medieval sense of the world to classify these poems as science, and adjust our notion of the medieval scientific mind, rather than as poetry, with the consequence of leaving medieval science to be more merely empirical than it probably was. But whether one calls it poetry about science, or science in a mythic form, the assimilative assumption remains the same. And not only does it justify such poems as the *De mundi universitate*; it also motivates commentators to gloss their inherited poetic texts with allegorizing paraphrases which were obviously and literally true, and to equate the one with the other. A reciprocal attitude, which one finds more and more in late commentary, takes the metaphoric and otherwise ornamented language of poetry as, in some sense, already literally true, and analyses the world so as to find what that truth might be. In addition to this relentlessly literal reading of metaphors, a third attitude is possible – that is, in which the poem as such is taken as parallel to, rather than as literally referring to. This third attitude, which operates within poems, between poems, and between poems on the one hand and the world on the other, I call the strategy of parallel systems.

The literal reading of metaphors harmonizes perfectly with the presence, in accessus terminology, of the radically discursive expectations defined by the modi of forma tractandi. Extended to metaphors, this literalism presumes that they involve some literal reference to real correspondences or structures in the universe. In practice, it involved a very considerable trust of poetic texts, literal word by literal word. For instance, one late medieval commentator on the medieval hymn-book, explaining the line 'suspensus in patibulo' from the *Vexilla regis*, insists that what would seem to be a mere piece of description is in fact far more than that, and that the whole range of significances for this suspension are in fact operative. Christ was suspended because this was a shameful way of death, because it was prophesied, and because to be suspended means to be hung in the air. This location is appropriate because air is the common element, which cannot be privately owned nor bought and sold, and because air is between heaven and earth as Christ is the mediator between man and God.[42] On the reference to the royal purple which decorates the cross in the same poem, the commentator informs us that there are three purples, white, black, and red, all of which fit. The red purple is the blood of Christ; the white purple is the water which came from his side, and the black purple is Christ's body, bruised (and therefore presumably blackened) according to descriptions found in Isaiah and the Apocalypse.[43] The first of these details is a literal fact; the second is a metaphor. Both are handled in the same way, by accepting and explaining as true all the possible literal meanings of the words involved.

This same literalism explains what are certainly figurative passages as if they referred to actual events. The *Pange lingua* of Fortunatus, for instance, joins the tree of the fall and the tree of the cross metaphorically centuries before the full history of the cross which appears in the *Legenda aurea* was formulated.[44]

On a simpler level, the line 'flecte ramos arbor alta' is interpreted in a very emotional and circumstantial way by a number of commentators. Originally, the poem was probably a daring metaphoric transposition of nativity and passion, obscured for the later Middle Ages by a textual corruption. Originally, the swaddling clothes 'pingit' – that is, made red welts as if the child had been scourged – but the 'cingit' of the usual corrupt text destroys the image. Developing the implications of 'pingit,' Fortunatus makes the manger 'arta' as a tomb, in which a body may be 'conditum.' Answeringly, the cross is metaphorically a mother, who holds the Christ 'mite' with bent arms. In this imagery, nativity, crucifixion, and pieta are assimilated to one another in a way which does violence to the literal facts for the sake of theological precision. But the late medieval commentators were deprived of this subtlety by their text. Therefore, they did not address the cross as a figurative mother, who should tenderly hold her child. Instead, they envision Mary at the foot of a cross too tall to let her reach her son, and with prearranged nail holes far too widely spaced for a body even the size of Christ's. The lines of the poem, then, are Mary's appeal to the cross to bend over so that she might touch her son, and to relax so that he might not be so cruelly stretched.[45]

This same literalism, of course, may turn up in pictures as well as in glosses. A fifteen-century copy of the *Metamorphoses*, for instance, contains an illustration of the Narcissus story, in which Narcissus' pool is really a mirror, in a jewelled frame. But from this mirror there flows a stream. The scene is set on a grass lawn, with three trees, flowers, one rabbit, a stake and wythe fence, and a gate.[46] Pictures like this, in which levels of reality are not presumed as we would presume them, in various modes characterize medieval art; what is important to note here is that they illustrate a world literally adapted to the act of poetic assimilatio. Again, the story of Prometheus, to which Ovid merely alludes in passing, turns out in some commentary to be literally true: 'Iste prometheus simulacrum fecit et ipsum arte diabolica spiritu incluso ambulare fecit, unde formatio hominis fabulose dicitur. / This Prometheus made a statue and having by magic art inserted a spirit, he made it walk; fabulously this is called the formation of man.'[47] This same literalism, I think, is what leads Giovanni del Virgilio to summarize the *Metamorphoses* in the realistic fashion of the novella,[48] and another Italian commentator to add his own development to the riddle of the Sphinx: 'Querebat enim quod esset illud quod primo est quadrupes postea tripes postea bipes, postea unipes, iterum bipes post tripes post quadrupes. / For she asked what that might be which is first four-footed, then three-footed, then two-footed, then one-footed, again two-footed, then three-footed, then four-footed.' The answer is the same, of course, but the medieval preference for full systems expresses itself by including the full count of numbers. The one-footed man is one hopping in play; the four-footed old one has two canes.[49]

When the commentator faces an inescapably metaphoric passage, he tends to presume that the correspondence it asserts is a real one, which can be trusted in all its implied details. For instance, in the medieval tradition of hymn commentary, on the famous metaphor of Mary, the 'stella maris,' one commentator has a very great deal to say. First, stars exist not just in the realm of fire, but operate also in air; similarly, the blessed Virgin does not exist in the fire of carnal cupidity, but in the air of piety and mercy, and the water of contrite tears. Again, because the kinds of metals are effects of stars, the stars work intrinsically rather than extrinsically; similarly, the blessed Virgin affects men intrinsically, that is, in their souls. Again, as the sunshine is not diffused without a mediating star, so the light of divinity is not diffused without the mediation of Mary, through whom Christ was sent to us. Again, the stars don't shine in the North because swamp vapours obscure their light; similarly, Mary gives no light in the Northern regions of human pride, because many vaporous vices prevent her.

But Mary is not only a star, she is a particular star, the stella maris. There are three reasons. As a pole star never sets, so Mary never sets for sinners; as the pole star makes the world intelligible, so the whole world of the Church revolves around Mary; as sailors navigate by the star, we navigate to the heavenly kingdom by Mary.[50]

Implicit in this literalism is not only a denial that figurative, poetic, or metaphoric language can be taken by itself as something essentially different or separate from the world it describes; positively, this literalism affirms all that other medieval discussions of assimilatio seem to imply. Most obviously, this willingness to trace metaphoric statements made in language to features of the real world presumes that the real world, as such, both as a whole and in detail, exists in a manner which is essentially, and not merely accidentally, linguistic or metaphoric – in medieval terms, assimilative. Further, this literalism also presumes what other commentaries, as we have seen, also require: that is, that the operations of the real world, as well as the material existence of its elements, are assimilative operations. As the world enacts itself, its operations are examples of assimilatio. The principle by which the medieval world is seen to enact itself in operations shaped by assimilatio I define as the principle of parallel systems.

A defining illustration of this principle of parallel systems can be found in the accessus to the *Metamorphoses* commentary of Arnulf of Orleans. There, in a context clearly dealing with scientific, moral, and spiritual matters, and above all with moral ones, he says that the kinds of transformations, or changes of substance, with which the book deals are:

de re animata ad rem animatam ut de licaone homine in lupum, de animata in inanimatam ut de domo Baucidis in templum, de inanimata ad animatam ut de statua Pigmalionis in virginem. De animata ad inanimatam ut de dracone mutato in saxum

from a living thing to a living thing as from Lycaeon the man into a wolf, from a living thing [sic] to a non-living thing as the house of Baucis into a temple, from a non-living thing into a living thing, as the statue of Pygmalion into a maiden. From a living thing to a non-living thing, as from a dragon changed into a stone.[51]

These are the same four relationships which define the kinds of metaphor, as explained by the commentary on the *Poetria nova* just cited, and as quoted from Donatus, the common knowledge of the entire Middle Ages. The structure of poetic change and the structure of moral change are the same. The *Metamorphoses* is a great book of metaphors, but it is classified in the Middle Ages as ethics, and is glossed as morality. Here again, the evidence might be misunderstood; medieval commentators might be accused of insensitivity to poetry, as they multiply their allegories. But properly we should see in their interpretations their belief in a universe which was already, in modern terms, so poetic that there was no need to claim for the poet greater powers than those of an honest reporter. If the structures of morality and the structures of metaphor are the same, if the forma tractandi of poetry is discursive, then obviously all that is poetic in medieval verse must, by medieval standards, be attributed to the world which that verse described and celebrated. The world and words assimilate because they are alike; the parallel systems of metaphor-making and moral change necessarily illustrate and define one another.

This structure of parallel systems is the most complex illustration of the medieval assimilatio only because more parts are involved. Whether the two terms of an assimilatio are a particular and its description, or the whole system of moral possibility on the one hand, and metaphoric possibility on the other, the nexus is the same interpenetrative and yet inextricably two-term act, by which two entities are joined in a way which preserves the integrity of each, and still enriches, glosses, explains, or defines each by the force of the presence of the other. This structure of parallel systems, this structure of assimilatio exists, as I have repeatedly affirmed, at all levels of medieval reality. In illustration, I have chosen only a few representative levels – from what might be called the merely practical world, a relation between human nature and ethics, and the relation between astronomy and human behaviour which is called astrology; from the world of the intellect, the fact of commentary; and from theology, allegorical exegesis.

In the commentary of Walter Burley on Aristotle's *Ethics*, there are a number of interesting marginal diagram outlines. Among them is one entitled: 'Nota quatuor virtutes corporales correspondent quatuor virtutibus cardinalibus.' The outline is as follows:

robur corporale	fortitudo anime
vivacitas sensuum	prudencie
pulcritudo	temperantie
sanitas	justicie

bodily strength	fortitude of spirit
sharpness of sense	prudence
beauty	temperance
health	justice[52]

The cardinal virtues, of course, are a hoary convention; the bodily virtues are not. A more conventional schema would have been made in terms of the vegetable, animal, and rational souls; this list gives every appearance of having been made up to fit the four cardinals. But regardless of its source, its appropriateness is both obvious and interesting. Separately, each bodily virtue fits the ethical virtue to which the commentator has related it. One can easily see that strength of body contributes to fortitude, even spiritual fortitude. Acuteness of perception, at all levels, is one way of defining the 'intelligentia' which is that third of prudence which operates on the present. Beauty of body, as one can learn from Daniel's exemplum of diet as well as from ordinary experience, is related to temperance – though the causal relation is the inverse of the preceding two. More important, perhaps, is the metaphoric relation – there is a similitude of integration, of moderation, which links beauty and temperance. And finally, the relation between health and justice is more metaphoric than anything else – and as the governing metaphor of Plato's *Republic*[53] it would have been well established. Beyond the local correspondence between single items, however, there is the more important total parallel. Formally, each of the two groups of four is a normative array – by being listed, and even more by being arrayed in parallel, each group makes implicit claims to completeness, and one can, in fact, develop a reasonable and distinctive ethical system by taking seriously this little scheme's claim to completeness. The mixture of material and metaphoric relationships is normal for the Middle Ages, as I have repeatedly shown; and the power of parallelism, or assimilatio between systems, as a strategy by which the two systems placed in parallel mutually illuminate one another is particularly well exemplified here.

Another illustration of precisely this structure – that is, of a parallelism which assimilates physical characteristics to moral ones, can be found in a eulogy which Sir Hector pronounces over the dead Sir Lancelot, in the version of Thomas Malory.

'A, Launcelot,' he sayd, 'thou were hede of al Crysten knyghtes! And now I dare say,' sayd syr Ector, 'thou sir Launcelot, there thou lyest, that thou were never matched of erthely knightes hande. And thou were the curtest knyght that ever bare shelde! And thou were the truest frende to thy lovar that ever bestrade hors, and thou were the trewest lover, of a synful man, that ever loved woman, and thou were the kyndest man that ever strake with swerde. And thou were the godelyest persone that ever cam emonge prees of knyghtes, and thou was the mekest man and the jentyllest that ever ete in halle emonge ladyes, and thou were the sternest knyght to thy mortal foo that ever put spere in the reeste.[54]

According to P.E. Tucker, the relations here asserted seem irrelevant and illogical unless we realize that for Malory chivalry was the outward and temporal expression of inner and timeless virtues.[55] This is true enough, but there is more. It is obvious that Malory admired chivalry; it is equally obvious that in the Middle Ages the relation between outward and visible characteristics of all sorts, and inward and ethical or spiritual graces equally various, achieved a harmony rooted in the perceived nature of things. But granting all this, the connections still call attention to themselves, because there are so many of them, and because the connections, in sum, form two different lists in parallel arrays, making strong isometric claims by their very formality. As an assimilatio of parallel systems, they contain more complex detail than does Walter Burley's array of parallel fours, and it is much less easy to see, in each particular case, how the fit works. It is not instantly obvious, for instance, how friendship is to be equated with horsemanship. But this very difficulty is its own solution – what it is most important to determine about this strategy of parallel systems is that it is a parallel of systems first, and only of details after. Malory's two lists do not, in combination, make a list of symbolic or referential equations, which the twelfth-century critic or C.S. Lewis might call allegorical. Rather, they assert an achieved assimilatio between two levels or two systems, one of behaviour and the other of ethical character.

The point of astrology is essentially the same. Mere fortune-telling is a cheap distortion of what intends, essentially, to assert that heavenly and human realities operate according to the same rules and forces and definitions, and therefore operate in parallel to one another. In his commentary on the *Anticlaudianus*, Raoul de Longchamp explains the fundamental similitude involved:

Homo vero dicitur mundus multiplici similitudine, quam habet ad maiorem mundum. In maiori autem firmamentum rationali motu movetur ab oriente versus occidentem. Planetae vero, qui septem sunt, irrationali motu moventur ab occidente versus orientem et motum firmamenti retardant.

Similiter in minori mundo motus rationis est ab oriente coelestium et post descendit ad terrena tamquam versus occidentem. Septem vero sunt, quae rationis motum impediunt, scilicet quinque sensus corporis, imaginatio et opinio. Ista enim semper versantur circa terrena et rationis motum impediunt, unde moveri dicuntur quasi ab occidente terrenorum et contra rationabilem motum. Imaginatio siquidem fallitur et opinio errat.

Item mundus est quasi civitas, ubi est respublica, ubi quidam sunt imperantes, quidam obtemperantes, quidam operantes. In coelo siquidem tres personae sunt imperantes quasi in palatio, in medio angeli milites et obtemperantes quia administratorii, in mundi suburbio quasi rustici et cupidinarii sunt homines.

Sic in microcosmo in cerebri palatio viget sapientia quasi imperatrix, in cordis meditullio est quasi militans audacia vel voluntas, in renum suburbio latitat voluptas. Item sicut mundus maior constat ex quattuor elementis, ita corpus humanum ex quattuor humoribus elementorum proprietates habentibus.

Man is said to be a world because of the manifold similitudes which he has with regard to the greater world. In the greater world the firmament is moved by a rational motion from east to west. But the planets, which are seven, are moved by an irrational motion from west to east and retard the motion of the firmament. Similarly in the lesser world the movement of reason is from the east of the heavens, and afterwards it descends to earthly things as if toward the west. There are seven things which impede the movement of reason, that is the five bodily senses, imagination, and opinion. These are preoccupied with earthly things and impede the movement of reason. Whence they are said to be moved as if from the west of earthly things and contrary to rational movement. Imagination obviously deceives and opinion makes errors. Also the world is like a city, where public matters occur, where some people are rulers, some courtiers, some workers. In the heavens there are three persons: rulers as if in a palace, soldier angels in the middle obeying like administrators, and in the suburb of the world, like peasants and makers of delicacies [reading 'cuppedinarii'] there are men. Thus in the microcosm in the palace of the brain wisdom flourishes like an empress, in the middle of the heart, like a soldier, audacity of willfulness, in the suburb of the loins sensuality lurks. Also the greater world is composed of four elements, and correspondingly the human body of four humours having the properties of the elements.[56]

An explanation of this contrary motion of the planets, very similar to this one of Raoul's, occurs in Arnulf's accessus to his commentary on the *Metamorphoses*. The basic similitude which astrology asserts justifies a great array of medieval poetry; the precise version of that similitude which is evoked in this discussion of the contrary motion of the planets finds its subtlest expression, I think, in the character of the Wife of Bath, whose determination by Mars and Venus precisely fits her desire to move contrarily through time, that is, to renew her youth.[57] More generally, there survives one commentary on the *Metamorphoses*, at least, which goes beyond seeing these changes as metaphors of morality, to find in them at many points an implicit treatment of astrology, or more generally of knowledge. The interpretations in this commentary very often equate the characters of Ovid's stories with 'quidam astrologus,' or 'quidam philosophus,' without necessarily distinguishing sharply between the two. For instance:

Sed aliter credo quod Siton magnus philosophus fuit qui considerando metaforice superclestia que activa dicuntur in eis peritus fuit et sic fuit homo, sed quia etiam peritus fuit in philosophia naturali consciderando speram activorum et paxivorum et in hiis peritissimus fuit ideo dictus est femina.

But otherwise I believe that Siton was a great philosopher, who, considering the supercelestial things which are called active, became an expert in them and thus was a man, and because also he was an expert in natural philosophy, by considering the sphere of the actives and the passives and being most expert in these things, he was called a woman.[58]

Or again:

Pheton vir fuit philosophys vanagloria plenius qui non teorica set pratica astrolaus fuit, unde feton idest utens practica filius climenes idest vanaglorie privignis [cod privinguis] meropis idest filius pratice meropes idest pratica climene idest vanagloria, philosophus idest sapientia celestis modo cum iste feton de solis proprietatibus specularet falsa de solis cursu nobis [cod inra] locutus est et sic mundus incendidit quia errores seminavit, sed cecidit in terram de plantis et vegetabilibus terrestribus postea tractavit.

Phaeton was a philosopher full of vainglory who was an astrologer in theory and in practice, whence 'feton' that is 'using practical things' the son of Climenes that is vainglory, philosopher that is heavenly wisdom. Now when this Phaeton speculated concerning the properties of the sun he told us false things about the course of the sun and thus set the earth on fire because he sowed errors, but afterwards he fell to earth, he treated of plants and terrestrial growing things. (f 3r–v)

Or again:

Vulcanus philosophus primus fuit, qui traderet dissiplinam de coniuntione martis et veneris, et sic eos cepit et propalavit, quia talem coniuntionem docuit. Sed quia talem coniuntionem scivit et collegit per motum et cursum solis, idcircho dictus est hoc fecisse, ex inditio philosophi. set per catenas et retia ita suctilia intendit, ita suctiles rationes ex quibus hoc habuit quod oculi videre non possunt, et sicut retia intueantur, ita ille rationes.

Vulcan was the first philosopher, who dealt with the discipline of the conjunction of Mars and Venus, and thus he caught them and made them public, because he taught of the conjunction. But because he found out about the conjunction because of the motion and course of the sun, he was said to have done thus, by the disclosure of the philosopher. But by the chains and net which were so fine he intends equally fine arguments by which he gets what the eyes cannot see, but perceives by arguments as if by a net. (f 6r)

Eventually the commentator makes the equation with poetry:

Per euridicem nos inteligimus pohesim seu philosophiam que inventa ab apolline per pratum scientie currens morsa ab uno philosopho sofista mortua est idest perdita. Orfeus autem diu speculatus est super ipsa et pulcro testu eam descripxit sed cum retro verterit se ad infernum idest ad errores perdidit eam.

By Euridice we understand poetry or philosophy which, invented by Apollo, running in the field of knowledge, was bitten by a sophist and was dead, that is, lost. Orpheus thought too much about her in a beautiful text, but when he turned back to Hell, that is, to errors, he lost her. (f 15r)

The implicit equation which this commentary asserts, that astrology equals philosophy equals poetry, is of course one which it would not be wise to push too far. But at the very least one can take seriously the assertation about assimilatio that the commentary generates – that is, that there is something about the structure of that parallel between the heavens and earthly history which resembles the structure of apprehension which is philosophy, and the structure of representatio or comparatio which is poetry. As a part of the great body of Ovidian commentary, this particular text is merely eccentric – the interpretations are often, by the author's own admission, his own personal opinions. At the same time, as a betrayal, the author only makes interpretations which state explicitly what other interpretations had presumed.

But commentaries not only define, explain, and presume assimilatio in what they say. Just as important, their existence, side by side with or surrounding their texts, is itself an example of assimilatio. Some twentieth-century poetic theorists have spoken of the heresy of paraphrase – medieval commentary exists as an assertion of the very orthodoxy of paraphrase, as implicit proof that the discursive force of the forma tractandi is correct, and as demonstration of the relation of assimilatio between text and its sentence.[59] This particular kind of assimilatio, as I have already said, is an assimilatio of parallel systems. The parallelism involved works at many levels. Obviously, in the most literal possible sense, one form of words, one text, exists in parallel to another, in a way which is always radically intimate, but never reductionist – in a way for which the two-term assertion of assimilatio is precisely appropriate. Far more important, however, is that the relation between text and commentary presumes, or generates, a relation between, or among, discrete levels considered both real and parallel.

The most elaborate example of this presumption of levels, of course, is the one illustrated by the medieval tradition of biblical exegesis. As far as this book is concerned, the medieval tradition of biblical exegesis is understood in its late medieval form – that is, as something achieved and conventional, whose techniques were so normal to interpretation that they were being applied unself-consciously to fictions as well as to the canonical narratives of the Bible.[60] In this tradition, as well as in the narrowly specific tradition of literary theory, as usually conceived, it is important to distinguish between twelfth-century and later understandings. For Augustine as for Hugh of St Victor, the relation between the biblical text and its sententia was a referential one, discussable in terms of an analogy with the theory of signs, and intended to achieve some ideal devotional conceptualization, either of God or of some aspect of God's truth or God's will. Therefore, the customary expectation was that an interpretation which had been made after the manner of biblical exegesis was such because it presented an explicitly Christian or spiritual content, either of something 'quod credas,' 'quod agas,' or 'quo tendas.' The important thing was not the relationship between the text and its interpretation, but rather that the interpretation was itself of a certain Christian character. Thus, the normal method of proving that an interpretation was true was not a defence of the relationship between text and interpretation – of, as it were, the fit, as one might claim to have reassembled the clock correctly because there were no parts left over and the things was running. Rather, one proved an interpretation was true by proving, usually by some confirming prooftext, that the interpretation itself made a true statement – as one might claim to have assembled the clock correctly because, at a certain instant, one could say on the basis of independent evidence that it was set at the right time.

The late medieval notion of assimilatio, and the implied doctrine of parallel systems, of which exegetical commentary is an ideally elaborate illustration, both suggest that, at least after the twelfth century, exegesis had achieved more than a power of symbolic reference. In addition, it had become a structural system. Obviously and necessarily the specific statements made in exegesis had Christian content, but as an array they were more than this – or better, were Christian in a different way. In order to see properly just what this structure was and how it worked, it is necessary for purposes of analysis to discuss it as a structure, without reference to this content. Considered abstractly as such, the great structural method by which typology operates simply implies that full explanation or understanding of any given anything is accomplished in terms of an ordered array of parallel narratives and figures and propositions, all related to each other by assimilatio, each resonating in terms of all the others, and all properly dealt with and analysed by a conscious elaboration to one-to-one parallels. The full explanation consists in the resonance – in the achievement of the assimilatio, rather than, or as much as, in the terms being assimilated to one another. The four usual elements in the assimilatio, of course, are the literal, the allegorical, the tropological, and the anagogical. Formally or structurally considered, the literal is obviously a text – a form of words whose appropriation of assimilation (or interpretation) will generate awareness of ordered parallels. The allegorical has to do with beliefs, and structurally asserts that one of the levels of reality which these assimilative structures may make coherently a part of the universe is the level of idea, or mind. The tropological level had to do with behaviour, and asserts that human action may also be explained and explain other things, by existing in or achieving a state of ordered parallelism with some thing or some things else. The anagogical level, finally, has to do with 'heaven,' or with spiritual reality, and asserts that theological, spiritual, teleogical, or psychic facts may also participate in the universe which parallels make meaningful and coherent.

In the Middle Ages, of course, all four of these categories existed independently. That they were all in some manner deemed to exist protected the Middle Ages from ever entertaining a merely existentialist philosophy; that they existed in some way independently guaranteed that there would always be a certain nominalism in medieval descriptions of the world. The achievement of this typological assimilatio, in that philosophically middle condition which all post-twelfth-century nominalisms inhabited, was to bring the weltering variousness of the category of words, and the equal variousness of the category of history into vital harmony with the simpler and centripetal categories of propositional and ideal thought – which, of course, they concretized as Christ and heaven. In accepting and conceptualizing this harmony, we must continually guard against a belief in merely reductionist criticism – we must continually remember that exegesis accomplished this harmony without violating the integrity or the independent existence of any of the elements which made it up. In fact, the first requirement of an entity which was to be considered a type, in traditional biblical terms, was that it be true, and therefore, in a manner, irreducible. Further, when fictions came to be included in the system, they were at least analogously irreducible.

However, in generalizing this structure in order to see it as the matrix for a system of systems in parallel, united by various acts of assimilatio, and capable of accounting for the textual material in whose textuality late medieval poetry and commentary actually exists, a problem arises. In biblical exegesis, except for rare exceptions which seemed not to make any difference to the great working of the system, the literal level was always the same – it was constituted by the literal words of the Bible.[61] In the larger world of acts, words, and ideas which late medieval poetry constitutes, the literal level, or rather the textual level, may occur at any or all levels of this fourfold schema. Dante's *Commedia*, the most obvious example, is literally anagogical, and the implied letter of ordinary history to which it assimilates must be, and most elaborately was, supplied by commentary. The Middle

English *Pearl* is similarly anagogical though with a more elaborated tropological frame. The textuality of Chaucer's stories exists mostly at the literal level, though once again there is a frame some of which might be taken as tropological, or at least as tropological irony.

What the fourfold schema of exegesis defines for literature is not a range of possible meanings of a text, considered referentially, but rather a range of possible kinds of reality a text may assimilate because of the interaction of words and the world, past and present and future. Thus the literal level normally includes all those remembered facts and stories, the 'individua cadentia in sensum' and their assimilated descriptions, which constitute the mode 'exemplorum positiva' of the forma tractandi. The consuetudines and credulitates which are really what poetry is about, and which as such exist only in language as universal propositions, correspond to the allegorical level. The tropological level is the reader or hearer, whom consideratio evokes, and who may occur dramatically within texts, as do Chaucer's pilgrims and the speakers of lyric, as well as in the more conventional place of audience. The anagogical level, literally presented, occurs as I have said as the *Commedia*. Normally, however, it is not the text, but something extra-textual which may be assimilated. Biblically, the anagogical level is prophetic – it evokes heaven, last things, ideal possibilities. Generalizing, anagogy is significance in some ideal sense. In medieval terms, the probable best term for this anagogy is figural prosopopoeia. Ideal doctrines, concepts, or possibilities for existence, taken not propositionally (that would be allegorical merely) but as if materially existing in their ideal form – these are the anagogy of a nominalist world, which has given up philosophical realism without yet being able to give up the need for the real presence of the true. When seen in linguistic terms, as a structure for the relation between words and things, this structure is probably exhaustive. If the tropological be taken as the category of action in the present – that is, fact undescribed and unverbalized because in the very act of being – then the allegorical may be taken as the category of language pure, and the literal as the category in which the two – language and act – are combined as we conceptualize and describe past events and pseudo-events. These three categories constitute a version of the modern semiotic triangle. But in the medieval scheme there are four categories, not three; the anagogical is the category in which literal events (that is, facts combined with words) achieve the status of words. Our modern word for this achievement is 'symbolism'; it is a word which I mention only to avoid it explicitly, because I think it confuses the issue. The medieval achievement of a figural universe was not a merely symbolic achievement, because it presumed an ontological as well as a linguistic ground. I therefore insist on the medieval terminology, as both fairer and less subject to mistake – figuralism, prosopopoeia, anagogy.

This structural, or even structuralist, analysis of the achievement of biblical exegesis is of course an interpretation of the medieval evidence, and not a report of medieval literal statements. Medieval discussions of four-level exegesis, as distinguished from their practice of interpretations of poems which in various ways assumed it, tend to be so conventional over such a long period of time that the distinctive character of late medieval practice is obscured. It is, however, literally clear that the metaphoric character of the allegory of the poets and the typological character of exegesis, which earlier writers had been at some pains to distinguish, eventually were discussed as if the same.[62] It is equally clear that the audience, the people to whose moral lives the application might be made, were related to tropology.[63] At the same time, there is medieval commentary on Dante's *Commedia* (for instance, the one just cited) which deals with the question of levels, and fails to identify the letter of the poem with anagogy, even though Dante clearly does.

This schematizing of the levels of exegesis as a four-part structure of parallel systems has a number of advantages for criticism. Above all, it permits one to deal with the textuality of any given poem in a medieval rather than a merely linguistic or aesthetic way, by defining it as a system of assimilatio located literally at a certain point, or over a range of points, in this whole structure. Thus located, it defines its expected commentary as a discussion of all of those parts of the structure not literally expressed. In addition, and with the reinforcement of the notion of consideratio discussed in chapter one, it can define the relation between text and audience in a way which is both two-term and assimilated. Further, such textuality presumes, even insists on, the indistinguishability of linguistic, moral, and material reality, and is therefore a fit basis for the criticism of a poetry for which there is no special category, either linguistic or aesthetic. Still further, it presumes, as a normative array of possible realities, a set of four which is at once arguably exhaustive and at the same time well adapted to affirm the kinds of values poems tend to insist on: the world of empirical experience, the world of the self, the world of discursive or definitional generalization, and the eschatalogical world figurally achieved.

This four-pole matrix for criticism tempts me to indulge in elaboration, after the manner of Northrop Frye; it is probably safer, however, left in the elucidating company of medieval examples rather than modern speculation. I shall propose four. First, I shall try to suggest how the grand chant courtois fits and is illuminated by this matrix. Second, I shall present a fifteenth-century Italian 'concordantiae poetarum philosophorum et theologorum' as a medieval analogue and illustration of the kind of analysis of levels I have just made. Third, I shall present the *Fulgentius metaforalis* of John Ridewall as a medieval exercise of the principle of parallel systems, and therefore as an exercise of commentary which illustrates the structure exegesis defines. Finally, I shall suggest several ways Dante's *Commedia* seems to parallel, or be illuminated by, the analysis which this structure of four makes possible.

The grand chant courtois presents objectively and dramatically the existence of an interior state of consciousness – as it happens, the consciousness which desires the ideal achievement of love in this world. Thus, textually the poems which are the grand chant courtois exist at the level of tropology, and at that level only. Though they literally express the desire for existence at both the empirical or 'literal' and anagogical or ideal levels, the desire is not the same thing as the fact. Criticism that finds in courtly love poetry a real adultery behind every sigh and languishing word makes the mistake of locating the poetry's textuality at the first level, the level of literal empiricism. Zumthor's mistake is to take the poetry as merely allegorical – that is, totally a linguistic phenomenon. If the poetry as text exists at the level of tropology only, then the elements which have to be located in the array of assimilationes outside the text are the audience and the commentary. What can properly be said about this poetry, or rather in the presence of it, and by what kind of person – by a person in what ideological or metaphysical location? I suggest that the most profitable arrangement is to admit the aspiration of the textuality. Though the grand chant courtois exists textually at the level of tropology only, what it strives for, wishes for, and points to is anagogy – the perfect, iconic life, in which persons find themselves transformed into personifications. Here, I suggest, is the proper place to locate the audience. In other words, the only fit use of the grand chant courtois, as a piece of language whose rhetorical effectiveness is to be classified as somehow ethical, is to teach ordinary mortal human nobles, kings, and queens how to exist as the personifications of their roles. In the light of this application, this posture of audience, then, commentary can proceed to discursive definition and discussion of those roles, and to analysis of the empirical achievements and shortcomings of the people who are supposed to live and be those roles.[64] In the synthesis of assimilatio which poems, audience, and commentary achieve, the highest and most important element probably should be seen as anagogy. The other elements serve this one. At least I speculate so, and can therefore suggest that this is what makes the difference, for the modern audience, between the grand chant courtois and such poetry as Chaucer's *Canterbury Tales* and Dante's *Commedia*. For both Chaucer and Dante, the audience exists in the 'right' place, at the level of tropology.

Dante's textuality exists at the level of anagogy; this explains why it is so amusing, and so profitable, to supply to it other examples – modern men and women who also deserve certain places in Hell – from the level of 'literal' empirical reality. Chaucer's text exists at the 'literal' empirical level, though with a certain ironic framing tropology of pilgrims (which must be reduced to the empirical too, before we can understand the tales); this fact explains why we can so easily receive his tales in the same way we deal with novels. But for us in the twentieth century, the anagogical audience of the grand chant courtois has disappeared, not only in fact, but even in conceptual possibility. The king now no longer has two bodies, and for the modern British sovereign to be called 'England' seems either an absurdity or a piece of antiquarian language, and not the inevitable prosopopoeia of politics.

I have repeatedly argued throughout this book that poetry in the Middle Ages occupies no separate and distinctive category, but participates in larger ones which are themselves normal parts of human life and thought. In this context, it is important to note here that this piece of criticism which I have just proposed implies that a poem, fully understood, is larger than its textuality, and includes, by assimilation, its audience and its commentary as well, by which and because of which it functions as a part of the system of parallel systems of which the world is composed. Here again, the medieval poetic is radically different from the modern one – much less a prisoner of words and of language, recoverable diachronically as well as synchronically, and both in the present and in the past.

My second example is a fantastic piece of late medieval intellectual synchretism. The title of its Renaissance edition is a fair description both of its character and its pretensions: 'Concordantiae poetarum philosophorum et theologorum, Joanne Calderia phisico authore, opus vere aureum, quod nunc primum in lucem prodiit ex antiquo exemplari authoris. Nemo igitur post hac poterit errare in via poetarum vel philosophorum nam ut apud theologos ita et apud hos, continentur dogmata salutis. / Concordance of the poets, philosophers, and theologians, by John Calderia physician, a work golden indeed, which is now first printed from the old exemplar of the author. After this no one will be able to err in the way of poets and philosophers, for in them just as in works of theology the doctrines of salvation are contained.'[65] John Calderia was a Venetian physician, sometime professor of medicine at Padua, and the father of at least one child, a daughter, for whom he wrote the *Concordantiae*[66] and an exposition of the *Distichs* of Cato at least. In the manuscript of this work now preserved in the British Library, there is quite a pretentious list of his writings, which includes citation of a commentary on Dante.[67] An Italian manuscript, now Munich, ms Clm 339, contains an 'Amphorismorum liber iohannis calderie phisici ad ieronimum lazarellum in quo omnes et usuales et particulares medicine canones continentur.' This corresponds to nothing in the British Library list, but may in fact be a version of the *Gemmam medicinalem*. Calderia died in Venice in 1474, apparently at an advanced age.

Calderia introduces his book with a discussion of the presence of divine truth in all being. 'Quattuor igitur communicationum genera divisimus quibus res divinas invenire homines possunt. / We distinguish therefore four kinds of communication in which men may find divine content.'[68] These four kinds of communications, or more properly, faculties, are life, cognition, understanding, and love – 'vita,' 'cognitio,' 'intellectio,' and 'appetitus sive amor.' It is through these faculties that one gains awareness of causes, of the first cause, and of the 'ratio' of being, which (or who) is divine, and ultimately God himself. Calderia's essay is not scholastic; he is at more pains to be Ciceronian than to be clear, and so the rhetorical structure of distinctio, of homologous parts and parts of parts, is missing. It can at least be said, however, that these four faculties are remarkably parallel to the four levels whose structure I have just tried to define. Life, of course, is basis, point of view – the self; it corresponds to tropology. Cognition is clearly that faculty which first inquires into empirical nature; intelligence is that faculty which comes clearly into play when one understands the Incarnation, though it was the basis of glimmerings of prophecy before that; love is that by which intuition comes in heaven. These three clearly correspond to the letter of empirical conceptualization, the allegory of the understanding of the truth and nature of Christ, and the anagogy of heaven.

The book itself is composed of three quite uneven parts. The first is a mythography, in which the cognitions of the pagans are interpreted so as to expose their truth. The second is an 'inquisitio liberalium disciplinarum.' Its content is largely doctrinal, but this doctrine is presented in the framework of an elaborated allegory, with personifications of the arts and an island of philosophy. The third part is entitled 'De tropheo beate Virginis Mariae'; in it, theology is presented in terms of a free adaptation of the triumphal procession of Beatrice in Dante's *Purgatorio*. As a document in the history of ideas, the content of the book deserves extended study; it is no work of genius, but it does represent what can fairly be termed an ultimate medieval extension of the traditions with which it deals. Beyond it are the different fantasies of the Renaissance, which Ariosto and Spenser represent.

For my narrower purpose, as a part of the enterprise of definition of late medieval literary theory, Calderia's book is interesting and important for a number of reasons. In the first place, he emphatically makes similitude the factor by which these three different but parallel arrays of information are made concordant. In the second place, though real pagan gods and late medieval emblem-like fictions are mingled in his mythography, his interpretations include some made after the manner of biblical exegesis; in typical late medieval fashion, he thus ignores the problem of historicity, and admits 'literary' and 'real' exempla on equal status into what can properly be classified the literal level of his world. Third, Calderia's use of allegorical figures at all three levels of his work permits me to refine my definition of prosopopoeia, and suggest a more limited and precise sense for it in the mode of anagogy which I suggested above. Fourth and most important, the very existence of such a work as this, claiming to reconcile three great areas of human experience for the sake of the moral and spiritual profit of a particular human being, is obvious testimony to the importance of this reconciliation and therefore implicit testimony to the correctness of viewing the exegetical levels as a structure of relationship rather than as a description of symbolic references. The first of these characteristics is obvious in interpretation after interpretation; as a conventional and obvious medieval habit, it needs no illustration. However, there is one more general statement, in the context of final apotheosis, which can be quoted as Calderia's own testimony about his practice.[69]

Calderia's use of figures which might technically be called examples of prosopopoeia at all three levels of his work imposes a useful distinctio. Dante, in his *Convivio*, proposed a distinction between the allegory of the poets and the allegory of the theologians. What he meant has been debated at great length;[70] it is perhaps possible to conclude now that the first of these covers, among other things, a wholly artificial figure whose characteristics are immediately reducible to the features of some abstract faculty or virtue; while the second has to do with figures which are neither destroyed nor reduced by their interpretations, but remain in some sense real. Two complementary tendencies seem to have been at work in late medieval literary Hermeneutik, by which these two were made into three. In the first place, the wholly artificial figures generated by the allegory of the poets, by the purely mechanical exercise of the figure of prosopopoeia, once generated and accepted by virtue of their presence in popular and accepted texts, began to acquire by processes of commentary which I shall examine later some textual existence apart from the particular literary context in which they were created, and in terms of which they were mere reducible metaphoric constructs. Once having acquired separate textual existence, they assimilated naturally to other figures, long traditional, which already had the same sort of existence. These other figures tended to be those of the pagan gods, though a few obviously 'historical' personages, such as Jason or Achilles, were also included. Thus by the later Middle Ages, Saturn and Venus, Achilles and Helen, and Friendship and Love, tended to array themselves along a common line of reality. Even while this process was going on, however, the exercise of the allegory of the poets continued to generate new artificialities, tightly tied to context and immediately reducible to the discursive statement or notion of which they are metaphorically equivalent; Chaucer's *Melibeus* is a good example. Calderia's allegorical personifications of the liberal arts also belong in this category.[71]

In addition to this process of commentary whereby allegorical figures having a local and discursive existence in a particular text came free of that text and began to associate with the pagan gods, a complementary commentary process was generating what I have above called anagogical prosopopoeia. In my *The Friar as Critic*, I referred to it as the trans-spiritual mode of poetry. The commentary process by which it was achieved was that extension of biblical exegesis which interpreted fictions as if they were Bible texts, thus transforming them into types. This commentary process, of course, cannot be credited with having created all the figures of this type which exist in late medieval poetry, but merely with being the explicit literal record of that transformation in sensibility because of which they could be created. The difference is perhaps easier to illustrate than to define discursively. Obviously, there is a difference in being between the personified virtues and vices of Prudentius, who behave in ways literally strange for human beings, but rationally appropriate to their definitions, and the Lady Meed of *Piers Plowman*, who behaves rather like Alice Perrers, without losing any of her power of presence as incarnate money. This difference exists as the intellectual and rational power of personification and the realistic presence of some example come together; in my former study, I tended to relate this synthesis to the nature of myth. I am now more inclined to relate it to late medieval ethics, though this is perhaps a distinction with little difference.[72]

In Calderia's *Concordantiae*, these figures are used with an awkwardness which betrays their nature clearly. He has created no great poetic world of his own, but has borrowed one in bits and pieces, whose arraying in these three parts defines them, and defines the system of relationship by which they sensibly cohere. In the section on poetry, for instance, Calderia uses two figures which may have came from the *Ymagines fulgencii* or from Robert Holkot's *Moralitates*, adapting the meaning slightly to fit his own context.[73] In the same way, Calderia includes many of the standard pagan gods, adding in many cases his own interpretations. Ericthonius, for instance, means both envy and Christ, because his serpent feet can be connected with the serpent lifted up in the wilderness. The interpretation of Io is confused by the presence of the bull-headed ship which is the normal euhemerism for the rape of Europa. Cybele, with her great crown, symbolizes the pope; Leda, the Church; Janus, John the Baptist; Eolus, a malignant spirit or the devil. Calderia's description of the Elysian fields, of poets, and of hell includes a reference to Dante. His treatment of Mercury permits him to bring in material from the *De nuptiis*, and to conclude that it is eloquence which not only ornaments history but also makes fables credible.[74] He describes the supercelestial and the terrestrial Venuses, and deals with Aeneas and Dido, Paolo and Francesca, and Circe and Ulysses. He tells us that Noah's flood was caused by a unique conjunction of planets. Finally, he concludes with Perseus and Bacchus, and discussion of the glory of the wise and the destiny of the wicked.

Calderia's second part, *De inquisitione liberalium disciplinarum*, he defines by saying: 'Hanc itaque poesim ... non veterum sed nostro ingenio elaboratam. / This poem, not copied from the ancients but made up by myself' (f 137r–v). It is an allegory in the standard tropical sense, with a temple of Jupiter in which one meets the liberal arts, and a wood, through which one must pass to reach the river of the island of the philosophers. This is a high marble place, reminiscent of Dante's *Inferno* IV and of the ice mountain of Chaucer's *House of Fame*. One gets to this island by means of seven bridges, which are stable only at the further end. Here live the philosophers, who discuss with Calderia their doctrines. Eventually he meets both Aristotle and Philosophy, and learns about the seven mechanical arts. The section eventually turns into praise of Franciscus Foscari and of Venice and her people, their dress, their navy, and other bases of Venetian patriotism.

Calderia's third part, entitled *De tropheo beate virginis Mariae*, is obviously adapted from the end of Dante's *Purgatorio*. It begins with a rough climb which ends at two flowing streams. Here Calderia meets an old man, apparently Noah, and other personages who compose a procession of biblical history. After John the Baptist comes the expected chariot, drawn by the bi-form Griffin, in which rides a glorious lady. Accompanying, in procession, are various allegorical characters, including the Gospels, the apostles (who represent the creed a phrase each), prophets, saint, martyrs, the pope, St Francis, the four doctors of the Church. In addition to Christian history, pagan history is summarized. The author is invited into the chariot himself, and gets various explanations and interpretations, a ride through the heavens, and a return trip home.

The most significant thing about this remarkable compilation is that it exists at all. Many of the axioms that it presumes, of course, are commonly presumed by the culture of the time – that there is divine truth in pagan fables, that the arts and philosophy are the outline of the known and knowable, that history is processional rather than just a succession of events, that fable, doctrine, and religion illuminate one another. But this rare and rather personal treatise of Calderia's is the most fully and pedestrianly enacted presumption of them that I know. As such, it is a particularly neat and telling example of the assimilatio of parallel systems which is, as I have said, the most complex mode in which the basic comparative strategy of poetry expresses itself. In addition, there is both in explicit and implicit statement here some comment on others of the features of late medieval literary theory which I have tried to define. Obviously, all three of his sections are poetry, even though the book is in prose. The first is labelled so. The second, he distinguishes from the first by naming it 'hanc itaque poesim ... non veterum sed nostro ingenio elaboratam.' The third, obviously, is borrowed from Dante, the greatest of then modern poets. In practice, the first section is the result of a certain exercise of the mode *exemplorum positivus*, which I defined in chapter two. The exempla which are most appropriate are obviously those already interpreted, or, as it were, 'put' – that is, those already received as significant fables. That it is significance, rather than the fabulous, which is important, is clear because the range of Calderia's material extends on the one hand from Noah and Aeneas to Holkot's *Amicitia* on the other. The second section, with its literally doctrinal intention, is Calderia's own poetry. In practice, it exists in the mode definitivus, ending explicitly in praise. The third part is literally eschatalogical, literally concerned to present the great figures and types of the great poem of Christian history, whose end and goal is heaven. Like the first section, its mode is exemplorum positivus, but like Dante's *Commedia*, its location in the structure of places is anagogical.

A more conventional but still very revealing example of the assimilatio of parallel systems is John Ridewall's *Fulgentius metaforalis*. Textually, it is a commentary, whose nature as such is obscured by the fact that its edition by Liebeschütz only contains half the full text.[75] With the full text in hand, as preserved for example in ms Bodleian 571, it is possible to see that Ridewall, in ordering his interpretations, has merely imposed new chapter groupings on a treatment which, in the manner of all commentary, deals seriatim with the items treated by Fulgentius in his mythography. At the same time, his work has a certain real independence. In no manuscript is it preserved as a commentary – that is, written out in the form of a glosa ordinaria, in the margin of the text of Fulgentius.[76] And it is clear even to the most casual reader that Ridewall is not really interested in the merely pedestrian work of commentary, but rather occupies himself with the pagan deities of Fulgentius only in order to give himself a framework for a discussion of essentially ethical material. His commentary, like so many other medieval ones, exists as much parallel to his text as dependent upon it or joined to it. The relation between text and commentary is not even as close as that between statement and paraphrase; it is a relationship which involves two real terms, not just one. It is, as I have already suggested, an assimilatio.

The original text of Fulgentius was itself a commentary – not on a previous text, but certainly in that its obvious purpose is to make sense of the data of an inherited corpus of mythological figures and stories. Fulgentius brings to bear the appropriate techniques – euhemerism, scientific and moral allegorization, etymologization. More often than not, the gods do not really survive the operation; they become their explanations. Saturn is just an ordinary king, Jupiter and Juno personifications of fire and air, Neptune of water, and Apollo of the sun. In Ridewall's commentary the atmosphere is quite different. Here the characters of myth are clearly set apart from their explanations. They are, admittedly, equated with certain ethical abstractions, but the equations are not so much derived from them as simply confirmed as true. The connections are merely asserted.

Except for small inconsistencies associated with Pluto and the population of Hell, Ridewall comments on the characters in the order in which they appear in Fulgentius. He does not always, as I have said, respect chapter divisions, but he does respect figures. This orderly procedure, of course, is what is expected of a commentary, and that Ridewall follows it is apparently too obvious to need comment. But it becomes important once one notices that the system of moral abstractions by which Ridewall interprets Fulgentius has also, at one revealing point at least, an order, and Ridewall follows that too. The children of Saturn, in order as Fulgentius specifies them, are Jupiter, Juno, Neptune, and Pluto. The order of the parts of prudence, both by convention and chronology, are memory, intelligence, and foresight.[77]

Structurally, what Ridewall has done is to assert that each of an already ordered set of gods has his or her own respective meaning, and at the same time assert that those meanings, in the order in which he relates them to these divinities, are already themselves an ordered set. What the rhetoric of commentary would seem to claim is that he has interpreted each of these deities by applying to each its own most appropriate ethical significance; what in fact has happened is that the whole system of mythology and the whole system of ethics have been placed in parallel, and then such individual equivalences as occur must be, and are, justified. The result is an assimilatio of parallel systems. An organized system of exempla, as it happens, the system of the pagan gods as authoritatively described by an accepted auctor, and an organized system of doctrine, as it happens, the parts of prudence have come together. Literal exempla and doctrinal allegory meet, as whole systems – since both are true, then they must be true part-by-part as well as whole-by-whole. The rest is argument.

What makes this achievement, this assimilatio of parallel systems, possible is that all its components are in some sense already established, systematic, true. For ethics, this truth is obvious. For mythography, it was the achievement of the very different allegoresis of such commentators as Alberic of London and Arnulf of Orleans, who in fact did explain, rationalize, euhemerize, and otherwise de-mythologize their inherited pagan material until it had become, in some sense, simply true. Even Ridewall is not completely beyond this stage. As the *Fulgentius metaforalis* progresses, the ethical realities which Ridewall attaches to the ordered series of Fulgentian figures are not themselves an ordered set, and some of them, such as the ambition which interprets Phaeton and the contemplative, active, and voluptuous life which are attached to Minerva, Juno, and Venus, had long been commentary conventions.

In these conventions, it would seem, these gods and goddesses have become merely moral personifications. But they do not, in so becoming, turn into merely rational constructs, after the allegorical fashion of Prudentius. They retain a certain exemplary reality, to which I have already referred in discussing Calderia's inclusion, in his mythographic section of poetry, of some of Holkot's *Moralitates* pictures. This exemplary reality, for the pagan gods as such and their stories, was an achievement of the commentary tradition of the twelfth century and before. It did not, I think, depend on the primal reality of the gods as such, but rather on the quality, character, and method of their acceptance by medieval culture, through commentaries which were preoccupied with explanations after the formula 'veritas huius est.' In order to see this process pure, one can see it in connection not with a pagan deity, or any other figure remotely true or historical, but with a figure originally only a trope, a personification in the purely verbal fashion of classical rhetorical and grammatical manuals. My illustration is a figure named 'Ratio.'

Ratio begins life in the *Anticlaudianus*, as an extended metaphor. The source passage is at the end of book one, where Prudence, after being elaborately described, appeals to Reason. In response, Reason rises and gets attentive silence with a gesture. She is described as merely like Prudence, only older; she also has a triple mirror, part glass, part silver, and part gold. In the glass, she sees what makes for being; in the silver, what makes for change; and in the gold, what makes for form and definition. All this is considerably spun out – the Lady Reason herself gets rather lost. She exists for the sake of having a mirror in which explanations can be hung; later, she exists for the sake of making reasonable speeches, and performing reasonable actions. The simply metaphoric character of poetic ladies such as this Reason is never fully lost sight of; the doctrine of the poem is ornamented by her presence, but it is the doctrine which is important, and literal ornament is never more than its integument.

The commentaries of the *Anticlaudianus* focus naturally on the mirror.[78] A gloss, attributed to Raoul de Longchamp, from a thirteenth-century Rheims manuscript, but different from Sulowski's text, explains the 'triplex speculum' as follows:

primum vitreum, per quod comprehenditur choerentia forme ad subiectum. Secundum argenteum per quod notatur tantum forma sine subiecto. Tertium auream per quod ydee comtemplantur. Primum dicitur ratio, secundum intellectus, tertium intellectuitas quod celestia tantum comprehendit.

the first glass, by which is understood the coherence between form and subject. The second silver by which is indicated form by itself without subject. The third gold by which ideas are contemplated. The first is called reason, the second understanding, the third insight, which understands heavenly things pure.[79]

The gloss of William Auxerre is briefer, and, in its use of a distinctio obviously and generally related to reason, and not specifically related to the *Anticlaudianus*, begins to make possible the detachment of the figure from its specific tropical context in the poem. By the triple mirror, says William, 'signatur naturalis, doctrinalis, et methafisica. / is signified natural, doctrinal, and metaphysical.'[80] Still another commentary, which survives so far as I know only in this excerpt, assembles details from various places in the *Anticlaudianus*, adds more details for the sake of verisimilitude, and isolates the complete picture as a picture. The text is very rough in all the copies I have seen, but its basic content is clear:

Ponunt antiqui philosophi ymaginem Rationis sub nomine Lesis, vel Lexis que talis erat: virgo crinibus aureis, in veste purpurea, fame honesta, oculi siderei, in manu tenens dextera[a] tria specula – aureum, argenteum, et vitreum. In aureo contemplabantur divina, in argenteo creaturas rationales et spirituales, in vitreo creaturas corporales et generabiles et corruptibiles, ad modum vitri frangibiles. Hec virgo consulit Nature de qua[b] supra quod peteret adiutorium ab altissimo nature quod est exemplar omnium virtutum ut complemur in ipso. Cuius legationem commisit et eis septem[c] artes liberales quasi equis ad currum iunxerunt, que fabricant currum idest ingenium quod quatuor rotis vehitur, in quod sunt septem artes, quinque equos ad currum iunxerunt,[d] super quem currum Lexim ad sidera transcurri servat.

The ancient philosophers put the image of Reason under the name of Lesis, or Lexis, which is as follows: a virgin with golden hair, in a purple dress, honest of reputation, with starry eyes, holding in her right hand three mirrors – gold, silver, and glass. In the golden one divine matters are contemplated, in the silver rational and spiritual creatures, in the glass corporal creatures who are born and who decay, fragile like glass. This virgin is concerned for Nature, about whom above, that she ask help from the highest nature that is the exemplar of all virtues that we be completed in it. Whose embassy she joined, and they added to them the seven liberal arts like horses to the chariot, who made the chariot, that is, genius, which went on four wheels, in which are the seven arts. They joined five horses to the chariot, on which chariot she watched Lexis be carried into the heavens.[81]

Reason has acquired a name, blonde hair, a purple dress, and a good reputation. One might imply the eyes from her commanding presence in Alanus' poem, but the other details are added. The triple mirror has become three mirrors, and we have still another interpretation of them. From her actions, anyone who knows the *Anticlaudianus* can still guess her source. But the source is not named, and if one did not know it one could not reconstruct from this summary more than the vaguest approximation of its point. Reason, having acquired a certain material verisimilitude, is detached; she is qualified to enter that society of exemplary figures asserted to be parallel to ethical and other discursive truths. And this is precisely what she does.

The final description of her, which I have just quoted, is preserved in a popular late medieval figure collection, called the *Ymagines Fulgencii*. Some of the figures in this collection are gods and goddesses. Condensations of all of Ridewall's figures except Ganymede appear. Other figures are inventions with the names of gods on them, such as the Jupiter with three wings who begins the collection.[82] Still others, like Ratio, are metaphors which have become people.

In this association of a personification like Ratio with a pseudo-pagan God equated with Christ, and a real one equated with Prudence, we have at work the same process of verisimilar concretion which had made False-seeming a friar, and gave us the Wife of Bath instead of Luxuria. All these figures, whether allegorical, inherited, or merely exemplary, get arrayed together and have much the same status – the same semi-fictional, semi-iconographic, semi-versimilar reality. The *Fulgentius metaforalis* and its derived *Ymagines*, along with other medieval commentaries, simply make explicit what would have been implicit in most late medieval acts of poetic inventio. Example and personification become qualified to be figura. As such, they have independent existence – they relate to interpretations as to parallels, not as to reductions. They and the systems they compose, are qualified to participate in assimilatio.

My final illustrations of this principle of assimilatio of parallel systems come from Dante. The first is made possible by an article by R.A. Shoaf, entitled 'Dante's *Colombi* and the Figuralism of Hope in the *Divine Comedy*.'[83] This is an article which accomplished a great many things at once. It of course sheds much light on the three contexts in Dante's poem where the image of the dove appears. As it does so, the medieval significance of the dove is elegantly and fully defined. More important still is the definition of Dante's poem as system which the article achieves. This system is one which most subtly exemplifies, and therefore helps to define, the strategy of assimilatio with which this chapter is concerned, and which, as a structure of comparison, I have called the basic material of late and medieval poetry. In order to make this exemplification clear in my context, I shall state it in my terms, without, I hope, distorting too much the argument from which it is borrowed.

The dove occurs in the *Commedia* three times, each time as half a simile. It is like Paolo and Francesca, like the poetry lovers who 'disperse at Cato's command,' and like Peter and James in *Paradiso* XXV. Things equal to the same thing are equal to (or relate to) each other; obviously, these three contexts, one from *Inferno*, one from *Purgatorio*, and one from *Paradiso*, must relate. The three cantiche are both parallel and progressive; the common relationship to the dove, at three points, deposits a normative array of figures which are themselves both parallel and progressive, to which the total figural meaning of the dove assimilates. The implied doctrines, of desire and hope and of poetic language, are never stated. Dante, as is his habit, lets his figures speak for themselves. Though most of us need the commentary as well, it is the genius of Dante's assimilatio which makes the commentary possible, as well as necessary. It is the structure of assimilatio which permits and requires the vast architectonic of parallels across three cantiche, based on what must never be allowed to seem a mere casual repetition of a simile. The poem itself exists as a system of parallel systems; it glosses itself. But because it exists literally as anagogy, and because it has in a sense appropriated tropology by having Dante the pilgrim as its definitive audience, it leaves for commentary to supply, after amusing itself with the particularities of the roman à clef, the doctrine, that is, the allegorical level of the structure. But Dante's assimilationes are powerful – allegoresis is not free. The doctrine of the poem remains unstated, but it is never undefined. Dante tells us, in a multitude of ways of which this repetition of doves is one, just where the parallels are, and therefore what they mean.

My last example is simpler, but it makes larger claims. Dante's assimilatio of doves defines the crucially important doctrines of love and hope. Beyond this is the world in which love and hope, and poetry as well, operate. In this world, which the existence of the *Commedia* to its audience defines, five people accompany Dante on his way: Virgil, Statius (who goes with Dante even further than Virgil), Matelda, Beatrice, and Bernard. Bernard, of course, is a saint – a character in a special kind of history which normally adjusted its facts to its meaning. Beatrice is a real girl, whom Dante knew personally – however much he transformed her after. Matelda is Astrea – that is, she is Justice, a personification. Virgil and Statius are authors – ultimately, they are books. They represent, in Dante's experience, four different orders of reality – holy history, personal experience, the rationality which can conceptualize and personify universals, and the ability to read and trust language which made books such authorities in the Middle Ages. The saint, the acquaintance, the abstraction, and the book – four different orders of reality, conversing with Dante in the same book.

Literally, of course, this is impossible. One venerates saints, one flirts with one's friend (or adores her), one thinks about concepts, and one reads story books of epic history. In our modern world, these four different types of activity have lost substantial contact with one another – though one person may, from time to time, do each of them. In the Middle Ages, they were radically related – they constituted, in fact, parallel systems between which assimilatio might operate. In the eschaton, all realities come together – the presence of these five figures, all equally on the same plane of reality, all guiding Dante in various ways to his confrontation with the Trinity and the Incarnation, is the assimilatio of anagogy. The parallels have met. But they have not become the same. Their presence to one another, under the common rubric of guide, is an implicit array in relation to Dante, like the array of characters compared to doves. As an array of four, they do not simply illustrate the four levels of exegetical structure which I have tried to define above – they are all anagogical. Nevertheless, they are related to that structure because each contains, in relation to the tropological Dante, all of it. Moreover, each contains all of this structure in a different and complementary way.

In the first place, all of them are literal exempla. Matelda-Astrea is a character in Ovid's *Metamorphoses* who has been detached from that poem, by an operation of sensibility analogous to that which gave independence to

Alanus' Ratio.[84] Essentially, she is the concept of Justice, embodied by veri-similar description. Beatrice is a part of ordinary life, of the world of Dante's real tropology – transformed by memory into his beatitude. Bernard, whose saint's life belongs to that medieval genre of narrative whose literal facts most conventionally endured an anagogical transformation, is to any living Christian both a literal and an ideal inhabitant of real heaven, and thus a perfected combination of letter and anagogy. Virgil and Statius personify the exemplary past whose narratives their poems contain, the memory of which is man's best basis for tropological wisdom, for doctrine, and for the under-standing which can at least point to heaven. Thus all these characters have a literal existence, in a range extending from the merely verbal through the historical to the sacramental; all of them are congenial to doctrinal allegoriza-tion and to tropological application; all of them, in Dante's poem, exist in perfect combination with their role-meanings in the manner I have labelled anagogic.

Characters like this do not all have to be at the same level – do not have to exist, as it were, together. I have argued elsewhere that it is the presence of the Green Knight, literally in Camelot, which is the problem, and that the poem exists to distance him into a proper parallel, in that morally instructive double universe whose literal human version is Sir Bercilak.[85] The resonance of parallel systems remains, of course; the complete universe, sub specie aeternitatis, must contain both the level of the Green Knight and the level of ordinary human experience, as well as other levels in addition. And it is the duty and the privilege of the wise to know, and understand the relation between these levels, as Gawain does. But whether the poem be the anagogi-cal *Commedia*, or the tropological grand chant courtois, or the literal *Canter-bury Tales*, or such texts as Canticles and *Piers Plowman*, in which forma tractandi and forma tractatus are the same, and therefore in which (I specu-late) tropology is assimilated into allegory, the important thing for the critic to do, whether he be medieval in truth, or modern in a way which desires to think medievally, is to draw the boundaries of his enterprise large enough to include all the parts, including proper commentary, and the proper applica-tion to audience which is ethics, as a part of the poetry if not a part of the textuality – and to see that this enterprise is one whose joints and couplings and articulations are made of assimilatio.

NOTES

1 *The Order of Things (Les mots et les choses)* (New York 1970) p 17. The four kinds of resemblance which Foucault chooses to define this behaviour of lan-

guage: '*convenientia, aemulatio, analogy*, and *sympathy*,' are brilliantly chosen, and deserve far more analysis and application as a normative array than he has, in the brief scope of his book, been able to give them.

2 Sheila Delany 'Undoing Substantial Connection: The Late Medieval Attack on Analogical Thought' *Mosaic* 5 (Summer 1972) 31–52. Robert Holkot is a perfect example of a philosopher who, though he expresses doubts as a sceptical philosopher of the validity of analogy, constantly depends on assumed analogies as the basis of his allegorizations of pagan stories.

3 Bartholomew refers to two *lemmata*, located as follows: 'et sermones poetici' (Averrois, ed Boggess, p 3, line 65), and 'et quemadmodum quidam hominum' (ibid, p 5, line 8).

4 Translation by cognate would be more prudent here, but the 'reason of the material' makes little sense. To translate 'ratio' which is explicitly the formal or metaphysical principle as 'theme' is to reverse form and content – at the same time, it agrees with the notion of double form defined by 'forma tractandi' and 'forma tractatus.' Thematic and even circumstantial explanations of lyrics of the 'grand chant courtois' were called their 'razos.' My translation is therefore at once serious, in that I take 'theme' as a possible modern equivalent of the meaning at this point, and also, perhaps more important, rhetorical in that I wish to underline the difference between medieval poetic formalism and modern ones.

5 Paris, Bibliothèque nationale, ms lat 16089, f 146v. For bibliography on Bartholomew, see Boggess 'Aristotle's Poetics' pp 282–3.

6 Douglas Kelly 'The Source and Meaning of Conjointure in Chrétien's *Erec* 14' *Viator* 1 (1970) 179–200

7 M.B. Parkes 'The Influence of the Concepts of *Ordinatio* and *Compilatio* on the Development of the Book' *Medieval Learning and Literature: Essays Presented to R.W. Hunt* ed J.J.G. Alexander and M. Gibson (Oxford 1975) pp 115–41

8 O.B. Hardison Jr and Leon Golden *Aristotle's Poetics: A Translation and Commentary for Students of Literature* (Englewood NJ 1968) pp 281–96

9 'primo poeta versatur circa assimilationem scilicet assimilans rem cum re et secundo circa ymaginationem scilicet faciendo estimare rem sic esse per talem assimilationem.' My rendering is more an interpretation than a translation; being more literal, however, would have obscured both the problem and the solution. These free-floating demonstratives 'sic' and 'talis' have to be taken as pointing to something.

10 It is, I think, quite an archetypal linguistic betrayal, that certain classes of speakers of English regularly introduce descriptions with the phrase, 'It is like ...' The same word, 'like,' may also function as a phatic demand for atten-

tion. This usage pertains to a culture in which there is an unusually large trust of analogical thinking.

11 In another place, Averroes says: 'Tragedia etenim non est ars representativa ipsorummet hominum prout sunt individua cadentia in sensum, sed est representativa consuetudinum eorum honestarum et actionum laudabilium et credulitatum beatificantium. Et consuetudines comprehendunt actiones et mores. / For tragedy is not an art which represents men as individuals capable of being sensed, but which represents their honest customs and praiseworthy actions and beatifying beliefs. And customs include actions and manners' (p 20). Again: 'Poeta vero non ponit nomina nisi rebus existentibus. Et fortassis loquuntur in universalibus. Et ideoque ars poetrie propinquior est philosophie quam sit ars adinventiva proverbiorum. / Poets do not name anything except existing things. And it may be that they name universals. And so the art of poetry is closer to philosophy than is the art which finds proverbs' (p 30).

12 Dragonetti 'Aux frontières'; Giuseppe Mazzotta *Dante, Poet of the Desert* (Princeton 1979)

13 *Didascalicon: A Medieval Guide to the Arts*, tr Jerome Taylor (New York 1961)

14 For example, Bernard Lonergan's *Verbum: Word and Idea in Aquinas* (Notre Dame 1967) and G.L. Bursill-Hall's *Speculative Grammars of the Middle Ages: The Doctrine of Partes Orationis of the Modistae* (The Hague 1971). Both these authors, in very different ways and for very different reasons, present medieval material or follow medieval procedure in a more than merely historical way, obviously betraying the belief that what they confront as medieval data is in some sense permanently true. One finds a truth remarkably parallel to Cassirer's analyses of language; the other a truth remarkably parallel to modern linguistics. In both cases, their quality of belief affects their use of medieval material – granting the inevitable distortions, the result is an assimilatio in itself. As such, it by analogy both informs and confirms Averroes' emphasis upon assimilatio as the fundamental structure of poetic language.

15 Paris, Bibliothèque nationale, ms lat 16089, f 146v

16 For a general discussion of imagination, see M.W. Bundy *The Theory of Imagination in Classical and Medieval Thought* (Urbana 1928).

17 Vatican Library, ms Reginesis lat 241, f 145r–v

18 In spite of the literal reference to the *Rhetoric*, the classification of praise as a 'vera pars poetica' is a clear evocation of the Averroistic *Poetics*.

19 Vienna, Österreichische Nationalbibliothek, ms Vindob 4959, f 68r. For a discussion of the genre of 'memoria technica' verses to which the commentator's quotation belongs, see Lynn Thorndike 'Unde versus' *Traditio* 11 (1955) 163–92.

20 E. de Bruyne *Études d'esthétique médiévale* (Brugge 1946)

21 Cambridge, University Library, ms Mm. I.18, f 8v

22 See chapter two, note 54.

23 In light of the argument I have here developed, it would probably be fair to say that the difference between description and naming, or indirect and direct expression, is partly the difference between language applied to particulars and language applied to universals, but partly also the condition of what medieval thinkers would call post-lapsarian language. In paradise, all names were at once proper names, which directly expressed what was named, and also perfect descriptions, which as language both revealed and perfectly corresponded to what was being named.

24 Gervais of Melkley *Ars poetica* ed Hans-Jurgen Grabner, Forschungen zur Romanischen Philologie 17 (Münster 1965) p 65

25 This is O.B. Hardison's phrase; he cites Thomas Aquinas, at the beginning of Aquinas' commentary on the *Posterior Analytics*. See 'The Place of Averroes' p 63.

26 Edmond Faral *Les arts poétiques du XIIe et du XIIIe siècle* (Paris 1958) p 275

27 The most elaborate use of this notation that I have seen is in Florence, Biblioteca nazionale, ms II.II.78, of Italian provenance and dated 1384. Listing them all would be tedious; for a sample, the note occurs in books five and six opposite the following lines: V 144, 165, 203, 231, 262, 330, 348, 389, 426, 528, 530, 543, 597, 704; VI 52, 107, 115, 186, 253, 299, 322, 451, 483, 522, 580, 597, 665, 685, 716, 787, 797, 854, 864, 880, 893. Other manuscripts of the *Thebaid* in which the same sort of notation occur include Padua, Biblioteca del Seminario Vescovile, ms 41; Oxford, Magdalen College, ms lat 18; Oxford, Bodleian Library, ms Canon class lat 79; Cambridge University Library, ms Ii.III.13; Cambridge, Corpus Christi College, ms 230, Cambridge, Trinity College, ms 0.9.12, London, British Library, ms Royal 15.C.10; British Library, ms Harley 2463; Leiden, Bibliotheck des Rijksuniversitcit, mss Voss lat Q.114; Gronov lat 14; BPL 136K.

28 Vatican Library, ms Palat lat 1690, f 23v. The commentator has apparently understood 'Haemonides' to mean the son of Jupiter, that is Mercury.

29 Ibid f 27v

30 Gervais of Melkley *Ars poetica* p 152

31 *Poetria nova* lines 765ff

32 *Lives of the English Poets, by Samuel Johnson, LL.D.* ed George Birkbeck Hill (Oxford 1905) vol I, p 20

33 *Poetria nova*, line 765. Faral's text reads 'verba decenter'; 'modeste' is recorded as a variant. 'Decenter' perhaps contains a bit more implication of reasonableness, but not much – it is clear that the commentator is not so much glossing the word as the notion which the word, as it were independently, modifies.

34 Munich, ms Clm 14482, f 94r. This fragment contains some material which is
conventionally found in some full commentaries on the *Poetria nova*, to which
it seems to have added an extra layer. This extra layer, not just a paraphrase
of Geoffrey's text, but rather an explanation of why the commentator thinks
that what Geoffrey says is important, is of course the one which most clearly
betrays the medieval doctrine. The complete commentary which corresponds
most closely to this fragment, both in fullness and in precisely equivalent language, is preserved in Assisi, Biblioteca communale, ms 309, ff 1r–74v. The
glosses in London, British Library, ms Add 37495, an Italian manuscript
dated 1382, collate roughly with the Munich fragment, but do not contain
more than the divisions and paraphrases. The more interesting dubitationes
are missing. In my very preliminary survey of manuscripts, I have found more
variety than coherence; but here, at least, there seem to be preserved evidence of a commentary succession. I am happy to thank Marjorie Curry
Woods for the information that the Assisi commentary is probably by Pace of
Ferrara.

35 'Consequenter in quinta parte format exemplum ut manifesta sit transumptio,
dicens, ex quo ita est quod predicte sunt proprietates rerum transumendarum,
igitur, O poeta, *dic dentes*, suple hominis quia de ipso fit sermo, ut dictum est,
sunt *nivei*, idest albi, et sic est *transumptio*. Nix enim ut dictum est de sui pro-
prietate dicitur alba; cum ergo dentes hominis propter suam albedinem dicuntur nivei, transumitur nix ad significandum albedinem dentium hominis. /
Consequently in the fifth section he makes an example to explain the metaphor, saying how it is true that the above are properties of the metaphoric
vehicles, thus: Oh poet, *say teeth*, supply "of man" because man is what the
passage is about, are *snowy*, that is white, and this is a metaphor. For snow,
as is said, is called white from its property; when therefore the teeth of a man
are called snowy on account of their whiteness, snow is appropriated to signify
the whiteness of the teeth of a man' (f 84v).

36 Cap de tropo, sv 'Metaphora'

37 The whole passage is as follows: 'Ad hoc etiam dubitari potest cur transumptio metaphorica de qua hic loquitur secundum Donatum fiat quatuor modis,
scilicet ab animali ad animale, ab animale ad inanimale, ab inanimali ad inanimale et ab inanimali ad animale, quia auctor iste non ponit nisi duos, scilicet
ab inanimali ad animale et econverso ab animali ad inanimale. Videtur enim ex
hoc insufficiens. Et dicendum quod cum fit transumptio ab animali ad inanimale vel econverso, artificialior est propter magnam distanciam extremorum,
quam si fiat ab animali ad animale vel ab inanimali ad inanimale et propter hoc
solum ponit duos predictos modos, et per illos subintelligit reliquos. Nam si
potest fieri transumptio ab animali ad inanimale, nullus dubitat quod possit

fieri ab animali ad animale. Item si potest fieri ab inanimali ad animale, sequitur quod multo fortius possit fieri ab inanimali ad inanimale, quia quanto
minor est distancia extremorum et maior similitudo tanto facilius est trans-
ferre. / On this subject one may wonder why metaphor as discussed here,
which according to Donatus may be made in four ways, that is from living to
living being, from living to non-living, from non-living to non-living, and
from non-living to living, is discussed here in terms of only two ways only,
that is, from non-living to living and vice versa from living to non-living. It
would seem that this is insufficient. And it must be said that to make a metaphor from the living to the non-living or vice versa is more artificial because
of the great distance of the extremes than [would be the distance] if it were
made from living to living or non-living to non-living, and for this reason the
author only includes these two modes, and in them understands the others.
For if one can make a metaphor from the living to the non-living, no one
doubts that one can be made from living to living. And if one can be made
from non-living to living, it follows that much more obviously one can be
made from non-living to non-living, because the less the distance between
extremes and the greater the similitude the easier it is to relate the two in
metaphor.' Munich, ms Clm 14482, f 94v

38 *Etymologiarum* I.xxxvii.5–6

39 A somewhat differing discussion, which is as close to an explanation as I
know, is to be found in a commentary on Donatus: 'Scire debetis tamen non
semper has translationes reciprocas esse. Reciprocae sunt, quotiens inter se
recurrunt, ut puta si conparationem facias a volatu ad navem aut a navi ad
volatum, istae reciprocae sunt. Habes in Vergilio utramque translationem
ipsius thematis. Volare proprie avium est, et transtulit ad vela; ecce ad naves
fecit conparationem ab avibus alio loco item a navibus transtulit ad aves,
"nare per aestatem liquidam," cum de apibus [sic] volantibus loqueretur. nare
est natare, quod vero est navis. istae reciprocae sunt, quotiens se respiciunt.
partis unius sunt, quotiens ab una parte transferimus, ab una vero non possumus. habemus in Miloniana "quidem ceteras tempestates et procellas in illis
dumtaxat fluctibus contionum semper putavi Miloni esse subeundas." Tempestates procellas fluctus, totum hoc maris est, et transtulit ad vim populi et
seditiones. e contrario non possumus ponere a populo ad pelagus. Numquid
enim possumus dicere, "talis tempestas populi fuit, qualis seditio maris."
tamen Statius demens dixit [Theb. IX.142] seditionem [rogi] maris. / You
should know nevertheless that these metaphors are not always reciprocal. They
are reciprocal, whenever they can go back and forth, as for example if you
make a comparison of a flying thing to a boat or a boat to a flying thing, the
comparisons are reciprocal. In Virgil you have both of the metaphors of this

subject. To fly is the property of birds, and he transfers it to sails, and so makes a comparison of birds to ships. In another place he transfers from boats to birds: "to swim through the liquid air," when he is speaking of flying bees [sic]. To swim is to float, which truly is a property of a boat. These are reciprocal, as often as they look back and forth. They are one way, whenever we transfer in one direction and cannot in the other. We have in Cicero's oration for Milo: "obviously in those flooding mobs I thought Milo had to endure further tempests and storms." The storms and tempests of the flood are entirely characteristics of the sea, and he transfers them to the strength and sedition of the people. And we cannot on the contrary do this from people to the sea. For we never say: "such a tempest of the people was like a sedition of the sea." But crazy Statius said, "sedition of the sea" of the struggle for the body of Oenides." *Grammatici Latine* ed H. Kiel, vol v, fasc 1 [Leipzig 1867] pp 305–6
40 Curtius *European Literature* p 545
41 Brian Stock *Myth and Science in the Twelfth Century* (Princeton 1972)
42 'Nota secundum dictum autoris, aliquis diceret quare Christus suspendi voluit in patibulo et non alia morte mori. Dicendum quod huius potest esse duplex causa quia non est aliqua mors nequior suspensionis morte et quia prophete prius predixerunt quod Christus mori deberet morte turpissima ideo suspendi voluit in patibulo. Secunda causa est illa quia omnis ille qui suspenditur sursum ad aera elevatur, sed deus voluit mori in aera et nullo alio elemento propter duplicem causam. Prima causa est illa quia aer est elementum commune omnibus quia aliquis potest habere propriam terram quia venditur et emitur. Similiter aliquis potest habere propriam aquam quia proprie ista aqua venditur et emitur et aliquis potest habere proprium ignem. Nullus autem potest habere propriam aerem quia aer est communis omnibus et per hoc Christus designavit quod passio sua deberet esse communis omnibus tam superioribus quam inferioribus ... Sed causa tertia est illa quare Christus volebat suspendi in aera quia recte sicut aer est medium inter celum et terram sic Christus fuit mediator inter deum et hominem dum stetit et affixus in cruce. Deus enim et homo discordes fuerunt quia deus conquerebatur de homine quod homo nollet servare mandata sua et econtra homo conquerebatur de deo quod nollet liberare creaturam suam. Modo Christus existit mediator et composuit hominem cum deo sicut patet per sanctum Paulum ad Gall. iiiº captiulo. Mediator unius noster non est sed duplicis scilicet divine et humane. / Note to explain what the author says here, someone should explain why Christ wished to be hanged on the cross and not die by some other death. It should be said that there are two causes for this because there is no other death more disgraceful than death by hanging, and because the prophets

earlier predicted that Christ should die by a shameful death, thus he wished to be hanged on the cross. The second cause is thus: because everyone who is hanged is lifted up into the air, and God wished to die in the air and in no other element for two reasons. The first reason is thus: because the air is the element common to all, since someone may own his own land which he can sell and buy. Similarly someone may have his own water since properly water is sold and bought, and someone may have his own fire. But no one can have his own air because air is common to all, and in this Christ designated that his passion ought to be common to all, as much to the superior as to the inferior ... And the third reason why Christ wished to be hanged in the air is thus: because rightly as air is the medium between sky and earth so Christ is mediator between God and man while he stood fixed on the cross. For God and man were in discord, because God complained against man that man would not serve his commandments and in response man complained against God that he would not make his creature free. Then Christ became mediator and reconciled man with God as is clear by St Paul's statement in Galatians the third chapter: Our mediator is not a mediator of one, but of two, that is, of the divine and the human.' Munich, ms Clm 13439, f 189v

43 'Nota circa hoc quod auctor dicit quod crux sit ornata purpura regis. Purpura dicitur esse triplex, quedam dicitur esse purpura alba, quedam nigra, quedam rubea. Modo Christus ornavit sanctam crucem primo rubea purpura et per hoc quod sanguinem suum effudit in cruce. Secundo ornavit sanctam crucem alba purpurea et hoc cum aquam dimisit in crucem. Tertia decoravit sanctam crucem nigra purpurea quia corpus Christi in hora mortis nigrum corpus Christi fuit sicut patet per ysayam quinquagesimo capitulo 3° ubi vulneratus est propter iniquitatem nostram accusatus est propter scelera nostra disciplina pacis nostre super eum et livore eius salvati sumus. Hod idem patet in Apoka- lipsis capitulo vi° sol factus est niger. / Note concerning this that the author says the cross is ornamented with the purple of the king. Purple is said to be triple – some purple is said to be white, some black, and some red. First Christ ornamented the holy cross with red purple because on the cross he shed his blood. Second he decorated the holy cross with white purple because he discharged water on the cross. Third he decorated the holy cross with black purple because the body of Christ in the hour of death was a black body of Christ as is clear from Isaiah, chapter fifty-three, where he was wounded for our iniquities, accused for our crimes, the discipline of our peace was on him and by his black bruise we are healed. The same is clear from Apocalypse chapter six, the sun was made black.' Munich, ms Clm 13439, f 190v.

44 For the history of this legend, see Esther Casier Quinn *The Quest of Seth for the Oil of Life* (Chicago 1962).

45 'In illa parte auctor facit inclamacionem ad sanctam crucem in persona virginis
gloriose dicens (et possunt [sic] esse vera virginis Marie que sub Christi cruce
stetit dicens) O alta arbor flecte idest inclina ramos tuos ut possim filium
meum osculare eius membra tangere et o alta arbor laxa idest remitte tensa
idest extensa viscera ne superne filius meus a te specie lanietur ... Nota sententia stat breviter in hoc quod auctor loquitur in persona beate virginis tria
petenda primo petit vel prima petitio stat in hoc O sancta crux inclina ramos
tuos ut possum fillium meum osculare. Secunda inclamacio est ibi O sancta
crux remitte tua extensa brachia ne filius meus a te sic lanietur ... Nota circa
primam inclamationem quia loquitur quod sancta crux tam alta fuit quod
mater Christi non poterat tangere pedes eius et igitur clamavit ut sancta crux
inclinet se ad eam ut posset tangere filium suum. Nota circa secundam clama-
cionem quod foramina sancte crucis in tanta distancia fuerunt ab invicem ita
quod Christus licet et homo magne stature erat non omnino poterat porrigere
foramina et ergo cum primo affixus fuit cum manu una tunc extendebat
ipsum ut perveniret ad aliud foramine et ergo Christus multum extensus fuit
in cruce modo stetit beata virgo ut sancta crux extensa viscera relaxat ut filius
eius mite extendatur. / In that part the author makes an exclamation to the
holy cross in the person of the glorious virgin saying (and it can be true of the
virgin Mary who stood under the cross of Christ saying) O high tree bend,
that is incline, your branches that I might kiss my son, touch his limbs, and O
high tree relax, that is loosen, the tense, that is extended fibres lest my son
be tormented on high by your nature. Note the meaning briefly is that the
author speaks in the person of the blessed virgin three requests. First she asks
or the first petition stands in this: O holy cross incline your limbs that I might
kiss my son. The second exclamation is there: O holy cross relax your extended
arms lest my son be thus tormented by you ... Note with regard to the first
exclamation that it is spoken because the holy cross was so high that the
mother of Christ could not touch his feet and therefore cried out that the holy
cross should incline itself to her that she might touch her son. Note with
regard to the second exclamation that the nail holes of the holy cross were at
such a great distance from one another that Christ, even though he was a
man of great stature, could not in any way reach the holes and therefore when
he was first fixed by one hand then they stretched him to reach the other hole
and therefore Christ was greatly stretched on the cross, and so the blessed virgin stood and asked that the holy cross relax its extended fibres that her son
be gently stretched.' Munich, ms Clm 13439, f 194r
46 Vienna, Österreichische Nationalbibliothek, ms Vindob 3145, f 30v
47 British Library, ms Add 15733, f 5r. The commentary is derived from that of
Arnulf of Orleans, though this interpretation is neither in Arnulf nor Gio-

vanni. The catalogue dates it fourteenth-century. Arnulf's own gloss insists on the metaphor: 'Prometheus re vera fuit quidam sapientissimus qui in Caucaso monte studens primus naturam hominis duplam esse consideravit secundum corpus terrenam ... secundum animam celestem. / In truth Prometheus was a certain very wise man who, studying in the mountain of the Causacus, first formulated the notion of the double nature of man – according to the body earthly ... according to the soul celestial.' (Arnulf p 201)

48 For a discussion of this point, see my *The Friar as Critic* pp 100–1.

49 Vatican Library, ms Vat lat 5222, f 248v (dated 1415)

50 'Nota primo ex quo auctor dicit Mariam esse stellam quia multiplicibus rationibus ostendi potest quod Maria stella dicitur. Prima ratio sic ista quia sic dicit philosophus super Thymo': Stella in ignem celestem non [cod vel] agit, sed bene agit in aerem aquam et terram et illud probatur que non agunt in ignem celestem illa non sunt de qualitatibus super celestium quia ignis semper manet sub eisdem qualitatibus et sub eadem extensione. Sed quod stella possit agere in aerem hoc patet per Averroem primo metrorum [sic] qui dicit in commento: Elementum stellarum clausat impressiones in aerum regione. Sed quod stella in aerem agat hoc patet per Avicennam in moralibus suis quia dicit constellacio atque saturnus agat in terrenis. Similiter quod stella agat in aquis hoc patet per Aristotelem tertio metrorum sic dicentem secundum ortum et occasum stellarum crescunt et decrescunt ipse aque. Sic similiter ipsa beata virgo Maria non agit in ignem idest in regionibus cupidatatis carnalis secundum eius pietatem et misericordiam sed agit in aerem idest in aquam tunc per devocionis lacrimas effudendo idest illis hominibus qui sunt devoti et contricionis diversas habent in illo agit et potencia eius misericordiam agit et etiam agit in terram idest in illos qui alicuius humilitatis seu humiles in corde sunt illi exultabuntur in hoc subsidium beate virginis. Secunda causa est illa quare beata virgo dicitur stella quia per Averroem primo celi et mundo: Stellam densior ipsis cordis. Sed nota ulterius quod ipsum lumen magnum accipitur in corpore aliquo denso seu umbroso quam in corpore claro et luminoso sicut patet per ipsum Avicennam in libro fontis, ymo lux magis incendium quam in lucem propter nimiam oppositionem vel propter nostram coniunctionem. Similiter beata virgo et densior pars totius orbis celestis est accepta quam aliarum stellarum facta in circulo et quod ipsa beata virgo tante luminositatis est hec patet per Johannem apok. tredecimo capitulo ubi dicit Vidi mulierem amictam sole et luna sub pedibus eius et in capite eius coronam stellarum et in humero habens filium. Hic enim describitur luminositas beate virginis. Primo enim luminosa fuit in parte superiori quia in capite portabat coronam novem stellarum et per istas novem stellas notantur novem choros angelorum turba virginum martirum et confessorum. Secundo denotatur quod ipsa lumi-

nosa fuit per totum corpus et hec ipse innuitur cum dicit amicta erat sole.
Tertio notatur quod luminosa fuit in parte inferiori et hoc innuitur cum dicit et
luna sub pedibus eius. Tertia ratio quia beata virgo dicitur stella quia sic dicit
causam eius. Stella fundat terra plus intrinsecus quam extrinsicus et causa est
illa quia sic dicit Avicenna in mineralibus suis sic: Metallorum genera stellarum sunt effectus sicut patet per Aristotelem 40 metrorum plus metalla
generantur intrinsecus quam extrinsecus igitur sequitur quod terra fecundat
intrinsecus sic simili modo beata virgo hominem fecundat seu fertilem facit
intrinsicus in ipsa anima et non extrinsicus id est in ipso corpore. Unde dicit
beata virgo plurimos salvos fecit in corpore et in anima cum pro maiori parte
plus salvat homo in anima quam in corpore. Quarta ratio est ista quare beata
virgo dicitur stella. Dicit Albertus in theorica planetarum lumen solis ampli-
andi partis non diffunditur nisi aliqua stella mediante et hoc ipse probat quad-
rupliciter ... sic simili modo lumen divinitatis cum ad inferos diffunditur idest
ad nos homines in stella idest Maria mediante unde de ea dicit sanctus Bern-
hardus nichil igitur in vobis salutis esse poterit quod non per Mariam Christus
vobis transmisit. Quinta ratio est ista et ultima quia Maria stella dicitur quia
dicit Allexander stella in aquilone non lucet et huius causa est quare iste
stelle in istis partibus [non] lucent causa est quia hic sint multe paludes ... ex
quibus paludibus exiunt multi vapores et isti vapores obumbrant ipsam stellam ne videri posset sic similiter beata virgo Maria non lucet in aquilone idest
in superbia seu in homine superbo quia ab isto homine exiunt multi vapores
idest multa vicia cum superbia sit radix omnium viciorum ... Nota auctor dicit
in littera nominando ipsam Mariam stellam maris. Unde beata virgo Maria
tribus de causis dicitur stella maris. Prima causa est ista quia stella maris occi-
dentalis nunquam occidit sic Maria nunquam occidit peccatoribus ... Sed omnibus veniam inpetrare promitto quare ipsa dicitur stella maris quare circa istam
stellam totus mundus intelligitur et ratio huius est ista quia stella maris infixa
est ipsi polo. Polus autem dicitur ipse punctus circa quod ipsum celum moratur
et ille polus est duplex scilicet polus articus et antarticus. Hec cum stella ista sit
infixa ipso polo sit [cod et i.] quod totus mundus tunc istam stellam volvens
et moveatur. Sic etiam circa Mariam totus mundus volvitur idest tota ecclesia
Katholica per ipsam regulatur et regitur. Tertia causa [cod stella] quia ista
stella omnis navigantes in hoc mundo ad regnum celorum perducit.' Munich,
ms Clm 13439, f 175r–v. Since this text is both quite long and exceedingly
corrupt, I have settled for the above summary in lieu of formal translation.
My transcription presents, but unfortunately does not solve, the scribe's con-
fusions.

51 Ghisalberti 'Arnolfo d'Orléans' 181
52 Paris, Bibliothèque nationale, ms lat 6459, f 3v

53 Known in the Middle Ages only at second hand, as for example from reference to it in the beginning of the *Timaeus*, but perhaps better known than one
might think. The Allegory of the Cave, for instance, occurs in a version only
mildly distorted in the 'Didascalia in rethoricam aristotelis ex glosa alfarabii,'
translated by Hermann the German, and preserved in Paris, Bibliothèque
nationale, ms lat 16097, ff 192v–3r.

54 Eugene Vinaver ed *The Works of Sir Thomas Malory* (2nd edition Oxford
1967) vol III, p 1259

55 Edmund Reiss *Sir Thomas Malory* (New York 1966) p 190

56 Raoul de Longchamp *In Anticlaudianum* ed Sulowski, pp 25–6

57 I have discussed this interpretation in a collaborative article with Patrick
Gallacher, 'Alisoun Through the Looking Glass.'

58 Vatican Library, ms Vat lat 2877, f 6v. This commentary deserves further
study for many reasons; at the linguistic level, for instance, it contains the
least normalized spelling I have seen in a late medieval Latin manuscript.

59 To use the word 'sentence' is perhaps to beg a question rather than treat it. I
use it, however, not to mean that all commentary should be considered 'sentential' in that it contains the 'meaning' in some abstract form of a poem
more concrete. Rather, I mean to claim that whatever sententia is, its status is
that of commentary. This status, as defined by medieval thinkers, is higher
than that enjoyed by commentary at other periods, no doubt – but not even in
the medieval case is commentary purely something to which a text can be
reduced. Sententia, in fact, does not necessarily mean something abstract or
universal. In the commentary of Giovanni del Virgilio on the *Metamorphoses*,
it clearly means narrative summary: 'Sententia primi capituli hoc est. Dicit
enim quod dum orpheus ita decantasset ecce magna turba mulierum baccan-
cium ... que cum audivissent orpheum ita decantantem cognoverunt eum, et
una ex ipsis iactatis capillis dixit: Ecce contemptor mei. Et proiecit astam fron-
dosam in vultum suum, sed non vulneravit propter folia. Et alia accepit lapidem et misit in eum, sed lapis ex dulcedine cantus orphei incecidit suplex ad
pedes eius ... etc. / The sentence of the first chapter is this: He says that while
Orpheus was singing thus, behold a great throng of the Bacchantes, who when
they heard Orpheus singing thus recognized him, and one of them, throwing
her hair about, said, "Behold the one who despises me." And she threw a
leafy spear in his face, but it didn't wound because of the leaves. And another
took a rock and threw it at him, but the rock, because of the sweetness of the
song of Orpheus fell suppliant at his feet ... etc.' Oxford, Bodleian Library, ms
Canonici misc 457, ff 50r

60 For the evidence which supports this generalization, see my *The Friar as
Critic*.

61 There was, admittedly, some medieval argument over such things as parable –
though here the question is not so much over whether the biblical words are
the literal level, as over how much of the reference of those words is also
literal. The clearest exception I know to the rule that the biblical words are the
literal level occurs in Nicholas of Lyra's commentary on *Canticles*, where he
asserts that the book has no literal level. *The Friar as Critic* p 10

62 The discussion occurs at the beginning of a commentary on the Hymns,
which is not quite merely a reporting of hoary convention, and is therefore
worth quoting at some length:

'Littera occidit, spiritus autem vivificat. Unde Aristoteles scribit scribit [sic]
primo elementorum res sunt multe et quasi infinite, nomina pauca. vero ideo
oportuit unam vocem et unam dictionem plures res representaret [sic]. Propter
ergo signatorum multiplicem vocum et dictionum tunc multi multipliciter et
diversi diverse dicta auctorum exponere ponantur, et ultra que voces representant ex impositionem voluntaria auctori exponunt aliter, ita ut hii exponunt hystoriace, hii allegorice, hii quidam anagoyce, hii vero tripoloyce.

'Historiace enim exponunt narrando eodem modo sicud res fuerunt peracte
et ob hoc hystoria sumit sibi nomen. Antiquitus enim habenti nulli licuit con-
scribere historiam nisi qui cognovit visu suo res fuerunt peracte. Alegorice
vero ut quando unum dicitur et aliud intenditur per sermonis transumptionem, sicut per ysaac intenditur christus, per arietem occisum caro humana,
per septem mulieres apprehendentes virum unum septem dona gratiarum
[two words illegible], per decem ascendentes [cod ascendere] in montem
altum, per [one word illegible] intelligimus eius excellenciam et sapientam eloquenciam etc. Secundum quod fit aliquando transumptio a re, aliquando a persona, aliquando a numero, aliquando a loco, aliquando a tempore, aliquando a
negotio, propter quod allegorica dicta est ab alios quasi alienum et gore locutio
quasi aliena locutio.

'Anagoyce vero quando loquimur de terrenis et intelligimus de supercelesti-
bus et ergo dicitur anagogia a gana quod est sursum et goge ductio quasi
ductio de terrenis ad supercelestia, unde secundum aliquos anagogia et allegorica sic differunt quod allegorica est sensus misticus pertinens ad ecclesiam
militantem, anagogia etiam est sensus misticus dum pertinet ad ecclesiam
triumphantem.

'Tropoloyce autem quando sermo convertitur ad informationem bonorum
operum ipsius anime ut cum dicimus david superast goliam intelligimus quod
humilitas devicit superbiam, sapientia maliciam etcetera. ideo tropoloya dicitur
a tropos quod est conversio et logos sermo quasi sermonis conversio vel quasi
sermo conversus.'

'They explain historically by narrating in the same manner as the thing was done and from this history gets its name. The requirement of the ancients was that no one should write history unless he has seen what happened with his own sight.

'Allegorically one explains when one thing is said and another is intended by the transfer of words, as by Isaac Christ is intended; by the ram killed, human flesh; by the seven women who catch one man, the seven gifts of grace; by ... we understand its excellence and wise eloquence, etc. According to this mode the transfer is sometimes made from a thing, sometimes from a person, sometimes from a number, sometimes from a place, sometimes from a time, sometimes from a piece of business, on account of which allegory gets its name from 'alios' or alien and 'gore' or saying, thus alien saying.

'The anagogical occurs when we speak of earthly things and mean heavenly, and therefore anagogy gets its name from 'gana' which means above and 'goge' leading, thus leading from earthly to the supercelestial, whence according to some anagogy and allegory differ in that allegory is a mystical sense pertaining to the church militant, and anagogy is a mystical sense when it pertains to the church triumphant.

'The tropological occurs when discourse is converted to the informing of good works of the soul itself, as when we say David overcame Goliath to mean that humility conquered pride, or wisdom malice, etc. Thus tropology gets its name from 'tropos' which is conversion and 'logos' or discourse, thus conversion of discourse or discourse converted.' Oxford, Bodleian Library, ms Hamilton 17, f 125r

63 The most overt statement of this relation between tropology and audience that I have found occurs in a commentary on Dante's *Commedia*. Once again, there is enough that is distinctive about the language to justify citation at some length. The commentary defines the four-sense understanding of the *Commedia* as 'quemadmodum scientia theologie,' and then explains 'Primus dico intellectus est hystoricus. Iste intellectus non se extendit nisi ad literam, sicut quando accipimus Mynoem iudicem et assessorem inferni qui disiudicat animas descendentes. Secundus intellectus est allegoricus, per quem intelligo quod litera sive hystoria unum significat in cortice et aliud in medulla et secundum istum intellectum allegoricum mynos tenet figuram divine iusticie. Tertius intellectus est tropologicus sive moralis per quem intelligo quomodo me ipsum debeo iudicare, et secundum istum intellectum Mynos tenet figuram rationis humane que debet regere totum hominem, sive remorsus consciencie que debet mala facta corrigere. Quartus vero et ultimus intellectus est anagogicus per quem sperare debeo digna recipere pro commissis. Et secundum istum intellectum Mynos tenet figuram spei qua mediante penam pro peccatis et

gloriam pro virtutibus sperare debemus. De personis autem quas hic ponit hoc accipe quod non debemus credere [cod cedere or redere] eos ibi esse, sed exemplariter intelligere quod cum ipse tractat de aliquo vicio ut melius illud vicium intelligamus aliquem hominem qui multum illo vicio plenus fuerit in exemplum adducit. / in some manner the science of philosophy ... I say the first meaning is the historical. This meaning has to do only with the letter, as when we take Minos the judge and sentencer of hell who judges the descending souls. The second meaning is allegorical, by which I understand that the letter or history signifies one thing in its shell and another in its marrow, and according to this allegorical meaning Minos holds the figure of divine justice. The third meaning is the tropological or moral by which I understand how I ought to judge myself, and according to this meaning Minos has the figure of human reason which ought to rule the whole man, or the prick of conscience which ought to correct evil deeds. The fourth and last meaning is the anagogical, by which I ought to hope to receive what I deserve for my deeds. And according to this meaning Minos holds the figure of hope, by whose mediation we should hope for punishment for sins and glory for virtues. Concerning the persons put here, understand this, that we should not believe that they are there, but understand them as exempla, as Dante deals with some vice he brings in some man who was quite full of that vice in order that we should better understand it.' Florence, Biblioteca Laurenziana, ms 42.14, f 176r

64 Judson B. Allen 'The *Grand chant courtois* and the Wholeness of the Poem: The medieval *assimiliatio* of text, audience, and commentary' *L'Esprit créateur* 18 (1978) 5–17

65 John Calderia *Concordantiae* (Venice 1547). The work is also preserved in Vatican Library, ms Palat lat 985

66 *Nouvelle Biographie générale* (Paris 1855) vol VIII

67 London, British Library, ms Add 15406 (dated 1450). The list of writings is as follows: Speculum divinale, Speculum sapientiale, Speculum historiale, Gemmam medicinalem, Lucidatorium, Omnes partes philosophie descripsimus, Librum de causis et causatis, Expositio psalmorum, Expositio comedie dantis aldigeri, Concordantia philosophorum, etc., Expositio Catonis, Familiares epistolas ad omnis mundi principes' f 100r–v

68 *Concordantiae* f 2v

69 'Sacrosancta illa parens me currum conscendere iussit et hiis verbis orationem prosequitur, Quia traditionibus gentilium philosophorum ac poetarum versatus quae a nostris animum abduxerunt necesse est ut Christi institutionibus diligentius erudiaris. Omnium ergo quae in coelo continentur in elementari mundo ipsa similitudo quaedam apparet, nam supercoelestis patris et filii et spiritus [cod spiuitus] sancti trinitas consimilem trinitatis in terris correspon-

dentiam habet, quia David pater Salomon filius sed Christus est amborum spiritus et ipsarum firma connexio. Angeli etiam suarum virium ac etiam suorum ordinum similitudinem faciunt. Similiter coelis atque sideribus sicut alio loco monstravimus etiam viae lactae similitudo quaedam apparet, haec igitur via inequalis et aspera per quam et currus et nos pariter vehimur, est sanctorum hominum iter per quod ad coelestia pertingunt ... Sed duo illa flumina quae intuentibus voluptatem afferunt, alterum a sapientia filii alterum a charitate sancti spiritus effluit, hoc etiam figmentum veteres poetae praeclare tradiderunt, nam Iupiter cum deos omnes ad supercoeleste atrium advocasset ut singulis suárum actionum leges imponeret non eadem qua caeteri via inces-serunt [cod in cessertunt] sed eminentiori et coeli partem quam pedibus com-praesserunt splendentem ac claram reddiderunt, per hoc significare volentes quod virtuosi clara et splendenti vià ad Iovem accedunt et sidera petunt ...' /
'That most holy parent ordered me to ascend the chariot, and with these words spoke: Because you have been occupied with the traditions of the pagan philosophers and poets which have taken away the spirit from us, it is neces-sary that you learn more diligently the instructions of Christ. A certain simili-tude of everything in the heaven appears in the material world, for the holy trinity of the supercelestial father and son and spirit has a corresponding trini-tarian similar in the earth, because David the father and Solomon the son have Christ as the spirit of both and their firm connection. The angels also make a similitude of their powers and their orders. Similarly, as I have shown elsewhere, there is in the heavenly stars of the milky way a certain similitude, for this uneven and difficult path along which we and the chariot are going together is the way by which holy men reach heaven ... But those two rivers which take away the lust of onlookers flow one from the wisdom of the son and the other from the love of the holy spirit, and this figure the old poets plainly also preserved, for Jupiter, when he assembled all the gods to his supernal court that he might make laws for each of their actions, they did not come by the way that others used, but by a more eminent one, and the sky where they walked they made splendid and radiant, wishing by this to signify that the virtuous come to Jupiter by a splendid and radiant way, and seek the stars' (ff 171v–2r)

70 The seminal articles are Richard H. Green 'Dante's "Allegory of Poets" and the Medieval Theory of Poetic Fiction' *Comparative Literature* 9 (1957) 118–28, and its answer, Singleton's 'The Irreducible Dove.' Dante's letter to Can-grande, and debate over its status and meaning, is of course involved here; the definitive article is Robert Hollander 'Dante *Theologus-Poeta*' *Dante Studies*, (1976) 91–136; it contains exhaustive bibliography.

71 With the difference that the earlier personifications classifiable as allegory of the poets, such as those of Prudentius and Alanus, appeal, admittedly with great power, to the intellect supremely; while those of Calderia, and even the *Melibeus* of Chaucer, have some energetic emotional appeal. Calderia's Rhetoric, for example, is a sexy creature, 'cuius aspectus habitus moresque omnes tantum voluptatis afferebant ut pro consuetudine amantium imo amentium sensus [sic] et animum omnem in hanc prorsus contuleram et caeterarum rerum imo et mei immemor factus velut stupens velut amens illius pulcritudine et lepore perfruebar. / whose appearance, dress, and total behaviour were so voluptuous that I devoted myself utterly to her, sense and soul, conforming to the custom of lovers, even madmen, and I forgot everything else, even myself, and enjoyed her beauty and charm like one charmed or crazed.' f 139r

72 It is awkward to refer to a book with which I now only partly agree, but in which facts are treated, and critical ideas defined, which are necessary background here. That the exegetical method was extended to fictions is important as a fact, as I tried to prove before. I now believe, in addition, that this is even more important as a betrayal – a betrayal of an attitude in terms of which one can account for what is most distinctive and most valuable about late medieval literature – that is, the quality of surrealism or super-realism one finds in figures and stories. This kind of (empirical) realism relates, I think, to nominalism; it is what makes Dante's Beatrice different from, say Prospero, as well as from Alanus' Dame Nature, though she resembles both of them more than she resembles Hester Prynne. It is a difference which, however one defines it, proves at least how much literature can benefit from, or at least be affected by, what society is willing to believe about everything else. See *The Friar as Critic*, especially chapter four, 'Applications,' pp 117–51.

73 '[M]aximum Deorum alatum oppinabatur et dextrae alae inscripserat promitto. Sinistrae expecto, prope cor remitto suprascriptio Deus clementiae. / He suggested that the greatest of the gods was winged, and on the right wing he wrote, I promise. On the left, I expect. Near the heart, I forgive. The superscription, God of clemency.' (*Concordantiae*, f 3r) With this compare Robert Holkot *Moralitates* (Venice 1514) ff 20r–1v, 'De passione et cruce Christi, Moralitas XVIII.'

'Ante templum amoris et benivolentiae Deum hoc modo formaverant, noverant, noverant enim quod si omnes essent amici nulla iustitia indigeremus, hic Deus aspectu Iuvenis et pulcer apparebat cuius caput et facies erant discoperta, et pedes nudos habebat, sed relique corporis partes indumento viridi tegetantur in fronte inscripserant hiems et aestas, in corde quod aperto latere videbatur prope et longe et in extremitate vestis mors et vita. / Before the temple of love and benevolence they made a god in this manner, for they knew that if all were friends we would need no justice. This god appeared like a youth, beautiful, whose head and face were uncovered, and who had bare feet, but the other parts of his body were covered with a green garment. On his forehead they wrote, winter and summer, on his heart, which was visible in his open side, near and far, and on the border of his garment, death and life. (*Concordantiae* ff 6v–7r) With this compare Holkot's 'De amore ad proximum, Moralitas xx' (*Moralitates* f 23r–v). Both figures also appear in a popular picture collection called the *Ymagines Fulgencii*; an illustration of the figure of Friendship can be found in Vatican Library, ms Palat lat 1726, Moralitas 17. On the *Ymagines*, see Beryl Smalley *English Friars and Antiquity* p 393 and passim; Allen *The Friar as Critic* pp 51–2, and 'Commentary as Criticism: The Text, Influence, and Literary Theory of the Fulgentius Metaphored of John Ridewall' *Acta Conventus Neo-Latini: Amstelodamensis* ed P. Tuynman et al (Munich 1979) pp 25–47. An edition of the *Ymagines* is in preparation by Nigel Palmer of Oriel College, Oxford; a very abbreviated indication of the text of each of the images is printed in *Fulgentius Metaforalis, ein Beitrag zur Geschichte der antiken Mythologie im Mittelalter* ed Hans Liebeschütz (Leipzig and Berlin 1926) pp 53–4.

74 'Nam et multorum disciplinarum rationem novit quia eloquenciam summa ratione profitetur etiam veritatem hystoriarum exornat et fabularum figmenta credere facit tanquam vera extitissent. / For he knows the content of many disciplines, because he professes eloquence according to the highest rule, ornamenting the truth of history and making fictional fables as credible as if they were true.' *Concordantiae* f 86v

75 I discuss the manuscript basis of the full text, and discuss the evidence that it is all Ridewall's, and not someone else's expansion, in my 'Fulgentius Metaphored.'

76 The most recent mythographic study I have seen, for instance, says of Ridewall's work that 'In the selection, arrangement, and interpretation of its pagan stories it more closely resembles Alberic than Fulgentius.' Earl G. Schreiber 'Venus in the Medieval Mythographic Tradition' *JEGP* 74 (October 1975) 520. This is not quite true. Ridewall's work resembles Alberic's by being a fairly short next step in the tradition beyond him; it is nevertheless still, textually speaking, a commentary on Fulgentius. It is certainly true, however, that these relationships are not nearly so clear from modern printed editions as they are in the manuscripts.

77 The *Summa de virtutibus et viciis* of William Peraldus is a popular late medieval authority; Peraldus gives this order as a commonplace: 'Secundum Tullium vero in rethoricis, distinguitur prudentia in memoriam, intelligenciam, provi-

denciam. Memoria est per quam animus repetit illa quae fuerunt. Intelligencia est, per quam ea prospicit quae sunt. Providencia est per quam futuri aliquid videtur antequam factum sit. / According to Cicero in the Rhetoric prudence is divided into memory, intelligence, and foresight. Memory is that by which the soul repeats what was. Intelligence is that by which it inspects what is. Foresight is that by which something of the future is seen before it has happened.' *Guillelmi Peraldi ordinis praedicatorum ... Summae virtutum ac vitiorum* (Lugduni 1618) p 201.

78 These have been studied by Denise Cornet-Bloch 'Les Commentaires de l'*Anticlaudianus* d'Alain de Lille d'après les manuscripts de Paris: Étude suivie de l'édition du commentaire de Raoul de Longchamp' École Nationale des Chartes *Positions des thèses soutenues par les élèves de la promotion de 1945 pour obtenir le diplôme d'archiviste paléographe* (1945).

79 Paris, Bibliothèque nationale, ms lat 11337, f 10r

80 Paris, Bibliothèque nationale, ms lat 8299, f 22v

81 Paris, Bibliothèque Mazarine, ms 986, f 16r. Textual corrections from Troyes Bibliothèque municipale, ms 1701, f 2r: a / ms Maz. had 'tria dextera tria'; b / *sic* Troyes, Maz. 'quo'; c / Troyes adds 'septem'; d / Troyes adds 'que fabricant currum ... iunxerunt.'

82 In its usual complete version, the *Ymagines* contains thirty-three chapters. They are, in the order of Vatican Library, ms Palat lat 1726: the Jupiter with three wings, Reason from Alanus, Charity in a red and white tunic, true Friendship in green (cf Holkot's *Moralitates* and John Calderia's *Concordantiae*, discussed above), the three Graces, Jupiter as the sun, the constellation Virgo, the Earth (looking rather like a complex Cybele), Woman (with Juno's peacock), Mortal sin, Vanity with a net, Love as Cupid, Cerberus as cupidity. Fortune, the tripartite life of man (that is, Juno, Minerva, and Venus), the Chimera, and Liber (that is, Bacchus), plus condensations of all the figures except Ganymede in the complete *Fulgentius metaforalis*, in Ridewall's order.

83 See chapter one, note 64.

84 I obviously accept here Charles Singleton's identification of her, in his *Dante Studies* II (Cambridge MA 1954).

85 *The Friar as Critic* pp 145–9

5

The assimilation of the real world

In the preceding chapter, I have tried to define the material of poetry by calling it assimilatio. In doing so I do not wish to deny that poems are obviously made out of words, but rather to suggest that under medieval presumptions words as such do not make a meaningful category. Taken as words only, as a self-referential linguistic entity, a poem may have modern existence, but would, in the Middle Ages, make ontological nonsense. It is, nevertheless, both possible and proper to begin to describe what a poem is by looking at the words, and by noticing that even the words as such, and the systems they make with regard to one another, enact or exist as comparisons – as likenings – as assimilatio. When we do so we discover two things, as I have tried to explain. One is that there are many comparisons, many indulgences of analogy, in the texts of medieval poems. At times these comparisons may even be generated by the structures of texts, rather than by their statements; I pointed to *Sir Gawain and the Green Knight*, and supremely to Dante's *Commedia*, as examples. The second and more important discovery is that the activity of assimilatio of which a text is composed does not exhaust itself within the borders of the text, but demands, as a part of one's proper attention to it, a simultaneous attention to an extrinsic meaning and to a tropologically defined audience. In these terms, I exploited the categories of four-level biblical exegesis to define a general semantic system, in which the power of language to implicate a system larger than words could be exercised and understood.

All of this discussion of assimilatio so far conducted has, however, paid attention primarily to the activity of texts, understood in their medieval sense. It remains to pay specific attention to reference – that is, to the world and to the audience which texts implicate, of whose larger system they are a part, and to which they relate by the same assimilation which I have defined in the last chapter. The question of audience is complicated by the fact that medieval poems have by now two audiences, that is, their medieval and their modern ones, and both of these must be accounted for by the power of consideratio. This question I reserve for my final chapter. Here, I consider the world – that reality to which reference is made. The claim that assimilatio makes about reference is that the world of words and the world of things are not two but one.

The critic can account for this unity by saying that the stuff of the real world is essentially, intrinsically, materially made already literary, because for people who classified poems as ethics and had no category for the 'literary,' the real world must already be so poetic in itself that there can be no need for poetry as a special case. But this does not account for the unity so much as state it. A proper accounting must explain the processes by which this unity comes to be, and enacts itself in human experience. This accounting, in a form which can be at once fair to the medieval facts and to the modern mind, consists of two parts, corresponding to the two inescapable aspects of modern epistemology – subject and object. It is possible, that is, to relate the existence of a medieval real world itself already so poetic that poems can exist in it without the support of a special category called 'literature,' to two aspects of that world – the manner in which it was perceived, and the manner in which it was deemed to exist, that is, to be true. These are not quite the same. The first aspect requires the description of the operative medieval faculty of human perception; the second, the description of the kinds of conclusions one might trust regarding the validity, truth, permanence, solidity, and importance of what had been perceived by that faculty. The first aspect, that is, requires a discussion of the medieval faculty of the memory. The second requires the discussion of the relation between fiction and fact, presuming that fact means both history and that other relation between story and the real world which I have called occasionality.

The particular kind of medieval memory which is relevant here, of course, is the artificial memory, that is, the firm memory, whose 'firmitudinem tantum habemus ex arte non ex natura' / firmness as such we have from art and not from nature.' Therefore, in the *Rhetorica ad Herennium*, 'ipse vero describit hic artificialem memoriam, non naturalem, que artificialis firma est, quia est habitus animi veniens ex arte' / he describes here the artificial memory, not the natural, which artificial memory is firm, because it is a psychological capability coming from art.'[1] My interest here in the artificial memory derives from its having effected, for the medieval sensibility, a certain erasure of the boundary which we now habitually erect between fiction and history.

In order to discuss this topic, I must first argue that the artificial memory is indeed firm and dependable, and must therefore come to terms with Giuseppe Mazzotta's recent discussion of memory in Dante and in Dante's *Commedia*.[2] For Mazzotta, Dante's memory fails, because it is incapable of preserving for representation the ultimate moments of recognition at the end of the *Paradiso*. This failure of memory is bound up, for Mazzotta, with the larger problem of the failure of language – of the ultimate duplicity of the sign which Adam trespassed, and whose using is a continual act of self-alienation in naming which is, for human beings who use language, both the chief evidence and the constant punishment of the fall. With this larger question I have already tried to deal by discussing the central strategies of *Paradiso* XXVI. I would of course agree with Mazzotta that the *Commedia* does, from time to time, deconstruct itself. In many places he has made a definitive description of the behaviour of Dante's language as such. But I would disagree that this behaviour results from the intrinsic failure of language; rather, I think, it is precisely this language which is required in order accurately to describe a human soul deconstructed by sin, whose utterance expresses his condition. Thus the language succeeds by enacting, over and over again, a failure which we can recognize as a failure, and in so recognizing, know the truth in terms of which the failure is what it is. The *Commedia* is the supreme philosophical poem, but even so it is not essentially a poem of statements, but a poem which grounds insight into the unstated. Thus language which must be transcended is language which one can transcend, and this is its success.

These are of course axiomatic matters, which argument cannot settle, and only commitment decides. Language is the central battleground of modern criticism and critical theory. To decide and define its powers, or to deny that it has powers in order to display one's critical panache, distrust of platonism, or existential honesty, are enterprises central to academe. One can settle the issue dogmatically, as far as Dante is concerned, by saying that if the divine Incarnation is true, then language is true, and the poem cannot presume the first, as it does, without both asserting and achieving the second in all the ways that matter.

One can deal with the problem critically by asking what kind of poem the *Commedia* is, so that one can know what memory must achieve in order to succeed. Dante says, in his letter to Cangrande, that his *Paradiso* (thus by necessary implication, the whole poem) is a treatise in ethics. I have already shown that this classification is utterly conventional. If the poem is a treatise in ethics, then its modus dicendi is ethical. This modus, as I showed from the preface of Aegidius' *De regimine principum*, is not logical and cognitive, but proceeds grosse et figuraliter, as does Dante's poem, and has as its end not that we may know, but that we may be. The cognitive failure at the end of the *Paradiso* is precisely that – a cognitive failure. Dante does not succeed in describing for us God as he really is. Within the action of the poem, he saw and understood, but memory and fantasy failed in reporting. But of course success is by definition impossible. What the memory does achieve, and does report with a clarity that is uncompromised by failure, is a condition of the perfection of the will. Dante's 'mente fu percossa' with the result that his will now moves perfectly, by the love that moves the sun and other stars. Since the poem is ethical discourse, this is its ideal end, which Dante perfectly achieves – and which, with all proper allowances for mortality, Dante leads many readers to achieve. Mazzotta is right to say that 'in *Paradiso* XXXIII Dante's language oscillates between efforts to remember and statements of oblivion which are simultaneously applied,' but he is wrong to say that they are 'simultaneously applied, not to the moral experience of the pilgrim, but to the constitution of the text' (p 266). The constitution of the text – and the re-constitution of the text which is every reader's experience of it – is precisely the *moral* experience of the pilgrim. At its highest, where insight becomes ineffable and the only possible next step is to be good, this is what moral experience is. To ask Dante's poem to be a self-trespassing sign is to ask for cognition at the price of life. The memory is not a failure, but the faculty which preserves what is needed in its needful form.

The importance and full significance of this firm memory, the artificial memory of classical rhetoric, for medieval literary theory, became clear only with the publication of Frances Yates' book, *The Art of Memory*.[3] She does not herself develop the implications of her work for literary theory, but they are clearly implicit in what she says, and I depend here on her work both for the medieval evidence itself and for what I consider a most elegant and illuminating explanation of what that evidence means. It is difficult enough to explain an art, even to a person who has some personal use for it, and in whose world it has some place – as those who have tried to read, or write, directions for the assembly of children's toys can testify. It is even more difficult to explain an art no longer in use, and for whose techniques and results our world has no practical use. These difficulties Frances Yates surmounts entirely; the result is that it is possible to understand the way in which memory and the medieval world interacted, and thus to understand how the resulting transformations were of great importance for literature.

For classical rhetoric, the artificial memory was the art of putting images in places in order that these ordered images might then remind one of the parts of one's speech. For practical reasons, the places had to be memorable as an ordered set, and the images to be put in those places needed to be the kind of fictional grotesques whose very absurdity was an effective reminder. For the purpose of structuring the memory, it does not matter whether the 'locis illustribus' to which Frances Yates refers are materially conceived 'well-lighted places,' or rhetorically conceived 'distinct topics.'[4] The point is that they form an intelligible array of distinct mental categories which can be remembered. The context from Martianus Capella's discussion of rhetoric features the ability of the poet and philosopher Simonides to remember the names and seating order of the guests at a banquet. Obviously, he must have done so by visualizing the table; the example presumes material places. Whether one remembers a table of guests or a table of topics, the purpose is to remember, by artfully placing images in 'locis illustribus.' What the artificial memory constructed, thus, were mnemonic devices. But in the Middle Ages, this artificial memory, defined and transmitted in a rhetorical tradition, eventually was used as the faculty by means of which were remembered the moral and theological examples of sacred and secular history. These examples, of course, were the guide to ethical behaviour. Inevitably, therefore, the positivist distinctions which we would make between fact and fiction tended to be blurred. What was remembered was remembered as an image or a story, because this was what memory had been invented and perfected to remember. Therefore, what medieval people in fact remembered, using this faculty, was related generically to the grotesques of classical rhetoric. Moreover in both cases what was being remembered was precious not because it existed, but because it reminded, meant, was significant. And for the Middle Ages what was remembered in this way was also dignified, both by being labelled as history, and by being connected with the rational through the platonic doctrine of reminiscence. History, then, is story, and as story has a primarily ethical and moral usefulness. But story, that is, fiction, is already classified as ethics. And the inherited and popular stories, which tended to be mythological, had in addition already been euhemerized and otherwise interpreted into a relation with human and natural history as well.

In all ages, the mechanical processes by which one keeps records determine what sort of records will be kept, and therefore to a great extent what use will be made of them. In oral cultures, the past exists in heirlooms and in remembered words. Given the normal attritions of use, the heirlooms will eventually be primarily cultic or ornamental objects, whose use involves little or no wear, and the words will probably be metred, because metred language is more easily remembered verbatim. In cultures which trust writing, the past exists in files and libraries, to which, barring the various calamities of history which affect paper and vellum, each successive generation may have direct access, and of which each successive generation may make its own interpretation. In the first of these cases, what is fixed is the mythologization, and scholarship makes hypotheses about the positivist data which might have been behind that mythologization. In the second of these cases, it is the facts, more or less, which do not change, and it is in the making of the mythologization that scholarship is free.

The medieval case is a combination of these two – possessed of written records, and even of the alphabetization which promised to reduce these records to data – medieval people tended to use their files as if they were resources of an oral culture. That is, they tended to be more interested in the mythologization than in the fact, more interested in the meaning of an event than in its bare material existence.

Frances Yates' book analyses a number of medieval witnesses to the nature and importance of this memory, which there is of course no need to repeat here. I shall, however, in a way partly supplementary and partly more focused on the problem of the literary, present four additional witnesses, one from Chaucer and three from Dante, which testify both to the importance and to the nature of this medieval artificial memory.

In the first place, remembrance is the appropriate reaction to something truly exemplary, as Chaucer makes clear:

When that the Knyght had thus his tale ytoold,
In al the route nas ther yong ne oold
That he ne sayde it was a noble storie,
And worthy for to drawen to memorie (*CT* I (A) 3109–12)

That is, the *Knight's Tale* is worthy of a place in the company of that great array of examples from the past, by means of which the present understands itself, its moral worth and its posture with regard to the future.

Second, as Charles Singleton has shown,[5] Dante's *Vita nuova* is transcribed from the larger book of his memory. In the textuality of the *Vita nuova*, which is of course only a part of the larger non-textual book from which it was taken, there is a complex fusing of autobiographical fact, the metaphor of the book, and the probable fiction of some of the poetry. Here the assimilatio between words and things is pushed very far back; it is pretextual. Implicitly, it exists already in the life itself, from whose memory the book is transcribed. This achieved assimilatio finds an analogue in a curious distinction which Dante himself makes in the next chapter of the same book – a distinction between fact and fiction.

E perocchè soprastare alle passioni ed atti di tanta gioventudine pare alcuno parlare fabuloso, mi partirò da esse; e trapassando molte cose, le quali si potrebbero trarre dall'esemplo onde nascono queste, verrò a quelle parole, le quali sono scritte nella mia memoria sotto maggiori paragrafi.

And because to pause too long over the passions and acts of youth might seem to some to speak fabulously, I leave them behind, and passing over much, which could be taken from the example whence the *Vita nuova* came, I come to those words, written in my memory under the large section headings.[6]

The passions and deeds of Dante's youth are of course not fiction, but they are classified as seeming such, by the word 'fabulously.' What the book does contain is example – 'esemplo' – the name given to a story when it most obviously and ostentatiously functioned as a carrier of moral meaning. In all this, the easy metaphoric equivalence of words and things is constantly assumed, and the crucial faculty which makes, or keeps, it all is memory. The distinction between fact and fiction is obscured, here in a most unusual way, not by believing in a fiction, but by disbelieving in (or perhaps better, by refusing to credit) a fact when it is of no exemplary value.

If the true is received as memorable only when it is of exemplary value, then it is also true, in relation to memory, that exemplary values are primarily dependent on memory, rather than on some other faculty. The relation is, as it were, reciprocal. Dante witnesses to this fact in a particularly telling way in his *Commedia*. Conventionally, of course, as I have already noticed in connection with the *Fulgentius metaforalis*, memory, along with intelligence and foresight, were the parts of prudence – that is, the moral faculty which was supposed to rule the continued behaviour which constituted history. With the help of remembered examples, a right understanding of the present guides the foresight which is the rule of future action. Therefore, when Dante faces in Hell the problem of dealing with the future, that is, with the soothsayers, he glosses the procession of these backwards-headed monsters with the story of the founding of Mantua. Virgil tells the story, really an euhemeristic legend and not the usual one at that, in considerable detail. It is in no sense a digression, because it implicitly recommends the use of remembered history, rather than soothsayers, as a means of dealing with the future. The connection with prophecy is underlined when

Dante responds to Virgil's instructions to ignore alternative explanations. Dante promises:

> ... Maestro, i tuoi ragionamenti
> mi son sì certi, e prendon sì mia fede,
> che gli altri mi sarien carboni spenti.

> Master, your arguments are to me so certain,
> and so hold my faith, that the others
> would be to me dead coals. (*Inferno* XX.100–2)

Singleton calls this 'a curious metaphor, though the meaning is plain enough,'[7] thus admitting that he does not know, and has not found, a rationalization of it. It is, I think, thoroughly justified by the burning coal from the heavenly altar in Isaiah 6, with which the angel cleansed the lips of the visionary penitent, and qualified him for prophecy. Virgil's exhortation to historical memory over soothsaying is, of course, just such a live coal.

The theoretical importance of memory, then, cannot be too highly emphasized. It fused under one faculty, by the happy accident that classical rhetoric was appropriated by the Middle Ages as it was, two quite different human habits – the tendency to use past events as precedent for future action, and the tendency to embroider the images of sense experience with a certain grotesquerie in order to make them more interesting or more memorable. Our modern habit is to insist that the historian separate these two kinds of thinking as rigidly and rigorously as possible. Medieval historians could exercise the same critical judgment. John Ridewall, for instance, was able to prove on the basis of literary evidence alone, that Dido could never have known Aeneas.[8] The anonymous mythographer of Bodleian ms Digby 221, using the same kinds of scholarly techniques but coming to an opposite, and characteristically medieval, conclusion, argued that Helen was an immortal.[9] But the techniques of positivist historiography had no particular virtue to medieval writers and thinkers, who tended normally to adjust their facts to fit their truths, and not the other way around. Thus history was mythologized as it was preserved, even though it was preserved in writing and depended, to some extent, on written records as well as written stories. And the attitudes appropriate to this kind of history permit and include most of the senses of formality, value, decorum, and meaning which in modern times are reserved exclusively for the belletristic or aesthetic experience. History, in short, was preserved in a description which, because of the peculiarly medieval mediation of an artificial memory, had already endured the preoccupation of an art, and existed as an achieved assimilatio.

It is thus difficult to draw a firm line between history and story; it is in fact morally advisable, or at least morally habitual, to fail to do so. This is the way memory works. Therefore, when a commentator honours both truth and history, and makes much of ancient eyewitnesses –

nulli licebat tractari antiquitus de hystoriis nisi esset inter res de quibus gesta est. Hystoria est testis temporum, narratrix veterum, magistra memorie, memoria vite, nutrix veritatis, nuncia vetustatis

In antiquity no one could deal with history unless he were involved in the business going on. History is the witness of the ages, the narrator of old things, the mistress of memory, the memory of life, the nurse of truth, the messenger of the past[10]

– it is wholly appropriate that he do so in connection with the *Eclogues* of Theodolus, in which the parallel legends of pagan and Christian history are brought together for the sake of being allegorized in assimilatio. I have already discussed in considerable detail the processes whereby the traditions of late medieval mythographic commentary and the extension of the procedures and attitudes of biblical exegesis to fictions witness to the medieval tendency to blur distinctions between fact and fiction, history and fable, the true and the false.[11] There is no need to repeat those arguments here, nor to present the conventional medieval definitions of fable, history, and argument[12] which make much of distinctions between true and false, verisimilar and non-verisimilar, without in practice generating the kind of attention to the verification of facts which is the chief preoccupation of more modern history. Instead, I wish to approach this problem from a slightly different tack, and examine a few medieval stories in use. From what was said about them, and from the character of the ways in which people were willing to trust them or at least professed faith in them, this category of story whose truth value is exemplary more than empirical can be defined.

In Chaucer's *Nun's Priest's Tale*, the narrator is permitted to say of his beast fable, which is of course by every possible medieval and modern standard a fiction:

This storie is also trewe, I undertake,
As is the book of Launcelot de Lake,
That wommen holde in ful greet reverence. (*CT*, VII.3211–13)

Fully to unpack the layers of Chaucer's irony here would involve truth in as many reversals as a soap opera, but it is certain that at one of these layers, and that a quite commonsense one, Chaucer agrees with us that both stories are false, and that the kind of people who are taken in by such are the conventional audience for what a more chauvinist age called women's magazine fiction. Dante magnificently transcends the issue; it is the story of Lancelot and Guenevere which speaks Love's message to Paolo and Francesca, but 'Galeotto fu 'l libro e chi lo scrisse. / Galeotto was the book and the one who wrote it' (*Inferno* V.137). To say that a book is true is a conventional synecdoche, which we translate by taking its content as reliable. But to call a book a pander makes a statement which we hear first as literal, and this is exactly right, because what makes the story of Lancelot and Guenevere both present and powerful is the book's auctoritas, and the pandering auctor who made it a book. The pander is the thing and not the story. At the same time, of course, it is also the story. The story is true because it is in a book, and the book tells a story because there was an event of ethical shape, whose narratio was worth remembering. In this metaphor of book as pander, reciprocity is total, and it is this reciprocity which precisely defines medieval historicity.

In the French compilation of Arthurian material which most closely corresponds to Malory, we get the basis of this metaphor. The author is writing 'le prologue du dernier libre du messere lancelot du lac qui parle de la grant queste du saint graal.' The following is a part of his invocation:

O glorieuse trinite ... [etc] de tres benigne et humble cueur vous supplie que me soies aidables a acomplir cest mieme derniere petite oeuvre. Car je nay entennoy de y mectre riens ne adiuster qui ne soit veritable et que je nay leu et viste en pluseurs livres anciens.

O glorious Trinity ... I pray you with benign and humble heart that you be helpful to me in accomplishing this same last little work. For I do not intend to put or add anything to it which is not true and which I have not read and seen in many old books.[13]

The basis, of course, is the conventional medieval authority of books, which supports, not the truth which can be verified, but the truth of 'fama,' the truth which is believed because everyone has said it.[14] Such a truth is of course credible but it is so in terms of a different set of uses for the truth than those which need a verified truth – uses at once more moral, and more dependent on and trustful of story.

One of the translators of the Tristan story also believes that his material is true. After wondering why no one else has translated a matter which contains such 'beles aventures et plaisantz,' he proposes to do it himself:

non mie pour ce que ie sache gramment francois, ainz apartient plus ma langue et ma parleure alamaniere dengleterre que a cele de france, comme cilz qui fu en engleterre nes. Mais tele est ma volentez et mon proposement que je en langue francoise et au miex que ie porrai, non mie entele maniere que ie y aquiere mencoigne, amis laverite toute aperte ce monsterai et ferai a savoir ce que li latins devise en francois de lestoire de Tristam, qui fu li plus souverains chevaliers qui onques fust ou [sic] Royaume de lagrant bretaigne et devant leroy artu et apres, fors seulement Galaad le bon chevalier et lancelot dou lac et li latins meismes de lestoire dou saint graal le devise apertement Que autans le Roy artus ne furent que iii tres bon chevalier, qui bien feissent aprisier de chevalerie, Galaad, Launcelot, Tristram. De ces iii fait li livres mencion sour touz les autres et plus les loe et plus en dit bien, et pour ce que ie sai bien que ce fu verite, vendroie ie en commencier en cestui point lestoire de tristam.

not at all because I know much French, for my language and my speech is more in the manner of England than France, like those born in England. But it is my will and my intention to show and make clear, in French as best I can, and in no way that will be a lie, but rather the truth entirely open, what the Latin tells in French of the history of Tristan, who was the best of all knights who ever were in the realm of Great Britain before and after Arthur the king, except only Galahad the good knight and Lancelot du Lac. And the Latin itself tells openly in the history of the holy grail that in comparison with King Arthur there were not but three great knights who exemplified chivalry well – Galahad, Lancelot, and Tristan. Of these three the books make mention above all others, and praise them and say well of them, and because I know well that this is true, I begin the history of Tristan in this place.[15]

Once again it is the testimony of books that is believed, and this belief is confirmed by praise.

According to T.H. White, simple British farmers believed, in 1940, that Arthur would return and rescue them from the hordes of the new Aryan barbarian. In a manner, so did C.S. Lewis. It is for this reason that I choose to begin to illustrate this medieval ability to blur the boundary between fact and fiction in stories, by reference to the Arthur stories, since they, probably more than any other corpus of stories which survives from the distant past, still have the power to evoke a certain quality of belief. It is a quality of belief which may not be taken too far, because in all ages, even the fourteenth century, there were ironists like Chaucer able to see the foolishness of all too oversimplified credulity. It is a quality of belief which never gets very far from books, and the fama that is made by 'beles aventures et plaisantz'; thus Dante is absolutely correct both to call the book a pander and to trust Virgil as guide. Yet at the same time it is a quality of belief that locates itself in the story, as such, and not just in the believer, because that would spoil it. At the same time it is a belief, because the audience desires it and wills it as well as simply receives it.

A distinction that medieval critics were perhaps more inclined to make than that positivist one between fact and false is a distinction between what might be called the essential and the accidental in a story. For instance, in a gloss on book ten of the *Thebaid*, one commentator says:

Obruit: hic incipit liber qui in parte extractus est a virgilio, ubi enim Virgilius duos iuvenes introducit, scilicet nisum et eurialum castra hostilia penetrantes, et magnam in illis stragem facientes, utrosque tamen occisos, sic statius hic inducit scilicet Opleum et dimatem in castra hostium irrumpentes et magnam stragem agentes utrumque tamen occisum. Hic ergo Virgilium. Virgilius Omerum imitat [cod imitāt], Qui quidem ulixem et diomedem castra devastantes inducit.

Obruit: Here begins the book which is partly taken from Virgil, for where Virgil introduces two youths, Nisus and Euryalus, who went into the enemy camp and made great slaughter among them, but were killed; so Statius here brings in Hopleus and Dymas bursting into the enemy camp and making a great slaughter, but both were killed. So he makes here something Virgilian. Virgil imitates Homer, who brought in Ulysses and Diomede devastating the camp.[16]

A not much better informed thirteenth-century commentator comments to the same purpose:

Obruta hesperia: hic incipit decimus liber in quo maxima eius pars sumpta est ex illo virgiliano ubi introducit actor nisum et eurialem de nocte egresso [sic] et maximam rutillorum stragem perpetrasse, tutum reversos fuisse. Similiter et actor iste inducit opleum tidei armigerum et dimam armigerum pertho' multos thebanorum de nocte interfecisse, non redisse sed interfectos fuisse.

Obruta hesperia: Here begins the tenth book in which the greater part is taken from that part of Virgil where the author introduces Nisus and Euryalus, who went out at night and made a slaughter of the Rutuli, and came back safe. Similarly this author introduces Hopleus the armour-bearer of Tydeus and Dymas the armour-bearer of Parthenopaeus who killed many Thebans by night and did not return but were slain.[17]

The commentators seem to agree without dissent that Statius is writing history, except for the bits of integumentum and allegory which one can easily distinguish. As such, history should be based on the facts, not on epic stories of entirely different events. Yet this particular incident in the history of the Theban wars is taken from the *Aeneid*. I take the words 'extractus' and 'sumptus' quite literally and seriously – not, of course, to mean that Statius took verbatim quotes from Virgil, but that the differences between verbatim quoting and similarity of shape was not a really serious one. Apparently, it is possible for history to be at once true, and the story of events which possess a canonical shape – as if history, in spite of its bewildering and at times absurd variety, will subject itself to a kind of medieval Proppean analysis, and furnish up, for every war, a heroic night invasion of the enemy camp. Since war is one of the most intrinsically mythic things human beings ever do, one can usually expect in it a predictable array of events. Nevertheless it is not really good historiography to recommend that one borrow an event from Virgil and put it in the history of the Seven against Thebes. What redeems the recommendation from absurdity, of course, is that what is borrowed is not an event but the shape of an event – in the faith that all epic wars assimilate to one another. And this willingness to presume for historical events their epic – or for that matter, hagiographic, or fabliau, or romance – form, is once again an evidence of the medieval willingness to blur the distinction between fact and false, and to receive stories as true more on the basis of their significance and their shape than their verifiability. This significance and this shape, obviously, are defined by bookish precedent – thus it is wholly natural that Virgil should shape the Theban war.[18]

The same comparison can exist between the book and veritable real life. Most of the biographies of Statius, which circulate attached to the *Thebaid*, mention the relation of the poet to Domitian; many of them say that the purpose of his writing his epic was to encourage Titus and Domitian to get along better than Eteocles and Polynices. In this connection, a number of commentators deal with the line addressed to Domitian: 'Tempus erit, cum Pierio tua fortior oestro facta canam. / A time will come when emboldened by Pierian frenzy I shall recount thy deeds' (I.32–3). Some medieval commentators knew that this line was ironic. A fourteenth-century Italian copy of the *Thebaid*, for instance, has the following comment:

Domicianus vero audiens ipsum statium esse probissimum in tractando, rogavit eum quod facta sua tractare deberet. Sed statius noscens quod dictus domicianus nil laude dignum commiserat, volens se excusare dixit quod prius in historia thebana suum volebat ingenium experiri, et imperator ipse contentus fuit.

Domitian, hearing that Statius was an excellent writer, asked him to treat his deeds. But Statius, knowing that the said Domitian had done nothing worthy of praise, wishing to excuse himself said that he wished to exercise his talent first on the history of Thebes, and the emperor was content.[19]

But his knowledge was most exceptional, and untypically based on careful historical criticism. A more normal, and I think more conventionally medieval opinion, is the following:

Scribit autem ad laudem domiciani imperatoris, non quia de thebana historia ad eum quicquam pertineat, sed dicit in hoc opere suum preacuere ingenium, ut post modum ad fortia eius facta describenda valeat sufficere.

For he wrote in praise of Domitian the Emperor, not because anything of the Theban history pertained to him, but he said that in this book he would sharpen his talent, so that afterwards he would be able to suffice for the description of his greater deeds.[20]

These commentators, one may be sure, knew little more of Domitian than that he was a Roman emperor, contemporary with Statius. They obviously believed, thus, that writing an epic poem about the legendary past was fit and proper preparation for writing contemporary history. In putting the point this way, of course, I take the betrayal at maximum strength. The commentator would not have distinguished, as I have done, between the legendary past and the immediate past – both are history, and both are worth remembering. But it is precisely this failure to distinguish which is the point – otherwise, unless the epic history of Thebes and the fit history of a contemporary Roman emperor were not generically the same, one could not practise on the one for the writing of the other. That they are the same, of course, is proof that they were remembered in the same way – by an artificial memory that preserved history precisely and only in so far as it was transformed into story – that is, into exemplary images, toward which one could behave with a quality of belief that was already, as it were, built into the story. When one understands a real event, it is because one has seen it in the shape of a literary event. The story of the past and the experience of the present really become true only as each rises to the character of what we would now call fiction. Thus, except for dogmatic purposes, the distinction between fact and false ceases to be interesting, and in common practice, most of the time, can be ignored.

By extension, then, Statius could have been taken, by virtue of this proper preparation, as one expert in the understanding of one's present. This is precisely what he becomes in Dante's *Commedia*. Like the risen Christ on the road to Emmaus, to whom Dante explicitly compares the newly appeared Statius, he is the expert on a present which is mysteriously but satisfactorily a fulfilment of the past. Ultimately, he accompanies Dante even into the earthly paradise from which Virgil is barred (*Purgatorio* XXXIII.134). Moreover, the city of his epic is also important. Even more than behind Chaucer's *Knight's Tale*, there haunts behind the *Commedia* the precedent of the city that failed – Capaneus the blasphemer, Amphiaraus and Tiresias, Eteocles and Polynices, Amphion, all figure in Hell, and the fit insult for the Pisa which is the 'vituperio de le genti del bel paese / shame of the people of the fair land' *Inferno* XXXIII.79–80) is that the city is 'novella Tebe / new Thebes' (89). These things work because the world, including the world of legendary and of such probably fabricated facts as the Christian faith of Statius, is a world in which parallel systems do work together; in which the border between fact and fiction can be crossed by assimilatio.

For the *Commedia* itself, the supreme fiction is the fiction 'that it is not fiction.'[21] Singleton makes this beautifully perceptive point in support of the fact that it is a figural poem. But even more telling, in a way, than its figural quality, in demonstration of this power of Dante's poem, is the later use to which it was put. Clearly, one's fama in Dante's great medieval roman à clef became, for succeeding generations, proof of one's real character and existence, and one could, as does one of Federigo di Montefeltro's early biographers, note that people are notable because Dante mentioned them.[22] The neatest evidence of this use of the *Commedia* that I know relates to the Christianity of Statius. At *Thebaid* VI.936, where Statius professes belief in omens, one commentator says:

praemissa fides: Hoc statius, et hoc antequam fuisset Christianus. et nullus poetarum fuit Christianus nisi ipse, et idem Dantes ipsum ponit.

praemissa fides: This is the statement of Statius, and this before he was a Christian, and there was no classical poet who was Christian except him, and Dante says the same.[23]

I have found no evidence in commentary on the *Thebaid*, other than reference to Dante, that Statius was a Christian. Dante very likely invented the detail himself. Once invented, however, and put in an authoritative poem, it becomes citable as true. Between the realm of poetry and the realm of fact there are few border guards, an indefinite boundary, and much traffic back and forth.

All these instances of the world in which memory believes are, among the kinds of assimilatio, descriptions. A literal story is literally told, as true (or, in the case of Chaucer, as not true). More complex than this is the relation that is generated by the occasionality of poetry. Particularly for medieval poetry, this dimension is largely hidden. The post-twelfth-century biographies which commentators attached to the names of troubadour poets certainly prove that medieval people were much interested in the occasions of poems, and inclined to believe that most poetry had occasional as well as absolute value. Dedications would tend to the same conclusion. That much poetry was performed – read aloud for some assembled and very often courtly audience – suggests that these readings were inevitably occasions, and must often have had, either in language or the emphasis of performance, some topical significance. In the nature of the case, however, knowledge of the occasion would tend to be lost, except for a very few poems like Gower's *Vox clamantis*, which is not so much an occasional poem as an occasional preachment. Therefore, it seems to me, much of the labour that has gone into arguing which historical characters are the butts of which bits of Chaucer's irony, or which ideological points of view the owl and the nightingale really support, is labour largely lost because its sole point has been to establish a fact of which one generally cannot be sure.

There is a difference, however, between discussing the probable occasion of a poem, and using a guess as to a poem's occasion as a basis on which to discuss the nature of occasionality. This discussion, it seems to me, is most important, particularly for medieval poetry, for two reasons. First, the ethical classification of poetry, if nothing else, guarantees that it will be more occasional, or more often occasional, or taken as occasional after the fact, than poetry written under more literary assumptions. Occasionality, whether in some general ethical sense or in the sense of some very particular and pointed observation about some human incident, story, or life, seems clearly one of the distinctives of medieval literature. In the second place, the relation between a poem and its occasion is a relation analogous to all the others impinging on and internal to poetry. It is a relation of assimilatio. This relation, under which the text of a poem per se is taken to include also all that larger field which constitutes the fullness of the thing – things remembered and person spoken to, material and audience – requires occasion at least as a rhetorical hypothesis in order that the poem under consideration may be considered complete. Therefore to understand occasionality is to enrich by one more exemplum in the normative array one's understanding of the crucial structural force in poetry, and therefore of its nature.

As examples in terms of which to discuss occasionality, I propose Chaucer's prologue to his *Legend of Good Women*, and Langland's *Piers Plowman*. In so doing, I deliberately avoid other perhaps more obvious possibilities, such as the *Book of the Duchess* and Gower's *Vox clamantis*, about whose specific occasions there is little serious doubt. But these poems raise questions of doctrine which are beside the point. I am not here concerned to discuss medieval theories of confession, or consolation, or revolution, but rather, in as pure a form as possible, to discuss the limiting case of poetic reference – that is, that relation between a poem and some specific human event or situation which the poem takes both as analogy to itself and as audience. Both the *Legend of Good Women* and *Piers Plowman*, in different and complementary ways, focus on this relation quite clearly and purely. The *Legend* does so both by its dedication to Queen Anne and by its explicit preoccupation with the relation between books and things. *Piers Plowman* does so because it is 'a commentary on an unknown text,' and therefore in its strategy of discourse glosses the relation of occasionality in a complex and tellingly medieval way.

The occasion of Chaucer's poem, I believe, is the poet's wish to praise Queen Anne for her bravery and console her for her loss, after her intercession before Arundel for the life of Simon Burley failed. It is in the nature of the case impossible to prove that this or any other event was the occasion, because Chaucer says nothing literally except that the poem is for the Queen. But this occasion does seem to fit both the poem and the external circumstances of Chaucer's life, as I shall show. And ultimately specifying the occasion is not an end in itself, but rather a means – I discuss occasion only as a means of having a specific base for considering occasionality.

Arundel's humiliation of King Richard and Queen Anne occurred as the events connected with the Merciless Parliament were drawing toward their climax and end. Our only full record of the incident is in the *Chronicle of the Betrayal and Death of Richard King of England*, in the context of Arundel's later trial and execution.

Et le commencement du parlement fu que le Roy fist sa complainte du gouuernement des ces seigneurs. Et comment ilz lauoyent despose de sa couronne en sa jeunesse. Et la Royne fut aussy iij heures a genoulx devant le conte Darondel pour le prier pour un sien chevalier appelle Jehan de Carnalay [ms Y Jehan de Beruelay, Rot. Parl. Symond de Burlee] lequel ot ce non obstant la teste copee. Et le quel conte respondi a la Royne, Mamie priez pour vous et pour vostre mary il le vault mieulx. Lautre jour apres le Roy fist sa complainte de la grant traison laquelle ilz auoyent encommence de faire enuers lui et enuers touz les seigneurs de son conseil. Pour laquelle traison le conte Darondel fu jugie a mourir et davoir la teste copee. Ansi come len fist.

It was at the beginning of parliament that the King made his complaint about the government of those lords, and how they had disposed of his crown in his minority. And the Queene was three hours on her knees before the Count of Arundel begging him for the life of one of her knights named Simon Burley, who was nevertheless beheaded. And the said count answered the Queen, 'My friend, it would be more worthwhile for you to pray for yourself and your husband.' The other day, after the King made his complaint of the great treason which they had begun to make against him and against all the lords of his counsel, for that treason the Count of Arundel was judged to die and to be beheaded, as thus it was done to him.[24]

Simon Burley was a particular favourite of the Queen, as well as of King Richard. Burley had been in charge of Richard's education, had assisted him through a long and tiring coronation ceremony, and had gone to Bohemia to win the Princess Anne, and again to escort her back to England to be King Richard's bride. Of the knights of the king's household, he was one of the most deeply and sincerely beloved. But he had made slighting remarks about Arundel's abilities as an admiral – before Sluys, obviously deserved – and the Lords Appellant were determined on revenge. Simon Burley was executed on 5 May 1388, presumably not long after the Queen's three-hour kneeling intercession. With his death, apparently, the rebellious lords of the Merciless Parliament, Gloucester, Arundel, and others, seem to have lost their zeal for judicial murder. They collected £20,000 of public money for their expenses in saving the state, and Arundel went off to sea.[25]

There is a curiously appropriate gap in the records of Chaucer's official life just at this point. He gave up his house over Aldgate in October 1386 and got what amounts to a passport in July 1387 to go to Calais with Sir William Beauchamp, but there is no record of him in Beauchamp's accounts. Certainly by the summer of 1386, when he was elected to Parliament, he was living in Kent. But he was not re-elected. Except for writs against him by creditors, issued between April and June 1388, we do not know where he was until the King declared himself of age in 1389, within two days of a year after Burley's death.[26] Chaucer was prudent to have disappeared. His friend and associate, Nicholas Bembre, had been executed with the full brutality reserved for traitors on the twentieth of February. Thomas Usk, who had imitated Chaucer's poetry and was probably his friend, was executed about the same time. During the early months of 1388, in fact, there seems to have been a systematic removal, from office and even from life, of everyone of substance belonging to what might be termed the royalist party. Of this party, of course, Chaucer was undoubtedly a conspicuous if not greatly powerful member.

To console the Queen in writing would have been a delicate business. The events connected with the Merciless Parliament were undoubtedly traumatic for both the King and the Queen, and would have cried out for sympathetic and loyal comment. But it is difficult to comment on failure. Too much praise would be ironic; too much openness, in the presence of powerful enemies, would be dangerous. The device of a poem in praise of Queen Alceste as daisy, introducing a series of denunciations of traitors against women, fills all requirements. To send such a poem to the Queen, whether she be at Eltham or at Shene, obviously invites the Queen to see herself as the referent of the glorious Alceste. That Alceste and her consort are so brilliantly attractive is of course a compliment in itself – had the two characters been merely Love and Lady the compliment could have stopped there. But naming Alceste and suppressing Admetus is suggestive; Chaucer is manipulating his material, and both the Queen and the modern critic are encouraged to look for more explicitly topical detail.

Ostensibly the poem is innocuous; it is 'about' Chaucer and his penance. But it contains veiled hints of secret meaning:

> But Goddes forbode, but men shulde leve
> Wel more thyng than men han seen with ye!²⁷

The subject here is writing, which must be believed. Again:

> But wherfore that I spak, to yive credence
> To olde stories and doon hem reverence,
> And that men mosten more thyng beleve
> Then men may seen at eye, or elles preve, –
> That shal I seyn, whanne that I see my tyme;
> I may not al at-ones speke in ryme. (lines 97ff)

Further, once we have Arundel in mind, the bird's defiance of the fowler strikes with powerful double meaning – the fowler that in winter 'hem made awhaped and distroyed hadde hire brood' (lines 132–3). In their song they despised 'the foule cherl that, for his coveytise, had hem betrayed with his sophistrye' (lines 136–7). Thus, though they found 'Daunger for a tyme a lord' (line 160), they sang proper praises to Summer, 'oure governour and lord' (line 170), for the sake of innocence, pity, mercy, and forgiveness. In addition, it is quite striking that Chaucer's treatment, as one accused of violating love's law, should contain on the one hand so much discussion of false accusation, liars at court, cunning tattler accusers, climaxing with envy (lines 345ff), and on the other, so clear an exposition of the obligation of the ruler to mercy (lines 376ff). Clearly, Queen Alceste is one whose intercessions in behalf of a penitent are based on good reasons, and the poignancy of the compliment to her, 'pite renneth soone in gentil herte' (line 503), is all the more obvious when we think of the pitiless gentlemen, the noble Lords Appellant.

Given these invitations to explicate Chaucer's compliment and consolation in more detail, we can find that Alceste, as he presents her, corresponds to the Queen quite precisely. Literally, Alceste was the wife of Admetus; she willingly died that his life might be spared, and afterwards was brought back out of Hades by Hercules. Allegorically, she is presumption, which mind, that is, the faculty to which fear can come ('possit adire metus' equals Admetus), needs for the undergoing of the difficulties which defend the soul. At the hour of death, virtue saves her from Hell.[28]

In Chaucer's literal poem, Alceste is the consort of the God of love, and Admetus has disappeared. At the level of real event, Queen Anne was presumptuous to the point of mortal danger for the sake of Simon Burley; Richard would have spared him had he had the power of his position. The most important feature of the correspondences between Queen Anne and Alceste is that the Queen's literal action corresponds to Alceste's allegory, while the Queen's allegory – that is, her proper glory as Queen – corresponds to the literal Alceste of Chaucer's poem. Literally, the Queen is presumptuous and at least potentially self-sacrificing; these are details which the *Legend* nowhere mentions in connection with Alceste, but which must be found by looking up the gloss and pursuing the allegorization. On the other hand, a queen, no matter how wretched her literal circumstances, means or figures a queen-ness for which the glorious literal Alceste of Chaucer's poem is a fit description. The poem thus compliments the Queen as glorious precisely when she is a nobly, even rashly self-sacrificing person, and at the same time pointedly ignores her loss, giving her as consort a Richard idealized as the God of love. The hidden meaning of Alceste's glory is presumptuous self-sacrifice; the hidden meaning of the Queen's humiliation is precisely her glory. The chiastic strategy of reference thus literalizes the Queen's glory, and reconciles her to her historical predicament by making it simultaneously that glory's integument and its privileged meaning.

Following up his compliment, Chaucer fulfils his 'penance.' In the legends of the saints of love which follow this prologue description of Alceste, there are repeated allusions which fit Arundel. Of the men who betray in these stories, Antony, Aeneas, Jason, Theseus, Tereus, and Demophon are explicitly sailors, as was Arundel. The words 'treason,' 'traitor,' and 'betray' occur frequently. Dido's kneeling to Aeneas is especially telling:

> She kneleth, cryeth, that routhe is to devyse;
> Conjureth hym, and profereth hym to be
> His thral, his servant in the leste degree;
> She falleth hym to fote and swouneth ther,
> Dischevele, with hire bryghte gilte her,
> And seyth, 'Have mercy!' (lines 1311ff)

Jason is denounced as a false lover, but the words apply equally well to a false courtier:

> ... thy statly aparaunce,
> And of thy wordes, farced with plesaunce,
> And of thy feyned trouthe and thy manere,
> With thyn obeÿsaunce and humble cheere,
> And with thy contrefeted peyne and wo.
> There othere false oon, thow falsest two! (lines 1372ff)

The two tales which do not obviously fit, the tale of Thisbe and the tale of Hypermnestra, compliment the Queen by praising self-sacrificial love and the showing of mercy which is rewarded only by imprisonment.

The compliment to the Queen finds confirmation even in small mythographic details. That the daisy was made by Cybele in her honour is appropriate because Cybele, under the name Berecynthia, means spring flower, or sole flower, and is thus more perfect. She means a kind of power and firmness of glory.[29] The Queen properly is both powerful and glorious. Mars also brings to bear an allegory which comments on what Arundel did, and points out virtues appropriate to royalty: 'Mars, that is fortitude and constancy, supporting the weak, and manfully defending them against she-wolves and dogs.'[30]

If this speculation is convincing, then Chaucer is praising Queen Anne by praising Alceste, honouring her self-sacrificing love for Burley with Alceste's implicit allegory, and denouncing Arundel both in many incidental details and by praising the sainted ladies of Love's train. The secret meaning of the poem, then, is the Queen, and the relation between Alceste and the Queen is that relation of assimilatio which normally relates text and commentary.

That in this case the appropriate 'commentary' for an elaborately allegorical text is a literal, particular human being, added to the fact that the relationships involved include two reals and two ideals, themselves as it were allegorically connected, in chiastic balance, suggests that one of the games Chaucer is playing in this poem is a game with the whole structure of relationship itself. It is in terms of this play that occasionality defines itself.

The most obvious feature of Chaucer's text is that it takes a very long time to get started. The prologue is over a third through before Alceste, who is presumably its subject, has appeared. But this approach to Alceste, long and detailed as it is, is also itself an exercise of levels and relationships, which gloss the central one between Alceste and the Queen. The poem of the prologue begins, in recommended medieval fashion, with a proverb:

> A thousand tymes have I herd men telle
> That ther ys joy in hevene and peyne in helle (lines 1–2)

Since the poem exists to compliment the queen, and by so doing, remind her that the actions of the merely powerful on this earth are not ultimately definitions either of truth or justice, this anagogic observation is thoroughly appropriate, and evokes the apotheosis of Alceste to which the prologue alludes at its end. But this proverb is not the poem's literal subject; rather, it is an excuse to begin a discussion of knowledge. One knows, primarily, what one reads. Books therefore are of great value. Chaucer apparently has in mind chiefly history books, because they deal with stories of holiness, reigns, victories, love, hate, and other sundry things. Books are the key of remembrance, and therefore should be honoured. This discussion, of course, reflects two medieval commonplaces – that truth for medieval people tended to be based on written authority, and more subtly, that everything which was to be remembered was in the process transformed into something bookish, or literary – a placed image preserved by the artificial memory.

But, says Chaucer, when May comes and the flowers spring, 'Farewel my bok, and my devocioun!' (line 39) Then he loves the daisy. This daisy, however, does not represent the reality of experience as opposed to the reality of books. The daisy is as literary as everything else. It is a flower whose praise can be helped by both 'flower' and 'leaf' parties in the French poetic debate. It is a flower which grows on 'enbrouded' (line 119) fields, which is associated with birds that sing in words, which has prosopopoeic rulers, which is praised by a reaping of words, and, most important of all, is adored in the pose iconographically conventional for dreamers in dream vision poetry.[31]

> Adoun ful softely I gan to synke,
> And lenynge on myn elbowe and my syde,
> The longe day I shoop me for t'abide
> For nothing elles, and I shal nat lye,
> But for to loke upon the dayesie. (lines 178ff)

This, in short, is no Wordsworthian ramble, but an 'olde storye, er swich stryf [of flower and leaf] was begonne' (line 196).

After this experience, which is literally described as an experience but whose iconographic shape is that of a dream vision, Chaucer gives us his literally announced dream vision. Here we meet Alceste, who, in Chaucer's invented source, 'turned was into a dayesye' (line 512). Here we find out why the daisy is so important, and thus incidentally why the books through which we came to get both the daisy and her allegorization are so important. In the rhetoric of this prologue, with its three sharply distinguished parts, we are involved in a dialectic of penetration, from container of remembrance (books), to symbol of remembrance (daisy), to that which must be remembered (Alceste). Beyond Alceste, of course, is Queen Anne. In its sequence, the poem is a literal emblem of the medieval act of reading, of understanding. What one finds in books is the daisy, what one finds in the daisy is Alceste, and what one finds in her is the Queen.

At the centre of this process is Alceste. The remembrance of the Queen is the end and purpose of the poem, but Alceste is the image of that remembrance. She reminds us of Queen Anne, and by virtue of her bookish existence as a mythographic character with a literal presence in the poem, a biography outside of it, and an allegorization in terms of psychology, she tells us what to remember and honour about Queen Anne. In the relation, therefore, between Alceste and Queen Anne, the process of transformation which artificial memory achieves comes full circle. The historical fact, figurally implicit in the glorified Alceste, is ready to be remembered. The dialectic of penetration which leads from books to bookish flowers to the allegory of flowers leads us to no fiction, but back out again into real contemporary history. The relation between literature and life is not mimetic, but assimilative – reciprocal. We do not move from life to words to meanings as from concrete to abstract; rather we move within a web of words, some literal, some figural, some in the natural language of the book of the creatures, some historical, so that what is now literal may become meaning and commentary, and what is now commentary may exist as letter.

In the reciprocity of this web of words we find the true meaning of a poetic occasion. Chaucer's *Legend of Good Women*, in its prologue, enacts a philosophy of poetic language.[32] Within the textuality of the poem, one begins in books – the key of remembrance – and through the dialectic of the three parts, penetrates to a meaning. These three parts might be properly seen as analogies of letter, sense, and sententia, if we allow that sentential is not discursive, but figural. Or, reflecting the four-pole structure defined by exegesis, we might label the discussion of books doctrinal-allegorical, and the two parts following two layers of anagogy. In any case the whole is bookish, verbal, assimilated, and the three parts which begin in memory and build, one upon the other, are as clear an enactment as I know of the full complexity of the meaning of meaning, as the Middle Ages understood it.

Chaucer was, I think, quite aware of these possibilities. The two surviving versions of his prologue prove that he was preoccupied with it, and returned to it quite late in his career, certainly after the death of the Queen in 1394. The character of his revision proves that what interested him was precisely his statement of a philosophy of poetic language; it was to him a poem about making poems, and even more fundamentally, about the precise power and authority that the words resulting from such making could and should have.

The poem in both versions concludes with a comparison between empirical and bookish experience. When the God of Love asks Chaucer if he knows the lady who has given him such light penance, he answers:

> 'Nay, sire, so I have blys,
> No moore but that I see wel she is good.' (F 505–6)

Love responds, 'That is a trewe tale, by myn hood!' He then suggests that Chaucer has a book in which he can find Alceste, and then Chaucer understands:

> 'Yis,
> Now knowe I hire. And is this good Alceste,
> The dayesie, and myn owene hertes reste?
> Now fele I weel the goodnesse of this wyf.' (F 517–20)

Love's words are ambiguous. I take them to mean that Chaucer's reaction, his sense that the lady is good, is a 'true tale,' that is, an honest report of his feelings. Perhaps it further means that the lady is indeed good. It is not, I think, to be taken as Chaucer's implicit claim of the truth of the story of

Alceste, nor of the validity of his seeing her goodness as proof of her story. Just the opposite, because the God of Love makes Chaucer's knowing well depend on his advising himself by consulting his book.

It is only when Chaucer thinks of his book that he can 'fele weel' the goodness of the lady, a goodness which he had already, within the action of the poem, seen well. The book validates the vision and makes it true. One verifies experience by looking it up in a book. This conclusion is even more bookish than Chaucer's beginning, which merely asserts that one must believe from books what one cannot verify by sight.

Chaucer's revisions underline this consciousness of books. A major addition is his list of books in G 271–310. A few lines later, he changes his description of the material of poetry from 'thynges' to 'bokes' (F 364 / G 342). He changes the location of the beginning of his dream so as to include his adoration of the literal daisy in the dream (G 102–3), thus making it explicitly rather than only by generic implication a verbal daisy. Even more, he is conscious that books are made things, and that he makes them, deliberately and wilfully, according to an intention which he imposes on his material:

> 'what so myn auctour mente,
> Algate, God wot, it was myn entente
> To forthere trouthe in love and it cheryce,
> And to be war fro falsnesse and fro vice
> By swich ensaumple; this was my menynge.' (G 460–4)

The God of Love says of him, 'He hath write many a bok er this' (G 348). Thus he defends received authority, knowing that it is made authority:

> 'But wherfore that I spak, to yeve credence
> To bokes olde and don hem reverence,
> Is for men shulde autoritees beleve,
> There as there lyth non other assay by preve.
> For myn entent is, or I fro yow fare,
> The naked text in English to declare
> Of many a story, or elles of many a geste,
> As autours seyn; leveth hem if yow leste!' (G 81–8)

I am not at all sure that I know what Chaucer means by a 'naked text in English.' It seems clear that some irony is involved, or some ironic pretending of irony, because the reader is essentially being dared to believe, in a context which suggests that Chaucer's naked texts will be harder to believe than will the old books and authorities from which, presumably, Chaucer has translated them. The closest analogue I know to Chaucer's notion, though it does not use his language, is the comment by Aegidius Romanus to which I have alluded already, made in the context of discussing the modus of ethical discourse, in which he says that 'gesta moralia complete sub narratione non cadunt. / one does not adequately treat moral activities by telling just what happened.' Narratio must be reinforced 'typo et figuraliter. / with the typical and the figural.' If this parallel is valid, then Chaucer's use of the phrase 'naked text' is the equivalent of saying that he will make an un-storial story – an un-bookish book – in a sense, a text that bears upon itself no signs that it is a made thing, that simply is. Such a text, which is made but does not seem made, answers to the paradox which Chaucer faces in dealing with all this bookishness, that is, that books constitute the reality they report. They constitute what constitutes them. In the plot of the prologue, Chaucer enacts the same circularity by letting Alceste be the allegory of the daisy, its meaning, and that which it constitutes, at the same time she is that which becomes the daisy and, by virtue of the honouring creation of Cybele, its cause. The daisy comes both before and after Alceste; cause causes cause.

It is possible for the modern reader, under the influence of Derrida, to take all this manoeuvring as proof that Chaucer is discovering deconstruction. But such influence is both perverse and irrelevant. Chaucer is indeed examining, in this discussion of the authority of books, the ground of his belief in language in general and in his own power to make true language in particular. This ground is, under medieval presumptions, the very circularity which seems to modern readers so paradoxical.

According to Freccero, it was Petrarch who first discovered the idolatry of language.[33] Chaucer faced the risk of this idolatry, while his black knight permitted himself fascination with an idealistic love language which had no referent. But he never, I think, committed it. As long as language can refer – as long as language can have true occasions, it can truly constitute them. This is what 'assimilatio,' in its largest sense, means. It is true, of course, that language reports the world, and so in a sense is caused by it, but to take this fact as a sufficient explanation of language is to fall into the naive sign theory of Gulliver's third voyage. It is equally true that we see only what we can name, and that thus language constitutes the world, but to take this fact as sufficient explanation is, at best, to achieve modern phenomenology. Chaucer's manoeuvring, in the prologue to the *Legend of Good Women*, presumes both truths at once – enacts, one might say, the condition of having it both ways – because Chaucer knows that language only works, and poets can only speak the truth, when there is precisely this circularity between language and the world.

Beyond all this, in Chaucer's first version, is Queen Anne. The dialectic of the meaning of meaning leads into a made book, in full consciousness of the bookishness and the human agency of books, but it enters the book in order to achieve the real world. Queen Anne is the poem's constituted result, but she is what constitutes it, and it says her truth. The poem is, in a sense, her commentary. She is also literally a part of the poem's audience, in that the poem was sent to her, and she read it or heard it. But there is also another audience, of which the Queen herself by imaginative projection can be a member – that is, the audience who know the poem's occasion, and can therefore regard Alceste and Queen Anne as assimilated equivalents, as mutually text and commentary, each making the other intelligible, within a relationship of perfectly circular assimilatio.

As long as a poem has an occasion, the distinction between the real world and the world of poetry disappears, and the textuality of poetry loses its priority and becomes commentary. The commentary is in the fullest sense real, in that one verifies material experience by the commentary, as Chaucer verified his experience of Alceste in his Ovid, and in doing so put into the action contained in his poem an experience exactly analogous to the experience which the reader has of the poem, when he verifies Queen Anne in it. The fundamental act of assimilatio is description or reference – the verbal activity in which the real world is appropriated, organized, remembered, understood. It begins as words refer to things, it grows more complex as things are compared or exchanged or likened, it becomes cosmic as systems of organized assimilation are themselves likened. This assimilatio presumes, of course, a world already fit to be assimilated – a world whose ethical nature, as I have already shown, is as such so literary in its formalities as to be easily assimilable. Medieval people appropriated and understood this world by remembering it – that is, by appropriating it as and into the textuality of a poem. When a poem has an occasion, the occasionality turns all these relationships upside down – the real world becomes the poem, and the textuality of the poem turns into a gloss, without, of course, being in any way diminished as such. When the occasion disappears, the textuality is all that is left, literally, but the occasion persists in the text, constituting it even while it is constituted by it. When Queen Anne was dead, the poem could no longer ask to be carried to her, and Chaucer deleted the lines. Dead, she was something which could no longer be seen by eye, and could only be remembered in a book, the key of remembrance. To be remembered is thus inevitably to be made bookish, to be made textual, but this is appropriate, because 'gesta moralia complete sub narratione non cadunt.' Chaucer's naked text, as he must have known behind his irony, is not really naked, because it is a text, and is constituitive of what it remembers. But real life does the same. Under medieval ethical presumptions, real life also aspires to textuality, aspires to become, as it lives, language – aspires to its prosopopoeia. Remembering constitutes fact, but only by making fact what it ideally is, in a world for which, even when faith was weakest, the definitive Word was a divine person, and the world was his book.

The prologue to the *Legend of Good Women*, thus, makes two important points at once. First, it defines occasionality by enacting a very complex reference: book to daisy to daisy's allegory Alceste to Alceste's meaning in the real Queen. Second, it surrounds this definition of reference with a complex, ironic discussion of books and texts and their making, whose implication is that this activity of reference is perfectly circular. Chaucer does not analyse or defend this circularity so much as enact it and act on it in making his celebrative language, and so leaves later readers grounded in weaker languages open to thinking him less comfortable than he is.

We should not, of course, do so. In order to explain more clearly why not, I turn to my second example of occasionality, *Piers Plowman*. In the activity of this text, the circularity of assimilatio is both more visible and more convincing, because it exists not in two terms but in three. As the *Legend of Good Women* is in reciprocity with the Queen, there are two terms. *Piers Plowman* implicates three. It is what happens as the Bible constitutes the world. Its textuality occupies as a third term the middle ground of an additional, external, and independently verifiable two-term activity between the Bible and the world. Further, it insists on being precisely and only itself. It frustrates misinterpretation by unintelligibility. Until we discover its own peculiar axioms of operation, it refuses to perform at all.

John Alford has shown, in his seminal article, that certain sections of *Piers Plowman* are organized in terms of biblical concordances.[34] Robert Adams has made an analogous point, by proving that the figure of Need occurs in the poem where it does because a verse in Job, medievally understood, specifies that after Need comes Antichrist.[35] What both these articles prove is that the text of the poem obeys no logic of its own, but occurs as commentary on or development of an array of themes already defined elsewhere as an ordered set – usually, by the Bible. I propose that the whole of the poem can be read in this way (and will define rather than violate Will in being so read). When this reading is accomplished we will not only understand why the poem contains the great miscellany of details we find in it, but more important still we will understand what kind of text it is which can be so constituted, and what its existence can tell us about the medieval understanding of the operation and authority of language.

Here, there is only room for a brief and quite speculative prediction of that reading, grounded in an analysis of the prologue of the B-text. My method, derived from and under the guidance of Alford's article, presumes that Langland begins by thinking about an array of Bible passages treating some common theme, and therefore, under medieval definitions, a concordance or a distinctio. In the light of this array, he will develop examples, illustrations, or explanations, whose coherence as an assembled text derives from and depends simultaneously on the Bible passages under consideration, and the human situation which Langland feels those passages instruct. The quotations in his text will not necessarily be the specific verses which carry the concordance or distinctio, though they may be, but they will certainly come from the same passage, and be an appropriate part of his amplification. The critic thus attempts to understand Langland's text by following this process of amplification backwards. Beginning with the quotations, especially those Langland emphasizes by using Latin originals, often followed by an 'etc' which is the medieval way of citing the larger context, one attempts to identify the concordance which justifies the particular array of quotations one confronts. The concordance names the theme; this theme is an interpretation of the human situation being instructed. This, to some extent, we know from history. Having, then, knowledge of the relevant human situation on the one hand, and the relevant biblical thematic concern on the other, we can correctly understand the text in the middle, which is at once their result and the argument of their relationship.

Understanding of the prologue of the B-text has been obscured, even if one wished to follow this method, by a wrong identification of its first quotation, 'Qui loquitur turpiloquium / He who utters foul speech' (line 39). Recent consensus indicates Ephesians 5:3–5, and specifically the reference in verse four to 'turpitudo et stultiloquium / filthiness and foolish talk.' But the correspondence is far from exact, and the context is not instructive. A better source, I think, is Colossians 3:8, 'turpem sermonem de ore vestro / filthy speech from your mouth.' The connection gains plausibility from the presence, in the interlinear glosa, of a variant reading, 'aliquis turpiloquium,' which is precisely Langland's term.[36]

Colossians 3 is a chapter which emphasizes the great contrast between the saved and the lost, the old man and the new man. It features lists, in one case a list of pairs: gentile and Jew, circumcised and uncircumcised, barbarian, Scythian, bond, and free (verse 11). After recommending various virtues, it reaches a climax in commendation of charity, which is the 'vinculum perfectionis / the bond of perfection' (verse 14). A concordance on Langland's quotation, which states the theme of filthy speech, leads *realiter* to Ecclesiastes 10, which uses the word 'stultus' and its derivatives numbers of times, and contains as well Langland's quotation, from later in the prologue: 'Vae tibi, terra, cuius rex puer est. / Woe to you, land, whose king is a child' (verse 16). This chapter also contains numbers of pairs of opposites, mentions the theme of hierarchy reversed, and concludes, after observing that money obeys all things, that one should not speak against the king lest he find out. Together, these two chapters from which Langland quotes establish *sermo* and *vinculum* as the major themes of the prologue, and suggest much of its literal content. Further, they point to yet other concordances on the theme of speech or on the theme of bonds or chains, which account for the rest.

The chapter in Colossians begins with a vision of Christ on high. *Piers Plowman* begins with a vision of a 'tour on a toft.' They are, as we find in Passus I, equivalent. Both texts then pass to the opposite: things of the earth, the 'deep dale bynethe' with its donjon. It is important, I think, to get this scene correctly visualized. The tower is the place of truth; the donjon, of falsehood. They represent the influences of Christ and the Devil, and may have been suggested, according to Skeat's note, by morality pageant wagons. The easiest interpretation is vertical: the tower on a hill, standing over the plain of folk, with that tower's dungeon deep below in the living rock of the earth. Allegorically, the folk are between heaven and hell. Though this is of course finally true, I now think that Langland's vision is a provisional, social, and historical one. There are two towers, not one. One of them is on a hill, the other, in a valley or dale, moated by a deep ditch, lower down and some distance away. Between there is a field, a territory. The scene is a perfectly realistic representation of rival lordships, appropriate to the truth and falsehood which rival one another in this life.[37]

Having defined his polarities, Langland then turns to specifics: the 'fair feeld ful of folk.' These are specified in chiastic terms, 'werchynge and wandrynge as the world asketh' (line 19). Then, for the next eighty lines, Langland gives a rigidly outlined set of examples. The first set, lines 20–38, are a series of pairs of workers, in each case one good and one bad. These come to a climax with Langland's quotation, 'Qui loquitur turpiloquium.' Then follow an equally neat set of wanderers. First there is a five-line introduction to 'bidderes and beggeres' and then there are three pairs of two, all more or less bad this time, who seek saints, and who preach, and who go off to London to chantries or the civil service. In imitation of Colossians 3, Langland has made his own exemplary list of human possibilities for good and evil.

The thing that surprises most about this whole passage is its architectonic neatness, constructed out of the welteringly energetic specification of folk. It is a neatness which is perfectly obvious once seen, but which it takes the guidance of Colossians to see properly in the first place. Once this is established, it is possible to see just what Langland means. His text, though it follows the thematic example of Colossians, is explicitly different from it in one important way. In Colossians, the specifications of moral and spiritual possibility are addressed to an audience which, though grammatically plural, is devotionally singular. Each Christian is being asked to address himself to the improvement of his own personal spiritual life, by rightly dealing with the specified possibilities. Langland, on the contrary, specifies a society – a number of people, living a number of mutually exclusive modes of life under the threatening castles of rival lords. I have already pointed out that Langland habitually raises the question of salvation in the singular only to answer it in the plural. Here at the very beginning of the poem, under the guidance of a biblical passage addressed to Christian individuals, Langland finds himself seeing a possibly Christian society. His choice of emphasis is all the more obvious because we know what guided it.

At the end of this passage of Colossians is the reference to charity, 'quod est vinculum perfectionis' (verse 14). Again Langland's reaction is political and corporate; he thinks of the Petrine power to bind and loose. He is pursuing a distinctio on the theme of vinculum. The biblical passage is, of course, Matthew 16:19; there are a number of details in the context, of which the most significant for Langland should be that it is here that the Pharisees ask for a sign from heaven, and the identity of Jesus is questioned and established. The first of these may have suggested to Langland the angel who speaks from heaven; the second, the whole discussion of the true function of the king. If so, then once again theological material generates a discussion of society as such.

Other texts may be involved, as well. In one of the English versions of the *Secreta secretorum* there is, in the context of a discussion of justice, a quotation from Seneca, 'Iusticia divina lex est, et vinculum societatis humane / The divine law is justice, and the bond of human society.'[38] This quotation concords realiter and litteraliter with Langland's distinctio, and it directly evokes his discussion of kingship. More telling still, it occurs in a context in the *Secreta secretorum* which concludes with the proverb, 'ffor whan al tresure is tried, trouthe is the beste,'[39] a verbatim statement of Langland's more pervasive theme, which occurs thus as the conclusion of Passus I (line 207).

In the part of his prologue immediately following this reference to the power to bind and loose, Langland discusses first pope-making, then king-making. These are, of course, the two powers; Langland will quote their biblical prooftext, 'Reddite Caesari,' at Passus I, line 52. Pope-making grows out of a pun on 'cardo' and 'cardinal,' evoking the gates which the keys of the kingdom open, and grounding the pope's existence in the cardinal or secular virtues. The king, though made by the commons, exists in a context of allegory, with Knighthood and Kind Wit. What is constituted is society as such. In both cases, because of pun and allegory, the constitutive power of language as such is evoked.

The king then has two witnesses, a lunatic and an angel. In a sense, they are the figural and literal versions of the same thing, because lunatics could be taken as speaking with a divine voice. What the lunatic says is a benediction or a blessing; the angel gives a definition of right rule under law, and quotes from Luke 6, the sermon on the plain. This passage, obviously appropriate for a fair field of folk, Langland uses as the central basis of the next Passus. All this gets two responses. From the educated goliard, a cautionary relating of the king and the law, using a linguistic metaphor, and from the commons, a tag affirming royal absolutism: 'Precepta regis sunt nobis vincula legis' / The precepts of the king are for us the chains of law.'[40]

The goliard is explicitly concerned for the relation between words and things, the angel for the spirit in which legal formulae should be applied, and the commons for the relation between legal authority and what the king says. All three, in complementary ways, are concerned to define language, and to define it for that crucially operative and powerful case, the law. Langland has chosen well. The law and legal process are verbal procedures which render the world true by describing it. In medieval pleadings, opposing lawyers would tell and re-tell the story of the case at issue until it could be decided what kind of story it was, and then judgment could be rendered. Pleading may thus permit the conclusion 'This man is a murderer,' and when the conclusion has been formally stated the man's nature and his fate are determined. But this determination intends only to be a true response to what he already is. Thus law is a language which seeks to be absolutely descriptive, and absolutely performative, at the same time. Further, and particularly in the English tradition, the law grounds itself not only in normative judgments logically derived, but also on the precedent of cases analogously related. In its activity in the world, legal language enacts much the same circularity of reference which Chaucer defines in the Legend of Good Women. This is especially true if the law is 'ius nudum' (naked law), undecorated by 'pietas' (goodness). Langland's description, here, of the king and the law makes it clear that he is thinking about language with just as much attentive clarity as Chaucer.

There follows the fable of the rats. Its political point is obvious, of course – common people have no real resource except obedience in dealing with the powerful. But Langland had already said this, as the statement of the commons themselves: 'Precepta regis, etc.' Langland's point has to do with metaphor, and thus continues his discussion of language, of 'nomen' and 'res,' which he had begun under the example of the law, now within a strong atmosphere of working assimilatio generated by the beast fable. What the mice want to do is bell the cat – that is, hang a bell around his neck. They get the idea for this, according to Langland's text, from having noticed the chains of office around the necks of London city burgesses. These chains are materially literal but metaphoric in meaning; conversely, the law, rightly instituted by a good king, is a chain which is only metaphoric materially but at the level of meaning does literally bind. Langland, thus, has gone from the nomen of vinculum to the res, and in so doing has lost its reality. The mice cannot bell the cat, and in fact should even follow the advice of Ecclesiastes 10 (from which Langland now quotes) and keep silent: 'Shal nevere the cat ne the kiton by my counsel be greved' (line 203). Then even nomen, or verbum, becomes corrupt; real lawyers, who come out all at once in a crowd exactly as the mice had done, will not speak their legal words except for money. The crowd expands to include other trades, including baxters, websters, and brewsters, and the passus ends with the crying of wares – sermo that is not exactly turpiloquium, but may sometimes be not far off. These wares, like the lawyers' words, are for sale. Money obeys all things, and Lady Meed will shortly appear, corrupting both nomen and res. In this conclusion, it is significant that a number of the specified trades are in a feminine form, though the trades themselves may well have been exercised by men. What is happening, I think, is that Langland's specification of trades is at the same time a notice of proper surnames, which by this time had become detachable from occupation. Geoffrey Chaucer was not a shoemaker, nor was his father. Thus, paradoxically, as a trade name becomes a surname, it becomes nomen sine re; eventually, a nomen quasi res.

The question which the whole of the poem asks and answers is the question of salvation – how may a person become a true person? Langland begins to discover that he can ask that question by thinking, under the guidance of the Bible, about a simpler one – what can a person be? The answer, crucially, has to do with language, with sermo which binds, which is a vinculum, supremely in the activity of right law under pietas, but also in one's own name, and in all the metaphors and relations of nomen and res in between proper naming and legal judgment.

This is, one might say, a strange way to begin to think about personal salvation. Even Bernard of Clairvaux, for all his allegories, recommends just what Colossians recommends – a procedure which an individual can follow as an individual. Langland reads his Bible, a form of words which by definition has the right and the authority to describe the world truthfully. As he does so, he asks his question, and looks at his world. The result is an intertextuality, which solves the problem of the relation between word and thing, in the definitive case of the Bible's word, by making a text which is simultaneously constituted by both, and in which the activity of language as such is carried on without ever being allowed to be self-existent, or independent.

It is therefore eminently appropriate that the literal text, as such, is both an allegory and a narratio of the achievement of salvation. Its location is the human self, its process of language is a process of knowledge, and its process of action is a process of will. In Langland's case, this allegory is complicated by the fact that Will is forced into so many social and plural modes of existence, but its intrinsic location is not changed. Thus to be between word and world is the inevitable location of any self or selfhood as such; this is where sermo takes place, whether it be turpis or beatus. The self is the vinculum in which reference takes place. Experience is always occasional, because it is composed of occasions. *Piers Plowman* is an experiencing text. This is what it means that its forma tractatus and its forma tractandi are the same.

The occasion of Chaucer's *Legend* was Queen Anne. *Piers Plowman* is the track of the Bible's occasional relations with fourteenth-century England. In both cases, the occasional relation means that the distinction between the real world and the world of poetry disappears, and the textuality of the poem loses its priority and becomes commentary. Nomen and res are reciprocal, each causes the other. Langland's own usage, in fact, contains the paradox. In one sense, the name 'king' fails to achieve the thing 'king' unless the king obeys the law; oppositely, the person who has and is the name 'king' fails to achieve the thing by failing to achieve that observance of law which is the king's definition. 'Res,' thus, may mean either the human person of the king, or his ideal definition as a law-keeper. The relation may be read either way, and with either term on either side. The vis transitionis is real, as Langland presumes by using grammatical metaphor. What his poem presumes by acting as it does is that the world answers, that the world is disposed to be genuinely and effectively named. Assimilatio rules throughout, in description, in comparison, in analogies between systems, because the world is fit to be assimilated. It is a world whose ethical nature is so literary in its formalities as to be easily assimilable. Medieval people appropriated and understood this world by remembering it – that is, by appropriating it as and into the textuality of a poem. But when the poem has an occasion, the occasionality turns all these relationships upside down – the real world becomes the poem, visibly, and the textuality of the poem turns into gloss, without, of course, being in any way diminished as such.

The modern critic can experience these reversals best, I think, in the world of painting, where one can find examples of occasionality which are still, as it were, alive. The clearest such example is portraiture. Many of the great masterpieces of painting are portraits; some of the greatest are self-portraits. Much of the critical discussion of these paintings is aesthetic – is the kind of discussion which might equally well fit a landscape or a still life having the same qualities of draftsmanship and chiaroscuro. But portraits, and especially self-portraits (because we are an introspective age), tempt us all to discussion of the subject. They are occasional art; they are commentary on their subject – in Rembrandt's self-portraiture, it is the painting which is the gloss; it is the painter who is the work of art. If we were more sympathetic to royalty, in this democratic age, the same temptation would be even stronger for the portraits of the great. Certainly when we see a portrait of someone we know personally, no matter how great the artist was, we take the painting first and foremost as commentary.

An equally clear example, at least for me, is the work of Canaletto, and other painters of Venice. These paintings are all occasional, in that they celebrate a town, and often a particular event in that town. They are masterpieces of composition, light, and description. But for anyone who has spent much time in Venice, the paintings, great as they are, nevertheless become commentary, and the aesthetic and moral centre of their existence is the town itself. To say this is in no way to denigrate the quality of the paintings, but rather, granting that to the fullest, to recognize that the city of Venice is itself an even greater work of art, composed of the daily lives and works of thousands of people over centuries, and now impossible to inhabit without being to some extent caught up in the theatricality of a real world which has not lost contact with rhetoric, and with the ethical poetic of the later Middle Ages.

Occasionality, then, is the reciprocity between life and poetry at its highest and most perfected level. Life, in its daily ordinariness, does not often rise high enough to be fit occasion. Much of the time, it must be assimilated – it must benefit from the preoccupation of an interpreting memory – before we can see what it really meant. Much of the time, it must be arrayed in poetry, side by side with all the proper illuminating comparisons and parallels, before we can see what its structure is. But some occasions are already poems. The glossed and inherited Alceste, as Chaucer presents her, is a great and beautiful lady. But Queen Anne, who held Arundel in her presence as queen for three hours even while she knelt before him as suppliant, and thus existed herself as the perfect iconic combination of fact and definition, is greater and more beautiful still. The Bible, a more powerful text and an even more relentlessly occasional one, dignifies all occasions into steps toward apocalypse. If one is perceptive as Langland was, one can see it happening. *Piers Plowman* is the track of that happening; as it tracks, it explains to us how Chaucer's occasional language not only can but must be caused by what it causes.

One must still admit that most occasional art – the work of laureates – tends to be second-rate. The *Legend of Good Women* is strange and fascinating, but it is not Chaucer's best work. In the genre that it defines, the only poem which one might rank as an unqualified success must be Virgil's *Aeneid*. The closest competitor in English is Spenser's *Faerie Queene*. The great medieval candidate, Dante's *Commedia*, is not a proper example, because in so far as it praises, it is not occasional, but an assimilatio of anagogy, and in so far as it is a poem occasional of Florentine politics, it blames, and the real people who can be made to exist to its characters as commentary, as Queen Anne exists to Alceste, lack entirely the moral weight of existence which might make themselves the centre, and transform the poem into commentary. Doubtless if we could literally know the heavenly Beatrice, then Dante's portrait of her as his beatitude would become the world's greatest occasional poem. Occasionality, in short, is the response of the real world to the possibility of its being remembered. It is, for a reason the Middle Ages would define in terms of the fall, a response often flawed, imperfect, and unworthy. Nevertheless, it is a response whose possibility defines the ideal – a real world already so poetic that poems, great as they are, can be happy to occupy the margins, and be the gloss of the book of life.

NOTES

1 Alanus de Insulis, Commentary on the *Rhetorica ad Herennium*, Paris, Bibliothèque nationale, ms lat 7757, f 12v. Though it is based on commonplace medieval opinion, it is perhaps worth emphasizing here that the notion of a 'habitus animi,' which can without too much stretching be translated as a 'psychological capability,' in combination with and the result of an art, neatly

expresses just that blurring of the border between extrinsic and intrinsic, between self and other, which defines the chief difference between modern and medieval epistemologies.

2 Mazzotta *Dante, Poet of the Desert* esp pp 253–74. This book was published after my own was written. I have revised occasionally under its guidance, and had of course already profited both from conversations with the author and from articles in which his position received preliminary statement. In details of interpretation and scholarship, the book is magisterial; my disagreements with it, when they exist, are doubtless axiomatic.

3 Frances Yates *The Art of Memory* (Harmondsworth 1966)

4 Richard Johnson, in his translation of the book on rhetoric from the *De nuptiis*, calls attention to his disagreement with Frances Yates in translating 'locis illustribus' as 'distinct topics.' In context, I would suggest that the Latin means both, without requiring so rigid a distinction between materially and rhetorically visualized topics as Johnson implies. See *Martianus Capella and the Seven Liberal Arts*, vol II *The Marriage of Philology and Mercury* tr William Harris Stahl and Richard Johnson, with E.L. Burge (New York 1977) p 203.

5 *An Essay on the Vita nuova* (Cambridge MA 1944)

6 *La vita nuova* II.60ff, *Opere* p 205

7 Charles S. Singleton *The Divine Comedy, translated with a commentary* (Princeton 1970) vol I.2, p 357

8 Smalley *English Friars and Antiquity* pp 130–1

9 'Helenam vero immortalem fuisse temporis probat diuturnitas. Nam constat fratres eius de Argonautis fuisse, Argonautarum vero filios cum Thebanis dimicasse. Item filii eorum contra Troianos bellum gesserunt. Si ergo immortalis Helena non fuisset, tot sine dubio per secula durare non potuisset. / The length of time proves Helen immortal. For it is true that her brothers were Argonauts, and the sons of the Argonauts fought with the Thebans, and their sons waged war against Troy. If therefore Helen had not been immortal, she doubtless would not have been able to last so long.' Text: Virginia Brown 'An Edition of an Anonymous Twelfth-Century *Liber de natura deorum*' *Mediaeval Studies* 34 (1972) 33.

10 Vatican Library, ms Vat lat 1479, f 15v. This is the same manuscript which contains text and commentary for a number of other works, including Ovid's *Metamorphoses* and the *Alexandreis* of Walter of Châtillon. It is of fourteenth-century French provenance.

11 *The Friar as Critic*

12 These are conveniently available in *The 'Parisiana Poetria'* pp 100–1.

13 Paris, Bibliothèque nationale, ms fr 112, book IV, f 1r

14 For a discussion of this 'fama,' see Sheila Delany *Chaucer's House of Fame, The Poetics of Skeptical Fideism* (Chicago 1972).

15 Vatican Library, ms Palat lat 1964, f 1r

16 Oxford, Bodleian Library, ms Canonici lat 74 (Italian, s XIV), f 78v

17 London, British Library, ms Add 16380, f 172vb

18 I am happy to thank R.A. Shoaf for telling me that the description of the Libyan march of the Republican army in Lucan's *Pharsalia* relates similarly to a desert crossing in the *Argonautica* of Apollonius. For his discussion of this fact, and his analysis of Lucan's intention for it, see '*Certius exemplar sapientis viri*: Rhetorical Subversion and Subversive Rhetoric in *Pharsalia* IX' *Philological Quarterly* 57 (1978) 143–54.

19 Padua, Biblioteca del Seminario Vescovile, ms 41, f 1v. Another commentary, of the same period and provenance, says: 'Notandum quod domicianus stacium ut de tributis suis scribet rogavit. Sed quia in eum nihil scriptura dignum videbat dimittens eius facta, honeste se in prologo excusat et ad grecam ystoriam se transfert. / Note that Domitian asked Statius to write about his contribution [to civilization], But because there was nothing in him worth writing about, [Statius], putting aside his deeds, excused himself honestly in his prologue and turned himself to Greek history.' (Cambridge University Library, ms Ii.III.13, 1r.)

20 London, British Library, ms Add 16830 (s XIII), f 144r. Virtually the same language can be found in Leiden, Bibliotheek der Rijksuniversiteit, ms BPL 191A, f 214r; and in Florence, Biblioteca Riccardiana, ms 842, f 1r.

21 Singleton 'The Irreducible Dove' p 129

22 This is Pierantonio Paltroni, who introduces his work with an interesting protestation of truth: 'Ho voluto fare questi brevi comentarii in materna lingua de la vita sua; et non sarà la mia opera ornata per mia eloquenza nè anche d'alcuna fittione, ma sarà ornatissima delle singolari opere di Sua Eccellenza et sarà ornata di verità. / I have wanted to make this brief commentary on his life in the mother tongue, and my work will not be ornamented by my eloquence nor by any fiction, but it will be exceedingly ornamented by the singular deeds of his Excellency, and it will be ornamented by the truth.' *Commentari della vita et gesti dell'illustrissimo Federico Duca d'Urbino* ed Walter Tommasoli (Urbino 1966) pp 39–40. Referring to Count Guido, who won a victory at Forlì in May 1282, Pierantonio says, 'della qual rotta scrive e fa mentione Dante / Of which rout Dante writes and makes mention' (p 41, cf *Inferno* XXVII.43). See also pp 42, 43.

23 Florence, Biblioteca nazionale, ms II.II.55, f 173. The accessus to this commentary is written over awkwardly at a crucial point, and it is impossible to be sure what the medieval text was. But the following is to the point: 'Statius potest dici a sto -are quia bene in scientia stetit et est dictus inter poetas christicolas et ista est causa, quia Dantes ipsum ponit in purgadorio quia erat antiquus et multa viderat et erat vir [reading past this point cannot be trusted]

bonus et iptissimus et ideo christicolas [sic] apellabatur. / Statius gets his name from "to stand" because he stands well in knowledge, and he is named among the Christian poets and this is the reason, because Dante put him in Purgatory because he was old and saw many things and he was a good man and ...' (f 123r).

24 *Chronique de la traison et mort de Richart Deux Roy Dengleterre* ed Benjamin Williams (London 1846) pp 9–10

25 These events are summarized in May McKisack *The Fourteenth Century 1307–1399* (Oxford 1959) pp 454–9; Thomas Costain's account, in *The Last Plantagenets* (New York 1963) pp 138–49, is imaginative but sound, and far more readable.

26 Martin M. Crow and Clair C. Olson eds *Chaucer Life-Records* (Oxford 1966). One of these writs for debt supposes that Chaucer 'latitat' in Kent, but he is not found (p 385). During this period, John Scalby received grant of Chaucer's Exchequer annuities (pp 336–9); Chaucer was possibly raising ready money. For record of the passport, see pp 61–2; he was, however, still definitely in England on 1 August 1387 (pp 376–8). The conclusion of the *Records* editors is cautious, but to the same point: 'The evidence found thus far in regard to the effect of these conditions caused by the actions connected with the Merciless Parliament upon Chaucer is inconclusive, but it suggests that Chaucer weathered the political storm with considerable skill' (p 339).

27 Robinson *Works* p 482, lines 10–11. Analysis is based on the F text; future references are to line number.

28 These glosses are from the most popular of medieval mythographies, called the Third Vatican Mythography, probably by Alberic of London. See Georg Heinrich Bode ed *Scriptores rerum mythicarum Latini tres Romae nuper reperti* (Celle 1834) pp 247–8.

29 Ibid pp 157–8

30 The allegorization occurs in Robert Holkot's commentary on the Twelve Prophets; he associates these planetary deities with prelates, not royalty – but the point is the same. 'Item habeat prelatus Martem, idest fortitudinem et constantiam, debiles supportando contra lupas et canes viriliter defendendo.' Oxford, Bodleian Library, ms Bodl 722, f 59v–60r.

31 For analysis and several reproductions of medieval illustrations, see John V. Fleming *The 'Roman de la Rose': A Study in Allegory and Iconography* (Princeton 1969).

32 This is basically the point of Robert O. Payne's *The Key of Remembrance: A Study of Chaucer's Poetics* (New Haven 1963). His book is especially to be commended because he described so well much of what rhetoric and memory *should* have done for Chaucer, before we had the full data, since discovered, which would have supported his arguments with elaborate external evidence.

33 John Freccero 'The Fig Tree and the Laurel: Petrarch's Poetics' *Diacritics* 5 (Spring 1975) 34–40

34 Alford 'The Role of Quotations'

35 Robert Adams 'The Nature of Need'

36 A.V.C. Schmidt ed *The Vision of Piers Plowman* (London 1978) p 305 notes the allusion to Ephesians 5:3–5 as a settled matter, citing Bennett's edition. J.F. Goodridge, in his translation, *Piers the Plowman* (Baltimore 1968) p 262, refers with equal doubt to Titus 1:10–12, Ephesians 5:4, and Colossians 3:8. The glosa, I think, settles the matter: *Biblia sacra* vol VI (Basel 1508) f 107v.

37 Elizabeth Salter's view of the scene is clearly vertical; see her *Piers Plowman, An Introduction* (Oxford 1962) p 71. Elizabeth D. Kirk recommends 'the landscape one still sees looking east from any point along the heights above Malvern.' She locates both towers in the east, against the sun, but provides place for only one, on 'the requisite "toft," Bredon Hill.' See *The Dream Thought of Piers Plowman* (New Haven 1972) p 20. I am happy to thank John Alford for having corrected my vertical visualization of the scene. His work in progress on *Piers Plowman* and the law, and the many insights which he has shared in conversation, have empowered me to begin for the first time to think with some originality and confidence about Langland's enigmatic poem, and I am happy to acknowledge here my grateful indebtedness.

38 Robert Steele ed *Three Prose Versions of the Secreta Secretorum* EETS Extra Series 74 (London 1898) vol I, p 169

39 Ibid., p. 170. I am happy to thank John Alford for the identification of this quotation.

40 Langland's concordance would doubtless have given him reference to 2 Maccabees 7:30, 'Non obedio praecepto regis sed praecepto legis, quae data est nobis per Moysen / I do not obey the command of the king but the command of the law, which was given us through Moses.' The statement was made in the context of persecution by a pagan ruler, but it enunciates a principle universally applicable.

6

'Consideratio' and the audiences of poetry

In the second part of Cervantes' *Don Quixote*, according to the analysis of Michel Foucault, 'Don Quixote meets characters who have read the first part of his story and recognize him, the real man, as the hero of the book. Cervantes's text turns back upon itself, thrusts back into its own density, and becomes the object of its own narrative. The first part of the hero's adventures plays in the second part the role originally assumed by chivalric romances ... Between the first and second parts of the novel, in the narrow gap between those two volumes, and by their power alone, Don Quixote achieved his reality – a reality he owes to language alone, and which resides entirely inside the words. Don Quixote's truth is not in the relation of the words to the world but in that slender and constant relation woven between themselves by verbal signs.'[1] And in Joyce's *Finnegans Wake*, the all-consuming word game, like the infinity of limited space, curves back upon itself in the endless circularity of its own solipsism, absorbing readers into its own verbal self, as if that were the only world there were. Since *Don Quixote*, from whose irony fictions that claimed to offer real advice to a real world have never recovered, the world of literature has cultivated more and more absolutely its own autonomy, and now in such works as *Finnegans Wake* may have ultimately achieved it. A medieval commentator on Ovid's *Heroides*, by contrast, tells us that the work is useful, at one level, 'quia cognito hoc libro cognoscemus dominas vel amicas nostras et cognantas [sic] caste amare / because when we know this book we can know our ladies or our girl friends, and having known them, chastely love.'[2] This contrast, between the linguistic autonomy of modern literature and the very practical usefulness in terms of which medieval critics received it, introduces the problem of this chapter, which is to define the audience of literature. This definition is double. I must define the medieval audience historically, and then the modern audience in terms which will permit us to relate to the posture of the medieval one. Difficulties here are enormous. In previous chapters I have been concerned to define medieval ideas, which as ideas are objective to anyone who thinks them, medieval or modern, and which can therefore be described well enough by describing them from the outside. But audience is point of view, and I must somehow therefore describe its interior so as to overcome the intrinsic difficulty that all descriptions are exterior to what they describe. My difficulties are compounded by the fact that the medieval audience and the modern one are, as the examples just cited indicate, so opposite as to be virtually incommensurable. In the light of these problems, I will depend less in this chapter on still further bulky medieval documentation, though I do provide some, and more on various invented analogies. We will not understand the medieval audience except by insight, if we wish, as we must, to understand it from the inside; analogies will generate this insight if it is to be generated at all.

As I have thus far tried to describe it, the late medieval theory of literature presumes that the content of literature is radically grounded in ethics, that the structures and procedures of literary thinking are no different from merely normal human thought, and that the true poem fully exists as its textuality is supplemented by audience and commentary, in a relationship of assimilation. Thus, because for medieval theory the audience of poetry was in a sense inside it, absorbed into it by virtue of that constant reciprocity acting between ordinary ethical life and its reflection in words, all the specific evidence by which I must define, in medieval terms, the concept of audience, has already been presented, in connection with the other topics already discussed. Medieval poetry is, in the modern sense of the word, constantly rhetorical, and it is thus impossible to have discussed its nature at any point without at the same time implicitly defining the notion of audience. For this reason, the narrowly historical part of this chapter will have to be an enterprise of recapitulation, in which I will merely try to bring together, in brief and summarizing synthesis, what I have already said about the topic of audience in a scattered way in the five preceding chapters. In this discussion, the contrast between *Don Quixote* and *Finnegans Wake* on the one hand, and Ovid's *Heroides* through medieval eyes on the other, is a contrast which I must simply accept as such, and try merely to make clear just what the difference is, and how the medieval audience differed from the modern reader.

But medieval poetry also has a modern audience. Obviously, I do not agree with Zumthor that nothing survives certainly of medieval poetry except its textuality;[3] I hope I have shown that it is possible to know what the medieval audience thought of its literature, and that in a good deal of detail. But it is simple-minded to recommend, to the modern reader of medieval poetry, that he simply 'become' a medieval reader, even though this 'becoming' is indeed imaginatively possible, to a sufficient degree to make plausible reading possible. Such readings, though plausible, would be of little use – though Arnulf of Orléans' commentary on the *Metamorphoses* of Ovid is a most interesting document, it would make little sense to read it, seriatim, to a modern classics class, or even to a class of medievalists who had been warned ahead of time. Historical scholarship does not exist to permit modern readers to imitate medieval ones, but rather to achieve in relation to them a profitably analogical reading. The problem, of course, is to decide on just what is profitably analogical. And this problem itself divides into two – first, by what means may we validate this analogy, since, per se, such reasoning is not in any way privileged to the modern mind; and second, how can we decide just what kind of profit we want? The first of these sub-problems leads to the difficult terrain of Hermeneutik, because that fairyland of phenomenology is the one in which the most persuasive analogies can be built. The second will lead to my proposing a medievally informed way of reading medieval poems which I hope has something new about it. In proposing this new way of reading, I realize that I discount some of the favourite strategies of 'literary' literary critics; I do so deliberately, in the belief that the medieval evidence defines for us a reader likely to be more culturally beneficial.

But I cannot deal with the modern audience until I have defined the medieval one. This audience can be very simply located – it is, or must become, a part of the poem. But this becoming in no way separates itself from or compromises that audience's ordinary practical existence – the world of poetry is one of the provinces of real life, which one can inhabit with total ontological, if not always ethical, comfort. The existence of a poem is larger than its textuality; the existence of the world includes its form. The two, as wholes, are the same.

The clearest statement of this fact, that the audience is a part of the poem, occurs in a commentary on the medieval hymn-book. The conventional definition of a hymn, as given in the *Expositio* of Hilarius for instance, is that 'hymnus dicitur laus dei cum cantico / a hymn is called the praise of God with song.'[4] A later commentary, possibly made in fourteenth-century France or Flanders, amplifies:

Hympnus ... est cantus, cum laude dei. Ubi [cod ibi] laudas deum et non cantas, hymnum non dicis; ubi [cod ibi] cantas et non laudas deum, non dicis hymnum, ubi [cod ibi] laudas aliud quod non pertinet ad laudem dei, et si cantando laudas non dicis hympnum. Hympnus ergo tria ista habet, et cantum et laudem et deum. Laus ergo dei in canticum hymnus dicitur. Sic Augustinus.

A hymn ... is a song, with the praise of God. Where you praise God and don't sing, you don't say a hymn, where you sing and don't praise God, you don't say a hymn, where you praise something that does not have to do with the praise of God, and if you praise by singing you don't say a hymn. Therefore, a hymn has three features: song and praise and God. A hymn is therefore called the praise of God in song. Thus Augustine.[5]

God, of course, is the audience of his praise. Hymns have three things, equally in the accusative – form, content, and audience, 'et cantum et laudem et deum.' It might be objected, on the basis of modern presumptions, that church-goers are the 'audience' of hymns, and God is merely a part of their subject matter. But to make this objection is to presume that the relationship with God which is the only proper excuse for going to church does not, in fact, exist. The human audience of ordinary poetry does not, of course, exercise a relationship so important as this one, but it is, I think, a relationship which this devotional one very powerfully informs. A hymn is worth nothing unless God exists and listens, the singing of the hymn evokes, includes, and describes both the presence of God and the God who is present. Since it presumes his presence to it, as an act of praise, it cannot exist except in terms of that presence. Its existence therefore includes – though of course it does not comprehend or constitute – that presence. The hymn is larger than its textuality.

Historically this is an easy enough point to see, because, from the point of view of the critical historian, the whole complex is something to which he is audience, and the praise of God is, as something involving both praise and God, the datum under consideration. From our point of view, and dismissing any possible distinctions between fact and fiction, these hymns, involving 'laus dei cum cantico,' involve precisely the same complex strategy of language which we meet in letters not addressed to ourselves. Sometimes, as in Ovid's *Heroides* or Richardson's *Pamela*, these letters are in fact addressed to fictions; at times, as in the case of Alexander Pope's, they are in fact addressed to us, as posterity, under the pose of an addressee more particular; at times, they are real letters. Textually, the thing before us in all cases is precisely the same – a form of words which presumes, as its completion, some particular and definite audience, an audience which is not in the textuality but definitely is in the letter. In order to understand the medieval audience, as the medieval critics define it, we must imagine ourselves at once the addressee of a letter, and as the reader of that same letter as if not addressed to ourselves. In so far as we exist as addressee, our existence as the audience of the letter guarantees the material continuity between its textuality and the real world we inhabit; in so far as we know both the letter and its addressee as a unity comprising the genre of letters – *Heroides* to any postcard – we permit to the textuality of the letter that possibly fictional existence which literature comprehends. The contradiction, of being both addressee and non-addressee, of course exists in anyone's ordinary experience, if he reads one of his old letter files, and the distancing of one's self into memory equally corresponds to the more comprehensive appropriation into self which medieval memory involved. The sense of material continuity between textuality and the real world is much harder to achieve, because our modern insistence on the difference between fact and fiction is so strong. The situation of the medieval audience is one which combines all these postures into one – the textuality of a poem presumes an audience, as a letter presumes an addressee, and at the same time universalizes that audience and appropriates it, in the way of which one is conscious when reading letters distanced by fiction or memory.

This is what I mean by having said, at several points, that a medieval person who wishes to be ethically good could achieve that condition by acting as if he were in a story – that is, by submitting to the assimilatio of becoming the story's tropology, or its letter, or (very occasionally), its anagogy. The 'as if,' of course, is completely achievable, because people who behave in this fashion tend to be remembered, and so in fact become story. However, in so doing, they are not absorbed, as are Don Quixote and his part two acquaintances absorbed, into mere words. Just the opposite. The world of merely textual words has expanded; the real has absorbed it by taking on its decorums. When Queen Eleanor and her Henry visit a new place, the people must recognize them (if the assimilatio was truly achieved) because they have read Thomas' *Tristan*. When Queen Eleanor went on Crusade, she is said to have dressed herself in the fashion of an Amazon, and was so recognized.[6] At one level, this is mere costume-party play-acting; but in medieval terms, it was in its way as serious as the Crusade itself, and iconographically it was precisely the same behaviour.

The medieval critics define this audience of poetry, which is a part of the poem in a way which makes words and world reciprocal and mutually continuous rather than distinct and alienated, in three ways. Most obviously, they make it clear both in definitions of intention and in commentary application, that poetry has practical, clear, ethical usefulness. One learns from poetry how to behave. Second, they explain one's willingness to accept this guidance in terms of that feature which distinguishes poetry from rhetoric – the consideratio because of which one accepts a poem as true, without having been 'persuaded,' but rather by having been at least hypothetically absorbed into the poem. Third, they define for some poems a special character as process, which as such is the process of some exercisable act of human knowing. The first of these is by far the most important, both in practice and in value. The second two are details – they explain how and why poetry is, as such, the kind of thing which is suitable to be so used.

I have already several times mentioned the *Heroides*, and the commentator's recommending to his medieval audience that they use the book as a guide to real amorous technique. The reader is to court his girl friend by the book. The advice given by the probable compiler of Bibliothèque nationale ms fr 112, Micheau Gonnot,[7] is precisely of the same character.

Il ne fait riens qui commence et ne fine. Et pource [cod pourc] est il necessite de finer leuvre par moy commence. Mais aux bons et vrais hystoriens prie de bon cueur que silz y treuvent faulte ne prolixite de langage leur plaise que par doulces et amyables paroles le veullent amender et corriger. Car selon mon petit entendement les jeunes chevaliers et excuiers y pourront aprendre moult de beaux faitz darmes, et quant Ils trouveront chose villaine ne de reprouche je leur conseille quilz ne le facent mie. Car les choses malfautes sont escriptes aux livres pour les fouir et eviter. Et les bonnes pour les ensuyvre et les accomplir chaque homme [cod chm] de bon voloir.

One who begins and doesn't finish does nothing, and therefore it is necessary to finish the work I have begun. But I pray good and true historians of good heart that if they find in my work any fault or prolixity of language they amend and correct it with sweet and amiable language. For according to my little intention young knights and squires should be able to learn from it much of beautiful deeds of arms, and when they find anything mean or reproachful I counsel them that they don't do it at all. For ill done things are written in books so that one can flee and avoid them, and the good so that every man of good will can follow and accomplish them.[8]

The difference that the modern reader senses, because he cannot imagine himself personally performing 'beaux faitz darmes,' but certainly does express interest in women, must not be allowed to distort the historical judgment. The medieval fact is that, whether the human act be a chivalric one, an ordinary amorous one, an idealized one such as might be contemplated in the grand chant courtois, or an ordinary ethical one such as might be recommended by a commentator on the *Metamorphoses*, the claim of poetry is the same – that the poetry is qualified to give guidance to life, and does so by insisting that life imitate poetry, that life be assimilated to, or into, poetry.

Thus Arnulf is perfectly serious when he says, speaking of the contrary motion of the planets, 'Quod Ovidius videns vult nobis ostendere per fabulosam narrationem motum anime qui fit intrinsecus / Seeing this, Ovid wishes to show us by fable narrative the motion of the soul which is made intrinsic.' And he continues in the same vein:

Vel intencio sua est nos ab amore temporalium immoderato revocare et adhortari ad unicum cultum nostri creatoris, ostendendo stabilitatem celestium et varietatem temporalium. Ethice supponitur quia docet nos ista temporalia, que transitoria et mutabilia, contempnere, quod pertinet ad moralitatem ... Vel utilitas est erudicio divinorum habita ex mutacione temporalium.

Or his intention is to recall us from the immoderate love of temporal things and exhort us to the worship of our creator, by showing the stability of the celestial and the variety of the temporal. The book is classified as ethics because it teaches us to hold in contempt these temporal things, which are transitory and mutable, and this has to do with morality ... Or the usefulness is the instruction in divine things derived from the changeableness of the temporal.[9]

In illustration one could pick an allegorization almost at random. I choose that for Perseus and Andromeda, since the story is familiar:

Cephei filiam, monstris maris expositam, Perseus cum harpe Mercurii et egida Palladis monstrum expugnando liberavit. Eam sibi Perseum coniugem habuit. Quam, dum interessent nupciis, Phineus et sui complices volentes ei eripere, viso capite Gorgonis, mutati sunt in lapides. Per Cepheum habemus creatorem, qui[a] Cepheus dicitur a cephe quod est caput. Creator enim qui caput est scilicet origo rerum omnium, cuius filiam idest animam quam creavit deus expositam monstris idest viciis, maris idest huius seculi quod mare potest appellari propter diversas fluctuaciones, Perseus idest virtus, Perseus enim interpretatur elatio – et quis magis est elatus virtuoso? – a mon[s]tris idest a viciis liberavit cum arpe Mercurii. Arpis enim ensis est recurvus et signat facundiam virtuosi que ad modum gladii curvi in se ipsam recurvans in supercilium iactantie numquam attolitur. Monstra maris interficit idest extirpat vicia. quibus extirpatis eam sibi coniugem assumsit. Anima enim a viciis liberata suo nubit creatori et coniungit. Sed eam Phineus et sui complices idest vicia volunt eripere Perseo idest virtuti, et hoc in ipsis nuptiis idest in leticia. Quoniam enim letior est homo citius subintrant vicia. Sed ostenso capite Gorgonis a Perseo idest cognito principio terroris, Gorgon siquidem terrorem signat, idest considerata bene causa quare metuendus sit virtuosus, mutantur in lapides idest fiunt stupidi ad modum lapidum.

With the falchion of Mercury and the shield of Pallas, Perseus liberated the daughter of Cepheus, who had been exposed to a sea monster, by defeating the monster. Perseus married her. Phineas and his accomplices wanted to kidnap her, while they were at the wedding, but were turned into stones by seeing the head of the Gorgon. By Cepheus we have the creator, because Cepheus is named from 'cephe' which means head. For the creator is the one who is the head, that is the origin of all things, whose daughter, that is the soul whom God created, exposed to monsters that is to vices, of the sea, that is of this age that may be named by the sea because of its diverse fluctuations, Perseus, that is virtue (Perseus is interpreted 'elation,' and who is more elated than the virtuous?), liberated from the monsters that is from vices with the falchion of Mercury. A falchion is a hooked sword and it signifies the eloquence of the virtuous which in the manner of a curved sword, curving back on itself, is never raised up in pride of boasting. He killed the monsters of the sea, that is extirpated vices, and having done so married her. For the soul, liberated from vices, marries her creator. But Phineas and his accomplices, that is vices, wish to take her away from Perseus, that is from virtue, and that in the midst of the wedding, that is, in happiness (since the happier a man is the more quickly vice steals in). But Perseus exhibited the head of the Gorgon, that is, recognition of the beginning of terror (for Gorgon means terror), and they were turned into stone, that is, they were made stupid in the manner of a stone, having considered well why they should fear a virtuous person. (pp 212–13)

In the *Metamorphoses*, the whole story occupies a substantial section at the end of the fourth book and the beginning of the fifth; it is told in considerable detail, and with a good deal of emotional power. The modern reader, for whom the rescue by helicopter of persons in exposed, dangerous, and inaccessible places is merely a part of normal life, has gained the right to believe in Perseus' flying rescue at the price of all wonder at it – perhaps there are some still for whom flying generates an 'elatio' which was in the Middle Ages available only in spiritual experience or by miracle. But one must believe in the 'elatio,' and the 'terror,' and all the rest. The point of the allegorization is not the reduction of a story to dull morality; the point is the assimilation of moral powers, already real and exciting in themselves as such, to the vivid physical adventures of exemplary heroism. The modern reader of course finds Ovid more exciting than Arnulf, myth more real than psychomachia, but this disability should not be permitted to distort the proper historical understanding of the medieval audience of poetry – an audience whose quality of belief, both in these fictions and in the powers which ruled the moral life, permitted the reality of each to enhance the other, in a relationship which, to our eyes, grasped as most real and most important the decorous, formal, theatrical, archetypal – in short, poetic – qualities of both. Thus the audience becomes a part of the poem, because the potential moral behaviour of the audience, in parallel and assimilatio with the words of the poem, enjoyed in relation to the textual story a real similitude – a similitude real in shape, in power, and in importance.

I could illustrate this point endlessly, and not just from the narrow period which I am especially trying to define. In a way, all cultures which believe in a literary paideia, from the ancient Greeks up to our own day, behave and believe as if the audience of poetry were, without losing any of its practical reality, assimilated into that poetry, and living a real life in constant similitude. Thus to suggest, as I have elsewhere, that Grendel can be allegorized in terms of the disordering of social bonds which produce good works[10] is not to reduce the *Beowulf* to trite morality, but rather to remind its audience that in an age of disorder that which caused it was as monstrous, terrifying, and banquet-hall-emptying as Grendel. In more modern times, it has been said that the distinctive culture of the American South can be explained in terms of too much reading of the novels of Sir Walter Scott.[11] I doubt, literally, that this was true, because too many Southerners behaved that way without having ever read Scott – though even they may have got him second-hand. A likelier source of the same sensibility would have been the Old Testament, preached through a sensibility that was typological, rhetorical, highly romantic, and individualistic. In either case it is certainly beyond question that the South, though less literate than other regions of the country, was more literary in cultural paideia, and the traditional rhetorical personalism which used to make Southerners the best demagogues, preachers, and light cavalry in America, as well as the people who still have the most noticeable manners, traces to a culture full of adventure stories, to which the real life of manners and morals assimilates.

The feature of poetry which makes it possible for the assimilatio to be credible, and the resulting patterns of moral behaviour to be achieved, is poetic consideration – consideratio. I have already discussed this notion in chapter one, and will here only recapitulate, developing especially such details as apply to the notion of audience. Consideratio along with consuetudo and credulitas are three of the six parts of tragedy, or praise. They are what is assimilated. Resemblance-making, heightened language, and charisma or expressive power are the three techniques by which assimilation is accomplished. Consideratio, in this array, is that which convinces; it is that quality of any given poetic content because of which the audience admits that it is true. One might call it, since Averroes equates it with meaningfulness, simply credibility.

In chapter one, I was concerned to define just what makes for credibility – just what features of the content of poetry are those which make one believe it – and settled for what might be called the archetypal quality, though with great reservation, and with a good deal of qualification made in order to distinguish this medieval credibility from that which one experiences in other poetry. Here, I am more concerned to define that credibility as such – as an act, or a posture implicating audience. First of all, it is clear both from Averroes' discussion and from the happy suitability of the English word 'credibility' that poetic consideration, consideratio, which is a feature of a poetic text, is at the same time the reflection of an act performed outside that text by an audience. Something is credible which is capable of being believed. The capability exists prior to the belief, both logically and absolutely. At the same time it is absurd to speak of anything's being credible unless somebody has been or will be able to believe it. The word presumes an eventual audience, and though that which the word names exists prior to audience, it cannot exist without it. Thus it names precisely that structure which I discussed in connection with the tropology of exegesis – that structure by which the textuality of a poem presumes something extra-textual which the poem as a whole must include.

Coleridge, for his version of poetry, defines this credibility as the result of the 'willing suspension of disbelief, which constitutes poetic faith.' In his definition Coleridge presumes a radical disjunction between the kind of belief one exercises in the daily practice of ordinary life, which has as its complement a disbelief in poetry, and the kind of poetic faith which results from the suspension of that disbelief. It is this disjunction, more than anything else, which the medieval doctrine of poetic consideration contradicts. Whatever consideratio is, it is a feature of poetry which generates ordinary belief – whatever ordinary belief is, it is that feature of the human psyche which responds affirmatively to consideratio. Neither corresponds to ordinary Coleridgean belief, nor to his disbelief. Rather, both consideratio and the belief which responds to it exist in such a way as to make the whole Coleridgean distinction irrelevant and meaningless. If one were to insist on his terms, then one might try to claim that the world, including poetry, existed as a range of merely practical objects of thought, and that belief, no matter what its object, was of the shape Coleridge labels 'poetic faith.' But this distorts too much. When poetry is ethics, then of course daily life becomes more decorous, more intentionally formed, more mannered, and ordinary belief becomes less positivist. But these differences are more differences in kind than in degree.

As differences in kind, they are ultimately impossible to illustrate, because we are the other side of Coleridge. What is required is to illustrate an act of knowing – in this case, that kind of knowing which is convinced by consideratio. This requires, in order to be fair to the medieval case, the exhibition of a thing 'containing' consideratio, which one can view from the outside and be convinced of, and at the same time an exhibition of the believing medieval person, within which one can be convinced in the right way. These exhibitions are manifestly impossible – one is always at the mercy of the epistemology of one's audience. One can hypothesize, on the basis of formal explanations – these I have tried to give. One can offer behavioural experiments, in the performance of which one acts medievally, in the hope that the act will trigger a corresponding posture of belief. These I have offered over and over again, in the discussion of many medieval poems; I repeat here only the most blatant one – that is, that one is acting medievally with Dante's *Commedia* by putting one's own contemporaries in their fit places in his great universe of moral places. But what is ultimately required is a quality of belief that is, if not strictly medieval, at least analogous to that. And this quality of belief either exists, or it does not, as a result of large historical forces. There is some reason to believe, as I shall show later, that we are beginning to be capable of something like it, but meanwhile, it is something for which criticism is neither licensed nor qualified to evangelize.

It is this lack of the right quality of belief – this lack of the right epistemology – which I think leads us to have so much trouble with those medieval poems which are themselves, in their textuality, epistemological. Here I mean those poems whose content occupies literally the tropological quadrant of the poetic universe, whose forma tractandi and forma tractatus are the same. That is, I mean clearly *Canticles*, for whose generic classification we have Aegidius Romanus' guarantee, and those other poems which I propose as of the same class – that is, *Piers Plowman* and, in its special pre-Aristotelian way, the grand chant courtois, as well as medieval lyric in general.

I have said, in chapter two, that the modi of the forma tractandi, though they name the operations of mind, do not name the operations of any particular mind. They analyse the activity of knowing in terms intrinsic to knowledge, rather than to a knower, and intrinsic therefore at the same time to the world of which knowledge is the coefficient. When the forma tractandi and the forma tractatus are the same, then the poem exists, in its textuality, as active knowledge. As such, it postulates an 'I' as focus, even while at the same time it also comprehends to the full the nature of modus as such, that is, a nature intrinsic to knowledge rather than (since we must make the distinction) to knowing. Therefore, when the modern reader comes to occupy, as a hypothetical commentator-audience, this 'I' focus, his epistemological expectations are necessarily frustrated, and the synthetic experience which the poem enacts – that is, an experience of knowledge which lacks the subject-object dichotomy – eludes or bewilders him. I have already suggested, most tentatively, that a distinctio which may illuminate *Piers Plowman* is one whose focus is indeed Will (Voluntas), but the will of God. In a state of perfect salvation, the distinction between the will of Christian man and will of God is a distinction without radical difference. The one exists as the expression of the other. But both the distinctio and *Piers Plowman* are obviously dynamic, dialectic, shifting. This behaviour, taken as the inevitable condition of the expressed will of God in a fallen world, can indeed act in resonance with a medieval Christian seeking will. But such doubleness – or multiplicity – is more difficult for a modern critical mind to assume. This specific suggestion about *Piers Plowman*, that is, that the cognitive will which is its 'I' is, at least in part, divine, may well be wrong. But in any case, it remains true that the cognition which is the dynamic act and continuity of the poem is one whose fundamental definitions are to be expected to be medieval, not modern. As such, this cognition must be informed by whatever else we can find out about medieval knowing. And the existence of the modi, in the enacted form in which they exist when forma tractandi and forma tractatus are the same, is obviously one important thing we can know about medieval cognition.

If these speculations are plausible, then poems of this type cease to be a frustrating critical problem, and become a central resource in helping us gain medieval access to medieval poems. If they enact the knowledge in terms of which medieval audiences and the textuality of medieval poems are assimilated – if their textuality, as it were, occupies the structural point of relationship between poem and reader, then proper modern attention to them will help the modern reader to read more correctly. I must, however, repeat and emphasize that these speculations, and these proposals, are made a priori, and do not arise out of any special inductive attention to *Piers Plowman*, or Canticles, or medieval lyrics in general. Inductively, I have a number of ideas about these texts, as well as a number of frustrations, but this is not the place to discuss either. I am here trying instead to define the a priori, that is, to suggest just what kind of reading of medieval poetry should be made, in terms of logical consistency with what actual medieval critics said about the literary texts which they read and commented on. For the *Canterbury Tales*, I am sure that this a priori is informing, because I have tried it in detail, and it works. For *Piers Plowman* and other works like it, I am only sure that the a priori predicts for their proper reading both unusual difficulties and larger than usual rewards.

At this point it would perhaps be prudent to stop. I have asked of the writings of the medieval critics the question, 'What kind of poetry do these writings presume?' I have answered that question in as much detail as the evidence permits, and have also, from time to time, suggested how medieval poetry does in fact answer to this presumption which the medieval critics define. In doing these things, I have defined a number of medieval facts, whose quondam existence is no less real for their being facts in the history of ideas more than of deeds, and for whose value their existence is sufficient argument. The historian is by definition under no obligation to pursue the question of value further.

But the historian is also a person. I do indeed believe that these medieval facts – attitudes and definitions of readers and readings of texts – are of absolute as well as historical value. The medieval critics have convinced me that their methods and theories are of use to reading which is modern and personal as well as modern and scholarly, and it is therefore appropriate that I speculate about the modern reader.

I said at the very beginning of this book that my chief theoretical presumption was that critics who write about literature betray themselves, in the long run, even more clearly than they inform what they are writing about. Therefore it should be possible to find the medieval definition of literature in what the medieval critics wrote about it. This I hope I have done. But in so doing I have myself written about literature, and in so doing have deposited a document which should fall under my own theoretical presumption, and betray me. This I happily admit, because I know that my mind functions in a post-Cartesian world, and understand my self-betrayal as that of one inevitably interested in point of view, subject-object relations, the phenomenological predicament. Further, I claim that my interest in the medieval critics' self-betrayal is not only an interest which my own epistemological make-up permits me to exercise – further, it is precisely that interest which, when exercised self-consciously, permits me to allow for the predicament of my own point of view. To allow for the medieval sensibility is, by exercising analogy, to allow for my own. For any given person, the semiotic triangle indeed defines a closed circle, and we are, as individuals, irretrievably relative. But if this is true for each of us, then it is equally true for all of us. The several circles defined by our semiotic triangles imply no spiral; all are, as whole circles, identical. All universes are equal, as wholes. Thus my study of the medieval point of view, my deliberate allowance for my own, and my

knowledge of the persisting textuality give me, as it were, more simultaneous equations than there are unknowns. By absolutizing the relativism
of point of view, I can escape it.

When I make this claim, however, I realize that there are modern critics
who would label it presumptuous. I need be no more specific than to call
them the post-structuralists, admitting that the designation is protean. For
them, my scenario would be more properly put as follows: 'In writing about
the medieval critics, I have myself written about literature – or at least (or
perhaps worse) written about writing about literature, and in so doing have
deposited a document which should also fall under my theoretical presumption, and betray me. At this point I am logically at the beginning of an
infinite regress – any analysis of this betrayal is itself a betrayal, which can be
analysed. But this analysis is also a betrayal ... and so on to infinity. On the
other hand, from inside my act of criticism, I should not be aware of this
betrayal, any more than Hamlet, already an adult when the play opens,
should be aware of the fact that he was never born. Therefore historical
criticism is not what I have done, but only what I think I have done – as the
medieval critic thought he was extracting ethical truth from literature, and
was perhaps unaware that he was in the process generating between himself
and his literary past a continuity so binding as to blind him to awareness of
anachronism, and therefore deprive him of the Renaissance. If I try to take
advantage of this analogy, and discover what my pretence at historical criticism blinded me to, I may perhaps discover solipsism, which deprives me of
direct access to facts (or texts) in themselves. So then I admit that I have no
texts, but only readings of texts, and in admitting this I make reading
primary, analyse that, find it inevitably of less than perfect congruence to the
noumenal text. This admission makes reading mis-reading, and I am free in
a never-never land of relativism. Beyond this point criticism must be piled
on criticism in layers of ever more rarified meta-verbalization.'

I must admit that I have descended to parody, and am of course guilty of
oversimplification. But I am not, I think, guilty of any distortion which is
essential in a platonist sense. I think I have indeed located this scenario in
the right world, and in the right place in that world. The world is the solipsism; the place is language, taken as a self-contained system, unforeclosed
with world, not a part of any real semiotic triangle. This place, language, does
have a certain structural integrity, as Saussure has shown; it does have a
history of its own, as philologists who work with sound changes have known
for over a century. The study of these things is a valid academic exercise, so
long as it is clearly recognized that this study is not of language, but of a
minor and relatively trivial aspect of language – that is, language considered

apart from its referential function. The fact that language 'brings Being into presence and holds it there' is the most important fact about language – no other fact about language would be interesting, or even possible of discussion, if this one were not true. To pretend, even heuristically, that it is not true, or at least for the moment not of interest, is a dangerous temptation to the critic. Instead of trying to cope with the solipsism, he is tempted to indulge it, or even (as my friend and colleague Robert Boyle tells me he does) take it for a functional equivalent of the world outside Plato's cave, where the incarnations of Poetry can take place.

The threat of an infinite regress of self-betrayals is only serious if one presumes the solipsism. It is of course not necessary to do so. The solipsism is itself self-contradictory, in that it makes absolute the relativism of an individual consciousness. But if relativism is absolute, then no axiom is privileged, including the relativist one, and any axiom can make itself true by the elegance with which it accounts for the world it grounds and explains. In our own day, two such axioms have been posited with what seems to be the greatest success. One generates the strategy of phenomenology, the other the strategy of that structuralism by which anthropologists explain facts under a linguistic analogy. The first absolutizes an act of knowing, of which both any knower and anything which can be known are derivative, and which is, as act, implicitly universalized; the second, generalizing still more largely, posits relationships as primary and entities as only secondary and derived. Both, in their respective ways, posit something other than an entity as such as the primary basis of thought and being, and so escape, or deal with, the solipsism, because that is the predicament of an entity (called a subject) conceived as primary, which in a manner collapses in a philosophical universe which contains no primary entities, but only derived ones.

My analysis of medieval criticism is, axiomatically, a phenomenological one. I begin with a species of the act of knowing, preserved textually in an array of commentaries. From this act I can hypothesize the knower and the known – that is, the axioms of the critic and the nature of his poem. But the textuality of the poem I have otherwise, and so can in a manner verify. If the verification proves out, I can be relatively sure of the knower – that is, of the axioms of the critic. But paradoxically, when I get the axioms of the critic, and when I conceive of his personhood, his axioms, his writings, and his poem in an array, I do not see a phenomenological situation. I do not see a critic interested in 'his view' of the poem, or even interested in the effect that his perceiving mind has upon the world. Rather, I see a situation which is structuralist in the anthropological sense, which the relationship of assimilatio constructs out of a universe comprising facts, words, and speakers, extended in both space and time. Further, I see that because assimilatio is essentially a relationship of linguistic character, the universe which it constitutes corresponds in fact to that universe which the modern anthropologist perceives under the guidance of the heuristic analogy of language. Thus, my having investigated and reconstructed the point of view of the medieval critic, an enterprise which is from my point of view phenomenological, permits me to learn how to do without point of view as a critical predicament, and read language and the world as a single coherent system both meaningful and real.

The solipsist critics, such as Zumthor, begin with what they call structuralism. But it is a structuralism which uses language as a metaphor only for language. With only one term, the metaphor lacks the power of a real analogia entis, and leaves the critic totally enclosed by language – that is, in a solipsism. My preference, of course, is obvious. I find the solipsism either arrogant, imprisoning, or both, and am at pains to analyse the effect of point of view only in order to allow for it as much as possible, and by allowing for it, dispense with it. The project permitted by the medieval critics, and by the literature they read and they and their contemporaries wrote, is a project of reintegration. One may inspect in actual operation a world in which point of view is, by consideratio, absorbed into poetry, and in which poetry, as words, both repeats and is absorbed into the parallel worlds of exemplary action and doctrinal ethical discourse. And all this, of course, without losing in the slightest any of the intrinsic qualities of decorum which we are wont to admire as aesthetic. Having inspected this world in actual operation, one may then by analogy profit from it.

This profit, I think, takes three possible forms, One may profit by being enabled to deal more fully with the significance of medieval literature. One may, by extension, profit by finding occasions in which the medieval axioms shed light on other literature and other art. Finally, one may use the medieval posture and method as an instrument of direct ethical analysis. The first of these profits is obvious, in a scholarly sense. But in a human sense, and allowing for the fact that the modern reader, not being medieval, must not imitate the medieval reader but must exist in a relationship of lively analogy with him, the medieval method works for us, in a sense, backwards. The medieval insistence on an essentially ethical character for something we know as literature was consistent with their tendency both to approve and to behave in terms of ethical patterns with a large component of what we would call the aesthetic. In the light of this consistency, but reading it backwards, we can use their literature as evidence for ethical behaviour, and read, in much more direct fashion than we would or could afford to permit ourselves in the case of some more modern art, ethically normative patterns from medieval stories.

Thus, in dealing with the *Canterbury Tales*, I tried among other things to account for the fact that nearly all the tales, most of them literally and a few at one analogical remove, deal with marriage. I said that marriage was a relationship between two people constructed in the light of both past and future tense stories – that is, in terms of stories of exemplary past marriages, and in terms of that sacramental vow which is in the most intentional possible sense a story in the future tense. For Chaucer, therefore, marriage is a real human action surrounded and conditioned by words. This whole complex, I think, is the paradigm in which he defines, or proposes a model for, a workable society.[12] This model, I think, is one which cannot have been conceived except in terms of the medieval definitions of literature – that is, of stories as something essentially ethical, and capable by assimilatio of including both doctrine and real life. Chaucer, being a medieval man and not a modern sociologist, lets his literal words be stories, and his doctrinal recommendation remain implicit. He does not generalize in jargon, and bury his exempla under their statistical and tabular reductions. But he is no less serious for being far more attractive.

His definition, I hasten to add, is as distinctive as it is serious. Chaucer's method may not be flexible enough to state all cases – no method is, in fact, and one gets out of any one method just what it was programmed to produce. In order clearly to see what Chaucer has chosen, and in its distinctiveness see just how the ethical reading of medieval literature may be more broadly informing than some others, it is necessary to take a brief excursus into sociology. One of the distinctions of modern social analysis is that made between what is called a status society and what is called a contract society.[13] This distinction is not exhaustive, but heuristic. It corresponds to the a priori assumptions of modern science; its primary value to modern thought is to permit us to distinguish modern and rationalist societies loosely descended from the social contract theories of the enlightenment, from previous and supposedly more primitive ones whose social bonding structures were less reasonable. Nevertheless, it is a distinction which permits us to begin. A status society is one whose primary elements are persons in personal relationships. As the child of certain parents, the husband or wife of a certain mate, the doer of specific works for specific other people, one has status. One exists as a person whom specific other people know to be significant, and the array of relationships which this existence implies is permanently attached to one's self. Such a society is full of homes and homeplaces and inheritances; it operates in terms of personal favours given and received; it finds it difficult to assimilate strangers; it cannot easily be regulated or operated by a bureau-cracy; it is rhetorically hierarchical but operationally democratic (in that it accords enormous respect to leaders and at the same time allows direct access to those leaders on the part of persons of quite low status); its chief administrative instrument is rhetoric, and it is relatively resistant to change.

The contract society, on the other hand, is one whose primary elements are functions whose nature and mutual relationships are defined by legal contracts. As a member of a contract society, one has the rights, duties, obligations, and privileges which the constitution of that society defines for one – one begins to have them by being admitted to that society, and one ceases to have them by ceasing to be a member. Such a society tends to treat persons as interchangeable – in fact, to prefer to deal only with parts of per-sons, as they are, from time to time, workers, taxpayers, voters, parents or children, or undertakers of journeys by foot or car. Such a society is easy to make bureaucratic; it is rhetorically democratic but operationally hierarchi-cal; its chief administrative instrument is executive decision carried out through a chain of command; it tends to value change as almost a confirma-tion of its operational existence; and it assimilates strangers easily, by con-tract – in fact by virtue of the fact that all its members are operationally temporary, and so strangers.

From the modern point of view, Chaucer's medieval society was almost entirely a status society. The possibility of making such contracts as that permitting entrance into a religious order complicates the issue, but only slightly – and modern analysis would tend to discount the element of con-tract even here, in order to talk about theological status, or the earlier ten-dency of people important in Cluny to be cadets of noble families. Chaucer's analysis of his own society was neither contract nor status. In these terms, one might define it as a status society continually being renewed by con-tracts, or alternatively, as a contract society whose chief executive is a status-creating God. But what goes wrong with these terms is that they inadequately account for the presence of language to Chaucer's society, by which, because of the presumed existence of the Incarnate Word, vows can be far more than contracts, and stories far more than fictions. For the Middle Ages, a vow was more than a contract, because it is made of words which, under medieval definition, constitute reality rather than merely refer to it, and which have, as pronounced, a sacramental dimension which makes their betrayal a sin. To break a contract involves loss of credit; to break a vow, the loss of both honour in this life and soul in the next. Reciprocally, a story – a kind of vow in the past tense – was the exemplary model whose form one's real life must assimilate. In return, life itself becomes assimilative and exemplary. A real marriage, in medieval terms, is more than a legal licensure of sex. In the Middle Ages, marriages existed not only for the practical purposes of avoiding sin and engendering children, but, more important, for the sake of figuring the supremely definitional relationship between Christ and his Church, and derivatively, all other relationships within which good order was created, fostered, and sustained.

For Plato, the fundamental reality was the human person, whose perfect internal harmony was the result of the philosophically perfect rule of body and spirit by mind. On the basis of analogy with this human person, the social Republic could be defined. But the actual Greek society of Plato's background, as Hannah Arendt describes it, was the fundamental reality of great words and deeds in public, of the political man acting rhetorically before an audience, on the basis of which a society could be both enacted and defined.[14] For Chaucer, the fundamental reality seems to be persons who have made a promise to be married. Taken altogether, his *Tales* are a great normative array of exempla of this reality, including failures and successes, good, bad, and indifferent, and even including the obvious analogy cases of ruler and kingdom and priest and church. Properly understood, this normative array exists as a subtle and powerful definition of a particular kind of achievable good society. Under the theme of marriage, the fundamental human relationship, we have an analogizing definition of human relationship in general. Because this relationship is created and sustained by vows and stories, that is, by words, we are permitted to include language as a constituent element in this assimilatio of relationship. This circularity between life and words is in no sense a fallacy, but the chief delight of the piece. If literature is ethics, then proper behaviour is story, and the best vow a man can make is to repeat for himself, as well as in himself, an exemplary story.

Thus understood, Chaucer's achieved ethical definition is of more than merely historical interest. It is perhaps unfair at this point to refer to *Love Story*, since that particular example of modern fictional marriage can be dismissed as merely popular. Nevertheless it is an important betrayal. Its central slogan, that love means never having to say one is sorry, really translates into the affirmation that all sorry selves are acceptable by definition. The fact that the marriage does not last points to the same conclusion – the deep presumption of the novel is that human relationships are of interest because they affect the existence of human individuals. Society is reduced to isolated individuals; value is firmly grounded in a reality out of which it is difficult, at best, to build society. Chaucer, for all his irony, was wiser.

Malory, I think, was less wise than Chaucer, but still wise enough. It is obvious that his central concern was the good society, and his definition of ultimate tragedy the failure of the society of the Round Table. His material did not give him any good marriages, and though he must have known Aegidius Romanus' distinctio for the good ruler in terms of self, family, and kingdom, he permitted Arthur to continue to fail to rule his family well. The love of man for woman in the book produces Arthur first, but Mordred and Galahad after, and there is no continuity for society when one's engendered successors are treason and the eschaton. Nevertheless, there is one paradigm in Malory which does, in normative array, constitute a subtle, important ethical definition, which is also central to Malory's concerns. The great question of his book, which many others have asked with as much agony if not so much power, is this – 'Why cannot great men of good will, who intend the good, achieve it for the society of this world?' The answer is Mordred and Galahad – this world is both fallen and provisional. But in the meanwhile there are good and great men.

The single event that happens more often in Malory than any other is the joust – the single combat between two knights. This combat, so often repeated, with such an infinity of small variations but always pointing to the same result, is a structure, I suggest, of comparison. What Mallory is telling us, implicitly by arraying his character in this pattern of combats, is that the good man can be defined only in terms of a series of one-on-one comparisons. As such, of course, comparison is a literary device, which structures all the relationships of poetry from description to the assimilatio of parallel systems. Out of a dialectic of repeated comparisons, each progressing a little further toward the establishment and defining of merit, there comes not so much agreement (since one knows that Lancelot is the best knight fairly early) as understanding. By the end one knows what he is, and knows that, tragically, that is not enough. But the point is not so much that Lancelot is the best, as that his definition is achieved by an essentially verbal, literary process. At the same time this is a literary process which life also enacts – in all circumstances from the fifth-grade playground combats which begin fast friendships, to the pecking-order-establishing behaviour of jackdaws. At all levels of the enactment, from romance to birds, there are elements of ritual, ceremony, decorum – at all levels, as it were, the ethical and the literary achieve each other.

It should by now be obvious that I take all this as significant at more than a merely historical level. I do in fact believe that human language and human behaviour belong together, that each can act properly only in terms of radical involvement in the other, and that all postures of philosophy or behaviour which tend to put barriers between language and fact are perverse, harmful, and unnecessary. I tend to think of societies that trust the literary paideia as more moral and more enjoyable than those which achieve their definitions in some other way, and I see no reason in logic or history why some version of the literary paideia should not operate as plausibly in our future as an analogous version of it operated in our human past. I therefore conclude by suggesting, with great diffidence about specific details but none at all about basic goals, that the medieval theory of literature may well be of some use to people of our own time, both as an instrument of analysis of other stories than the medieval ones, and as an instrument of ethical analysis in the absolute.

These ways of being of use are more subtle than the one I have just explained. That they can exist at all is due to what may be called the self-authenticating quality of art, which I now wish to expand slightly to include human life as well. That is, whatever it is in the Venus de Milo which persuades both me and the ancient Greeks and all who have seen the statue in between that it is a thing of importance also exists in a living human being. Regardless of cultural differences, human beings recognize each other as significant others, when they confront one another personally – and failure to do so is universally recognized as a sign either of war or psychosis. Over against this self-authenticating quality, any given person stands in encounter in terms of his own axioms, his own presumptions, his own definitions. In terms of these he will feel, receive, and define his sense of this authenticity which confronts him. It is for this reason, as I have said, that both Benvenuto da Imola and Benedetto Croce, with quite different presumptions, could find Dante's *Commedia* supremely admirable. If then, it is true that I may confront any art of any period with whatever critical assumptions I happen to possess, whether they be aesthetic, ethical, idolatrous, or whatever, and find something of good, then it must also be true that this same experience would occur to any other critic. There is no a priori reason, or experimental one either that I can think of, why this principle should be affected by chronology, and therefore no reason to deny that the medieval critic's axioms might well be able to make something of art later than medieval, even if only assumed hypothetically. Thus assuming hypothetically, one might very well make something quite strange – but whatever it might be, it could be guaranteed at least to be a response to that self-authentication which is art.

I have, for example, from time to time been given to teach certain modern novels. When I confront *The Scarlet Letter*, I may experimentally presume that it too is an ethical piece, whose beginning will indicate its concern, and whose order and outline, descending from that beginning, will exemplify some discursive ethical definition. The beginning of the piece is a chapter called 'The Custom House,' in which Hawthorne (or his persona) confronts the radical existence of people in separation from their roles, and attributes this disaster to lack of transplanting. There follows a complex exemplum of a transplanted people, the result of which is a child who can return to the old soil of Europe, achieve a coat of arms (thus uniting self and role), and re-establish continuity. Thus briefly put, this summary of an interpretation seems as blatantly reductive as anything in medieval commentary. But it really is so, I submit, only if definitive statements and structures in general, and ethics in particular, are thought intrinsically reductive. The problem of human continuity is a very real and serious one, and one which tends to express its difficulties in terms of conflict between 'existential' persons and petrified roles. This notion of transplanting, if the removal to the New World for one generation can be called that, is more conventionally thought of within a single life, and takes the form of pilgrimage or puberty rite. But there are cultural forms of it as well, of which the Babylonian captivity of Israel is the most obvious example.

Once this is said, one can still talk about characters, about the symbolism of Pearl, of light and dark and glitter, of polarities between forest and town, new world and old, of structure in terms of scaffold scenes, of the real history of New England, of the doctrine of evil according to Hawthorne and Melville and its relation to transcendentalism, and perhaps even of Freud and Marx. But I submit that if one wishes to talk about the novel as something ethically exemplary, in a way which does not reduce or compromise its high allegorical existence as something self-authenticatingly powerful, then one could hardly do better than to presume that it assimilates real life, rather than exists as a mimesis of it, and so is in continuity with the real life of a sometime American civil servant, whose essay about a custom house had in it, at least emotionally, a truth which one need not distinguish too carefully from fiction.

Again, I think it can be affirmed as a general principle in William Faulkner's works that conflict continues until one side cheats in some way, and then the other side suddenly (at least in terms of the verbal space of the piece of fiction) wins. To say this is to presume that whatever providence rules the plots of these books knows what cheating is – this again seems to me a safe presumption. The thing that most distinguishes twentieth-century Southern fiction from most other American fiction is that there is justice in it – and that justice of a very peculiar kind. It is justice abstract – not attached to the desire or value or even life of any human being, but rather something one submits to at a level far below consciousness, as one either submits to the laws of metabolism or is sick. Thus detached, but attached to normality and definition as such, its actions often seem unjust, capricious, or grotesque –

but only because it controls the lives of people whose pathos of existence demands our sympathy in a way which prevents our seeing how perverse they are. Quentin Compson's pilgrimage into the meditation of death is no crazier than Henderson the Rain King's more successful one, and their authors successfully involve us in both. But for Quentin we are supposed to remember that one who tells about the South by recounting the grandiloquent failure of a poor white trash arriviste does not really understand.

One will understand none of these things, thus, unless Faulkner's books are permitted to assimilate real life, and their commentary, which includes Faulkner's own insistence that he was by vocation a farmer, and his country-gentleman fondness for fox-hunting when he lived at the University of Virginia. This assimilation, of course, should not be mistaken for mere biographical criticism, which makes too much of the 'individua cadentia in sensum.' Rather, it defines those consuetudines and credulitates whose examples the assimilatio connects. The ethical understanding which results is not a medieval one, but it is a very persuasive one. Very few of Faulkner's characters measure up to it, because the ones who are virtuous lack the power of which they might be stewards, and the ones who have power lack virtue. Justice is therefore triangulated by exemplary failures, not successes. Of them all, one of the most cryptic, and at the same time most telling, is Caroline Bascomb Compson, who interpreted Benjy as 'my punishment for putting aside my pride and marrying a man who held himself above me,' and who was right both about her pride and about the social status of her husband.[15]

Neither of these examples is precisely fair, I realize, because both Hawthorne and Faulkner are in sensibility and technique closer to the medieval than most of their greatest contemporaries. It would be even less fair to cite contemporary science fiction – such books as Heinlein's *Stranger in a Strange Land* and Ursula K. LeGuin's *The Left Hand of Darkness*, to name only two of a multitude. I do so only to suggest that the kind of writing the medieval analysis most clearly presumed as its object – that is, writing in which exemplary fictions link, by assimilatio, the ethical values of ordinary life with some perhaps experimental but at the same time very clear, hard conceptualization – is not only still being written, but is in the genre of science fiction a literature of great and growing popularity and importance.

But beyond the possible analysis of a Hawthorne novel, or a Faulkner novel, and even beyond the enterprise of critical bolstering for a genre dismissed as popular trash by critics and writers still fascinated with the linguistic solipsism, or its psychiatric versions, there is the enterprise of ethical analysis in the absolute sense. If the medieval critics remind us, by classifying literature as ethics, that a body of poetry we were axiomatically prepared to receive in terms primarily aesthetic could be just as well, and with just as much art, seen as ethics, then in absolute ethical analysis they can help us do a thing precisely complementary. That is, they can help us become aware of the literary qualities in ordinary life – and this as an instrument of ethical analysis.

One of the most interesting developments in modern college curricula, as I observe them, is a double shift into the social sciences. It has now been going on for some time, and can, I think, be taken as a confirmed and probably irreversible trend. This shift has taken place at two levels. First and most obviously, the numbers of students involved has vastly increased, largely at the expense of other disciplines which have traditionally considered themselves more humanistic. The second level is perhaps surprising, but should not be. At the same time that students have flocked to the social sciences, the books they have been given to read have included more and more works of literature. I seriously doubt that what is done with those works of literature, in that context, is fully fair to them. But even so it is often fairer than what had been done with them by the New Criticism.

As best I can understand, social scientists who use works of literature in their curricula and in their research take these works either as a kind of empirical description or as a betrayal of a human being's mind – an author's reaction to the situation he has made fiction in his book. That is, they have taken literary words as a language belonging to the subject-object epistemology which is normal both to the modern common mind and to the scientific method as it is usually understood. Literary words, of course, have undergone a simple transformation, but this can be allowed for and reversed in analysis. This done, literary words become evidence, along with a host of other data, for the normative description of human behaviour. In using the word 'normative,' of course, I do not mean in any way to deny the inductive character of the social science enterprise, but merely to say that when, on the basis of his data, the social scientist does permit himself a descriptive generalization, it is in fact a generalization, and as such, makes a definition.

The medieval critics would say, I think, that the enterprise of the normative description of human behaviour is the only fit enterprise for the literary critic, since literature is ethics. At the same time, they would suggest that the social scientists are likely to get flawed descriptions, because they have an understanding of language which filters out of the textuality of literature most of what it properly should be contributing to that normative description – that is, that theory of language which presumes the substantial interaction of language and fact, of which 'subject' is the assimilated audience, and 'object' at its noblest is that which justifies occasionality. Thus the social scientist is likely to miss altogether, or misinterpret functionally, those formal dimensions of human behaviour which range from the figural to the mannerist, as well as those final causes, which make behaviour into myth by explaining such human actions as war, marriage, and inheritance.

All of this is to say, very simply, that the social scientists are, in modern academe, asking most of the most interesting and important questions, but that the people really most likely to get good answers to those most important questions are the people who best understand story-telling. Time was and may still be in some quarters that the people who understand story-telling best were the theologians. But of late most theologians have been more interested in the fact that their stories were probably not true than they were in the fact that they were stories. The literary critics, whose stories never had been true, were not distracted by this problem. But they did make the mistake of believing that stories were made by words, and began to look at the structures of texts rather than the forms of act. The social scientists have stories that are real facts, but the stories lack language, and cannot be remembered. The medieval critics, by contrast, had stories, and language, and a truth which was not the mere slave of fact, but in terms of which facts could find their meanings. The besetting modern temptation, in a world full of meaningless facts and impotent meanings, where public language tends to be either jargon or propaganda, and comforting language seems always merely personal and private, has been to seek refuge, either in the solipsism, or in mere power over facts. But neither refuge is a safe one, or a human one either. Our predicament is of our own making, since we have in all cases gotten out of life precisely what the axioms we presume have asked for.

When Dante found himself lost in the dark wood – be it exile, or personal and political frustration, or accidia over the failure and loss of love, or the accidia of a clever man who has borne fools too long and knows that his frustration is both morally proper and a species of pride – he had sense enough to realize where he was, and what he needed. That is, he knew he was just the other side of a metaphoric Red Sea from Hell, and he needed guides who had been there before. Real life, in short, heals itself by becoming a character in the allegory. The world of truth can be reached at any point from the world of fact, simply by naming it properly, and by telling the story. It is this truth which medieval literature enacts; it is this truth which the medieval critics define. And it is this truth, I think, which is the only thing which can make the mere words and stories of literature worth the life of a commentator, much less of an audience, who otherwise would have more important things to do.

NOTES

1 Michel Foucault *The Order of Things* (New York 1973) p 48
2 Assisi, Biblioteca communale, ms 302, 138v
3 Paul Zumthor *Essai de poétique médiévale* (Paris 1972) esp pp 19–20. Obviously in this statement I mean the word 'certainly' at maximum strength; otherwise what I have just said would not be literally true. It would, however, be methodologically true, since Zumthor establishes his understanding of medieval poetic almost exclusively from reading this textuality – with, of course, much modern criticism.
4 *Expositio pulcherrima hymnorum per annum secundum Curiam non amplius impressa* (Venice 1513) 1v
5 Vatican Library, ms Reg lat 138, f 286r
6 Amy Kelly *Eleanor of Aquitaine and the Four Kings* (Cambridge MA 1971) p 35
7 For discussion of this probability, see Pickford *L'Évolution du roman aurthurien* pp 14–24.
8 Paris, Bibliothèque nationale, ms fr 112, book IV, f 1r–v
9 Ghisalberti 'Arnolfo d'Orléans' p 181
10 'God's Society and Grendel's Shoulder Joint: Gregory and the Poem of the Beowulf' *Neuphilologische Mitteilungen* 78 (1977) 239–40
11 I do not know where this notion originates. Mark Twain certainly makes much of it, in *Life on the Mississippi*, though with more pejorative intent than the fact will support. For a more balanced view, see W.J. Cash *The Mind of the South* (New York 1965).
12 Allen and Moritz *A Distinction of Stories*
13 The distinction probably traces to Sir Henry Maine *Ancient Law* (London 1954) esp pp 99–100. Maine sees these as successive rather than alternative.
14 Arendt *The Human Condition* (Chicago 1958). My specific reference is to her quotation of the *Iliad*, where Achilles is to be 'the doer of great deeds and the speaker of great words' (p 25), but it presumes, of course, her whole discussion of the public realm.
15 Quentin, who reports this opinion, gives the reason for it one page earlier: 'because one of our forefathers was a governor and three were generals and Mother's weren't.' His willingness to exclude his mother from the group 'our' is shocking at the human level, but correct at the level of abstract justice. See William Faulkner, *'The Sound and the Fury' and 'As I Lay Dying'* (New York 1946) pp 121, 122.

Index of subjects and authors

accessus 5, 37–8

Adams, Robert 275; 'The Nature of Need' 93, 112n44, 287n35

Aegidius Romanus 99, 273, 298, 307; and particulars 195; *De differentia Rhetoricae* 17–18; *De regimine principum* 13–14, 17, 59n30, 97, 159, 160, 250; on Canticles 91–2, 111 n41, 149; on duties of a prince 160–1; on forma tractandi 114–16; on Romans 115n54

Aesop: *Fables* 74, 166n4

aesthetic, medieval 193

Alanus de Insulis 79; *Anticlaudianus* 10, 50; commentary on *Anticlaudianus* 58n26, 224–6; on *Rhetorica ad Herennium* 7–8, 18, 51n4, 283n1

Alberic of London 224, 286n28

Alexander de Villa Dei: *Doctrinale* 74, 76, 166n4

Alexander, J.J.G. 230n7

Alexander of Hales 81

Alford, John A. 40, 61n48, 275–6, 287n37, n39; 'The Role of Quotations' 62n60, 287n34

allegoresis 69–70

Allen, Judson B.: 'Alisoun Through the Looking Glass' 116n65, 240n57;

'Commentary as Criticism' 51n3, 107n9; 'Fulgentius Metaphored' 246n73, n75; *A Distinction of Stories* 60n42, 62n58, 115n59, 116n64, 168n16, 173n51, 313n12; 'The Education of the Public Man' 61n54; *The Friar as Critic* 95, 111n39, 115n56, 170n33, 173n53, 220, 238n48, 240n60, 241n61, 245n72, 246n73, 247n85, 284n11; 'God's Society' 313n10; 'The *Grand chant courtois*' 243n64; 'Hermann the German' 59n34; 'The Library of a Classicizer' xviin4

alphabetization 67–8

Anouilh, Jean: *The Rehearsal* 32

Aquinas, Thomas 19, 197

Arendt, Hannah 306; *The Human Condition* 313n14

arete, of motorcycles x–xi

Ariosto, Ludovico 218

Aristotle: *Elenchorum* 167n7; *Poetics* 13. *See also* Averroes: *Poetics*

Arnulf of Orleans 53n14, 135, 169n23, 170n28, 209, 224, 237n47, 239n51, 290, 294–5, 313n9; on *Metamorphoses* 135, 205; on poetry as ethics 53n14

Index of manuscripts